Ladino Rabbinic Literature
and
Ottoman Sephardic Culture

Jewish Literature and Culture
Series Editor, Alvin H. Rosenfeld

Ladino Rabbinic Literature
and
Ottoman Sephardic Culture

Matthias B. Lehmann

INDIANA UNIVERSITY PRESS
BLOOMINGTON AND INDIANAPOLIS

Publication of this book is made possible in part by generous support from the Koret Foundation.
This book is a publication of

Indiana University Press
601 North Morton Street
Bloomington, IN 47404-3797 USA

http://iupress.indiana.edu

Telephone orders 800-842-6796
Fax orders 812-855-7931
Orders by e-mail iuporder@indiana.edu

© 2005 by Matthias B. Lehmann

The paper used in this publication meets the minimum requirements of
American National Standard for Information Sciences—Permanence of
Paper for Printed Library Materials, ANSI Z39.48-1984.

Manufactured in the United States of America

Library of Congress Cataloging-in-Publication Data

Lehmann, Matthias B., date
  Ladino rabbinic literature and Ottoman Sephardic culture / Matthias B. Lehmann.
      p. cm. — (Jewish literature and culture)
  Includes bibliographical references and index.
  ISBN 0-253-34630-4 (cloth : alk. paper)
  1. Sephardim—Middle East—Intellectual life—19th century. 2. Rabbinical literature—Middle East—History
and criticism. 3. Ladino literature—19th century—History and criticism. 4. Ladino literature—Middle East—
History and criticism. 5. Ethics in rabbinical literature. 6. Sephardim—Middle East—Social conditions—19th
century. I. Title. II. Series.
  DS135.L4L44 2005
  956.1′004924046—dc22

                                                                                2005004206

1 2 3 4 5 10 09 08 07 06 05

CONTENTS

CONTENTS

Acknowledgments

I am deeply thankful for the unfailing support of Peter Schäfer at the Institute for Jewish Studies at Freie Universität Berlin as well as that of Joseph Dan. I am indebted to both these formidable scholars for their insightful comments as I developed this book. I also wish to thank Aron Rodrigue, who read an earlier version of the manuscript and for whose invaluable input I am very grateful.

Most of this work was researched and written in Madrid, where I was a research fellow at the Institute for Hebrew and Sephardic Studies of the Consejo Superior de Investigaciones Científicas (CSIC). Iacob M. Hassán and Elena Romero introduced me to the field of Ladino literature and provided much support along the way. In Jerusalem, thanks are due above all to Dov Cohen of the Ben-Zvi Institute, without whose help my research there could never have been as productive. Both in Spain and Israel, librarians and staff at the libraries of the CSIC in Madrid, the Ben-Zvi Institute, and the Jewish National and University Library in Jerusalem have been very helpful.

Colleagues and friends have offered their advice, shared their research, and volunteered their comments during various stages of research and writing: Esther Benbassa, Olga Borovaya, Javier Castaño, Harvey Goldberg, Uffa Jensen, Habbo Knoch, Sarah Abrevaya Stein, and Thorsten Wagner. Two other scholars whose encouragement and support have accompanied me since the days of being an undergraduate student of Jewish studies are Mark R. Cohen and Paul Mendes-Flohr. I am also deeply grateful to Rabbi Moshe Bendahan of Madrid, to whom I owe so much. Joel Rotenberg was very generous with his time in helping me to render my prose into more readable English.

Since I moved to Bloomington in 2002, Indiana University's Jewish Studies Program and History Department have provided an extraordinarily supportive and enriching environment. I am very grateful to my colleagues and friends who have helped to make this transatlantic transition a pleasant and successful one, in particular the successive directors of the Borns Jewish Studies Program, Alvin Rosenfeld and Steven Weitzman.

Working with Janet Rabinowitch and the staff at Indiana University Press has been most rewarding. The perceptive comments of the anonymous readers have also helped a great deal in making this book possible.

Over the years, my work has benefited from the kind support of various institutions, and it is a pleasure to acknowledge their help: fellowships from the German Academic Exchange Service (DAAD) and the Senate of Berlin, a research grant from the Maurice Amado Foundation of Los Angeles, and more recently a faculty summer fellowship from Indiana University that has allowed me to finish work on this book. A grant from the Koret Foundation has helped with its publication.

Portions of chapter 3 were previously published as "The Intended Reader of Ladino Rabbinic Literature and Judeo-Spanish Reading Culture" in *Jewish History* 16 (2002). I am grateful to Kluwer Academic Publishers for permission to reprint these segments here. Thanks also to Scott Taylor of Indiana University's Graphic Services, who prepared the map. All translations, unless otherwise noted, are my own.

I owe more than I can possibly say here to my parents, Ute and Reinhard Lehmann, and I thank my wife, Miriam, for all those precious moments in our years together. It is to them that I dedicate this book.

Ladino Rabbinic Literature
and
Ottoman Sephardic Culture

The Ottoman Empire in the mid-nineteenth century

Introduction

Ottoman Jewry in the nineteenth century was a society in transition. Sephardic communities in places such as Istanbul, Salonika, or Izmir underwent a process of profound cultural, political, and social transformation that changed the parameters of its cultural identity, the patterns of authority and power within the communities, and the economic basis of Jewish life. By the end of the century, Ottoman Sephardic identity had been redefined by a prolonged process of westernization, promoted by the local economic elites and advanced by European organizations such as the Paris-based Alliance Israélite Universelle. The political authority of the rabbinic establishment was challenged by alternative sources of power and authority, individuals and institutions that represented the politics of westernization and the secularization of Sephardic culture. In addition, Jewish life that had been molded by the Ottoman imperial order was now reshaped by a superimposed political and economic order dominated by the West that transformed the once overwhelmingly powerful Ottoman Empire into a semi-colonial setting.

Yet the story of Ottoman Jewry in the nineteenth century is by no means one of a straightforward and unambiguous modernization. Like modernization elsewhere, this was a long process in which old and new, tradition and modernity, religious and secular culture continued to coexist, but with contrasts and dissonances probably even more striking than in the West. French was promoted as the new language of civilization, both by the Alliance and by the secular Jewish press, and the study of Turkish as the language of the country was praised, yet still at the turn of the twentieth century some 85 percent of Turkish Jews identified Ladino (Judeo-Spanish) as their mother tongue.[1] Likewise, secularization eroded the political power of the rabbis, but religious tradition continued to play an important, if changing, role in Ottoman Sephardic society. Religious instruction, even in the modern schools established by the Alliance, was still a prerogative of the rabbis, and if the religious establishment faced the challenge of westernization, there was no attempt to create a religious reform movement like in Germany or North America at the time. In addition, westernization was also a function of social status: Western education did by no means reach all strata of Ottoman Jewish society in the same way, while exposure to Western ideas and fashions led to different, socially determined ways of appropriation.

In this book, I read the transformation of Ottoman Sephardic society through the lens of popular rabbinic ethical (in Hebrew, *musar*) literature. Being conceived as a medium of rabbinic instruction and education directed not only at a reading audience of rabbinic peers but also, and perhaps primarily, at a popular readership, musar literature mediates between rabbinic elite and popular discourses.[2] If this is true for popular rabbinic literature in Hebrew, it is even more so of musar literature published in Ladino, the vernacular language of the Ottoman Sephardim. Musar literature is an eminently conservative genre, trying to preserve and perpetuate religious tradition, but it also mediates between continuity and change as it cautiously introduces new ideas or responds to new trends. What we gain by looking at rabbinic literature in Ladino is a more nuanced picture of Ottoman Sephardic culture in an era of change, and probably a better understanding of how the social, cultural, and political changes experienced by Ottoman Jewry in the nineteenth century transformed the *mentalité* of this traditional society in transition.

As becomes clear in the course of this study, and as has been pointed out by other historians of Sephardic Jewry,[3] the modern Ottoman Jewish experience deviates in many ways from the trodden paths established by modern Jewish historiography, which is dominated by the intertwined narratives of emancipation and assimilation, the rise of modern antisemitism, and the emergence of Jewish nationalism, embourgeoisement, and secularization. Yet at the same time, we also encounter many themes familiar from the study of other Jewish societies, thus questioning the counter-myth of an essential difference and otherness of modern Sephardic history. In fact, it is not unproblematic to speak of a singular "Sephardic" experience, given the great diversity of contexts, ranging from the colonial setting in nineteenth- and twentieth-century North Africa to the Judeo-Spanish communities in the Ottoman Empire, that will concern us here.[4]

In the remainder of this introduction, I give a brief overview of the chapters that follow and discuss both the nature of rabbinic musar literature and its use as a historical source. I also provide a review of the original sources that I analyze in this book.

Chapter 1 offers some historical background on the Sephardim of the Ottoman Empire, describing where they came from, introducing the main institutions of their communities, and pointing out some of the changes and challenges that they encountered in the nineteenth century. The textual analysis that ensues is not a classical intellectual history of themes and concepts of rabbinic ethical literature, but focuses on those issues that establish Judeo-Spanish musar literature as a cultural factor, striking a path between continuity and change in the transformation of Ottoman Sephardic Jewry in the nineteenth century. Chapter 2 therefore discusses the emergence and development of Ladino print culture and establishes in broad terms its impact on Ottoman Sephardic culture.

The chapters of the second section explore the interrelations between authors, translators, and readers. Chapter 3 traces the patterns of translation of Hebrew rabbinic discourse into Judeo-Spanish, how the authors and translators imagined the reception of their books, and what this tells us about Judeo-Spanish reading culture. Then, in chapter 4, I examine different forms of sociability as represented in Ladino musar—suggesting an opposition between *meldar*, or religious study, and leisure—and I will assess the place of vernacular musar literature in this framework.

The representation of the social order is the common theme of the chapters in the third section. Chapter 5 asks how the rabbis represent and legitimize the social order, real and ideal. Chapter 6 offers a close reading of three social types—the wealthy, the poor, and the learned—as they are portrayed in musar literature, showing how the stability of the social order is a central concern of the rabbinic educational effort to perpetuate the traditional symbolic universe. Then, in chapter 7, a discussion of the representation of gender and gender roles completes the account of Sephardic musar's picture of society and the social order.

The fourth section turns from the social to the symbolic order and explores representations of exile and history, themes that will allow us to understand the mentality expressed in Ladino ethical literature and gain insights into the dynamics of continuity and change within Ottoman Sephardic rabbinic tradition. Chapter 8 asks how exile, *galut,* is represented and argues that the primary concern of the rabbis is to establish and maintain boundaries: social boundaries around the Jewish community to separate it from its gentile neighbors, and symbolic boundaries around the universe of rabbinic tradition to separate it from alternative worldviews and what they called "foreign knowledge." Chapter 9 investigates the apparent opposite of exile—the notion of the center, the role of the Land of Israel. It becomes clear that for the rabbis, unimpressed by European Zionism, home remains a distant utopia. Chapter 10 centers on the dimension of time, explaining how the rabbis understand history as suffering and how suffering is interpreted as punishment and atonement for sins. We see how, in the 1840s, two rabbis begin to cautiously include non-rabbinic knowledge into Ladino musar, presenting a new perspective on history and opening the horizons of rabbinic literature just at the time when the first secular Ladino newspaper appeared in Izmir.

In the final section we see how the Sephardic authors of vernacular musar responded to the challenge of modernity and the proliferation of competing secular ways of understanding the world: I examine in chapter 11 the clash between scientific and rabbinic knowledge and the appearance of a new vision of change as progress.

Ladino Musar Literature as a Source for Ottoman Jewish History

The few books published in Ladino before the eighteenth century were mostly for the benefit of Marranos returning to Judaism after having escaped the Portuguese or Spanish Inquisitions.[5] These early Judeo-Spanish publications were not yet part of mainstream Ottoman Jewish literature, which continued to be written and published in Hebrew.[6] Yet by the 1730s, under circumstances discussed in a later chapter, a new rabbinic literature in the Judeo-Spanish vernacular emerged. Throughout the eighteenth and nineteenth centuries, dozens of Judeo-Spanish translations of the Bible, prayer books, and popular digests of rabbinic law appeared, as did a growing number of original works written in Ladino. Particularly numerous was the output of rabbinic musar literature, both original and translated, which can be read as a source for the history of this transitional period of Ottoman Judaism.

Musar is one of the oldest and most influential, yet also most understudied, genres of Jewish literature. Commonly denoted as ethical literature, musar has been defined as "prose literature that presents to a wide public views, ideas, and ways of life in order to shape the everyday behavior, thought, and beliefs of this public,"[7] and thus is, by definition, an educational, didactic literature. Typically addressing a broad audience (unlike specialized works of rabbinic law or those dealing with philosophy or mysticism, written for a small elite readership), musar literature makes ample use of fables, stories, epigrams, and hagiography to render its message accessible for an extensive audience.[8]

Joseph Dan, one of the pioneers in the study of musar literature, points out that rabbinic ethical literature has always played a major role in Jewish history, "as the force that absorbed the revolutionary new ideas of philosophers, pietists, and mystics and turned them into a constructive and conservative ideology." Dan adds that "as far as traditional, orthodox Judaism is concerned, what was true in the Middle Ages is even more so in the period starting in the seventeenth century. The role of ethical literature, especially mystical ethics, only increased during these centuries."[9] The proliferation of musar literature in the eighteenth- and nineteenth-century Ottoman Empire thus was not an isolated phenomenon. The literature of Hasidism that emerged in eastern Europe in the eighteenth century, for example, was mostly an "ethical" literature. According to one bibliographer, 516 musar books were published in Hebrew, Yiddish, and Ladino during the eighteenth century alone, as opposed to 285 in the preceding centuries since the beginning of Hebrew print.[10] The social dynamics behind these parallel literary developments in the Ashkenazic and Sephardic worlds were very different, to be sure, although all musar literature of the period shared certain cultural ideals and an approach to Jewish tradition strongly influenced by post-Lurianic mysticism.

Musar literature may not seem an obvious choice for historical study. After all, it is not only a traditional but, indeed, a highly conventional literary genre. If we are looking for the representation of particular events and "social reality," the rewards of a study of musar literature will be disappointing. Rabbinic responsa literature, which deals with specific questions of Jewish law, lends itself more easily to a social-historical analysis (and it has, in fact, been used widely by historians of Ottoman Jewish history in the sixteenth and seventeenth centuries, though neglected in studies of the modern period).[11]

In musar literature, there are few instances in which social or cultural change is addressed directly (though these cases exist), and we need to understand that musar literature cannot be read as representing or documenting social reality. Unlike practical guides for religious observance (another genre of considerable popularity in eighteenth- and nineteenth-century Ladino literature), musar does not dwell on the minute details of religious law (*halakhah*). Instead, musar literature presents a meta-halakhic discourse that constructs a symbolic universe in which religious observance becomes meaningful in the first place.[12] Following the influential study of the sociology of knowledge by Peter L. Berger and Thomas Luckmann, I use the term "symbolic universe" in the sense of bodies of theoretical tradition that integrate different provinces of meaning and encompass the institutional order in a symbolic totality. . . . *All* the sectors of the institutional order are integrated in an all-embracing frame of reference, which now constitutes a universe in the literal sense of the word, because *all* human experience can now be conceived of as taking place *within* it. The symbolic universe is conceived of as the matrix of *all* socially objectivated and subjectively real meanings; the entire historic society and the entire biography of the individual are seen as events taking place *within* this universe.[13]

Musar literature is a literary system that represents the symbolic universe of rabbinic tradition. Such a symbolic universe does not simply exist but needs to be constructed and perpetuated through communication, and it needs to be translated into social order. In traditional Jewish society, rabbinic literary communication is the central (though not the only) means of representing and perpetuating the symbolic universe, providing a "sheltering canop[y] over the institutional order as well as over individual biography."[14] Musar literature is a prime instrument in the construction of a meaningful set of cultural references for its readers, who are invited to see and understand the world through the prism of musar's worldview.

Here lies the historical relevance of musar literature. I propose to read Ladino musar literature neither as document of something exterior to itself (e.g., the "author's intention" or social reality)[15] nor as a treasure-house of source materials for a classical history of ideas (tracing concepts and ideas such as repentance or metempsychosis and showing how new ideas were presented in old flasks, or old ideas in new flasks). Instead, I argue that Judeo-Spanish musar literature played a central role in the construction and maintenance of the symbolic and social order of Ottoman Sephardic tradition in the era of transition and that it contributes significantly to our understanding of this period. I submit that Judeo-Spanish musar literature played a central role in defining the path chosen between continuity and change in Ottoman Sephardic society in the late eighteenth and nineteenth centuries: that, instead of representing or responding to these processes, this literature was itself part of the transformation of eastern Sephardic Jewry.

Any study that purports to be an exercise in the close reading of certain texts must provide an account of how the texts were chosen in the first place. Unsystematic factors, such as the availability and condition of books in the libraries consulted, certainly influence the process. Nonetheless, I have applied certain *a priori* criteria to the inclusion or exclusion of texts, and I believe that the corpus upon which the present study is based does indeed represent the literary field of Judeo-Spanish musar literature to a very satisfying degree. Five major criteria were used in selecting the books.

The first criterion is, obviously, the Judeo-Spanish language of the publications. I have also included works that were Ladino translations from the Hebrew, among other reasons because the disdain for Judeo-Spanish translated literature as "derivative" has been shown to be groundless[16] and because it is sometimes impossible to distinguish clearly between cases in which Ladino works refer to a Hebrew source and those in which they are "original" (to the degree that the notion of originality makes sense in an intertextually interrelated literary field).

A second criterion is the date of first publication. Whether the original was in Hebrew or Judeo-Spanish, I decided to focus on works from the nineteenth century, the period when the transformation of Ottoman Sephardic society was most pronounced. (The only exception is Elijah ha-Kohen's immensely popular *Shevet Musar*, which was first published in Ladino in 1748 but reprinted several times throughout the nineteenth century.) Consequently I have not included the Ladino translations of Bahya ibn Paquda's *Hovot ha-Levavot* (eleventh century; first Judeo-Spanish translation by Joseph Firmón, published in Istanbul in 1569 and in Venice in 1713—one of the earliest Ladino translations of rabbinic literature and one of the few that predate the eighteenth century), of Isaac Aboab's *Menorat ha-Ma'or* (late fifteenth century; translated by Abraham Asa and first published in Istanbul in 1762), and of Yehi'el bar Yequti'el's *Bet Midot* (thirteenth century; published in Judeo-Spanish as *Ma'alot ha-Midot* in Istanbul in 1824).

Legal literature and practical halakhic manuals are excluded from this study. Though *musar* and digests of religious law are often discussed together in the existing histories of Judeo-Spanish literature,[17] and though guides to halakhic practice do sometimes include musar material and vice-versa, I maintain the distinction between the two genres.

In attempting to study the representation of the symbolic universe of rabbinic culture, and given the necessity of restricting the corpus, it appeared best to limit the study to musar books with general subject matter, that is, to exclude those which are monographic treatments of one specific ethical concept. I am convinced, however, that a micro-study of single-issue treatises would confirm the findings presented here.

A final criterion was that the books should have been printed at least twice (though I allowed two exceptions to this rule). In the absence of any data on the number of copies printed and the impossibility of tracing the distribution and diffusion of the works, this seemed to be the only (flexible) criterion which would avoid including books that remained just too marginal in their own times. I am aware, however, that the mere fact that a book was republished is not sufficient evidence of how it was received.

Thus, I have chosen nine from among some twenty-nine titles which Elena Romero has included in the section on musar in her history of Judeo-Spanish literature—the best and most extensive treatment to date.[18] Fourteen of these works are classified by Romero as being of "general contents," and three of them are Ladino translations of medieval Hebrew literature. I have chosen the following nine titles:

1. Elijah ha-Kohen, *Shevet Musar*, translated by Abraham Asa, ed. princ. Istanbul 1748, Istanbul 1766, Salonika 1800, Izmir 1860, Izmir 1889 (Hebrew ed. princ. Istanbul 1712).[19]

Elijah ha-Kohen was born around 1645 and died in 1729 in Izmir. The *Shevet*

Musar was among the ten most popular books of Jewish musar, according to Joseph Dan.[20] Its author was a rabbi and preacher in the turbulent period after the Sabbatean upheaval. Gershom Scholem has argued that his works "prove beyond any doubt that the famous preacher was profoundly and clearly influenced in his conception of messianism by Sabbatian writings and teachings."[21] Lurianic concepts and ideas abound in his writings. The Ladino translation was prepared by the prolific author and translator Abraham Asa of Istanbul, to whom we owe a good number of the Ladino classics of the eighteenth century.[22]

2. Isaac Bekhor Amarachi and Joseph ben Meir Sason, *Darkhe ha-Adam*, ed. princ. Salonika 1843, Salonika 1849, Salonika 1892.[23]

3. Isaac Bekhor Amarachi and Joseph ben Meir Sason, *Musar Haskel*, ed. princ. Salonika 1843, Salonika 1849, Salonika 1892.[24]

Rabbi Amarachi was among those Judeo-Spanish authors who were also entrepreneurs in the printing business: he operated a printing press between 1845 and 1847 and imported Hebrew letters from Vienna and Livorno; among the books published by Amarachi were parts of the *Zohar*, the classic of kabbalistic literature (part 3 on Leviticus, Numbers, Deuteronomy, published 1845), and the Ladino translation of Pinhas Horovitz's *Sefer ha-Berit* (1847).[25] Amarachi also translated a few works from Hebrew to Ladino, such as a biography of the English Sephardic philanthropist Moses Montefiore, A. M. Mendel's *Keter Shem Tov*.[26] I have not found any data on Amarachi's partner in the publication of these two works, Joseph ben Meir Sason.

4. Isaac Farhi, *Imre Binah*, ed. princ. Belgrade 1836, Salonika 1863, Salonika 1887.[27]

5. Isaac Farhi, *Zekhut u-Mishor*, ed. princ. Izmir 1850, Salonika 1868 (Sacadi ha-Levi), Salonika 1868 (Qupah de gemilut hasadim), Salonika 1887.[28]

Isaac Farhi was born in 1779 (or 1782) in Safed and died in 1853 in Jerusalem.[29] Farhi was sent abroad twice by the community in Jerusalem and once by the community in Hebron to raise funds for the support of the *yeshivot* in Palestine: in the years 1828–30 and 1837 he went to Turkey and the Balkans, including the cities of Izmir, Istanbul, and Belgrade. In 1848–49, he was sent to Italy and France, visiting among other cities the large Sephardic community of Livorno and the major French entrepôt of Marseilles. Farhi, a prolific author of numerous musar books in both Hebrew and Ladino, seized the opportunity to have some of his books printed in the cities that he visited during his mission; it was a common practice among many rabbis from the Land of Israel who raised funds in the Diaspora to seek sponsors for the publication of their writings as well.

6. Abraham Palachi, *Ve-hokhiah Avraham*, ed. princ. Salonika 1853 (vol. 1), Izmir 1862 (vol. 2), Izmir 1877 (in one volume).[30]

Abraham Palachi (Izmir 1809–99) followed his famous father, Hayim Palachi, as chief rabbi of Izmir in 1869 after a long conflict that had erupted in 1865. He recognized the need for improving education and teaching foreign languages (in particular French) for the Sephardic community of Izmir and delivered a sermon on the occasion of the opening of the new school established by the Alliance Is-

ספר

שבט מוסר

ח״ב

ליברו לוזייו אי איסטימאד׳ו קי לו אינג׳יניין אי
לו איזו איל רב גראנדי אי סאנטו עט״ר
מו״ר מר קשישא **הכהן** הגדול כמוהר״ר **אליהו**
הכהן האיתמרי   זכר צדיק לברכה
פארה קי סי קאסטיגי איל אומברי אי סי
אינביזי פארה קונוסיר אאיל ש״ת אי סו זכות סירה
מגן אנוזוטרוס קומפאנייא סאנטה די ישראל קי מו
סי אב׳לרה איל קוראסון איל סירא׳רו פארה טורנאר
אין תשובה אמן :

פה אזמיר יע״א

ממ״א המלך סולטון עבדול מג׳יד יר״ה וממ״א

כדפוס של החכם כמוה״ר ז׳ ציון בנימן רוריטי

נר׳ו בכר **יאושע משה** זנ״ל

אמן שנת כת״ר מורה

Title page of Elijah ha-Kohen's *Shevet Musar* (vol. 2) in the edition of Izmir 1860,
produced by Ben-Tsion Roditi

raélite Universelle in 1873.[31] Although his rabbinic writings present a decidedly conservative outlook, even someone like the Western-educated Alliance teacher and community leader Gabriel Arié referred to Palachi in his autobiography as "a man of great intelligence and vast Talmudic erudition" with whom he had "maintained the best of relations."[32]

7. Eliᶜezer Papo, *Pele Yoᶜets*, trans. Judah Papo, ed. princ. Vienna 1870 (vol. 1), Vienna 1872 (vol. 2), Salonika 1899–1900 (both volumes) (Hebrew ed. princ. Istanbul 1824).[33]

We know very little about Judah Papo, who translated his father's *Pele Yoᶜets* into Ladino. He died in Jerusalem in 1873. Though it is not clear when he arrived in the Holy Land, he is mentioned as a rabbi in Jerusalem in 1856.[34] His father, Eliᶜezer Papo (1785–1828), was born in Sarajevo and became rabbi of Silistra, a small community in Bulgaria near the Rumanian border, in about 1821. Among his students was Rabbi Judah Alkalai, who is often cited as a Sephardic forerunner of Zionism.[35]

Papo's *Pele Yoᶜets* is in many ways one of the most interesting examples of Ladino musar literature. It would seem that, together with Elijah ha-Kohen's *Shevet Musar*, it was among the most successful works of Sephardic musar, even far beyond the Judeo-Spanish world: in addition to its Ladino version, it was also published in Judeo-German, Yiddish, and Judeo-Arabic translations in the nineteenth century, and the Hebrew original is still widely available in modern editions today. The Ladino version of *Pele Yoᶜets* represents the cultural values of the Ottoman Sephardic rabbinate in the nineteenth century in a particularly eloquent way, and its captivating Judeo-Spanish style and its breadth of subjects make it an especially rewarding source.

8. Ben-Tsion Roditi, *Ki Ze Kol ha-Adam*, Izmir 1884.[36]

Roditi was probably better known as a printer and publisher than as an author: in 1857, he established a printing house in Izmir that continued to operate until 1884. Among the seventy-one books printed by Roditi was a series of commentaries on the Pentateuch called the *Meᶜam Loᶜez* (1864–68), as well as another edition of the *Meᶜam Loᶜez* on Genesis in 1878, and the 1860 edition of the *Shevet Musar*.[37]

9. Isaac Badhab, *Nehemadim mi-Zahav*, Jerusalem 1899.[38]

Badhab, the author of the latest book discussed in the present study, was born in 1860 in Jerusalem, where he became a rabbi and lived with few interruptions until his death in 1947. He was sent on a mission to Tripoli in 1887 and returned a year later. In 1899, he raised a loan in order to import books from Livorno, but the venture was not successful. Nevertheless, Badhab, while suffering from ill health, collected old and new books and assembled a considerable library.[39]

All of these books appeared as octavo volumes. Unfortunately, we have no information on the number of copies printed. Of the first edition of Huli's biblical commentary *Meᶜam Loᶜez* on Genesis (1730), 1,000 copies were printed, certainly an unusually high number and probably never matched by later rabbinic works in

פלא יועץ

דיטו ליב׳רו קונטיינו טימור אי מורא׳
דולסי מאס קי טייל אי נוטר׳ די פאנאל
טודו קיין אין איל טילדארה אי לו אפ׳ירמארה
אין טודום סום אינ׳ום אי קאריראם פרוטפיריארה

פ׳ואי אג׳ונטאדו אין לשון הקודש

די איל

חסידא קדישא ופרישא הרב המובהק כמוהר״ר

אליעזר פאפו זיעא

אי חואי טריזלאדאדו אין לאדינו פור מאני

די סו איזו

הרב הכולל בישראל להלל כמוהר״ר

יאודה אליעזר פאפו יצ״ו נ״סוא

שנת חכו מ׳מ׳ת׳ק׳י׳ם וכלו מחמדים לפ״ק

מיטטאמפאדו אין לם איסטאמפאקייאם די קי׳ יעקב הכהן שלוסבירג
אין ב׳יינה

Wien, 1870.
Druck von Jacob Schlossberg.

Title page of Judah Papo's Ladino version of the *Pele Yo'ets* (Vienna, 1870)

Ladino.[40] The source texts listed above include single volumes of around 160–180 pages and three two-volume sets (*Shevet Musar, Pele Yo‛ets, Ve-hokhiah Avraham*), each volume having from slightly over 200 pages (vol. 2 of *Ve-hokhiah Avraham*) to well over 300 pages (vol. 1 of the *Pele Yo‛ets*).

We do have a little more information about the forms of publication and distribution, and about the price of at least one title. In the first edition of his Judeo-Spanish *Pele Yo‛ets*, Judah Papo asks the reader in a note following the preface to contribute one *mecidiye* and promises in return to publish the rest of his father's book and have it bound. At the end of the first volume, however, he laments that he has not received sufficient contributions and thus would delay publication of the second volume, which indeed only appeared two years later.[41] From this we know that the book appeared in installments, and that publication was financed by their sale: apparently the usual method of publication that had been introduced by Hebrew printers in the Ottoman Empire in the sixteenth century.[42] In the second edition, the publisher, Immanuel Castro, writes that it was practically impossible to find any more copies of the *Pele Yo‛ets* and that those copies that did exist were too expensive. He announces that he is planning to publish the *Pele Yo‛ets* in weekly installments of three leaves (twelve pages) each and encourages readers to enter a subscription (*abonamiento*) for one *grush* (the Ottoman *kurush*) a week.[43]

In the bimetallic system of the Ottoman Empire adopted after 1844, one *mecidiye* was the equivalent of 20 silver *kurush*. The *kurush* was relatively stable until late in the eighteenth century; after 1760, its debasement gained momentum (one pound sterling was 5–7 *kurush* in 1736, 15 *kurush* in 1798, and 108–111 *kurush* in 1844).[44] What were the prices of Ladino *secular* literature published around the turn of the twentieth century? The books listed by the Shayich library in Jerusalem in 1913–14 were priced between as little as 0.20 and 16 *kurush* (though many had only around twenty pages). A subscription to the Smyrniote newspaper *El Meseret* was two *mecidiye* a year (2.5 outside Izmir).[45] Contrast these prices with two other numbers: the monthly fee for students attending the schools of the Alliance Israélite Universelle initially oscillated from 5 to 75 *kurush*— which was quite substantial considering that "75 *kurush* represented in 1897 the average weekly wage of a sales assistant in a shop in Istanbul after many years of service."[46]

Other books were published with the help of sponsors. At the end of the second volume of Elijah ha-Kohen's *Shevet Musar*, edited by Ben-Tsion Roditi in 1860, the printer gives a list of the members of the Izmir community who had made possible the publication of the book—a list that occupies a little over four pages.[47] But there were also cases of one single wealthy individual sponsoring the printing of an entire musar book. Isaac Farhi, for example, relates that a prominent person from Belgrade who regularly contributed to Farhi's yeshivah in Jerusalem volunteered to have his musar book *Imre Binah* printed in the "printing house of the prince of Serbia."[48]

As for the geographic distribution of our texts, the major centers of the Ladino-speaking world are represented. While some books (those by Amarachi and Sason) were always printed in one place and may only have reached the readership of that particular region, other titles were reprinted in various places, suggesting that they found an audience across the empire. It should be added that the books were not necessarily published in the same city where their authors lived. Not surprisingly, the bulk of Ladino material was printed in the most important centers of Ottoman Jewish printing—Constantinople, Salonika, Izmir—but our corpus also includes works published in Jerusalem and places outside the Ottoman Empire, such as Vienna, Livorno, and Belgrade (in then-autonomous Serbia).

At the crossroads of rabbinic and "popular" culture, of Hebrew and Ladino discourse, rabbinic ethical literature in the Judeo-Spanish vernacular is particularly apt to serve as the point of departure for a study that is interested in the cultural and social relevance of musar. "Popular" ethical literature was above all an act of translation: the authors translated rabbinic expert knowledge into what they believed approached popular discourse. In this sense, vernacular Judeo-Spanish musar literature was a representation of what the rabbis understood as popular, but was not "popular" per se. Rabbinic musar literature in the vernacular was thus a mediating literature, a literature that tried to translate knowledge from one discourse—the expert rabbinic discourse in Hebrew—into another—non-elite, everyday communication in Ladino.

It is on this level of translation that Judeo-Spanish musar literature worked as a cultural factor. The act of translating elite knowledge into a non-elite discourse—though always, to be sure, from the perspective of the experts and never a "popular" discourse "by the people"[49]—stood at the juncture of the rabbinic symbolic universe and the social order. In translating rabbinic knowledge into the idiom of everyday discourse, the Sephardic rabbis were forced to submit their idea of the world to the test of social reality and thus *respond* to developments they observed. But they also tried to *shape* the ideological mindset and social practice of their readers and to inscribe their knowledge into the everyday reality of their readers.

Part I

Vernacular Musar Literature
as a Cultural Factor

Historical Background

1

A Sephardic Renaissance in the Ottoman Empire

One of the greatest rabbinic authorities in the sixteenth century Ottoman Empire, Samuel de Medina, was once approached by a congregation of German Jews residing in the Ottoman city of Salonika with a question regarding the prayer rite used in their synagogue. Over the years, they explained to de Medina, more and more members of the congregation had abandoned their German-Ashkenazic tradition and had switched to the Sephardic rite. A minority resisted this change, which had also affected numerous other congregations in the city that had originated in various parts of western Europe. To this minority, the change of the prayer rite from one tradition to another seemed to be a straightforward violation of the biblical admonition, "Hear my son the instruction of thy father and forsake not the teaching of thy mother" (Prov. 1:8), as it was usually understood by the rabbis. Samuel de Medina reviewed the issue and, after discussing a whole range of different arguments and sources, came forth with the following advice for those who had recently switched to the Sephardic order of services: "I, therefore, regard it as your religious duty to continue using the Sephardic rite since it is beneficial to those who follow it. Besides, it has become the general practice among all the Jews of Turkey."[1]

How does one account for the emerging dominance of Sephardic, Judeo-Spanish culture in Ottoman Jewry? The expulsion of Jews from Spain and the exodus of Jews after the forced conversions in Portugal in the late fifteenth century coincided with the great expansion of the Ottoman Empire from a regional power to a world empire.[2] Established around 1300 by the founder of the Ottoman dynasty, Osman I, and driven by an ideology of holy war (*ghaza*), the new Turkic state quickly became the dominant power in Anatolia and began its centuries-long expansion into southeastern Europe. The Ottomans achieved their greatest triumph when they captured the capital city of Eastern Christianity, Constantinople, in 1453, and thus brought the Byzantine Empire to an end. Fourteen fifty-three marked the transition of the Ottoman state to an empire, and the Ottoman sultan responsible for the conquest of Constantinople, Mehmet II (ruled 1451–81), has been referred to as the "true founder" of the empire. He was followed by other highly successful sultans, namely Selim I (1512–20) and Süleyman I (1520–66). Selim conquered Syria (including Palestine), Egypt, and the Muslim holy sites of the Hejaz from the Mamluks, firmly establishing the Ottoman Empire as the foremost power in the Islamic world. The long reign of Süleyman, known as "the Magnificent" in Western and as "the Lawgiver" in Turkish sources, is often associated with the high point of the Ottoman Empire. Under his rule, Ottoman forces destroyed the Hungarian state in the Battle of Mohács and extended their rule through North Africa in the West and to the Persian Gulf in the East.

The state established by the holy warriors was transformed into an elaborate imperial system, creating a unique Ottoman civilization that is best described as a bricolage of different influences incorporated into the tapestry of the emerging Ottoman imperial order. These included the frontier Islam of the early Ottoman *ghazis*, now undergoing a process of institutionalization and further transformed through their encounter with the orthodox Sunni Islam of the Arab provinces conquered by subsequent Ottoman sultans, as well as the culture and administrative practices of the former Byzantine territories, the dismantled outposts of the Latin presence in the eastern Mediterranean going back to the period of the Crusades, and their diverse, mostly Christian populations.

The Constantinople that fell to the Ottomans in 1453 was only a shadow of its former self. The Byzantine capital had never recovered from the Fourth Crusade in 1204 when the Crusaders sacked the city and destroyed or carried off much of its legendary wealth. When the Ottomans made the city their new capital, they faced the challenge of restoring this symbol of Byzantine imperial power and civilization both economically and culturally.

A key to their success was the repopulation of the city in the years following the conquest. To this end, the Ottoman authorities forcibly transferred population groups from the provinces to the new capital, a process known as *sürgün*. Among the people brought to Constantinople was a large number of Greek-speaking Jews (called Romaniots), sometimes entire communities, who joined the ranks of the old Romaniot community that had existed in the Byzantine capital for centuries.[3] The forced transfer was resented by the Greek Jews who were affected by the drastic measures of Ottoman population politics,[4] but even at this early point Jewish sources began to paint a rather positive picture of their conditions under Ottoman rule. Invariably cited in books on Ottoman Jewry is the famous letter composed in the 1430s by Rabbi Isaac Zarfati, a European Jew who had immigrated to the Ottoman Empire and who wrote to his coreligionists in Germany, encouraging them to follow his example: "I proclaim to you that Turkey is a land wherein nothing is lacking, and where, if you will, all shall yet be well for you. . . . Is it not better for you to live under Muslims than under Christians?"[5]

While the Ottomans were establishing themselves firmly as the foremost power in the eastern Mediterranean, the Catholic kings of Castile and Aragon, Isabella and Ferdinand, defeated and conquered Granada, last remnant of the century-old Muslim presence in medieval Spain. Among the first measures of the victorious kings was to decree the expulsion of the Jews from all their lands. By July 1492, the last Jews had left Spain, once the largest and one of the most creative and affluent Jewish communities in Europe.[6] It is practically impossible to establish a reliable number for the Sephardic exiles, though a reasonable guess puts their number between 100,000 and 150,000.[7] Many of these Spanish Jews arrived in the Ottoman Empire in various waves of migration. Some appeared soon after the expulsions, in Istanbul as early as the summer of 1492. Others arrived by way of

North Africa or Italy, and still others after the forced conversion in 1497 of the Jews in Portugal, where many of the Spanish exiles had gone. They were later joined by Portuguese *conversos,* or converted Jews, who were able to leave Portugal and reverted to Judaism abroad in the course of the sixteenth century, especially after the establishment of the Portuguese Inquisition in 1536.[8]

In 1523, Rabbi Elijah Capsali of Crete wrote a history of the Ottoman Empire, *Seder Eliyahu Zuta,* in which he gave an enthusiastic account of the Ottoman treatment of the Jews. In fact, much of his description attributes messianic significance to the Ottoman victories over Christian forces in southeastern Europe, in particular their conquest of Constantinople, and over the Mamluks of Egypt in 1516–17. Capsali interpreted the expulsion of the Jews from Spain and their settlement in the Ottoman Empire as the workings of divine providence, the beginning of the ingathering of the Jews from exile. According to this early Jewish historiographer, Sultan Bayezid II (1491–1512) actually invited the Sephardic Jews to come and settle in his empire, throwing open the gates of the Ottoman cities in a conscious decision to promote Jewish immigration. While this is not implausible in light of the Ottoman interest in Jewish settlement—witness the politics of *sürgün*—no Ottoman document has been found that corroborates Capsali's account.[9] On the other hand, Capsali's enthusiasm is echoed by the self-perception of the Sephardic Jews in the empire, both of the generation of the Spanish expulsion and during subsequent centuries. An example of this attitude, expressing both gratitude to the Ottoman rulers and messianic expectation, are the colophons of Hebrew books printed in the Ottoman Empire during the sixteenth century. Thus the title page of a collection of responsa published in Istanbul in 1556 declared that "this book was completed . . . in Istanbul, the fine city, the city of a great king, a faithful shepherd, our master the Sultan Süleyman, may his splendor be exalted, and his honor grow, and in his times and ours may Judea and Israel be redeemed and may the redeemer come to Zion."[10]

Whether the Ottoman authorities made a conscious decision to invite the Sephardic refugees or simply tolerated their settling in the cities of the empire, the Spanish Jews were remarkably successful in their new home. A community traumatized and uprooted by the pogroms and mass-conversions in Spain in 1391 and by the expulsion of 1492, the Sephardic Jews in the Ottoman Empire not only reasserted themselves in a new environment, but managed to establish what became one of the foremost centers of Jewish culture in the early modern period. Rabbinic learning flourished in sixteenth-century Ottoman communities such as Istanbul,[11] the Macedonian port city of Salonika,[12] and Safed in the Galilee,[13] each making major contributions to Jewish culture in many different areas.

In these communities, as from the seventeenth century onward in Izmir (Smyrna),[14] the Sephardim were successful in imposing their rite, culture, and language on the indigenous communities, though the process was slower in Istanbul than in the other cities of the empire.[15] The case of the German congregation changing to the Sephardic prayer rite in sixteenth-century Salonika is one example of this complex process, at the end of which Ottoman Jewry had undergone an almost complete Sephardization.[16] Indeed, the rich heritage of Spanish Judaism which they had brought with them, in addition to their demographic dominance, soon firmly established their cultural and economic hegemony within Ottoman Jewry.

The foundation of this cultural renaissance under Ottoman rule was the economic prosperity of the Sephardim in the sixteenth century. The Sephardic Jews soon encountered their niche in the expanding Ottoman economy, as tax farmers and tax collectors, providing financial services to the Ottoman court, and in international trade, relying on their knowledge of European languages and the network of Sephardic Jews throughout the Mediterranean basin—and beyond.[17] Salonika became a center for the manufacture of textiles, and the Jewish community was so much identified with this industry that they began to pay their poll tax in cloth to provide for the Janissary corps, a crucial element of Ottoman military success in the classical age. In subsequent centuries, however, this dependence on the textile industry proved to be more a liability than an asset, as it became increasingly difficult to compete with the much cheaper textiles imported from Europe. Moreover, after a long period of decline, the Janissary corps was abolished in 1826.[18]

Most important, however, was the laissez-faire attitude of the Ottoman authorities. In stark contrast to the governments of Christian Europe before Emancipation, Ottoman rulers did not impose any restrictions on the economic activities of their Jewish subjects (or other non-Muslim groups, for that matter). Samuel de Medina testified to this fact in a responsum dealing with the Jews of Janina (Greece) who tried to limit competition by excluding visiting Jewish merchants from doing business in their city. "Considering the fact that Moslem and Christian merchants are permitted to sell their wares all over the Empire," reasoned de Medina, "why should Jews discriminate against Jewish merchants, especially since the law of the land offers freedom to all people to pursue their mercantile activities in every part of the Empire?"[19]

A conspicuous feature of Ottoman Sephardic culture was the preservation of their Spanish language. While there are different opinions as to whether it is possible to speak of a distinctively Jewish form of Spanish prior to the expulsion, in its new Ottoman environment the Spanish of the Sephardic Jews developed into an autonomous linguistic system, Ladino (also known as Judeo-Spanish).[20] The closest parallel to this phenomenon is, of course, the Yiddish language that continued to flourish after the migration of Ashkenazic Jews to Poland-Lithuania since the Middle Ages.[21] Maintaining their own autonomous language was the most obvious sign of the multi-ethnic and multi-religious fabric of a profoundly heterogeneous Ottoman society in which the different communities, Muslim and non-Muslim alike, lived side by side without much interference from the state (except to levy taxes and guarantee military security).

Both the success of the Sephardic Jews and the continuous use of their own language throws light on their condition as Jews living within the Ottoman imperial order. The treatment of the non-Muslim population was essentially based on the Islamic legal concept of granting protection (*dhimma*, in Arabic, or *zimmet*, in Turkish) to the "people of the book" (Jews and Christians), who, in turn, were expected to recognize the political primacy of Islam, pay a special poll tax, and be confined to a legally guaranteed yet inferior place within Ottoman society.[22] In practice, the implementation of the legal restrictions imposed on the "protected" non-Muslim population was subject to the pragmatic considerations of the governing Ottoman authorities and to the varying degrees of control exercised by the central government and the balance of power between different political interests at various times and places. In this context it is important to remember that in many parts of the Ottoman Empire, such as the Balkan heartlands, non-Muslims continued to represent the majority of the population, and even in Istanbul and in the major cities of Asia Minor, the percentage of non-Muslims was relatively high. For centuries in Salonika, Jews constituted the majority of the population.[23] In other words, the relative tolerance of Ottoman authorities toward Christians and Jews was dictated by the necessity to ensure the stability of the empire and the rule of the Ottoman dynasty over a vast non-Muslim population as much as it was a function of the demands of the *shariʿa*, or Islamic law.

The corporate character of the traditional Ottoman system excluded Jews, like all other non-Muslims, from state affairs, but it guaranteed the far-reaching autonomy of the Jewish community and its institutions. These were dominated by rabbis and notables and were subject to the rules of Jewish religious law (*halakhah*) and congregational bylaws. Upon their arrival in the Ottoman Empire, the Sephardic immigrants established a separate community structure alongside the existing Romaniot institutions.[24] The cornerstone of this structure was the congregation, or *qahal*, centered around its synagogue, ruled by a board of dignitaries, the *maʿamad*, which hired a rabbi (known as *marbits Torah* in the classical age)[25] to guide the congregation as its judge and teacher. Some synagogue buildings had already been in existence in pre-Ottoman times or were established with the official permit of the Ottoman authorities; many others were established in private houses or as part of a study house (*bet midrash*).[26]

The congregation's rabbi was also the head of the religious court and supervised other functionaries such as the *hazan*, who led prayers in the synagogue, the ritual slaughterers (*shohatim*), and the teachers, as well as the schools (both the public *talmud torah* and the privately endowed *meldar*). In the eighteenth century, Ottoman communities began to establish a principal rabbinate in each city, typically shared by two, three, or even four rabbis (known as *rabanut ha-kolelet*) who shared in the task of providing rabbinic leadership for the city. The most powerful sanction at the disposal of the rabbinic leadership was the ban, or *herem*, excluding an individual from the community in order to enforce discipline. Unlike certain Jewish communities in medieval Christian Spain,[27] the communities in the Ottoman Empire did not have the right of jurisdiction in criminal law and the authorities only recognized the authority of the rabbis in religious matters (including, of course, family law).[28] In reality, rabbis served as judges and arbiters in all kinds of questions involving members of their congregations, just as Jews had at times recourse to the Ottoman *shari'a* courts and thus circumvented rabbinic jurisdiction—a scenario often deplored by the rabbis and yet by no means uncommon.

The individual congregations established by the Sephardic Jews (and other immigrants) were originally based on the common origin of its members, reflected in the name of the *qahal* such as Gerush Sefarad, Cordova, Aragon, Portugal, and so on. Later there were also congregations that derived their name from the individual initiating their establishment, for example the Señora *qahal*, named after Doña Gracia Mendes, the famous sixteenth-century benefactor of Portuguese *converso* origin. Over time, the difference of origin began to lose its importance because of interethnic marriages, internal migrations between different Ottoman regions, or the relocation of individuals and entire congregations as a result of the great fires plaguing Ottoman cities. Henceforth, congregations were increasingly based on the quarter (*mahalle*) where their members lived, and the difference of origin was blurred. This led, over time, to a more unified set of rites and customs that can be defined as the Ottoman Judeo-Spanish tradition.

In spite of this cultural convergence and unlike the situation in the traditional Ashkenazic communities in central and eastern Europe, structures of a city-wide community (*qehilah*) remained weak in the Ottoman context.[29] To quote once again from a responsum by Samuel de Medina, the guiding principle in the relation between *qahal* and *qehilah* was that "in this city [Salonika], while all congregations enjoy complete autonomy, yet when matters arise which concern the entire community, such as those of the Talmud Torah or the communal lodging house, then all congregations act as one organization and follow the rulings of the majority."[30] In addition, to be sure, the Jewish community at large faced the Ottoman authorities, in particular in terms of their fiscal responsibilities, as a city-wide unit.

From the seventeenth century onward, one sees a trend to centralization and institutionalization of the community structure, namely the establishment of the *rabanut ha-kolelet*, first and foremost in the more recent communities such as Izmir that asserted itself as a major Jewish center besides Istanbul and Salonika since the first decade of the seventeenth century. Structures beyond the limits of one city, however, in particular an Ottoman chief rabbinate and an imperial institutional framework for all Jewish communities, did not emerge until much later, then in the context of the administrative reforms of the Ottoman state in the nineteenth century.[31]

In the aftermath of the expulsion from Spain, the Sephardic communities of the Ottoman Empire emerged as prime centers of rabbinic culture. During the sixteenth century, the capital, Istanbul, the thriving port of Salonika, and the city of Safed in the Galilee assumed a leading role in the production of Hebrew elite culture. The Ottoman rabbis produced a vast corpus of halakhic literature, interpreting the classical works of Jewish tradition and offering solutions to newly emerging problems in the numerous volumes of their responsa. A second field of inquiry that the Sephardic Jews brought with them from Spain was the study of philosophy, although it was opposed by leading rabbinic scholars, such as

Menachem de Lonzano in his polemical book *Derekh Hayim* (1575); nevertheless, philosophy generated little interest until the Jews' exposure to what was considered foreign knowledge in the nineteenth century.[32] The third major field was Jewish mysticism, or Kabbalah, which originated in southern France and Spain in the twelfth and early thirteenth centuries and found its classical expression in the *Sefer ha-Zohar*, written around 1280 in Castile. Kabbalah set out to discover the secrets of the universe, divinity, and the role of the Jewish people in the story of mankind within the text of the Torah.

The remarkable productivity of the Ottoman rabbinic elite in the sixteenth century is evident in the output of Hebrew printing in the Ottoman capital and other cities of the empire. The first printing press anywhere in Ottoman lands was the Hebrew printing business established in 1493 by David ibn Nahmias, who had received his skills in Spain, and the first book printed was one of the classical codes of halakhah, the *Arba'ah Turim*. Between 1504 and 1566, more than 120 Hebrew books were printed in Istanbul alone.[33] In fact, the Jewish printers of the Ottoman Empire printed many of the standard texts of rabbinic culture, major works of the eminent Jewish scholars from Spain, and also published for the first time in print manuscripts that they had brought from Spain. Numerous works of the Midrash, collections of rabbinic interpretations and exegesis of the biblical text, were first printed in sixteenth-century Constantinople, such as *Midrash Rabah* (1512), *Pirqe de-Rabbi Eli'ezer* (1514), and *Midrash Tanhuma* (1520).

The fact that all this printing activity took place in the century following the expulsion from Spain is hardly a coincidence, of course. On the one hand, it testifies to the success—both economically and intellectually—of the Sephardic Jews in the Ottoman Empire. On the other hand, however, it bears witness to the perceived necessity to collect their traditions and make them available for a broader reading public in order to preserve the cultural heritage of a community uprooted and dislocated by the expulsion.

Printing extant works of rabbinic Judaism was not the only contribution of Ottoman Jewry in the sixteenth century, however. Both in terms of Jewish law and Jewish mysticism, Ottoman Safed in the century after the expulsion from Spain brought forward major original contributions that have shaped the outlook of traditional Judaism in subsequent centuries. Joseph Caro (1488–1575), born in either Portugal or Spain, arrived in Safed in the mid-1530s. He authored a monumental compendium of rabbinic law under the title *Bet Yosef* and is best known for the condensed version of this code, the *Shulhan Arukh*, a practical digest of Jewish law that is still considered the most authoritative legal compendium of traditional Judaism.[34] Like the major Hebrew printing enterprises of the century, Caro's daring project of providing a new law code for his times, supplanting such revered classics as Jacob ben Asher's *Arba'ah Turim* or Maimonides' *Mishneh Torah*, marks a cultural crossroads. The transition from Spain to the Ottoman world generated a need for codification and unification of religious practice in the face of Sephardic mass migration.

The second luminary of sixteenth-century Safed who left his imprint on

Jewish tradition was Isaac Luria (1534–72).[35] Though Luria, born in Egypt, lived in Safed for less than three years at the end of his short life, his teachings profoundly transformed the texture of Jewish mysticism. Luria himself did not write down his teachings; we owe all our knowledge about Lurianic Kabbalah to the accounts of his disciples, in particular Hayim Vital (1543–1620). Originally, Lurianic thought—as was the case with Kabbalah generally—was meant to be an esoteric body of knowledge available only to a small group of initiates. A particularly fascinating chapter in the intellectual history of Jewish thought is the subsequent wide dissemination of Lurianic ideas through various channels of communication, introducing many of its ideas and its performative practices into the Jewish mainstream, both in the Sephardic and the Ashkenazic worlds. Though the popularization of kabbalistic knowledge that Gershom Scholem identified with the spread of Lurianic Kabbalah has been questioned by more recent scholarship, many aspects of the Lurianic tradition became pervasive throughout Jewish literature in the seventeenth and eighteenth centuries, not least of all in the literature of musar.

This includes aspects of the Lurianic myth, such as the notion of *shevirat ha-kelim* (breaking of the vessels), an image representing a catastrophic rupture in the process of creation ultimately responsible for the existence of evil. This concept is tied to the idea of *tiqun*, mending or restoration, that understands the performance of the divine commandments (*mitsvot*), recitation of the prescribed prayers, and the study of Torah as being part of the universal process of restoring the primordial order. As in earlier Spanish Kabbalah, the assumption is that there is a parallel structure of the divine and the material worlds, represented in the complex imagery of the ten heavenly spheres, or *sefirot*, and human behavior is understood to have an impact on the upper worlds. Indeed, *tiqun* is the ultimate purpose of performing the commandments, praying, and studying. God's will, as Vital noted,

> can only be achieved by one who knows the [kabbalistic] intentions of prayer and mitsvot, and who intends to mend [*le-taqen*] the upper worlds, and to unite the name of the Holy One, blessed be He, with His *Shekhinah* [the divine presence in this world, and the lowest of the ten *sefirot*]. And his intention should have nothing to do with receiving reward in this world, nor even for his benefit in the world to come. . . . Even in connection to the study of Torah, do not think that it is for the purpose of learning its contents, but do so . . . in order to unite the Holy One, blessed be He, and His *Shekhinah*.[36]

New Challenges and New Responses

The so-called "golden age" of Ottoman Jewry, its culturally most creative and economically most successful phase, coincided with the classical age of the empire at the height of its power. By the seventeenth century, however, new challenges arose. In the existing literature on Ottoman Jewry, the period from the early seventeenth through the mid-nineteenth century is often presented as one of general decline, both economically and culturally. This simplifies the course of Ottoman and Ottoman Jewish history and often seems to be written with the knowledge of hindsight, telling Ottoman history from the perspective of a disintegrating empire defeated by European powers in World War I.

It is true, of course, that the military expansion of the Ottoman Empire came to a halt and that the Ottomans began to suffer defeats at the hands of West European powers and Russia. It is also true that the central government in Istanbul found it increasingly difficult to control the vast provinces of the empire in which local elites asserted themselves and, at times, effectively wrestled local control from the central authorities. Just as the "pax ottomanica" had proven beneficial to the Jews in the century of the empire's expansion, the shifting of fortunes to the disadvantage of the Ottomans likewise had an adverse effect on its Jewish inhabitants.

The difficulties of the Ottoman Empire were not only military and political: even more important, the empire that had once occupied a central position at the crossroads of world trade, linking three continents and controlling the eastern Mediterranean, found itself increasingly marginalized in the economy of the colonial world order.[37] The emerging powers of the Atlantic seaboard began to dominate trade and encroached upon the economy of an Ottoman Empire that proved to be ill-prepared to face the onslaught. This change did not remain unnoticed by Ottoman observers; as early as 1625, a certain Ömer Talib wrote:

> Now the Europeans have learnt to know the whole world; they send their ships everywhere and seize important ports. Formerly, the goods of India, Sind, and China used to come to Suez, and were distributed by Muslims to all the world. But now these goods are carried on Portuguese, Dutch, and English ships to Frangistan, and are spread all over the world from there. What they do not need themselves they bring to Istanbul and other Islamic lands, and sell it for five times the price.[38]

This state of affairs had a negative impact on the economic status also of Ottoman Jews. In addition, their relative position in the fabric of Ottoman economic life declined as the Jews lost ground to other minorities, particularly the Greeks (in trade) and the Armenians (in money-lending).[39] The vanishing fortunes of the Jewish elite did not leave the educational and cultural standards of the Sephardic communities unaffected: the institutions of elementary and higher education no less than the publishing houses responsible for the dissemination of rabbinic knowledge relied on the generous sponsorship of prominent Jews and suffered from the economic crisis that affected Ottoman Jewry.

And yet, the picture is more complex; regional differences need to be taken into account. Consider the case of the Ottoman port city of Izmir in the seventeenth and eighteenth centuries: of no particular importance at the end of the sixteenth century, the city emerged as a major port for Ottoman-European trade and experienced a remarkable boom since the early seventeenth century. An indication of Izmir's tremendous growth is the fact that the tax revenue of Izmir and its surroundings, farmed out to a single tax collector by the Ottoman authorities, almost doubled between 1589 and 1626.[40] As a result, Izmir attracted a large number of Ottomans, particularly members of the Greek, Armenian, and Jewish minorities, leading to a great population increase: by the end of the nineteenth century, it had become the second largest city in the empire after Istanbul, but outnumbering Alexandria, Damascus, and Salonika.[41] Likewise, Izmir became one of the three largest and most productive Jewish communities in the empire and, indeed, one of the communities that we encounter time and again in the present study.[42]

The growth of Izmir was largely due to its "discovery" by the Dutch, English, and French trading interests. Izmir, just as the Ottoman economy at large, was integrated into a superimposed commercial network in which the Ottoman Empire provided raw materials demanded in Europe and became a market for finished European products. In the semi-colonial relationship between the Ottoman Empire and the European powers, Izmir served as a major point of exchange. Thus, while the economic transformation can be described as part of the story of increasing Ottoman dependence on the West and ultimately Ottoman decline, the immediate effect on those cities and those social groups involved in and profiting from this exchange created renewed growth. Because they wished to promote trade and were in need of local intermediaries who both knew the languages and were familiar with Ottoman administrative practices, the European trading companies employed members of the non-Muslim Ottoman population, mostly Christians but at times also Jews. As part of the so-called "capitulations" negotiated between the European states and the Ottoman authorities, these local representatives of European trading interests were placed under consular protection. While this eroded further Ottoman sovereignty, it provided a formidable opportunity for an economic-commercial elite among the Christian and Jewish populations to lift themselves above the century-old Ottoman system of *zimmet*.

In a similar vein, it is important to point out that the Ottoman Empire still attracted some immigrants in the eighteenth century, namely Jewish merchants from Livorno in Tuscany, who settled in Ottoman trading centers under the protection of the French consulate and contributed considerably to the well-being of the local Jewish economy. Later, these Livornese Jews—the *francos* or "Europeans," as they were known—were an important factor in the modernization of Ottoman Jewry, serving as intermediaries between Western and Ottoman culture and between Jewish communities in Europe and in the Ottoman Empire.[43] In both the cases of Izmir and the immigration of the Livornese Jews it is clear how, since the seventeenth century and more clearly in the eighteenth and nineteenth centuries, a new local elite emerged that derived much of its social and economic status from the interaction with Europe.

The eighteenth century came on the heels of an abortive messianic movement around the false messiah Sabbatai Sevi of Izmir (1626–76),[44] who had attracted a large number of followers throughout the Ottoman Empire and Europe and across the entire spectrum of Jewish society. Preparing himself for the role of messiah, Sabbatai Sevi carried out all kinds of bizarre acts in direct violation of Jewish law, which he legitimized by asserting that many of these laws would become obsolete in the redeemed world; he expressed this symbolically in a blessing that declared, "Blessed art Thou who has permitted the forbidden." In spite of the antinomianism of the Sabbatean message, its followers included some of the leading rabbis in the empire. In Izmir, Sabbatai Sevi was so powerful that he had the acting chief rabbi, Aaron Lapapa, removed from office and replaced by a figure more sympathetic to his case, Hayim Benveniste. Sabbatai Sevi declared that redemption would occur in June 1666, but when given a choice between death or conversion to Islam when the Ottoman authorities grew wary of the uproar, he converted to Islam. Some Sabbateans continued to believe in his messianic mission and a few hundred families in Salonika even chose to follow his example and converted to Islam (the *dönme* sect that continues today). Most Jews, however, in the empire and beyond, were profoundly disillusioned.

Part of the broad attraction to Sabbatean messianism and the longing for redemption was clearly a reflection of the declining fortunes of Ottoman Jewry. In addition, in the aftermath of the Spanish expulsion, messianic expectations had been an important feature of Ottoman Jewish culture, and the messianic branch of Lurianic Kabbalah, though probably not widely popularized in the generation prior to Sabbatai Sevi, also played an important role. What seems most remarkable about this episode, however, is the sheer range of the messianic excitement and the speed with which both followers and opponents of Sabbatai Sevi exchanged information about the movement and were aware of developments in far-away communities. In fact, communication about Sabbateanism catalyzed patterns of communication in the Sephardic and, indeed, the entire Jewish world in the early modern age. As Jacob Barnai has pointed out, "One common thread becomes evident: that ideas and events achieved prominence as a result of the continuous flow of information among the Jewish communities and between the Jewish and non-Jewish worlds." Sabbateanism was "an important catalyst for the development of communication channels and the scope of information transmitted."[45] From a historical perspective, it would seem that this was the most important and lasting impact of Sabbateanism.

While many historians have identified the Sabbatean crisis as a turning point in Ottoman Jewish history, others have called this assumption into question. Avigdor Levy, for example, holds that "Ottoman Jewry's decline . . . had been set in motion almost a century before the Shabbetai Tzevi affair, and it was destined to continue. . . . From a broad historical perspective . . . [Sabbateanism's] impact on Ottoman Jewry's position within the Ottoman body politic appears to have been episodic and with mixed results."[46] In fact, though the conversion of the alleged messiah and the subsequent meltdown of Sabbateanism as a mass movement may have triggered a crisis of authority for the Ottoman rabbinate, there is no evidence of a shift toward alternative sources of authority, much less a wholesale assault on the values of traditional rabbinic culture. Rather than a turning point, then, the Sabbatean movement seems to have aggravated a crisis of Ottoman Jewry that had its origins in the decline of its economic fortunes since the seventeenth century.

It is at this juncture between the "classical" age of Ottoman Jewish tradition that came to an end by the late seventeenth century and the European-style modernization of the late nineteenth century that the present study begins. Against the conventional portrayal of this transitional period in Ottoman Jewish history as one of decline and stagnation,[47] I argue in this book that the first half of the eighteenth century through the latter half of the nineteenth was a period of profound social and cultural transformation. I suggest that "transformation" (in contrast to change in general) should be understood as a "change of the existing institutional symbolic premises," to adapt a phrase from S. N. Eisenstadt.[48] During the eighteenth and nineteenth centuries, the Sephardic communities of the Ottoman Empire underwent a multi-faceted process of transformation that changed their symbolic world order. Unlike some historians who have maintained that "all trends among Ottoman Jewry in the modern age were imported,"[49] I argue that internal processes of transformation were already under way when Ottoman Jewry began to be exposed to a full-fledged modernizing project in the second half of the nineteenth century. The vernacular rabbinic literature discussed here is not only a valuable source for our understanding of this period of transformation but was, in fact, one of the cultural factors that helped generate this transformation even before the advent of the westernizing forces in the mid-nineteenth century.

Yet a close reading of the rabbinic literature published in this period also reveals that, though the transformation of Ottoman Sephardic culture began much before the mid-nineteenth century, the processes of change affecting Ottoman Jewry did accelerate considerably from the 1840s onward. Three factors played a key role: first, changes in the political status of the Jewish communities in the empire, namely the reforms implemented by the Ottoman state (known as the *tanzimat*) throughout the nineteenth century, and the challenge of the emerging ethnic nationalisms among the Ottoman subject peoples in the Balkans. Second, the already noticeable European presence was now reinforced by the direct intervention of European Jewish institutions, such as the Paris-based Alliance Israélite Universelle and their educational network in the eastern Mediterranean, which proved to be a powerful force in the westernization of Ottoman Jewry. Third, a genuine secular Judeo-Spanish public sphere emerged, particularly through the proliferation of Ladino newspapers since the mid-nineteenth century (more about which in chapter 2). What sets these developments of the mid- and late nineteenth century apart from the earlier and contemporary processes studied here is that they challenged the traditional order from the outside, questioning and contesting the authority of the leaders of traditional society and the values and symbolic order of traditional Sephardic culture at large.

The Ottoman tanzimat movement was a series of attempts to safeguard the empire from its perceived decline through reforming its military, administrative, and educational institutions.[50] Some of these reforms affected the situation of the Jews (and other non-Muslims) directly and transformed their status in the imperial order. As early as 1829, Sultan Mahmut II abolished the dress code which (in line with Islamic law) had distinguished Muslims from the various non-Muslim groups. The Ottoman reform edicts of 1839 and 1856, which were at once the result of the state elites' attempt to modernize the state and a response to European pressure,[51] abolished—at least theoretically—the old corporate structure of the Ottoman Empire and declared the equality of all subjects regardless of religion. The process of political change reached its high point with the promulgation of an Ottoman constitution in 1876 and members of the non-Muslim population groups, including several Jews, were elected to the new Ottoman parliament. The constitutional regime was of short duration, however, and came to an abrupt halt when Sultan Abdülhamid II (1876–1909) suspended the constitution and dissolved the parliament soon after he ascended to the throne. The constitutional order was restored only after the Young Turk revolution of 1908.[52]

The political reforms of the tanzimat era were accompanied by a new imperial ideology that was supposed to promote "Ottomanism," or an Ottoman patriotism, bracketing the religious and ethnic diversity of the empire's population. In an age of nationalism and unconcealed European support for the national movements of the different Christian peoples living under Ottoman rule, Ottomanism met with little success. Though embraced by the Ottoman elite, it arguably elicited little enthusiasm even among the general Muslim population, and failed entirely as a counter-model to separatist nationalisms. In the Jewish public, however, Ottomanism did find some resonance and the editors of numerous Jewish newspapers still embraced and defended the virtue of the imperial ideology at a time when Muslim Turks themselves abandoned it and embraced Turkish nationalism instead.[53] Thus, the reforms of the nineteenth century never overcame the compartmentalization of Ottoman society. In fact, the capitulation regime placing numerous non-Muslim Ottoman subjects under European consular protection and European support for the national aspirations of Christian nations on the Balkans only reinforced the ethnic-religious differences in Ottoman society.

But the changes in the Ottoman political order, declaring legal equality of all subjects regardless of religion, did have an impact on the Jews of the empire. State-imposed centralizing reforms of the non-Muslim "nations" (*millets*) and their community institutions, in particular after the reform decree of 1856, challenged the established patterns of authority and strengthened secular leadership vis-à-vis the religious elites. The tanzimat and the surge of Christian nationalisms suggested that there were alternative models of political and cultural identification than in the traditional Ottoman order. Patterns of identity, authority, and leadership began to be secularized and disentangled from religion. The modernization of Ottoman Jewry in the late Ottoman period needs to be understood in the context of these trends in general Ottoman history.

To be sure, the vast majority of Jews, Muslims, and Christians in the Ottoman Empire remained traditional and their values continued to be determined by religion throughout the period of Ottoman reforms. Though the Ottoman reforms were accompanied by an attempt to centralize and modernize the administrative structure of the non-Muslim *millets*, Ottoman Jewry never underwent a formal process of emancipation with all the exigencies that it implied elsewhere. In Europe, emancipation was a process that linked civil and political rights for the Jewish minority to its "regeneration," a term that implied its integration into bourgeois society as much as the dissolution of the old corporate structure of the traditional Jewish community. As it was famously expressed in the aftermath of the French Revolution, "To the Jews as a Nation, nothing; to the Jews as individuals, everything."[54] European Jews thus faced the challenge of how to preserve Jewish continuity and yet meet the expectation, and desire, of full integration into European society, giving rise to a whole range of modern Jewish identities from a radical assimilationist ideology through various forms of religious reform and accommodation to emancipation to the traditionalist rejection of modernity by an emerging ultra-Orthodoxy.

In the Ottoman Empire, by contrast, the state encouraged a modernization of community structures and occasionally supported reforming elements within the community against more traditionalist forces, but an ideology of emancipation and assimilation was foreign to the multinational Ottoman imperial order. Modernization in the case of Ottoman Jewry in the second half of the nineteenth and the early twentieth century meant a process of embourgeoisement, a cultural transformation that is best described as westernization, and even a degree of secularization among the westernized elite, but it did not entail the weakening of a sense of Jewish difference. Jewish identity was transformed, but it was not questioned.[55]

In this process of embourgeoisement and westernization, the educational work of the Alliance Israélite Universelle played a central role.[56] Established in 1860 in Paris, the Alliance translated the ideology of "regeneration" embraced by French Jewry in the seventy years or so since its emancipation into a non-European context. Establishing a network of Jewish schools throughout the Islamic lands, the Alliance pursued an agenda of westernization in order "to cast a ray of the civilization of the Occident into the communities degenerated by centuries of oppression and ignorance," in the words of an Alliance circular of 1896 echoing the "civilizing mission" of French colonialism at the time.[57] Since the opening of its first schools in the 1860s, the Alliance transformed the cultural outlook of the Ottoman Sephardim. It is hardly an exaggeration to say that the Alliance and the graduates of its schools were able to dominate the modernizing discourse among Ottoman Jewry well into the early twentieth century,[58] while other forms of Jewish modernity, namely Jewish nationalism or Zionism, remained marginal until the period following the Young Turk revolution.[59]

The Alliance schools set out to modernize the traditional Jewish education in the Ottoman Empire. The main educational institutions of traditional Ottoman Jewish society were the talmud torah and the *meldar* for young children and the *yeshivah* for advanced study;[60] a small wealthy elite received their training from private teachers at home.[61] There was no formal schooling for girls. In some cases, various congregations joined forces to establish a school, as was the case with the famous talmud torah of Salonika, which even in the late nineteenth century, well past its most glorious days, had as many as 1,280 students in 1890.[62]

We have different accounts as to when schooling began and how many years children typically attended the talmud torah or *meldar.* Dov Cohen speaks of a general schooling age between five and ten years, while Aron Rodrigue mentions seven to thirteen.[63] This might reflect the differences between various communities; it is also clear that some parents sent their children to school even earlier, at age three, and that many children were forced to abandon school early, after only three or four years, in order to help support their families.

Education, a prerogative of the rabbis and one of the most important sources of employment for those having received rabbinic training, began with teaching the Hebrew alphabet and reading the Torah. Familiarity with the order and text of prayers was the first and most basic goal of education. Then, the text of the Torah and its cantillations were learned by heart, accompanied by a word-to-word translation into Ladino and the standard commentary by Rashi. Those who continued would begin to study the Talmud, while other matters, such as basic arithmetic, were also typically part of the curriculum. The educational standard of the vast majority of Ottoman Sephardim would thus not exceed a certain degree of literacy in Ladino and Hebrew and a familiarity with the texts of prayers and the Torah.

The material conditions in the *meldarim* were difficult. Often between fifty and sixty children were studying in a crowded room adjacent to a synagogue. Books were scarce, although the matter probably improved with the revitalization of Hebrew print in the nineteenth century, and much of the teaching and learning was done orally. The most ardent critics of the traditional schools were predictably the westernized intellectuals of the late nineteenth and early twentieth centuries, for example Alexander Ben-Guiat, one of the most prolific translators and authors of modern Ladino literature, who published in 1920 a short pamphlet entitled "Suvenires del meldar."[64] These intellectuals denounced the poverty, lack of preparation of the teachers, and backwardness of the curriculum, and praised the Alliance for its modernizing efforts. In fact, the critique of the standards of traditional education was much older and had first been voiced among the rabbinic elite itself who lamented that not even the humble expectations of traditional mass education were always met by reality. Take, for example, Jacob Huli, the author of the first volume of the *Meʿam Loʿez,* published in 1730, who proclaimed that "because of our sins . . . there are very few who know how to read a verse [of the Bible] correctly."[65]

Only a relatively small number of students went on to study at the yeshivah after finishing the talmud torah or *meldar.* In the yeshivah, they would receive a higher education, based on the study and discussion of traditional rabbinic literature and, according to the Sephardic educational tradition, focus on practical halakhah. According to the bylaws of one yeshivah in Izmir, the students had to leave that institution no later than three years after getting married—a rule that probably is representative for the practice in other places as well.[66] Classes were typically small, with seven students that were admitted free of charge and to whom the teacher could add three more against payment in the case of the Izmir yeshivah. Unfortunately, we have no data on the absolute numbers or percentage of students attending these institutions of higher learning; it is clear, however, that they represented a rather small portion of the Jewish population. An even smaller elite finally obtained the training that led to rabbinic ordination and qualified them to exercise rabbinic functions in the congregation or community. While there was no universal standard or curriculum, the focus was to prepare the *talmid hakham* (advanced student) for the two central tasks of a rabbi: jurisdiction and teaching. Thus, a mentor would introduce his student to the art of rendering legal decisions in the form of responsa and to the art of delivering a sermon in public, as well as teaching the values of traditional rabbinic culture to a broader audience.

As pointed out above, it was the Alliance that transformed the patterns of Jewish education in the Ottoman Empire in the latter half of the nineteenth century. Alongside religious education, which it largely left to the local rabbis, the Alliance promoted the study of French and of secular subjects. The battle over the modernization of education, however, was fought even before the opening of the first Alliance schools. The "main conflict between the traditionalists and reformers," as Aron Rodrigue has pointed out, "was played out *before* the Alliance came on the scene. . . . Even though the end result was a political stalemate, the principle of education in European ways was tacitly accepted."[67] In particular, the elite of European, mostly Italian Jews living in the urban centers of the empire played an influential role in promoting the study of foreign languages and secular studies, and the case was taken up by the secular Ladino press from its inception in the mid-nineteenth century. However, the way was prepared by the rabbinic literature in Ladino that began to expand the educational agenda of traditional Ottoman Jewish society.

Print and the Vernacular: The Emergence of Ladino Reading Culture

2

The Eighteenth-Century Classic: Huli's *Me'am Lo'ez*

Frank Kermode once dubbed the "classics" of literature somewhat irreverently as "old books which people still read." He adds: "The books we call classics possess intrinsic qualities that endure, but possess also an openness to accommodation which keeps them alive under endlessly varying dispositions."[1] This seems to be an appropriate description of the "classical" status of the *Me'am Lo'ez* in Judeo-Spanish literature. Published in Istanbul in 1730, the first volume of Jacob Huli's encyclopedic Bible commentary—the *Me'am Lo'ez* on Genesis—inaugurated what has been called the "golden age" of Judeo-Spanish (Ladino) literature in the eastern Sephardic diaspora.[2] It has even been claimed that the *Me'am Lo'ez* "set the contours of the popular religious universe of the Sephardim well into the modern period."[3] It certainly set the contours of the new Judeo-Spanish literary system and provided a frame of reference for the considerable output of Ladino religious literature during the following two centuries.

Among modern scholars who study the *Me'am Lo'ez,* there is hardly a work that does not describe it as an "encyclopedia" of Sephardic Judaism or rabbinic knowledge. Moshe Gaon called the book a "*kol bo*" (everything within), and Michael Molho subtitled a brief overview of the work "*Encyclopédie populaire du séphardisme levantin.*"[4] The best definition has been offered by Arnold Goldberg, who called the *Me'am Lo'ez* an "encyclopedic commentary" organized around the biblical text, a mixture of the Palestinian *targum* ("amplifying Bible translation"), *perush* (commentary), and *yalqut* (thesaurus), drawing on a broad range of traditional rabbinic sources.[5] Jacob Huli himself invoked the great encyclopedic and anthological milestones of Jewish literature as a model for his work, beginning with Mishnah and Talmud and leading to Moses Maimonides' *Mishneh Torah* (twelfth century), Jacob ben Asher's *Arba'ah Turim* (fourteenth century) and Joseph Caro's *Shulhan Arukh* (sixteenth century). Of Maimonides' landmark work, Huli writes in terms strikingly similar to those he uses to describe his own time: "In that period, afflictions grew and wisdom was lost, and thus God enlightened His world by sending us a great sage"—that is, Maimonides, who explained the entire Torah in his *Mishneh Torah* (literally, "repetition of the Torah"). "It was enough for a person to read the pericope and then to read his book [the *Mishneh Torah*], and from there he would be informed about all novellae, ordinances, and laws, and would not need to read any other book."[6]

Huli decided to produce a new, all-encompassing "repetition of the Torah" for his own times, and, audaciously, he did so in the vernacular. This encyclopedic approach—together with his decision to write his work in Ladino—was a remarkable departure from what has been described as the overall preoccupation of Ottoman Sephardic rabbis with minute halakhic questions, from a rabbinic culture which is said to have limited itself to the *Shulhan ʿArukh* and non-messianic Kabbalah after the Sabbatean crisis.[7] It is true, of course, that the Ottoman rabbis produced a tremendous output of responsa literature during that time, but Huli's *Meʿam Loʿez* and the Judeo-Spanish literature that followed is evidence of the remarkable self-confidence of these vernacular rabbis in their ambition to remap the territory of rabbinic knowledge for a popular readership. This notable literary innovation, I submit, marks a cultural crossroads in the Ottoman Sephardic world well before European models of modernity erupted into Ottoman Jewish life and transformed it even further.

The *Meʿam Loʿez* was continued by a dozen authors for more than a century and a half, with the last volume published in 1899. Iacob M. Hassán and Elena Romero have differentiated between the "classic" (or early) *Meʿam Loʿez* volumes on the Pentateuch that were published in Istanbul between 1730 and 1772, the middle volumes (Joshua in 1851 and Esther in 1864), and the late *Meʿam Loʿez* (Ruth, Isaiah, Ecclesiastes, and Song of Songs, between 1882 and 1899).[8] While later volumes retain certain features of Huli's original commentary on Genesis, new and sometimes quite different literary structures appear. Michael Molho has remarked that the last volume to be published, Shaki's commentary on the Song of Songs, hardly resembles the earlier volumes at all in content, style, even typography, and is clearly the work of a new generation influenced by its education in the modern Alliance schools.[9] The *Meʿam Loʿez* as a whole is thus a highly diverse series written by many different authors and published in various centers of Judeo-Spanish print culture over almost two centuries. It might best be seen as a genre unto itself, first established by Huli and then continued, transformed, and adapted to varying new contexts by many others.

Huli's work on Genesis and the first part of Exodus (through 26:33) became a classic by virtue of the standards it set for Judeo-Spanish literature and written language, and no less so by virtue of its potential adaptability to the needs of the generations of Sephardic authors and readers following its inception.[10] Curiously, however, the *Meʿam Loʿez* continued to be seen as a popular work and did not acquire rabbinic or scholarly authority. It is quoted only rarely in Judeo-Spanish literature, and (needless to say) even less in Hebrew rabbinic books. When the nineteenth-century *Pele Yoʿets* (both Hebrew and Ladino) notes that one who is not sufficiently familiar with the laws of mourning should read the relevant passages from the *Meʿam Loʿez*—one of the few explicit mentions of Huli's work I have come across in Judeo-Spanish musar—it is not cited as a supporting reference but as recommended reading for an unlearned audience.[11]

From the perspective of literary history, Judeo-Spanish musar literature and the *Meʿam Loʿez* clearly represent different genres. For all its diversity in style and contents, the *Meʿam Loʿez* is first and foremost a commentary on the biblical text.[12] In the architecture of the *Meʿam Loʿez*, it is the biblical narrative that provides the basic structure of the commentary; Huli always returns to the text he comments upon, and the largest literary sub-unit in the *Me'am Lo'ez* is determined by the weekly Torah reading. He divides his commentary on each reading into chapters of unequal length, usually revolving around one or several overarching themes of educational concern to him, themes that largely inform his selection of material from rabbinic tradition.[13] Huli explains and elaborates on the biblical text, but he also wants to entertain and educate. Extensive excursions tell stories adapted from traditional rabbinic literature and Sephardic oral traditions, provide detailed information about correct religious practice, introduce legal concepts, teach moral lessons, and then always return to the framing narrative of the biblical text itself.[14]

The literary structure of musar, by way of contrast, is usually determined by its subject matter. Typically, each chapter forms a discourse on a single topic, which can be either a musar value (e.g., fear of God, repentance, charity), a date in the cycle of the year (Passover, Yom Kippur), or a life event (birth, circumcision, marriage, death). Despite the differences between the genres, however, many Ottoman Sephardim read the *Me'am Lo'ez* as a book of musar, as evidenced by a remark in the *Sefer Ze Eliyahu* (Istanbul 1863): "[In Izmir,] they learn even from an early age how to read musar books like the *Me'am Lo'ez, Kav ha-Yashar, Shevet Musar* and other books of moral chastisement."[15] In other words, the patterns of consumption by the reading community and the social impact of the *Me'am Lo'ez* and of Ladino musar literature were similar.

Though later authors writing in Ladino did not necessarily follow the literary model established by the *Me'am Lo'ez,* Huli's classic marked the beginning of the new Judeo-Spanish print culture of the Sephardic communities of the eastern Mediterranean: it made traditional knowledge available in the vernacular and provided the basis for a broad reading public that had not existed in this form prior to the pioneering work of Huli and other authors in the early eighteenth century.

In discussing the role of anthologies in Jewish literature, Jacob Elbaum has remarked that "creativity in this sphere reemerges at specific cultural junctures, and that is certainly not happenstance."[16] This is also true of other attempts at a synthesis of Judaism like Maimonides' *Mishneh Torah* or Karo's *Shulhan 'Arukh.* Huli's *Me'am Lo'ez* should also be seen as marking such a "cultural juncture"—the complete transformation of patterns of communication by vernacular print culture in the early-eighteenth-century Ottoman Empire. The *Me'am Lo'ez* stands out for the novelty of its literary architecture and the audaciousness of its encyclopedic approach. Together with the other Judeo-Spanish works that were published in the first decades of the eighteenth century, it marks the beginning of a Judeo-Spanish rabbinic literature that left its mark on the age of transformation of Ottoman Jewry.

Eighteenth-Century Ladino Literature

There had been Judeo-Spanish books before the eighteenth century, but they were isolated cases which did not generate a whole Judeo-Spanish literary culture—

witness Moses Almosnino (ca. 1515–ca. 1580) and his *Regimento de la Vida,* a collection of religious precepts, or his *Crónica de los reyes otomanos,* books that were still written in Castilian Spanish and cannot be called Ladino. Huli, in the introduction to his *Me'am Lo'ez,* asserts that his contemporaries found the language of Almosnino's *Regimento de la Vida* unintelligible and calls it a "lucid book, but its words are very sealed."[17] Similarly, Spanish translations of the Bible appeared in the sixteenth century, most importantly the trilingual version of the Pentateuch (in Hebrew, Judeo-Spanish, and modern Greek, all in Hebrew characters) published in Constantinople in 1547, and, in Latin characters, the famous Bible of Ferrara (1553).[18] But these are isolated cases, however important they may have been (I refer to the Sephardic literature in Spanish/Judeo-Spanish in the *eastern* Mediterranean; obviously, there was a tremendously rich literary production of both original and translated works in Spanish—and Portuguese—among the Sephardic Jews of Amsterdam).[19]

In the eighteenth century, by contrast, Huli's *Me'am Lo'ez* marks the beginning of a prolonged period of a flourishing literary creativity in Ladino. Another towering figure of Ladino letters of that generation is Abraham Asa (ca. 1710–ca. 1768).[20] To call Asa a prolific translator would be an understatement. Between 1739 and 1745, he published a Judeo-Spanish translation of the Bible—the first complete one in Hebrew characters.[21] In his introduction to one of the volumes, Asa makes clear the educational ideal behind his efforts: "David Qimhi[22] explains that what sustains the Jews in this exile is their ceaseless reading of the Bible. And Isaac Abrabanel[23] says that the reason for the expulsion from Spain was that people did not read the written Law [i.e., the Bible]; while there were, in those places, more than five thousand rabbis of universal fame, the masses did not read the Bible." Since most people do not understand what they are reading when they recite the biblical text in Hebrew, "the publisher Jonah [Ashkenazi] wanted . . . to print the Bible in Ladino, well translated [*bien ladinado*], and including Rashi's commentary."[24] It is worth noting that the initiative for the Judeo-Spanish Bible translation is attributed here to the publisher, which points up the important role of the editors and publishers in the emergence and flourishing of the vernacular literature.

Asa's efforts to present the essentials of Judaism to a broad audience gave birth to much more. More than ten years before his Bible translation, he had published his brief *Sipur Malkhe 'Otmanlis* (History of the Ottoman Kings), translated from the Hebrew *Sipur Devarim,* which had been published the same year in Istanbul and was based on Joseph Sambari's unpublished *Divre Yosef* (Istanbul 1728). A year later, Asa's translation of *Otiyot de-Rabi 'Aqiba* appeared as *Letras de Rabi 'Aqiba* (Istanbul 1729). Many more translations would follow: the complete prayer book, *Bet Tefilah* (Istanbul 1739); the treatise *Orah Hayim* from Joseph Karo's *Shulhan 'Arukh,* published as *Shulhan ha-Melekh* (Istanbul 1749); Isaac Aboab's musar classic *Menorat ha-Ma'or* (Istanbul 1762); Elijah ha-Kohen's *Shevet Musar* (Istanbul 1742); and *Sefer Yosipon* or *Sefer Yosef bin Gorion* (Istanbul 1743). As an author, Abraham Asa also composed the fascinating work *Sefer Tsorkhe Tsibur* (Istanbul 1733), which presented the major precepts of Judaism in the form of rhymed *coplas.*

The sheer number of Judeo-Spanish translations that Abraham Asa prepared and the pioneering character of his work are remarkable and demonstrate his strong ideological commitment to educating the masses who were unable to read all this in Hebrew. However, the titles he selected and found worthy of translation into Ladino require some comment. I argue that the list of Asa's translations parallels the integrative, comprehensive approach we have seen in Huli's *Me'am Lo'ez*. There is a bit of everything, from the basics of Jewish knowledge and practice like the Bible, the prayer book, and the *Orah Hayim*, to the handy recompilation of the religious duties of the Jew in the *Tsorkhe Tsibur*, to some Kabbalah and to Ottoman and Jewish history. While Huli began a Sephardic encyclopedic Bible commentary, integrating everything he deemed important for a non-learned public, Abraham Asa tried to make a library of important books available to the Ladino reader. The educational ideal behind the two enterprises, however, was the same: to at last make accessible the heritage of Jewish tradition, which had been locked away in books unreadable by the masses and administered by an elite of rabbinic learned men. The vernacular print culture which emerged at that time popularized rabbinic knowledge: Jacob Huli with his encyclopedia and Abraham Asa with his library of Jewish knowledge are the prime representatives of this movement.

Elena Romero has related these towering figures of Judeo-Spanish rabbinic literature in the 1730s to the authors of another genre that flourished in the eighteenth century, the *coplas*.[25] "The authors of these *coplas*," she writes, "in terms of their intentions and their achievements, seem to be part of a group of rabbis and scholars who dedicated themselves, together with . . . Abraham Asa . . . and Jacob Huli and his successors, since the beginning of the eighteenth century to overcome the lack of knowledge of the cultural and religious traditions among ample sectors of the Sephardic world of the time."[26]

My thesis is that we should read Ottoman Sephardic history in the eighteenth and nineteenth century in the light of these literary developments. The emergence and flowering of a rich vernacular print culture in the eighteenth century led to the formation of a broad reading public which included social groups that had been all but excluded from printed Hebrew elite communication, and this new audience was the basis for the emergence of a Judeo-Spanish public sphere in the nineteenth century. I suggest that the new patterns of communication generated by the Judeo-Spanish rabbinic literature of the eighteenth century and the religious and secular Judeo-Spanish literature of the nineteenth call for a reappraisal of modern eastern Sephardic history.

The New Educational Ideal

Although Jacob Huli and many other vernacular rabbis claimed that they produced a Judeo-Spanish rabbinic literature for the masses because of the insufficient knowledge of Hebrew among the common folk, there must have been more that impelled these authors to undertake this new educational enterprise. There clearly was a sense of educational crisis expressed as a decline of knowledge and loss of

Hebrew proficiency, as when Huli held in a passage quoted earlier that "because of our sins, the world changed and came down and regressed to the degree that there are very few who know how to read a verse [of the Bible] correctly."[27] This and numerous similar remarks express a view of a "decline of generations" that became almost a commonplace in rabbinic literature from the tenth century on. In the words of Moses Hayim Luzzatto, "The most learned among us is no greater than the most insignificant disciple of former generations."[28] It is evident that this talk of spiritual and intellectual decline should not be taken as a description of the real intellectual or spiritual standards of the time; rather, it is part of an ideological model justifying the overwhelming authority of the rabbis of the Talmud (the *tanaʾim* and *amoraʾim*) over that of later scholars.

Likewise, it seems a bit rash in Huli's case to take his pronouncements of educational decline at face value. It might be accurate to speak of a decline of knowledge if we compare the 1730s with what Joseph Hacker has described as the intellectual ferment among sixteenth-century Ottoman Jews.[29] The claim that people did not know enough Hebrew was certainly true, and perhaps knowledge of Hebrew really had been declining. But we miss the point if we read Huli's and other authors' pronouncements of decline as historical evidence of real change in educational standards. Rather than truly expressing the difference between one generation and the next, the image of "decline" is a literary formula and expresses the difference between the rabbis' social ideal and the social reality as they perceived it. Huli's complaint about the decline in Hebrew knowledge and thus in religious practice often has been taken at face value; in fact it echoes a time-honored literary convention that can be seen, for example, in almost the same words as Huli's, in Maimonides' introduction to the *Mishneh Torah:* "In our days, severe vicissitudes prevail, and all feel the pressure of hard times. The wisdom of our wise men has disappeared; the understanding of our prudent men is hidden. . . . On these grounds, I . . . intently studied all these works, with the view of putting together the results obtained from them . . . all in plain language and terse style, so that thus the entire Oral Law might become systematically known to all [and] so that all the rules shall be accessible to young and old."[30]

Yet the mere fact of people's relative ignorance of Hebrew and rabbinic knowledge, whether more pronounced than in earlier generations or not, is not sufficient to explain the flourishing of rabbinic literature in Judeo-Spanish in the eighteenth century. What stimulated the creation of a popular didactic literature in the vernacular was the dissatisfaction of a group of rabbis with the educational standards of the time. Once these rabbis developed an ideal of popular learning and learnedness, once they began to care about what people beyond the rabbinic elite knew, they were forced to acknowledge the difference between their social ideal of a learning society and reality as they observed it. They responded by expressing this difference between ideal and reality using a time-honored literary topos, that of decline over the generations, and set out to find a remedy: a vernacular rabbinic literature accessible in language and structure to the average Sephardic Jew of their day.

In the introduction to the *Me°am Lo°ez,* Huli writes that "my soul desired to make a good and permanent remedy for the masses: to explain the Bible in Ladino, chapter by chapter, drawing on *Gemara* and *midrash* and other books of the great sages, of all the novellae and ordinances, the same issues which Moses [Maimonides] and Joseph Karo have brought out, not issues that are a matter of piety, but only those which are everyone's obligation."[31] Huli does not promote an ideology of piousness but seeks to inform the masses about their religious duties, the halakhic standards which the average person is expected to meet. A century later, Eli°ezer Papo expresses the same educational ideal in the Hebrew version of the *Pele Yo°ets:* "There are now many ignoramuses who do not understand the holy tongue.... The one who wishes to benefit Israel should undertake to write prayer books, compendia of law (*qitsure dinim*), and books of ethical instruction in the vernacular, which is better than to publish books of learned discussions (*pilpulim*) or homiletics (*derushim*) ... which do not serve more than one person in a town once in fifty years, but rather books in the vernacular which will go through the hands of many men and women."[32]

The new pedagogical thinking of the vernacular rabbis is patent here too, combined with a polemic against the subtleties of expert knowledge. It could reasonably be compared to the critique of education as we find it, for example, in the writings of the Maharal of Prague. As in Ashkenazic Europe, such a critique within the rabbinic elite, the primacy of morality over specialized learnedness, and the broadening of the public to include those who only read the vernacular would lay the ground for later educational projects of the Jewish Enlightenment.

But where did the new educational ideal of men like Jacob Huli and Abraham Asa and the authors who followed them come from? An argument advanced by Marc Angel seems persuasive: "Musar literature is a logical outgrowth of Lurianic thought. Musar authors felt a responsibility for the collective spiritual health of the Jewish people."[33] Though this claim is made with regard to Hebrew musar literature, it seems reasonable to extend its logic to the creation of a popular, vernacular musar literature. "Ethics in Lurianic Kabbalah," to quote Joseph Dan, "is no longer an attempt to achieve personal perfection. It is a set of instructions directing the individual how to participate in the common struggle of the Jewish people.... The individual's deeds are not his own private affair, because they profoundly influence the fate of the people as a whole."[34] In Lurianic Kabbalah, "the intrinsic, extramundane process of *Tikkun* [mending the world], symbolically described as the birth of God's personality, corresponds to the process of mundane history. The historical process and its innermost soul, the religious act of the Jew, prepare the way for the final restitution of all the scattered and exiled lights and sparks."[35] The restoration of the divine order is a collective effort of all Jews carried out by scrupulously fulfilling the religious commandments, and should be seen as forming the basis for the new educational ideal; this in turn leads to the creation of a new form of popular didactic literature in the vernacular.

The prominence of Lurianic thought among the Sephardic rabbis writing in

Judeo-Spanish can easily be traced in their musar books. Although they nowhere present a consistent Lurianic-kabbalistic theosophical worldview in their books written for a broad audience, Lurianic terminology and concepts abound. Ladino rabbinic literature in the eighteenth and nineteenth centuries thus forms part of a broader trend in Jewish literature at the time: "The cumulative effect . . . of what is generally called Kabbalistic Mussar literature and the emergence of Hasidism [in eastern Europe]," argues Moshe Idel,

> contributed to the dissemination of some Kabbalistic concepts, rituals, and motifs even when their broader theosophical framework remained unknown to the larger public. The belief in transmigration of souls (*gilgul*), demonic possession (*dibbuk*), and homunculus (*golem*), as well as the plethora of Kabbalistic terms that infiltrated ordinary Hebrew and the performance of customs and rituals incorporating Kabbalistic elements, such as the Tikkun of *Shavuᶜot* night, are evidence of the penetration of Kabbalah into the non-Kabbalistic Jewish public.[36]

The question remains why it was only in the eighteenth century that a new educational ideal engendered a Judeo-Spanish rabbinic literature. Some historians have attributed an important role to the Sabbatean movement and the crisis of authority that it purportedly created and to which the Judeo-Spanish vernacular rabbis would have reacted—a view for which we lack evidence, however.[37] Jacob Barnai and others have argued that it was the Sabbatean meltdown which caused the alleged "stagnation of the Ottoman communities . . . in contrast to the liveliness of the European communities," and that the Ottoman rabbis "cloistered themselves, returning to their former habitual religious life based upon the halakhah of the *Shulḥan ᶜArukh* and kabbalah free of Sabbatean theological interpretation."[38] This does not account for the emergence of a whole new literature, now in Ladino, a little over half a century after the Sabbatean crisis.

Neither is there any clear evidence that the authors of this new literature were in fact responding to a perceived post-Sabbatean threat to traditional authority. Even works by authors with clear Sabbatean leanings are cited with some naturalness and frequency in Judeo-Spanish and Hebrew musar literature of the period. One also must differentiate between Istanbul and the provinces when assessing the impact of Sabbateanism; it seems that the social disruption caused by the spread of the Sabbatean movement was largely overcome in the capital city in the eighteenth century—and it was precisely here that Judeo-Spanish rabbinic literature began to flourish. In Izmir, by contrast, sympathizers with Sabbateanism continued to hold key positions in the community and in 1731 edited the three-volume ethical work *Hemdat Yamim* with clear Sabbatean tendencies, while the Salonika community continued to live with the *dönme* sect until the twentieth century.

If Ladino literature did not come as a response to Sabbateanism, the importance of the messianic movement may lie elsewhere, however. Sabbatean propaganda, as it was shaped by Sabbatai Sevi's prophet, Nathan of Gaza (1653/4–1680), helped to spread Lurianic ideas and practices. While the exact nature of Lurianic influence on Sabbateanism may still be debated, it is clear that Nathan's ideology was deeply suffused with Lurianic thinking and that the followers of Sabbateanism employed an imagery and terminology that was Lurianic.[39] Not necessarily widely popularized, the ideas of Luria's teachings were disseminated, thanks to Sabbatean propaganda and the widespread exchange of information about the movement, throughout the rabbinic circles of the empire, and in turn had an important, if sometimes indirect, impact on the emergence of a vernacular musar literature translating the collective responsibility for *tiqun* into a universal educational program. As mentioned earlier, Lurianic concepts made their way into the mainstream of Jewish literature and thus also into the Ladino musar books.

The importance of Sabbateanism for the emergence of Judeo-Spanish musar thus does not lie in the fact that it had caused an educational crisis or in the fact that it called for an active response on the part of the rabbis, but in the fact that it catalyzed the spread of Lurianic ideas which, in turn, strengthened a new, socially more inclusive educational ideal.[40]

The Emergence of Judeo-Spanish Print Culture

In her influential study *The Printing Press as an Agent of Change,* Elizabeth Eisenstein claimed that "among historians dealing with the post-Reformation era, the invisibility of the cumulative impact exerted by the new communications system is particularly marked. The intellectual and political revolutions of the sixteenth and seventeenth centuries are placed in the context not of a post-print but of a pre-industrialized society."[41] A similar point could be made for modern Sephardic history: while most studies have treated the history of Ottoman Jewry before the late nineteenth century as a "pre-westernized" society, I propose that it be understood as the history of a society after the emergence of a Judeo-Spanish print culture.

To be sure, Hebrew printing had been known in the Ottoman Empire well before the eighteenth century; the transformation into a print culture goes back to the early sixteenth century.[42] There had been a decline in Hebrew printing in the empire between the late 1590s and the early eighteenth century, however, and books often had to be imported, notably from Italy.[43] The reestablishment of Hebrew printing in the early eighteenth century coincided with the flourishing of Judeo-Spanish literature, when Jonah Ashkenazi established a press in Istanbul in 1710. It will be remembered that he was the publisher who was the force behind Abraham Asa's Bible translation, and he also was the publisher of Huli's *Me'am Lo'ez* on Genesis and other volumes from that series—in fact, of the 210 Hebrew and Ladino books published between 1710 and the first decade of the nineteenth century in Istanbul, 188 were printed by Jonah Ashkenazi's publishing house.[44] The development of Judeo-Spanish vernacular literature and the resurgent Hebrew print culture are thus closely interrelated. Though Hebrew print culture already had a rich history in the Ottoman Empire, it gained renewed momentum in the early eighteenth century and contributed to the emergence of a Judeo-Spanish print culture which transformed the patterns of communication in the eastern Sephardic world.

Hebrew print and vernacular literature were more than "interrelated" developments, however. Preservation through printing was a crucial factor in the development of vernacular literature. Even after the advent of printing, many rabbinic books in Hebrew remained unpublished (i.e., not printed) and circulated in manuscript form among the limited circle of the learned elite. For example, many works of one of the outstanding Sephardic rabbis, Elijah ha-Kohen of Izmir, were never printed. Nonetheless, such works were referred to and cited by other rabbis; although they were not widely disseminated and were easily lost in the many blazes which plagued Ottoman cities, they were publicly available to at least a limited, local group of learned persons. By contrast, printing was a precondition for the very existence of Judeo-Spanish literature. It had to be a mass literature, printed and widely diffused, to exist at all. The vernacular literature could never be a substitute for the Hebrew elite literature, but relied on wide diffusion among a general audience by means of the printed word. It was only print that made the existence of a vernacular literature feasible; a Judeo-Spanish book in manuscript effectively did not exist, because it would not generate interest among the limited elite audience that would have access to such a manuscript. A good example is the larger portion of the *Me'am Lo'ez* on Deuteronomy, which is said to have been finished in manuscript but never printed, and thus is lost from the records of Ladino literary history.[45]

The revival of Ottoman Jewish print culture in the eighteenth century was not an isolated development. The same period also saw the emergence of Ottoman-Turkish print in Arabic script. Up to that point, Islamic and Ottoman authorities had rejected the use of print for Arabic or Turkish works.[46] While Jews and later various Christian minorities had established their own printing presses in the Ottoman Empire before, it was only in the late 1720s that we find the timid beginnings of an Ottoman Turkish print culture.[47]

An emblematic figure in the advancement of printing in the Ottoman Empire was Ibrahim Müteferrika, who also is known as one of the first Ottoman diplomats to have advocated a new openness toward the West and the reformation of the Ottoman military on European models. In 1726 he submitted a treatise, "The Means of Printing," to the Grand Vizier and the leading Islamic authorities; after obtaining authorization to establish a press, he began operation a year later. None other than Jonah Ashkenazi was among those credited with having helped Müteferrika establish his press.[48] Müteferrika even applied to exempt his Jewish associate from the poll tax, for he had, as he explained, "profited from the services of the Jew names Yuna [i.e., Jonah], who possesses all the important elements [needed for printing]."[49] In 1744, Müteferrika established the first Ottoman paper mill, and again sought the assistance of an Ottoman Jew whom he sent to Poland to hire three experts to come for a year to Istanbul and teach their profession to local craftsmen.[50]

The first printed Ottoman Turkish book appeared in 1729. It is noteworthy that the Sultan's authorization explicitly prohibited the publication of religious works; thus, in marked contrast to the Jewish case, early Ottoman print was limited to secular subjects, namely geographic and historiographic works. The Muslim religious authorities were concerned about the undesired consequences of print and the uncontrolled spread of knowledge to a general public.[51] Not until the early nineteenth century would there be continuous Ottoman printing in Constantinople.[52]

All vernacular print cultures, including Ladino, developed much later in Ottoman lands than in western or central Europe. It is true that popular literature in Greek was being printed in the Greek diaspora in Venice from the sixteenth century onward and was distributed in the Ottoman Empire until the nineteenth; the first Greek printing press in the empire itself was opened in the early seventeenth century, whereas the first Armenian printing press was founded in Istanbul in 1567.[53] But popular literature in the southern Slavic vernacular languages of the Balkans developed only after 1800, that is, during the period of nation building among the Christian peoples under Ottoman rule. The first book in modern Bulgarian, for example, was published as late as 1806.[54] Hence, the Jews of the Ottoman Empire not only pioneered printing in general (the first Hebrew press had been established in Constantinople in 1493 by Jews exiled from Spain); they were also among the bellwethers of the flowering of modern vernacular print culture in Ottoman lands in the early eighteenth century, which was belated only from a western European perspective.

As early as the late eighteenth century, Ottoman observers were quite conscious of the potentially disruptive impact of print in the vernacular on the traditional social order. This can be seen in a report about the French Revolution prepared by a high-ranking Ottoman official for the Ottoman administration in 1798:

> It is one of the things known to all well-informed persons that the conflagration of sedition and wickedness that broke out a few years ago in France . . . had been conceived many years previously in the minds of certain accursed heretics. . . . The known and famous atheists Voltaire and Rousseau . . . had printed and published various works . . . all expressed in easily intelligible words and phrases, in the form of mockery, in the language of the common people. Finding the pleasure of novelty in these writings, most of the people, even youths and women, inclined towards them and paid close attention to them.[55]

Both Ottoman print and Ladino print in the empire remained within the confines of tradition until a much later date, to be sure, but it is remarkable that Ottoman observers in the late eighteenth century were no less conscious about the potential social consequences of the spread of vernacular print culture to the traditional order than were later historians of the French Revolution.

The Impact of Vernacular Print Culture

Just as the invention of printing had a revolutionary impact on European culture since the mid-fifteenth century, so it did in Ottoman Jewish society in the eighteenth and nineteenth centuries. The advent of a print culture in the Ladino vernacular catalyzed the effect of printing and generated trends that transformed the geographical dissemination of knowledge and standardized it while transforming patterns of rabbinic social control and creating new social contexts for the communication of traditional knowledge.

GEOGRAPHICAL DISSEMINATION AND STANDARDIZATION

Any discussion of the dissemination of books through printing and the use of the vernacular must be concerned with data on actual circulation. Unfortunately, such data are not available in our case; we have no reliable information on the numbers of copies printed or the geographic patterns of distribution. As far as we can tell from the places of publication, subsequent editions of a book were often reprinted in different cities which were not necessarily the author's hometown. Thus, the diffusion of Judeo-Spanish literature was not confined to a particular region; indeed, it extended throughout the Ladino-speaking world, including places outside the Ottoman Empire like Vienna and Livorno, and from Livorno to North Africa.[56] It would nonetheless seem prudent to assume that a higher concentration of printed material was available where the necessary infrastructure existed, that is, printing houses, book dealerships, libraries, and institutions of higher learning (*yeshivot*). Ottoman print culture thus reinforced the centrality of certain urban centers (Istanbul, Salonika, Izmir, and a few more) as centers of Jewish learning, and presses and book dealerships developed into new cultural foci in the urban topography of these cities.

Whereas the printed book standardized texts to a degree which was inconceivable in manuscript culture, popular rabbinic literature in Judeo-Spanish standardized knowledge. This is, to be sure, a somewhat idealized description of a complex process. As Natalie Zemon Davis has demonstrated for early modern France, the transition to print did not affect all parts of society equally and by no means substituted for or even significantly weakened oral culture in France for the first 125 years or so after the first presses were established in the country.[57] The same is true of Sephardic culture in the eighteenth and nineteenth centuries, when oral traditions persisted, notwithstanding the advent of Judeo-Spanish print, and the printed versions of stories (*maʿasiyot*) integrated into the *Meʿam Loʿez* and musar literature did not immediately replace the repertoire of the oral tradition. But it is significant in this context that in the eighteenth century, we also see the flourishing of another genre of Judeo-Spanish literature, the *coplas*. Though written, *coplas* carried on older oral traditions which occasionally went back to pre-expulsion Hispano-Jewish culture. In turn, many *coplas* composed (or recomposed) in the eighteenth century became part of a repertoire of orally transmitted folk culture.[58] Thus we see the emergence of new intersections of written and oral culture, which had hitherto been rather strictly divided along linguistic lines (Hebrew versus vernacular).

The standardization of folk tradition through printing paralleled a standardization of knowledge of correct religious practice. Much like earlier compendia that promised to standardize religious practice, such as the *Shulhan ʿArukh* (the printing of which had provoked significant opposition among Ashkenazic rabbis in the sixteenth century for this very reason),[59] the *Me'am Lo'ez* and Judeo-Spanish musar and halakhic literature contributed to the crystallization of a more uniform halakhic practice. The *Me'am Lo'ez*, by representing rabbinic and folk culture on the same pages, and the many Ladino works that followed it, served to integrate multiple, regionally different eastern Sephardic traditions into a new, more uniform Judeo-Spanish culture. Building upon a common language and common historical memories and aided by inner-Ottoman Jewish migrations, the emerging Ladino reading culture created, as Avigdor Levy called it, "a new type of Ottoman Jew . . . who was equally at home in Safed, Bursa, Izmir or Istanbul."[60]

SOCIAL DISSEMINATION AND TRANSFORMATION OF RABBINIC CONTROL

Vernacular print culture opened the world of traditional knowledge to a broader audience than manuscript or Hebrew print culture ever could have done. While the diffusion of written knowledge to the lower classes should not be exaggerated—most people still did not have access to books, much less own them—the production of vernacular rabbinic literature opened the field of traditional knowledge to sectors of the community which had been virtually excluded from it; as we see in chapter 3, the implicit, and at times explicit, inclusion of women in the reading public is of particular importance. Traditional knowledge now was being mediated by printed books, in addition to the pulpit of the synagogue and other oral routes within the family and between individuals and the rabbi.

This broadening of the social spectrum of (at least potential) recipients of rabbinic literature both restricted and enhanced the degree of rabbinic control over society. On the one hand, individual readers now could pursue knowledge without necessarily depending on the personal mediation of someone with special training. This decentralization of rabbinic control over the communication of knowledge is among the most important consequences of Ladino print culture. On the other hand, the vernacular literature enabled the rabbis to shape and standardize popular religious practices and attitudes much more effectively than before.

The importance of individual reading must not be overstated, however, as reading was evidently not predominantly individual. The social institution of the *meldado*—familiar from other traditional cultures as the *veillée*, the evening gathering to read and hear books being read—was an important institution in the dissemination of printed knowledge. Sometimes a *talmid hakham*, a student of Torah, would be present at these *meldados* (as was recommended by the musar authors), but obviously this need not always have been the case. Collective reading in a *meldado* contributed to the decentralization of rabbinic control over the communication of knowledge, as did an individual's reading of Ladino literature.

New literary forms, such as the *Me'am Lo'ez* series, were created and old forms of Hebrew musar transformed in order to integrate entertainment and instruction, narrative and pedagogical elements, and in order to make the canon of traditional knowledge more accessible to untrained readers. The prominent role of popular stories—*ma'asim*—in the *Me'am Lo'ez* and books of musar represents this quest for creating entertaining and didactic works and the confluence of rabbinic and popular traditions.[61]

In addition, the vernacular rabbis tried to make knowledge manageable to the non-expert reader by categorizing and restructuring it, by using convenience to the reader as an organizing principle. The outstanding example is again the *Me'am Lo'ez* and its elaborate system of indexes that lead the less learned reader to passages of interest.[62] In the nineteenth century, Eli'ezer and Judah Papo's musar text book, the *Pele Yo'ets,* had thematic sections arranged in alphabetical order. Features such as the index—very much a product of print culture and the new possibilities of reproduction—and alphabetically ordered sections transformed books like the *Me'am Lo'ez* or *Pele Yo'ets* into reference works that the reader could navigate far more easily than earlier volumes. Even those musar books that did not feature indexes or the convenience of alphabetical order still attempted to present rabbinic knowledge in simple language and make it accessible for the average reader.

All this notwithstanding, the readers still depended on the mediation of the translator who selected books to be rendered into Judeo-Spanish, or the author of vernacular books who decided what his public should know. While non-experts were now potentially freer in the choice and practice of their reading, rabbinic control also increased in a certain sense. Vernacular literature now reached a public distinct from those who read didactic treatises in Hebrew, and popular works affected these readers more strongly than instruction from the synagogue pulpit. Judeo-Spanish rabbinic literature thus served a purpose similar to that of Yiddish rabbinic literature of earlier times, though the Sephardic rabbis were not as explicit or as conscious about this consequence as were their counterparts writing in Yiddish, one of whom stated, "For the people hear sermons in the synagogues and do not understand what the sermon is. They speak too rapidly in the synagogue, but in this book one can read slowly, so that he himself will understand."[63]

The social spectrum of rabbinic literature was extended not only in the sense that it reached a new, broader audience; in addition, a new group of authors emerged, those whom I call the vernacular rabbis. It is noteworthy that—with very few exceptions, and only from the second half of the nineteenth century onward[64]—Judeo-Spanish rabbinic musar books were not written by the most prominent rabbis of their time. Jacob Huli, for example, did not hold the position of the rabbi of a *qahal,* although he did serve as *dayan*—a member of the rabbinic court—in Istanbul.[65] There was opposition among the rabbinic establishment to his daring project of a vernacular encyclopedic Bible commentary[66] and we have some evidence of a debate over the legitimacy of vernacular rabbinic literature.[67] It was not only the use of the vernacular that made Ladino musar literature a marginal enterprise from the viewpoint of the rabbinic establishment: in Ottoman rabbinic culture, evident both in education and publication, expertise in halakhah ranked far higher than in *aggadah,* the nonlegal literary traditions. Elijah ha-Kohen of Izmir, for example, was widely respected as a preacher and author of numerous popular works of musar. But he was also mocked by rabbinic colleagues for an occasional legal ruling that they felt was based on the moralizing worldview of the popular preacher and author rather than on knowledge of the pertinent legal litera-ture.[68] The transition to a vernacular print culture thus opened the way for a new group of authors who were, though not opposed to the rabbinic establishment, standing on its margins.

Moreover, there were now people like Ben-Tsion Benjamin Roditi or Isaac Amarachi who are known to us not only as authors of musar works (*Sefer Ki Ze Kol ha-Adam* in Roditi's case, *Sefer Musar Haskel* and *Sefer Darkhe ha-Adam* in Amarachi's), but also as publishers. Amarachi established a press in Salonika in 1845 although it shut down only two years later.[69] Roditi was an active publisher in Izmir (he printed the 1860 edition of the *Shevet Musar* and a complete set of the *Me'am Lo'ez* on the Pentateuch) and operated a printing house which at that time had been in business longer than any other in the city, from 1857 to 1884.[70]

These publisher-rabbi-authors represented a new social type, though Roditi is certainly an outstanding figure. While Ottoman rabbis in the seventeenth and eighteenth centuries were generally known for their halakhic erudition and their huge output of responsa but much less so for their literary creativity in other areas, the vernacular print revolution produced a group of authors with different priori-ties. Though socially not a homogeneous group, they shared an ideal of reaching out to the masses to entertain and educate. They had to ally themselves with pub-lishers and find sponsors to support their ambitious projects, and a social network of authors, publishers, and patrons was established to promote the Judeo-Spanish vernacular literature, notwithstanding the financial difficulties amply evidenced in many introductions to the *Me'am Lo'ez* or musar books.[71]

The Development of Ladino Rabbinic Literature in the Nineteenth Century

After the initial phase marked by the ground-breaking works of Huli, Asa, and others in the first half of the eighteenth century, additional volumes of the *Me'am Lo'ez* series were published through 1772 and a few musar titles were published or reedited. During the last quarter of the eighteenth century and until the 1820s (when most of the *Me'am Lo'ez* series was published in Livorno), the publication of Ladino books declined in the Ottoman Empire. The publication of translated and original Ladino rabbinic literature regained momentum by the late 1830s and early 1840s and reached its peak in the period from the 1860s through the end of the century.

This uneven development of Ladino print culture in the latter part of the eighteenth and the early nineteenth centuries was due to the vicissitudes of Hebrew print in general in the Ottoman Empire and was certainly related to the economic crisis of the Jewish communities in the empire at the time and, indeed, the eco-nomic and political crisis of the Ottoman state at large in the decades between 1770 and 1830. In Istanbul, after the press operated by Jonah Ashkenazi and his sons closed in the late 1770s, Raphael Hayim Pardo printed just six books in his printing house between 1799 and 1808, and printing did not fully resume until the 1820s. In Izmir, which had become one of the foremost centers of Hebrew print and rabbinic scholarship in the Ottoman Empire, Ashkenazi established a branch of his printing business that was active from 1728 to 1739. Printing in the city resumed in 1754 in a new publishing house and was interrupted again between the late 1760s and 1838. Only in Salonika were Hebrew books printed continuously since the early eighteenth century by publishers of variable success and longevity.[72] Hebrew books continued to be printed abroad, to be sure, and it is hardly a coincidence that the publication of Ladino literature resumed in the 1820s with the publication of the *Me'am Lo'ez* in the thriving Italian port city of Livorno.

While many of the titles under discussion here were published originally well before the advent of secular Ladino literature and before the project of westernization gained momentum among Ottoman Jewry, the development of rabbinic literature in the Judeo-Spanish vernacular in the second half of the nineteenth century overlaps with the emergence and expansion of secular Ladino literature. The first newspaper in Ladino was the short-lived *La Buena Esperanza* of 1842 in Izmir, followed a few years later by *Sha'are Mizrah* (later *Puertas de Oriente*) published in the same city.[73] In one of its earliest numbers, *Sha'are Mizrah* expressed the educational agenda of the nascent Ladino press: it acknowledged the permit by the Ottoman authorities to publish the newspaper which, the editor confidently proclaimed, was due to the desire of Sultan Abdülhamid's government to see its subjects educated, "being certainly aware that the benefits of printing are such that we can learn about every science, like the most civilized nations of Europe" and expressing the hope that "thus we will be able to prosper in everything" and be considered "worthy subjects of such a gracious and just sovereign."[74] We find here the themes that set the agenda for the political and cultural changes in Ottoman Sephardic society promoted by the secular Ladino press through the second half of the nineteenth century: Ottoman patriotism, the desire for a regained prosperity through modern education, and the rhetoric of "civilizational progress" inspired by the European model.

After timid beginnings in the 1840s, the newspapers in Ladino flourished from the 1860s onward and were the most important vehicle in spreading the politics of westernization. *El Jurnal Yisra'elit* was published in Istanbul since 1860 and replaced by *El Nacional* and *El Telegrafo* in the 1870s. In 1875, Sa'adi Halevi of Salonika—incidentally also known as a publisher of rabbinic literature in Ladino—began to publish *La Epoca*, which existed well into the twentieth century.[75] Secular genres in Ladino literature, such as the novel, adapted from Western (in particular French) literature, developed in the framework of the new Judeo-Spanish public sphere emerging in the second half of the nineteenth century.[76]

It seems fair to say that whereas the beginning of rabbinic literature in Ladino was marked by the educational implications of Lurianic Kabbalah, its expansion in the second half of the nineteenth century was part of a general expansion of Judeo-Spanish literary creativity and in part a response to the social transformation of Ottoman Jewry. It would be wrong, however, to depict this later stage of Ladino

rabbinic literature as merely a reaction or response to social and cultural developments on the outside or to see it as just another modern phenomenon, alongside
newspapers and novels, in the history of Ladino literature. Nineteenth-century
rabbinic literature in Ladino continued the literary patterns established by the pioneers of the early eighteenth century. In fact, rabbinic literature in Ladino often
anticipated features of the emerging secular Judeo-Spanish reading culture. This
is true both for patterns of consumption of such literature (namely the reading
circles) as it is for the educational intentions of the authors of Ladino literature,
and it even is true for the introduction of secular subject matter into the Judeo-
Spanish literary canon. Rabbinic literature in Ladino created a Judeo-Spanish
reading culture, and it created the reading public that was to be the basis for the
development of secular Ladino literature in the second half of the nineteenth and
early twentieth centuries.

Though with a different educational agenda, latter-day Sephardic intellectuals
producing the Ladino newspapers and other secular literature were able to build
upon the precedents set by their rabbinic predecessors in the eighteenth century. By
the mid-nineteenth century, rabbinic and secular literature existed side by side and
responded to each other, sometimes explicitly and often implicitly. But even then,
intersections between rabbinic and secular literary cultures and their reading publics were numerous. Consider Saᶜadi Halevi, publisher of *La Epoca*, one of the most
successful Ladino newspapers in nineteenth-century Salonika. Scion of a veteran
printing family there, Halevi also was the translator into Judeo-Spanish of Moses
Almosnino's sixteenth-century popularized halakhic work *Regimiento de la vida*,
as well as the publisher of more than 200 books between 1840 and 1902. These
included most of the halakhic and homiletic works by Hayim Palachi, the re-
nowned chief rabbi of Izmir, rabbinic responsa, and Ladino rabbinic literature such
as Isaac Farhi's widely popular musar book *Zekhut u-Mishor*.[77] The development of
the Judeo-Spanish literary public, from its beginnings with Huli and Asa in the
eighteenth century through its secularization toward the end of the nineteenth and
early twentieth centuries, should be seen as the unfolding of *one* literary history,
rather than the history of competing rabbinic *versus* secular literatures.

What is true for the history of Judeo-Spanish literary culture in the Ottoman
Empire is also true for Ottoman culture at large. As far as some of the social
consequences of vernacular print culture are concerned (the wider social dissemination and thus democratization of knowledge, the decentralization of control, the
development of a vernacular literature), similar developments as those within the
emerging Judeo-Spanish print culture have been described for Ottoman culture in
general: "The emergence of the Ottoman printing press in the early eighteenth
century followed by the establishment of newspapers and periodicals in the early
nineteenth altered the existing relation between knowledge and control," one historian of the Ottoman Empire has recently remarked. "By purchasing and reading an Ottoman or translated Western book, or, if one was illiterate, by attending
one of the many reading cum coffeehouses in the capital where certain newspapers
were read out loud, one could have direct personal access to knowledge outside the

household structure."[78] This transformation in acquiring knowledge through the printed vernacular book, read individually or publicly in a group, leading to a decentralization of social control and a democratization of knowledge, was a feature of the transformation of Ottoman Sephardic society, just as it was of Ottoman society at large in the nineteenth century.

Part II

Authors, Translators, Readers

The Translation and Reception of Musar

3

In a recent article, Olga Borovaya has examined the translation of *Gulliver's Travels* into Ladino as an example of an effort by a westernized elite to educate the Sephardic masses in the early twentieth century. Having defined translations broadly as the transfer from one literary system to another and as an act of rewriting, she focuses on this Ladino work as an adaptation of the literary classic to the Judeo-Spanish cultural context. "Most often we deal with adaptations when reading children's books, no matter whether translated or original," she argues, adding that "behavior patterns of children's literature are similar to those of cultural adaptations."[1]

It seems to me that the westernizing strategy of Sephardic intellectuals in the second half of the nineteenth century and in the twentieth century, adapting works from one literary system (mostly French) to another (Ladino), continued in a certain sense what the vernacular rabbis had done since the early eighteenth century when they rewrote rabbinic knowledge as a non-elite discourse for a broad public. Works of Ladino rabbinic literature, whether rewritings of Hebrew works or the *Me'am Lo'ez*, can be seen as cultural adaptations that follow patterns similar to those of the literary adaptations studied by Borovaya. Rabbinic vernacular literature, meant to educate and enlighten the masses, arguably provided the model for and legitimized the later efforts of westernizing intellectuals who translated and rewrote European literature into Ladino.

The production of Judeo-Spanish musar literature as a cultural adaptation was guided by the author/translator's image of the intended reader. Vernacular moralizing literature was a paternalistic discourse in which the rabbis translated Hebrew knowledge into literary patterns they deemed fit for a popular readership. Below, I trace the major principles guiding these translations. I then discuss how the Sephardic vernacularizing authors reflected both on their own literary enterprise and on the roles they imagined or intended for themselves and their readers. They assumed their readers would take an essentially affirmative attitude and believed that musar literature would indeed shape socio-religious practice. They recognized the coexistence of collective learning and individual reading but insisted, in both cases, on the mediating role of a *talmid hakham* (Torah scholar) in order to control the reception of vernacular literature. Beginning in the latter half of the nineteenth century, however, we begin to find references to reading practices that deviate from the patterns intended by the authors and translators of Judeo-Spanish musar.

Musar as Translation

JUDAH PAPO ON TRANSLATION

The dynamics of rewriting Hebrew musar into Ladino can be seen particularly well by studying Judah Papo's Ladino "translation" of his father Eliᶜezer Papo's Hebrew *Pele Yoᶜets*, first published in Istanbul in 1824. This work is of great interest not only because it is one of the most important works of Sephardic musar in modern times, but because the author of the Judeo-Spanish version shows an exceptionally eloquent awareness of the difficulties of translation. In the introduction he writes:

> It is known that the work of translating [*copiar*] from one language into another is very difficult, for if one wants to render it into Ladino [*ladinar*] word for word, the flavor of the speech is lost. And if one wishes to take up the [most] important of what the author wanted to say and to rewrite the speech according to one's own understanding, one might miss the point and go beyond what the author intended. But I am very sure about this, because I am very familiar with [my father's] books in manuscript and in print, and my ears resound with what his mouth was saying. Therefore I am very sure that I do not depart from his will and his intention.[2]

While this quotation has been used in the (to my mind, futile) discussion of Séphiha's theory of Ladino as the "*judéo-espagnol calque*,"[3] I do not think that Papo's distinction between "*ladinar* word for word" or a rewriting more removed from the original is referring to the issue of the "calque" translations typical of the Ladino Bible versions as opposed to non-"calque" Judeo-Spanish. The phrase "*ladinar* word for word" could of course refer to calque translation—imitating the Hebrew original as closely as possible syntactically and even lexically—but this would not make much sense since no one translated musar literature that way. The alternative faced by Papo was either to produce a translation fairly close to the Hebrew base text like Abraham Asa's Ladino version of the *Shevet Musar*, for example—or to rewrite it freely, adapting the original text to a new public and to changed circumstances, presumably keeping the "main ideas" of the Hebrew text but reshaping it considerably.

Judah Papo's claim that he faithfully adheres to his father's intention is an important legitimizing device. Because he sees his father as one of the outstanding authorities of his generation, his assertion that he does not deviate from his father's teachings also enhances the authority of his own Ladino *Pele Yoᶜets*.

While invoking his father's authority, he admits his own authorship of an extensive chapter which he added to the original *Pele Yoᶜets*, entitled "*Mitsvot*." This chapter, addressing new questions that seemed of burning importance to the author when he published the Judeo-Spanish version of the book in the early 1870s, could be considered an Ottoman-Sephardic rabbi's response to modernity. Judah Papo's brief introduction to this new chapter further illuminates his understanding of translation:

קי לה ויריקיאה די פידריד גרוש . אי סוצ'רי איסטו דישו איל
פסוק „אשרי אדם מפחד תמיד".

הקדמה אל המצות.

אמר הבן . מי דיקלארו סינייוריס, קי אין לה קופיא די איסטי
ליצרו סאבנו , אפילו קי אה לה פאריינסייה פארידֿי
קי אי אונגֿאם קוזאם מואיצֿאם, קי נו איסטאבֿן אין איל פלא יועץ
די לשון הקדש , אונה לה צֿידֿאד איס קי עודו איס סו ליי די **מי
סיכ'** פֿאדֿרי זלוק"ל , או קי איסטה איספארֿארֿדו אין אונדרוש לו„
גֿאריס דיל **פלא יועץ** פֿרופ'ייו אין אונדֿראם ליגֿאראם . אי יין מאכֿני
ליגֿאראם אי לו ריקוֿ'י אין אובֿה ליגֿרה עודו לוקי איס פֿ די און דים„
קורסו , אי טֿאכצ'יין קי מי סירצֿ'י די אובֿנדרוש ליצֿדֿרוש סֿרייוֿם קי
טֿיֿיכי אין כֿתיצֿה אי אין איסטאמֿאכֿפֿה , אי פֿוכֿו אי פֿולֿאדֿו , קי לה
פֿיכֿדֿולֿה אצֿלֿה אי פֿוזֿה אלֿבֿונֿה קֿוזֿה . אונֿה אין איסטֿה ליצֿרֿה די
מצות אי אוכֿגֿאם קֿוזֿאם די לוקי מי מיֿנֿיירֿון אין כֿיֿכֿו די לֿוש
סֿיֿלֿוֿם קי סֿוֿן קֿוזֿאם איכֿפֿורֿטֿאֿכֿטֿיֿם אי מֿיֿכֿסֿטֿיֿרֿוֿזֿאם פֿור מֿוֿאֿיֿם„
טֿרו טֿיֿיֿכֿפֿו . אי פֿוֿר איסטֿה רֿאֿזֿון מֿי טֿוֿמֿי איל קֿוֿרֿאֿזֿ'י אֿי איֿזֿי
איל איֿכֿצֿ'ֿיֿכֿייֿו די אלֿה אצֿלֿה קֿוֿמֿו קֿי סֿו יֿו איל אֿצֿֿלֿאֿדֿוֿר . אי סֿיֿיֿכֿדֿו
קי אין איסטֿה ליצֿֿרֿה , פֿוֿר פֿרֿוֿבֿאֿם אֿה דֿאֿר אֿה סֿאֿבֿ'ֿיֿר לֿה צֿ'ֿיֿר„
דֿאֿדֿיֿרֿיֿאֿה די לֿאֿם קֿוֿזֿאם, עֿוֿצֿ'ֿי קֿי מֿיֿכֿסֿטֿֿיֿר די סֿיֿרֿצ'ֿיֿרֿמֿי אֿי
אֿיֿיֿוֿדֿֿאֿרֿמֿי די מֿוֿכֿגֿֿום פֿֿסֿוֿקֿיֿם די לֿה לֿיֿי . אֿי סֿי מֿיֿטֿֿיֿאֿה קֿאֿדֿֿם
פֿֿסֿוֿק אֿיֿן לֿשֿֿון אֿי אֿיֿן לֿאֿדֿֿיֿנֿו קֿוֿמֿו לֿה רֿיֿגֿֿלֿֿה דֿֿיֿל לֿיֿצֿֿֿרֿו , סֿֿי אֿחֿֿזֿֿאֿֿה„
לֿאֿֿרֿגֿֿיֿֿאֿֿה אֿי אֿֿטֿֿכֿֿאֿֿגֿֿֿאֿֿכֿֿֿכֿֿֿֿֿו פֿֿֿֿֿור אֿיֿֿל מֿיֿלֿֿדֿֿֿאֿֿדֿֿֿוֿֿר . פֿֿוֿֿר אֿיֿֿֿסֿֿֿטֿֿֿו אֿֿֿקֿֿוֿֿֿרֿֿֿֿמֿֿֿי
אֿֿֿֿיֿֿֿן אֿֿֿֿיֿֿֿֿל דֿֿֿֿיֿֿֿקֿֿֿֿלֿֿֿֿֿאֿֿֿֿֿרֿֿֿֿו די לֿֿֿוֿֿֿֿֿם פֿֿֿֿֿֿסֿֿֿוֿֿֿֿֿקֿֿֿֿֿיֿֿֿֿֿֿֿם אֿֿֿיֿֿֿֿֿן לֿֿֿֿאֿֿֿֿֿֿדֿֿֿֿֿֿֿיֿֿֿֿֿֿֿכֿֿֿֿֿֿו . אֿֿֿֿי אֿֿֿֿֿפֿֿֿֿֿֿיֿֿֿֿֿלֿֿֿֿֿֿו קֿֿֿֿֿי אֿֿֿֿֿי
אֿֿֿֿֿֿֿוֿֿֿֿֿֿכֿֿֿֿֿֿֿגֿֿֿ

In the translation [*copia*] of this holy book, although it seems that there are many new things which were not in the [original] *Pele Yoʿets* in the holy tongue [i.e., Hebrew], in fact everything is my father's doctrine [drawn from other sources] or dispersed in other places in the same *Pele Yoʿets* in other chapters. I did not have enough [space to include all] chapters [of the original] and I assembled in one chapter everything that belongs to one discourse [*discurso*]. I also used other books of his in manuscript or in print, and there is very little that has been added, for in the act of writing, one sometimes unconsciously adds something [*la pendula habla y puja alguna cosa*].—But in this chapter on "*mitsvot*," there are many issues that I have been inspired by the heavens [to address], and they are important and necessary issues for our times. And thus I took courage and wrote these words on my own [*como que so yo el hablador*]. In this chapter, I had to have recourse to many verses from the Torah in order to adduce proofs for the verity of what I say, and had I given every verse in the [holy] tongue and in Ladino as is the rule in this book, it would have become very long and an annoyance for the reader, and this is why I left out the translation [*declaro*] of the verses in Ladino. And though there are many things in this chapter which are already mentioned and explained elsewhere in this book, I had to return to them in order to follow the thread of the speech in one sequence [*por caminar el hilo de la habla en un pedazo*].[4]

A close reading of this passage allows us to make some remarks on Judah Papo's understanding of translation which, as I submit, neatly summarizes how the vernacular rabbis understood their task of translating (elite) Hebrew into (popularized) Ladino musar. To begin with, the young Papo readily acknowledges that his version is a quite different text from his father's. He has shortened some chapters and expanded others, he has freely rearranged the material which he found in the Hebrew base text, and he has even made use of other writings of his father's unrelated to the *Pele Yoʿets;* since they were written by the same author, Judah finds it legitimate to add them here. He also admits that he might have added something of his own during the writing (or rewriting). In the first volume (letters aleph through yod), most chapters of the Hebrew book (120 out of 178) have equivalents in the Judeo-Spanish version, though the two versions are not always the same length; but in the second volume, the ratio is only 61 out of 213. The second volume does include the extraordinarily long chapter on *mitsvot* which Judah Papo added to the *Pele Yoʿets* (89 pages). All this does not prevent Judah from calling his Ladino *Pele Yoʿets* a "translation," as the first page clearly states: "Pele *Yoʿets* . . . composed in the holy tongue by . . . Eliʿezer Papo . . . and translated [*tresladado*] to Ladino by his son . . . Yeʾudah Eliʿezer Papo."

What does this say about how the vernacular rabbis understood their work of translation? It is significant that Judah Papo uses the terms "tresladar" (to translate), "copiar" (to copy), and "declarar" (to explain) interchangeably in his writings; to him, these are not really contradictory or even simply different concepts. For the Sephardic rabbinic translator, it is important to preserve the original author's intention and *not* the linguistic or discursive structure of the original text, and Papo claims to know more about his father's intentions than anyone else. In reality, however, Judah Papo does sometimes clearly depart from what his father said (so it seems from the modern historian's perspective, at least), as we will see in the chapters below on the Land of Israel and the different understandings of exile. He would not have seen this as a betrayal of the Hebrew author's intentions, of course, but rather as a way of accommodation to the supposed expectations of his intended readers and to his own educational agenda. The Sephardic translators obviously did not share the modern feeling that there is an important difference between a literal translation and a free adaptation.

The most telling evidence of how Papo imagines his intended readers is often what is just assumed and passed over in silence. His introductory remarks to the chapter on *mitsvot* are also relevant in this regard. While Judah Papo quotes and translates biblical verses in the other sections of the book, in this new chapter he wants to spare his readers excessively lengthy biblical references. Papo does not omit the Hebrew but decides to do without the Judeo-Spanish translation of the verses in question. Other Judeo-Spanish musar books confirm the general impression that the rabbis writing in the vernacular usually assumed that the reader would understand the biblical verses given in the original, whereas they translate—with very few exceptions—all references from the rabbinic literature, whether in Hebrew or Aramaic. It was thus the consensus among the vernacular rabbis that one could not cite verses from the Bible, the divine revelation in Hebrew, *only* in translation. Moreover, quotations from biblical verses were an important legitimizing device which invested the rabbinic discourse with authority, and the rabbis might have cared more about providing biblical proofs than about whether the average reader would understand these verses. Nevertheless it seems that the rabbis counted on a reading public that would be able to make sense of the biblical references in a musar book, taking for granted that people were familiar with the Pentateuch as read in synagogues and that they had studied it in the traditional schools (the *meldar*) which many still attended in the nineteenth century.

There are many other unspoken assumptions that produce lacunae in the text and tell us a good deal about the intended reader of this literature. Even in the works of the latter half of the nineteenth century, the standards of observance that are taken for granted in the musar works are remarkable. Consider, for example, what the *Pele Yo'ets* has to say on the dietary laws (*kashrut*) or daily prayer. The author does not, and does not have to, explain the basic rules of *kashrut*. Huli, in the *Me'am Lo'ez*, discusses the dietary laws at length, but he does so to provide a handbook for halakhically doubtful cases. Judah Papo simply assumes that his readers observe *kashrut* and only reminds them of the necessity to check legumes and vegetables for insects, something which is often neglected.[5] With regard to prayers, the *Pele Yo'ets* condemns those who recite their prayers alone at home and do not attend synagogue services—but that someone might not be praying regularly at all seems unimaginable to him.[6]

Papo's introduction to his new chapter on *mitsvot* raises another interesting point: he says that he "assembled in one chapter everything that belongs to one discourse," and later states that certain repetitions are inevitable in order "to follow the thread of the speech in one sequence," that is, in order to provide consistent, progressive reasoning. Thus the young Papo's rewriting of the *Pele Yo*ʿ*ets* has its own literary structure independent of the Hebrew "original." He tries to organize his material into "discourses" rather than emulate the complicated patchwork of sources that we find in many other musar works of the time. Judah Papo thus carries his father's alphabetical reorganization of rabbinic knowledge a step further. No less important, he is conscious of what he does and, if only in passing, reflects on his literary strategies in the text itself.

THE DYNAMICS OF REWRITING HEBREW MUSAR IN LADINO

It is beyond the scope of this work to present anything approaching a comprehensive comparative study of the Hebrew and Judeo-Spanish versions of the *Pele Yo*ʿ*ets*. It shall suffice to give three examples that provide some insight into Judah Papo's image of his intended reader and his educational program.

1. The chapter "*Sod*" ("secret") in the Ladino version of the *Pele Yo*ʿ*ets* opens by saying: "The *gemara* said, may you have many friends, but do not reveal a secret to more than one person among a thousand."[7] The entire chapter deals with guarding one's secrets and the value of being discreet. The author reprimands those who try to discover others' secrets by asking insistently, eavesdropping, or reading other people's letters. All this follows rather closely the second part of the chapter entitled "*Sod*" as we find it in the Hebrew *Pele Yo*ʿ*ets*. The opening part of the Hebrew passage, however—half the chapter—is totally absent in the Ladino version. It begins by stating that "the study of the secrets of Torah is higher than all other studies. Fortunate the one to whom God has allocated a share in understanding [*binah*], and who has a sign and a name [*yad va-shem*] in the wisdom of Kabbalah [*be-hokhmat ha-qabalah*] and follows the right intention in fulfilling the commandments, in his prayers, and in his study according to their secret [meaning]."[8] The Hebrew text then goes on to call on the *talmide hakhamim* to "turn to travel *pardes*," that is, to study the secrets of Kabbalah, after their study of Talmud and religious law. But even the person who lacks understanding of the secrets of Kabbalah should read books of kabbalistic instruction and interpretation of the prayers and commandments, and thus "his heart will burn" and he will realize the deep significance of all the *mitsvot* and all the prayers. "The one who has not tasted of this wisdom [of Kabbalah] did not taste the taste of the fear of sin, and to serve God with fear and love and joy." Reading books of Kabbalah reveals that even in the most mundane matters—eating, drinking, marital relations—"there are elevated secrets" of cosmic importance (*u-vone* ʿ*olamot*).[9]

The fact that Judah Papo omits any reference to Kabbalah in his version of the chapter "*Sod*" does not mean that he disagrees with his father. Some of the ideas expressed in the Hebrew passage cited here are found elsewhere in the Ladino version. In the chapter on eating and drinking, for example, Judah Papo insists that "we have the merit to cause secret processes in the heavens by eating and drinking, doing everything according to our obligations [i.e., saying the appropriate blessing before eating etc.]."[10] Thus, if the Ladino *Pele Yo*ʿ*ets* omits the first half of the chapter "*Sod*," we could simply explain this as part of the necessary rearrangement of material and shortening of some chapters. But why would he have chosen to omit precisely this part of the chapter if Kabbalah is indeed superior to all other fields of study, as the Hebrew text affirms?

It seems that, while the Ladino text shares the theological assumptions of (particularly Lurianic) Kabbalah, the vernacular Papo has decided that the *study* of Kabbalah is not relevant to his intended reader. It is true that on another occasion he cites the merit of reading *Sefer ha-Zohar* even without understanding it.[11] But he does not repeat the claim of the Hebrew *Pele Yoʿets* that the study of Kabbalah is preeminent over all other Torah study.

A further indication of how Judah understands the study of Kabbalah is found in his chapter on *mitsvot*.

> The wisdom of Kabbalah: this is the tremendous wisdom from which it is possible to know the secrets and the sanctification and the spirituality which is done through the Law and the commandments in the upper worlds, and that everything depends on the Law and the commandments which Israel affirms. . . . The capital of this wisdom is Jerusalem. The appropriate place for [studying] this wisdom is the *Qehal Hasidim* [in Jerusalem]. . . . It is a unique place and there is no place like it in the whole world.[12]

Kabbalah is praised by Judah Papo no less than in the Hebrew *Pele Yoʿets*, and the Lurianic reading of study and performing the commandments is evident. It is also clear, however, that he believes the systematic study of Kabbalah is not meant for the masses. The center of this wisdom is Jerusalem and the study of Kabbalah is limited to an elite of learned men who deserve to study it because of their great piety. Kabbalah, for Judah Papo, is clearly elite knowledge and thus, by definition, beyond the limits of a vernacular, popular discourse.

All this is consistent with the fact that kabbalistic books are almost entirely absent from vernacular rabbinic literature. While kabbalistic ideas inform most of Judeo-Spanish musar literature and are prominent in the *Meʿam Loʿez* as well, there seems to be no kabbalistic literature in Ladino. Some Judeo-Spanish "rewriters" draw on kabbalistic material and invoke it in their titles, such as Abraham Asa in his *Letras de Rabi ʿAqiba* (mentioned above), and Abraham Finçi in his translation of selected passages from the *Zohar*, published as *Sefer Leqet ha-Zohar* in Belgrade (1859) and reedited in Salonika (1867) and Izmir (1877). To these works one might add the legendary tales on some of the great heroes of Kabbalah, such as the *Shivhe Rabi Shimʿon bar Yohai* taken from the *Zohar* (Izmir 1877), the *Shivhe ha-Ari* (Istanbul 1766), or the *Shivhe Morenu ha-R' H[ayim] V[ital]* (Salonika 1892).[13] But, at least according to my cursory review, the *Leqet ha-Zohar* is actually a work of moral instruction, not a presentation of kabbalistic lore.[14]

What clearly emerges is an apparent resistance on the part of the Sephardic rabbis writing in Ladino to making kabbalistic texts accessible to the general public. Switching from one literary system to another—from Hebrew to Judeo-Spanish—is more than a linguistic matter; the educational ideal is transformed as well. The rabbis, when deciding what knowledge they deem relevant for a broad public, apparently preserve Kabbalah for the learned rabbinic elite, while certain ideas—from the uplifting of fallen sparks to the transmigration of souls—inform the ideological fabric of the texts and become part of the popular imagery.[15]

2. Another example pointing in a similar direction is the chapter "*Mishpat va-din.*" The following points are made in this chapter of the Judeo-Spanish version of the *Pele Yo'ets:*

- It is important to appoint a rabbi, even in small towns. Papo explains what the community should look for when searching for a rabbi (erudition in halakhah, moral integrity) and recommends—not totally without self-interest, one suspects—that the community should pay the rabbi well. Rich and poor alike must honor him.[16]
- All cases of internal community conflict must be brought before the rabbinic court and all parties must accept whatever judgment is handed down.[17]
- In every town, a lay leadership—"*grandes y rejidores*"—must be named in order to administer all community affairs. Judah Papo insists that these community leaders "should not be only rich persons; along with them, there should be honorable and wise people even if they have no money." Papo encourages these community leaders not to despair when they encounter opposition, asserting that "being leader of the Jews is not greatness but slavery. . . . Not even Moses satisfied all Jews." The leaders should always try to establish consensus and unity in all matters.[18]

The most obvious feature of the chapter as a whole is that it is directed toward the lay public of the community and is meant to enhance the authority of rabbis and community leaders. This contrasts sharply with the Hebrew *Pele Yo'ets* which, unlike the Ladino version, addresses *talmide hakhamim* along with the lay public. To begin with, the Hebrew chapter is much longer and more detailed. The community should appoint a judge, and the importance of the rule of religious law and its administration by a learned *talmid hakham* is pointed out. If there is no *talmid hakham,* however, or if the community cannot pay him, "God-fearing merchants [*anashim soharim*] with the common sense to judge between two persons" should be appointed as arbitrators so that the parties will not bring their case before a gentile court.[19] Eli'ezer Papo gives preference to the learned elite, of course, but the "lesser evil," as he calls it, in the absence of a rabbi would be to appoint members of the economic elite in the community (this significant statement contrasts with Judah's remark that not only the wealthy should serve as community leaders). The Ladino *Pele Yo'ets* mentions nothing like this. Consequently, when it comes to the obligation to name a *parnas,* the Hebrew *Pele Yo'ets* suggests that this position should be filled by a *talmid hakham.* His decisions—even if they are wrong—must be upheld by the community "*gedolim,*" the economic elite.[20] For Eli'ezer, the ideal is a harmonious alliance between the learned and the wealthy.

Most important, however, the Hebrew *Pele Yo'ets* also directly addresses the rabbis and *talmide hakhamim* themselves, tells them how to behave, and instructs them not to take pride in their appointed positions. He points out the difficulties of rabbinic leadership and suggests that the *talmid hakham* should avoid such positions of leadership rather than pursue them. Several pages of this chapter are dedicated to telling the *talmid hakham* how to behave as the rabbi and judge of the community (*more tsedeq*).[21] The leadership of the appointed judge must be respected by all, including the other *talmide hakhamim,* who should not assume the function of "lawyers" and should not instruct conflicting parties in the best legal argument lest they increase strife within the community.[22]

The chapters of the Hebrew *Pele Yoʿets* and its Judeo-Spanish version assume two entirely different publics. The intended reader of Eliʿezer Papo's book includes learned lay people and *talmide hakhamim* alike, while Judah's version is clearly meant as a "popular" book directed toward a non-learned, non-rabbinic readership; his remark on the social make-up of the community leadership (that it should include poor people) would appeal to such a "popular," non-elite public.

Judah Papo's work thus has much to teach us about the selective process behind the educational rabbinic enterprise of Judeo-Spanish musar. The masses are to be educated and should have access to traditional knowledge; but there are clear limits, and nothing indicates that the younger Papo is willing to challenge the authority and ultimate interpretative monopoly of the rabbis. Still, the dynamic set in motion by his and so many other vernacular rabbinic books might have contributed to precisely such erosion of the rabbinic monopoly on knowledge.

3. So far, I have described differences in content between the Hebrew and Judeo-Spanish versions of the *Pele Yoʿets.* Perhaps one literary aspect of Judeo-Spanish musar literature—the marked prominence of stories and exempla, *maʿasiyot* and *mashalim*—is even more important in assessing the role of the intended reader in the shaping of vernacular musar. Obviously, these were also a feature of Hebrew ethical literature, but they are particularly frequent and important in the vernacular books. Throughout the Judeo-Spanish *Pele Yoʿets* we find examples where Papo introduces a *maʿaseh* or *mashal* into the text where the original did not have one, or he amplifies and relates at length a *maʿaseh* from the rabbinic tradition which had only been hinted at in the Hebrew original.

For example, as the *Pele Yoʿets* deliberates on the passing quality of material wealth, insisting that true wealth is knowledge of Torah, this is illustrated by a *maʿaseh* which also can be found elsewhere in Ladino musar but is absent from the Hebrew *Pele Yoʿets:* A rabbinic scholar is traveling in the company of wealthy merchants who ridicule him when he tells them that he guards his wealth, that is, his learnedness in Torah, in a place where nobody can see it. The ship is attacked by pirates, and when they arrive at the port, the *talmid hakham* is recognized there as the great scholar he is and honored accordingly, while the merchants, robbed of all their goods, have to beg for food.[23]

Also frequent are cases in which the Hebrew *Pele Yoʿets* alludes to a *maʿaseh* from the rabbinic sources, which remains enigmatic to the reader not already familiar with the story. Consider the following passage from the Hebrew text: "All women should learn musar from the story in the Talmud concerning Baba ben Buta about the woman who rendered honor to her husband and hit Baba ben Buta on his head in order to do her husband's will. Thus all women '*will show respect to their husbands, great and small alike*' [Est. 1:20]."[24]

The reader who does not know the story will hardly be able to make sense of this; the Ladino version, however, is more extensive and intelligible to the average reader:

> In the *gemara* there is a story about a woman who married a man and the two spoke different languages. The husband told his wife in his language to bring two pumpkins, and it seemed to the woman, in her language, that he had requested candles. She brought candles. In his anger, the husband told her to smash them against the door. In the husband's language, door was called "baba." The wife did not understand. She knew that the city's rabbi was called Baba ben Buta and she thought that he wanted to tell her to smash [the candles] on his head, and thus she did. The rabbi knew how it came to pass and was very pleased to see the goodness of the woman who did not think back and forth before doing the will of her husband.[25]

This remarkable lesson in Judeo-Spanish musar understanding of gender roles is illustrated in the Hebrew version by alluding to a *ma'aseh* which is assumed to be familiar to the reader. The Ladino version, however, gives the entire story, assuming that its intended reader will not necessarily recognize what it is about, and translates the moral message into the graphic language of a story.

The elaboration and, even more important, the addition of *ma'asim* in the Ladino version of the *Pele Yo'ets* show how the vernacularization of Hebrew musar involved translation of knowledge not only from one idiom into another, but also from one literary system into another. This translation was determined very much by the intended reader and the translator's educational ideal. Readability, intelligibility, and entertainment are important features of the vernacularization of rabbinic knowledge. Moral values are being translated into the imagery of illustrative and entertaining *ma'asim*.

A cursory comparison of the Hebrew and Judeo-Spanish versions of the *Pele Yo'ets* thus shows some important features of the educational enterprise of presenting a new library of rabbinic knowledge in the vernacular, which was begun by Jacob Huli and Abraham Asa and continued in the nineteenth century by author-translators such as Judah Papo. First, vernacularization had its limits. Kabbalistic knowledge and practices were largely withheld from the non-learned public, though kabbalistic ideas are dominant throughout. Second, the rabbis had in mind a clear image of an intended reading public, and their texts must thus be understood as representation of what *they* as an elite believed appropriate for the non-learned public to whom their writings were addressed. The vernacular musar literature is a paternalizing discourse translating elite knowledge into an accessible, vernacular language.

The Reception of Musar

THE TRANSITION FROM COLLECTIVE
LEARNING TO INDIVIDUAL READING

Abraham Palachi, who succeeded his father, Hayim, as chief rabbi in Izmir after a prolonged power struggle in the community in the 1860s, was a prolific writer in Hebrew, publishing both works of musar and responsa. He also wrote one musar book in Ladino, "to be studied by schoolchildren and ignorant people, everyone with his friend and his neighbor, so that they may learn from its teaching to walk the right path."[26] Some Hebrew sermons were appended to the second volume of the first edition and omitted from the subsequent single-volume reprint.

The most striking feature of Palachi's book is his frequent use of Hebrew terms, expressions, and entire phrases alongside the basic Judeo-Spanish of the text. Two different linguistic registers coexist in Palachi's *Ve-hokhiah Avraham:* the Hebrew of the rabbinic discourse often determines Palachi's choice of words or phrases, and his syntax is often dictated by the incorporated Hebrew elements.[27] The translation from one code (the language of the rabbinic discourse) into another (Ladino, the language of the masses) thus remains incomplete, producing a text that represents an extreme example of the diglossia of vernacular rabbinic culture (and curiously calling to mind the [Ladino-French] diglossia of the westernizing intellectuals of later periods).

When I first read Palachi's volumes, I found it difficult to imagine this text being enjoyed by a reader who was not familiar with Hebrew. The many hermeneutic digressions throughout the book would certainly have been unintelligible to someone who did not know a good deal of Hebrew or was uncomfortable with rabbinic hermeneutics. What had been a mere suspicion was confirmed by the discovery of an unlikely use of one chapter of Palachi's book: it was incorporated into a 1868 reprint of Isaac Farhi's book *Zekhut u-Mishor,* an apparently very successful musar treatise which was first published in Izmir in 1850 and reprinted several times. The edition is a bibliographical curiosity which was rediscovered only recently.[28] It was published by the *Estamparía de la Qupah de Gemilut Hasadim* in Salonika in the same year as another edition, which also appeared in Salonika (published by the printing house of Saʿadi ha-Levi). The editor of the *Qupah* edition chose to integrate part of the chapter on Purim from Palachi's *Ve-hokhiah Avraham.* Important lexical changes were introduced in this version of Palachi's chapter, giving us the opportunity to assess how the Ladino-Hebrew mixture of *Sefer Ve-hokhiah Avraham* might have appeared to its popular readers.

A comparison of the two versions of the chapter leads to some obvious conclusions. Apart from minor adjustments of dialect and local usage ("*no*" instead of "*non*" and the like), the editor of the 1868 text consistently replaces all the Hebraisms in the Judeo-Spanish text which he doubts can be understood by the average reader. Certain Hebrew terms like *ba'al ha-bait* or *hayot ra'ot,* which either form part of the Judeo-Spanish lexicon or can be reasonably assumed to be commonly understood, are kept, but the many Hebrew terms and phrases that characterize Palachi's text have been replaced by their Ladino equivalents. Thus *"shikor gamur"* (drunkard) becomes *"boracho pedrido,"* and where it says of those who try to avoid giving Purim gifts to the poor *"se fuyen de casa ke-tinoq ha-boreah mi-vet ha-sefer"* (they escape from their homes like a child that escapes from school) in the original, the 1868 edition has *"se fuyen de casa como la criatura que se fuye de onde el melamed."* The 1868 edition also spells out the numerous abbreviations used by Palachi, all to make it easier to read (although there are, of course, plenty of Judeo-Spanish works that make ample use of abbreviations).

Palachi's book hardly seems to be the most appropriate text for individual reading by "schoolchildren" and "ignorant people," as claimed on the first page of the book. Indeed, as the author also suggests, one should read the book "together with his friend and his neighbor," in a small study group (*meldado*). The recommendation that study groups be formed and learned persons be invited to teach musar can be found throughout Judeo-Spanish rabbinic literature, as we see in detail in the next chapter. This incomplete "popularization" in the *Ve-hokhiah Avraham* is thus not to be attributed to the inability of its author to produce a truly "popular" book—after all, he had plenty of literary precedents to draw on. Rather, Palachi's book should be understood as a reference guide for those who *taught* a popular audience, and not so much as reading material for unlearned individuals. It made rabbinic musar conveniently available to those who assembled study groups in order to teach the rules and practices of Judaism. From this standpoint, *Ve-hokhiah Avraham* was only the first step in the process of cultural translation; the translation had to be completed by the mediating authority of a *talmid hakham.*

The integration of Palachi's chapter on Purim into Farhi's *Zekhut u-Mishor* and the numerous lexical changes meant to enhance its readability mark a transition toward opening vernacular literature to individual reading. The rabbinic authors maintained the ideal of the study group under the guidance of a *talmid hakham,* not least because they feared that they would lose control over the communication of knowledge if the vernacular book supplanted the mediating authority of a rabbinic scholar. They nevertheless sought to produce "popular" books that were appropriate for individual reading and communicated knowledge in a manner intelligible to the average reader not trained in Hebrew and rabbinical studies.

I do not wish to imply that there was a linear, one-way development from collective study to individual reading. Both modes existed side by side throughout the period under consideration here; but with increasing literacy (notably of women) and the increasing production and availability of books in the vernacular, the importance of individual reading grew, particularly from the mid-nineteenth century onward (although it never totally replaced other modes of reading). The way in which the editor of Farhi's "popular" text integrated and transformed Palachi's chapter, smoothing over the difficulties in the original, illustrates this movement toward replacing textbooks meant for those teaching musar to others with a musar literature explicitly (though not exclusively) written for individual readers.

The transition from reference manuals for teachers to textbooks both for individual readers and collective study also underlies the Judeo-Spanish adaptation of the Hebrew *Pele Yo'ets* by Judah Papo. In the introduction to his Hebrew *Pele Yo'ets*, Eli'ezer Papo explicitly expresses the idea of the book serving as a guide for musar teachers:

> Perhaps God will have mercy on me and grant me that my booklets find grace in the eyes of my contemporaries, and that they study them and teach them publicly [*va-yidreshum la-rabim*]. . . . There are things which it is inappropriate to teach to the masses [*bifne hamon ha-'am*], and there are expressions that are better omitted out of respect for those who listen and [terms like] "ignoramus" [*'am ha-arets*] and the like that are better left unmentioned, and I myself have indicated the places that the one who teaches publicly would do better to omit by two half-moons [he illustrates with semicircles].[29]

The Judeo-Spanish version prepared by Judah Papo can be used as a reference work, but it is primarily designed to be a musar text book accessible to the individual, unlearned reader. However, he does not heed his father's advice that potentially offending terms like "ignoramus" be omitted (none of the Ladino musar authors did).

IMAGINING THE RECEPTION OF MUSAR

The authors' images of their readers were formed in a two-stage process. Authors/ translators observed how their works and those by others were being received, and this feedback in turn informed their assumptions about their reading audience and their readers' expectations. Here I discuss two examples of how musar authors imagined the reception of their work, and how they hoped to shape the communication with their readers. Their remarks, of course, are not to be understood as "objective" descriptions of Judeo-Spanish reading culture, but rather as their own images of the reading public which, in turn, determined their literary production.

Abraham Palachi, in his *Ve-hokhiah Avraham*, presents the following description of how best to teach musar in public:

> When he teaches musar in public, and when he reads [aloud from] musar books in order to benefit others [*a-ser mezake et ha-rabim*], he should take care in three things: *First*, if there is among those listening someone who has stumbled into a certain sin, and accidentally he comes to pass censure upon this matter, he should take care not to dwell on this too long, for he would embarrass [the other], but [should speak] briefly and in kind words. In any event, it is appropriate not to prolong the passage [to be read] more than the rule, lest people become impatient and fall asleep and be annoyed by him, for he would cause them to sin, but [he

should teach] in moderation and according to the time. *Second,* the pace he takes must be appropriate to the time he has and to those who are listening. *Third,* he should not choose matters of piety and abstemiousness. . . . Moral chatisement is required in the basic teachings of the Law. If the teacher sees that many stumble into great sins, it is not appropriate to go and teach how to do virtuous things, but first, *"shun evil,"* and thereafter, *"and do good"* [Ps 34:15]. Much wisdom is required to pass censure on the basic teachings of Judaism.[30]

Two practices of teaching musar are mentioned here. Palachi speaks of the sermon or public lecture in the synagogue, study house, or private setting. But the second practice is of more interest here: the public reading of musar books in a study session (*meldado*) for which Palachi gives his three pieces of advice as to how best to catch the attention of the audience and most efficiently convey the educational message.

First, it is inappropriate to embarrass one's audience. Musar is chastisement, but it must not publicly expose anyone to embarrassment. The teacher should show respect for the audience and speak with kindness and empathy rather than harsh and threatening words. This is what Papo means when he says his work "is no chastisement that annoys, it does not come with fire and flame, but with sweetness."[31] This empathy for the listener/reader and the insistence on kindness are shared by most Judeo-Spanish musar books, the major exception being the eighteenth-century fire-and-brimstone rhetoric of Elijah ha-Kohen's *Shevet Musar.* Did the authors in the nineteenth century feel that their audiences no longer would appreciate this kind of uncompromising moral chastising and public exposure of their faults?

Second, the section of a musar book which is read to others should not be too long, and the pace of teaching should be appropriate to the audience. One might expect, then, that musar authors themselves tried to heed this advice in their writings. The editor of Farhi's *Zekhut u-Mishor* does exactly what Palachi recommends here for the adaptation of written musar to public teaching when he includes a chapter from Palachi's *Ve-hokhiah Avraham* (which is not the best example of brevity, and, as we have seen, abounds with Hebraisms and difficult language): the chapter is considerably shortened, the language is stripped of its many Hebraisms, and what is retained of the chapter is the entertaining *ma'aseh* it tells rather than the lengthy moralizing discourse.

Finally, in terms of content, Palachi's advice reiterates Jacob Huli's (and, before him, Maimonides') programmatic understanding of popular education as being about the "basic teachings of Judaism" (Palachi), and "not things that are a matter of piety but duties which are incumbent upon every person" (Huli).[32] The educational ideal of Judeo-Spanish musar thus establishes a standard which can be met by all, rather than an ideal of righteousness accessible only to a few virtuous people. However demanding musar texts can be in detail, they are intended to impart moral standards and a model of religious observance to the average Sephardic Jews of their time rather than an elitist ideal of piety.

Thus far, we have seen how musar literature was imagined as being read collectively in the *meldado*. But we also find evidence of individual reading practice. Here is what Isaac Farhi says in his *Imre Binah*:

> I will tell what happened to me in Jerusalem . . . in the month of *Shevat* in the year 5585 [1825]. The first day of the week I had to visit an individual [*ba'al ha-bait*] . . . and I found him reading the holy *Zohar*. When he saw me, he received me with much honor. . . . He asked me, saying: "Last night I had a dream of the pious rabbi [no name given] who told me to read the Book of Proverbs. What is the meaning of this?" I told him that the answer was very clear, and that he wanted to tell him to read books of musar, things that he understands, and the time for [reading] the *Zohar* will come. He promised to read a portion of the *Reshit Hokhma* regularly, and I told him that he should first take the *Shevet Musar* by Elijah ha-Kohen, which is easier to understand, and so he promised to do. I went off to my work and a week later I returned for my entreaty. From outside I heard that he was reading with much pain. I entered the room and did not even have time to greet him. As soon as he looked up and noticed me, he raised his voice with . . . great weeping as if I were—God forbid—lying dead before him. In a loud voice he said to me: "What have you done to me, what have you done to me? Woe to me, what will be my end, where will I bear my shame, unfortunate me. . . . Which medicine can I find for my illness? . . . " I did not speak to him either kindly or ill but, hearing these sacred words, my eyes spread tears like fountains. After half an hour I went to him with kind words, and I was there more than three hours in order to settle his heart with words of Torah about that matter. From this day on, that man sanctified himself more and more.[33]

Farhi's anecdote tells us three things about how the authors conceived the reception of musar: it tells us about the hierarchy of study, it indicates the overlapping of individual reading and the mediating authority of the *talmid hakham*, and it testifies to the impact which the rabbis believed their musar books would have. (Incidentally, we also learn that individual study was reading aloud from a book for oneself, as Farhi says that "from the outside I heard that he was reading.")

To begin with, the biblical Book of Proverbs is interpreted as a reference to ethical literature, and Farhi encourages the man to study musar rather than the *Zohar*. As it was in Aramaic, the *Zohar* was obviously even less accessible to the average Sephardic Jew than Hebrew rabbinic literature, and, as I have indicated above, the vernacular rabbis did not find it appropriate for uninitiated people to study kabbalistic knowledge. When the man proposes to study Elijah de Vidas's *Reshit Hokhmah*, a musar treatise in the spirit of Lurianic Kabbalah,[34] Farhi responds that he should begin instead with Elijah ha-Kohen's *Shevet Musar* because it is easier to understand (there is no indication that he is referring to the Judeo-Spanish translation, and not the original *Shevet Musar*, whose Hebrew is indeed quite readable).

The hierarchy of rabbinic study is obvious: "popular" works like Elijah ha-Kohen's *Shevet Musar* are the ideal starting point (which is why it was translated into Ladino) and represent adequate reading material for unlearned lay people. Next in the hierarchy of study is the musar work *Reshit Hokhmah*, initiating the reader into more profound insights than the popularizations of Lurianic ideas in the *Shevet Musar*. At the top stands the *Zohar*, reserved for those who have mastered the lower steps (the rabbis encouraged ritual reading of the *Zohar*, but it was not considered good to begin with it). Absent from this list is, not surprisingly, halakhic literature, which is reserved for the rabbinic elite itself and is not seen as an appropriate subject for popular study.[35]

Second, Farhi himself, representing the *talmide hakhamim* as a social group, plays a key role in shaping the reading practice of the *ba'al ha-bait*. The individual reader does not even know how to choose the most appropriate reading material, and thus Farhi first suggests to the man what to read. When he goes back to see him, reading the *Shevet Musar* has raised more questions than it has provided answers and Farhi, the *talmid hakham*, is called upon to help the individual reader out of his despair over his sins. Thus, while the authors of vernacular musar reckon with the practice of individual reading and encourage it, they never see their own mediating role as superfluous. The ideal of vernacular musar retains a role for the rabbis as mediators of knowledge. In praising his hometown, Izmir, Abraham Palachi writes that "most *ba'ale batim* have their particular *talmid hakham* to go to them after Sabbath or during the week" in order to explain musar and other material to them.[36] In fact, the vernacular rabbis emphatically defend the primacy of guided study, reading in the company of a *talmid hakham*. "One should not think," says Palachi, "that he already meets his obligations by reading alone what he understands. He should invite a *hakham* to his home, so that he might learn something more, or should go to the study house in order to learn from the *hakhamim*."[37]

Third, the fire-and-brimstone rhetoric of the *Shevet Musar* has not failed to impress its reader. While musar authors usually advocated teaching with kindness, they were convinced that they could mold their readers' thoughts and practice as educators. The expression to "engrave musar in the reader's heart,"[38] which is found often in Judeo-Spanish musar, is indicative of this belief. Thus, in assessing the role of the intended reader in Ladino musar literature, we must bear in mind that the authors really believed that what they wrote would shape socio-religious practice. The whole enterprise of a vernacular rabbinic literature is built on the premise that didactic rabbinic literature has the power not only to remedy people's ignorance, but to change their actual behavior.

In the psychology of musar, men and women are constantly challenged by their evil impulse, their *yetser ha-ra'*,[39] and it is the task of musar literature to assist them to overcome the temptation of sin. "And thus said the *gemara*," affirms Judah Papo,

> when the evil inclination meets you, bring it to the study house. If it is of stone, it will dissolve, and if it is of iron, it will break. . . . It is obvious that one who persists in reading or hearing musar being read becomes a good Jew and fearful of the Creator. And he who does not read and does not look for [an opportunity to] hear musar being read falls further back every day. But the most important thing is to persist in [the study of] musar with frequency for thus it is like the constant dripping of water that wears away the stone. In the same way, persisting

in [the study of] musar penetrates man's heart of stone. And if he is not persistent, it is of little use to him and if he hears [the teaching of musar] once in a thousand occasions, it goes in one ear and out the other.[40]

This passage echoes the talmudic pronouncement, "If this repulsive wretch [the evil impulse] meets you, drag him into the Beth Hamidrash. If he is of stone, he will dissolve . . . for it is written, *Ho, every one that thirsteth come ye to the water* [Isa 55:1][41] and it is written, *The waters wear the stones* [Job 14:19]."[42] The metaphor of water wearing the stone expresses the educational optimism of the musar rabbis. Continuous study conquers both the evil impulse *and* ignorance. Study ultimately leads to piety as "second nature": "with learning, his nature turns around," in the words of the *Darkhe ha-Adam.*[43]

This optimism is an important precondition for the functioning of the literary system of vernacular musar. The authors believed that their readers' character and social practice were malleable, and imagined them as children learning to understand the world. No less than the Sephardic intellectuals, the *maskilim* of the nineteenth century, the rabbis believed in the pedagogical power of books and in the civilizing power of education.[44]

THE MYTH OF THE LONG WINTER NIGHTS

Rabbinic authors' statements about the reception of their work should not be understood uncritically as accurate descriptions of actual reading practice. Jacob Huli recommends the *Me'am Lo'ez* with the oft-quoted remark that "during the very long winter nights you will have something to distract yourselves, and you will enjoy reading every part of this book,"[45] or "when the person returns from the shop, and also on the Sabbath or festival when he has nothing to do, he will distract himself with this book and read the portion he likes from the Torah or prophets or writings."[46] The same image is invoked by Judah Papo in the Judeo-Spanish *Pele Yo'ets:* "Everyone should read [this book] at home with his family on the Sabbaths and festivals and the long winter nights. The neighbors should gather and read it together. Those women who can read should assemble friends and relatives and should read it with them."[47]

There is a problem, however, with taking this as a true description of actual reading practices rather than as recommendations. In fact, the image drawn here is challenged by an observation voiced by Isaac ha-Kohen Perahia, who wrote in the introduction to the Exodus volume of his Judeo-Spanish *Sefer ha-Yashar* (1898):

> Everyone returns home at night tired from his work earning a living for his household, and even if he takes up the *Me'am Lo'ez,* he won't understand anything and it seems a heavy burden to him . . . and sleep overcomes him because it is reading without understanding. And this leads [people] to waste the winter nights and the hours when they cannot work, like Sabbaths and festivals, reading secular stories [novels] and pastimes.[48]

That is to say, even a work like the *Me'am Lo'ez* would later be subject to the critique Huli directed against the works of his predecessors—namely, that it was too difficult and too long winded to serve the average Sephardic Jew in free moments after work when he or she is tired from the day's labor. It is clear that authors like Huli and Papo are speaking primarily of what they hope will be the reception of their books, but this does not mean that people actually read (exclusively) Me*am Lo*ez and musar during the "long winter nights."

In connection with the *veillée* in early modern France—an informal evening gathering to read from printed books—Natalie Zemon Davis has warned that talk of "long winter nights" should not be taken at face value anyway, as people often had to work until late in summer *and* winter, if necessary by candlelight.[49] Before accepting what the vernacular rabbis say in their introductions to promote their books, a serious study of Sephardic reading culture would first have to consider the patterns of working life and how they varied historically and geographically; it would then be possible to assess how much time people had to read and whether they could reasonably be expected to study a long, difficult text. Again, it is easy to talk about the intended reader as imagined by the author and inscribed into the text, but the actual conditions of reading culture are far more difficult to assess and certainly varied across time and space.

THE DISCOVERY OF WOMEN AS READING PUBLIC

The pedagogical initiative of vernacular musar is not limited to the male public of Hebrew rabbinic literature. One of the most important consequences of the vernacularization of rabbinic knowledge is a new openness toward a female public, hitherto all but excluded from traditional study.[50] Whereas the "we" employed in musar books almost always refers to the author and his male readers, later titles would explicitly include a female public. In the eighteenth century *Shevet Musar,* the author still addresses women in an indirect way, including them as a public to be instructed in Judaism, but not as a *reading* public: "The ignorant who does not know to read," writes Elijah ha-Kohen, "should go on the Sabbath and festivals and at any time of the day to the study house to listen to words of Torah and *derekh erets* [proper deportment]. And what he hears, he should tell his wife and the people of his household when he returns home in the evening."[51]

The ordinary man attending the rabbis' studies at the *bet midrash* is thus understood as a broadcaster of the rabbis' educational message, taking it beyond the immediate audience of listeners and readers. In the nineteenth-century *Pele Yo*ets, the panorama is different and Judah Papo explicitly spells out the ideal of addressing a female reading public alongside his male readers. He suggests the establishment of particular women's *meldados:* "How good it is if women, friends and relatives, meet, one Sabbath at the home of one friend, and another Sabbath at another friend's home, and each group appoints a woman who can read and they spend the hour with [study]. An advantage is that they will look for ways to teach their daughters [how to read as well]."[52]

Significantly, however, Judah Papo encourages women to learn to read and write not only for the sake of religious study. He explicitly mentions profane communication like reading and writing letters among the things women should be able to do.[53] Other Sephardic rabbis who published vernacular musar at the time also insisted on the importance of educating girls. Isaac Amarachi and Joseph Sason wrote, for example, that it is appropriate "to teach the daughters the holy tongue [Hebrew] and the language of the land in which one lives, and teach them to understand the prayers they say, and how to write and how to calculate, and then teach them a profession, because idleness leads to promiscuity."[54]

The vernacular rabbis anticipated opposition to their inclusion of women in the educational ideal of musar. Many people will claim that women do not have time to study and learn their prayers and blessings because they are occupied with their domestic duties, writes Judah Papo; against this claim, he holds that "there is time for everything," and that the tasks of running a household should certainly not deter women from learning.[55] It is obvious that the rabbis writing in Ladino included women in their educational ideal and their potential readership without ever trying to change the traditional understanding of gender roles. Nor does Papo question the assumption that domestic duties are female duties. In terms of subject matter, there was still a gendering of knowledge: witness the publication of books directed exclusively toward a female public, such as the *Sefer Dat Yehudit* of Abraham Laredo and Isaac Ha-Levi (first published in Livorno in 1827 and then in Jerusalem [1878] and again in Vienna [1881]), which explains women's duties related to family purity, the lighting of Sabbath candles, and the laws of *halah* (separating dough) and *kashrut*. But what is most important for our purposes is the fact that women were discovered as a reading public, and that (at least some) vernacular rabbis took an increasing interest in the education of young girls and women.

Obviously not all women took advantage of the new possibilities opened up to them by vernacular rabbinic literature, just as not all men flocked to the study sessions or read the new volumes of Judeo-Spanish musar. But reading and study were now increasingly stripped of their gender-specific association with a male public. Although not all musar books were part of this development (and some authors may very well have resisted it), the social consequences of this development are important. By including women among the intended readers of their popular books, the authors of popular Ladino rabbinic literature paved the way for the emergence of a female reading public that would prove a most receptive audience for new, secular genres of Judeo-Spanish literature that began to flourish in the nineteenth century.

MELDAR AS PART OF THE RITUAL OF REPENTANCE

Study, *meldar*, is not only a means of acquiring knowledge; it also is the ritual performance of a divine commandment. The idea of *meldar* as ritual is well expressed in the following:

> The use of study [*meldar*] is not only that through *meldar* we know what the commandments of our Creator are ... like an order [*firman*] from the king which only serves to proclaim the king's will. The Law is not like this, because

just reading the royal order is nothing and the reward is only for doing what the order declares as the king's will, not for reading the commandment. But for *meldar* [Torah], he [the reader] deserves a reward for the *meldar* itself, for it is one of the Law's commandments.[56]

The ritualistic reading of sacred texts, which Robert Bonfil has described as a medieval element inherited by modern Jewish reading culture, included texts which were esoteric and difficult to understand, such as the *Zohar*. Whereas medieval societies were still characterized by a generally high rate of illiteracy, this illiteracy was largely reduced to Hebrew, to the sacred sphere, in the modern era. Anthropological studies among "Oriental" Jews have established the parameters of this ritualistic reading: reading aloud in a group, often in a singing tone, of units of text defined without regard to their content.[57] This practice was further influenced and popularized by the Lurianic notion of Torah study as a mystical rite, evident in the emergence of study circles under the impact of Lurianic Kabbalah.[58] An example of the wide diffusion of ritual daily Torah study, particularly from the eighteenth century onward, is the great success of the anthology *Hoq le-Yisraʾel*, published for the first time in Egypt in 1740. This work, spreading also in eastern Europe since the 1880s, presented a selection of texts to be studied, or recited, on a daily basis, beginning with a part from the Torah portion of the week, followed by passages from the Prophets, Mishnah, and Talmud, notably ending with a passage from the *Zohar*.[59]

But what was the function of ritualistic reading of *vernacular* rabbinic literature? Obviously, the reader was expected to understand what he or she read. The basic function of vernacular literature is didactic, and the authors set out to write their Judeo-Spanish books precisely with the objective of providing the average Sephardic Jew with reading material that was not esoteric. Beyond their pedagogical interest, however, the vernacular rabbis insisted on the ritual importance of the act of reading. *Meldar* occupied a central place in the rabbinic religious universe, as was well expressed in a prayer to be said before studying a musar book—"*nosah de tefilah por decirse antes de meldar libro de musar*"—which was appended to the 1868 *Qupah* edition of Isaac Farhi's *Zekhut u-Mishor*. The final paragraph reads:

Therefore we are reading books of musar to make our hearts repent and to know our flaws. . . . All the words of musar that we are reading, let them enter the innermost parts of our hearts and let them be forever on our mind to cleanse our thoughts, reconstruct what we have damaged, rebuild what we have destroyed, and straighten what we have bent. And as we know that your will, Lord of the universe, is repentance, we ask you . . . to open our eyes, so that we may distance ourselves from the evil inclination and cleave to the good inclination.[60]

Studying (vernacular) musar thus is part of *teshuvah* (repentance), and understanding what one reads is part of the ritual reaffirmation of the symbolic universe of religious knowledge that has been challenged by transgression. *Teshuvah* as a ritual reaffirmation of the universe of rabbinic tradition includes here the reading of rabbinic ethical literature in order to "engrave" the values of musar on the reader's heart and mind. A particularly interesting example of a vernacularized version of a *tiqun*, or anthology of texts to be studied ritually, combined with musar, is Ben-Tsion Roditi's *Ki Ze Kol ha-Adam*. Intended for a sick reader hoping to recover from illness, Roditi encourages the regular study of texts that he provides at the end of each chapter of his own musar treatise.[61] These include texts from the Torah, the Prophets, and other biblical passages, given in Hebrew with complete *niqud* (the vowel points), facilitating their recitation, if not understanding. This is followed by passages from the Talmud, midrash, and other sources, including musar books like *Shevet Musar* and *Pele Yoʻets*, all in Ladino.

Reading and understanding vernacular musar are thus part of the reaffirming ritual of *teshuvah:* if transgressing divine law causes damage to the integrity of the traditional symbolic universe (and, as the Lurianic kabbalists and our musar authors would see it, to the cosmic order at large), the study (*meldar*) of the precepts of rabbinic laws and ethics reaffirms and mends the disrupted order. It is significant that the reading of vernacular Judeo-Spanish musar and the study of the classical texts of Hebrew rabbinic tradition are both referred to as *meldar,* according them an inherent religious value apart from their didactic purpose and investing them with authority for their fulfillment of one of the most important commandments of divine law, *talmud Torah.* When the vernacular rabbis ascribe the same ritual importance to the reading of Hebrew and vernacular Judeo-Spanish rabbinic literature, they ultimately invest the vernacular literary field with authority formerly monopolized by Hebrew (and Aramaic) rabbinic discourse. As the reading of Judeo-Spanish rabbinic literature is made into the ritual performance of a commandment beyond its immediate pedagogical function, the vernacular rabbis enhance their own authority and legitimacy.

The ritual character of *meldar* presupposes an intended reader who shares the worldview of rabbinic tradition and is interested in reaffirming it through study as an act of *teshuvah.* Reading as ritual by necessity implies an *affirmative* reading. In reality, however, "there are problems with presuming that these cultural products are read in an accepting and uncritical way, that the message is absorbed, unmodified and that the reader or consumer then lives the image they have read."[62] Below, I briefly review the evidence from within Judeo-Spanish musar bearing on how a critical reader might have approached this literature.

THE CRITICAL READER

We have no indications in the texts themselves about how they might have been read by a critical or skeptical reader until the second half of the nineteenth century. Then we find attacks against westernizing intellectuals, dubbed "epicureans" or "philosophers" by the rabbis. They are constructed as the "other" of the traditional universe and excluded from the literary community of the "we" constructed in the texts to include the author and the intended reader. Arguably the most important nineteenth-century work of Judeo-Spanish musar, Papo's Ladino *Pele Yoʻets* mounts an attack (not found in the earlier Hebrew version) against these "epicureans," who are *hakhamim* in their own eyes and do away with the fear and honor of the *hak-hamim*, and they reply to the words of the *hakhamim*, saying: this is not good, and here they were very strict. . . . If it were left to everybody to explain the Law according to his own mind, there would be thousands of laws, everyone a law according to his mind. . . . Those who rebel against the words of the *hakhamim* only do so because they want to get rid of the yoke of the Law and the command-ments and want to enjoy this world.[63]

This can be read as a description of the unwanted critical reader of rabbinic literature, the reader who declines a ritual, affirmative study of rabbinic literature leading to religious practice but takes the liberty of thinking about and accepting or rejecting what he or she reads. These readers take advantage of the new ways of individual reading which vernacular rabbinic literature made accessible to them in the first place, adopting a stance as critical readers which the rabbinic authors never wanted to permit their non-expert audience. But once rabbinic knowledge has been opened up to a broad public, this audience begins to respond actively to what it reads instead of silently consuming the portions of knowledge prepared by the authors of vernacular rabbinic literature. They thus challenge the rabbinic mo-nopoly over the administration and interpretation of traditional knowledge.

As a matter of fact, the rabbis dismiss the possibility of educating critical, secularized readers who reject the fundamental basis of the traditional universe out of hand. "In the world, there are all kinds of different people," writes Papo. "There are some people who are heretics against God and do not believe in recompense for the righteous or punishment for the wicked." These people only want to enjoy this world, and "nothing is achieved by all that one tells them, for they are lost and there is no medicine for them. But"—and here the author tells us how the vernacular rabbis understood the sociocultural environment within which they wrote—"there are only few people like this. The majority know that there is a God in heaven and that the world is not ownerless [*hefqer*], and that the one who does good is re-warded."[64] The reading public imagined by the authors of Judeo-Spanish musar is one whose great majority is loyal to the basic assumptions of the traditional uni-verse.

What do the rabbis describe as the reason for deviant practices of critical read-ing? The following remark by Isaac Farhi seems representative of Judeo-Spanish rabbinic literature in general:

How many people have, because of our sins, begun to read non-Jewish books of stories [*libros de historias de goyim*] and do not put them down day or night, which rather should be the case for [studying] Torah. . . . And because of our sins it is clearly seen that they were good Jews, fearful of the Holy One, before they lost themselves with these books. As this deadly poison enters their body, they turn from right to wrong, are disgusted by the Law, scoff at those who learn [Torah] and ridicule the commandments and consider themselves to be *hakhamim* . . . and they are not ashamed to say about the words of the *hakhamim* that they did not know what they were saying.[65]

The increasing exposure to Western ideas and fashions through European literature is identified as causing a growing number of people to question the truths of rabbinic knowledge. However, the secularization of the Judeo-Spanish literary public sphere in the late nineteenth century was aided by the vernacularization of Sephardic reading culture and the subsequent democratization of knowledge since the eighteenth century. Now, in the latter half of the nineteenth century, the Judeo-Spanish reading public was confronted with European ideas and fashions as a result of its exposure to Western literature in translations and adaptations and to new, secular literary genres. A growing number of Ottoman Jews were acquiring knowledge of European languages (particularly French) and thus had even more direct access to European literature. More significant, however, was mediation through (original or translated) novels, newspapers, historiography, and the theater in an increasingly secular Judeo-Spanish public sphere.

It would be erroneous to assume that the Ottoman Sephardic rabbis generally opposed the new genres of literature; Judah Papo, for example, was full of praise for the Ladino press.[66] Nevertheless, reading, to the rabbis, was dangerous if not controlled. They thus recommend that their own books be read in study groups under the supervision of a *talmid hakham,* though they recognized the need to make rabbinic literature suitable for individual reading too, lest people read only secular and foreign literature. Readers of foreign, non-Jewish books were exposed to dangerous foreign ideas, leading them to oppose secular to traditional rabbinic knowledge. They arrogated to themselves the position of critical readers of rabbinic literature, ultimately challenging the integrity of traditional knowledge and traditional social practice. Thus, the rabbis disapproved of readers' venturing beyond the confines of the traditional symbolic universe, and certainly beyond the confines of literature in a Jewish language (Hebrew or Ladino). Though they did not deny the usefulness of knowing foreign languages for business, they rejected the reading of books outside the Hebrew and Ladino literary fields as a dangerous breach of boundaries.

AVAILABILITY OF BOOKS

How widely available was Judeo-Spanish rabbinic literature to its imagined readers? As I have indicated in the introduction, we do not have any data on the number of copies printed or the patterns of distribution of this literature. An important role in the dissemination of this literature and the amplification of its message was played by the formal and informal *meldados,* or reading groups, the establishment of which was advocated by the authors of Ladino musar. Just as in the case of secular literature, namely the newspapers, in the late nineteenth and twentieth century, such collective reading and reading aloud made these books available to a public that did not necessarily need to have access to the books individually. We have also seen that these books were mostly published in installments which were typically sold in the synagogue. It is not unreasonable to assume that people did not only buy and collect these texts, but shared them with each other. In fact, readers would have seen individual installments of a given book without perhaps ever having access to the finished book itself.

For all the shortcomings of traditional education and literacy, it also needs to be taken into account that in Jewish society, in the Ottoman Empire as elsewhere, there were precedents of public libraries. Simha Assaf has argued that the collections of books available in every synagogue, *bet midrash*, or yeshivah were open to the public and played the role of public libraries, so that access to books— other than in Christian Europe where libraries usually were part of monasteries, universities, or the court—was never an exclusive privilege of the learned or wealthy elite.[67] Also in Ottoman Muslim society, publicly accessible libraries were not uncommon by the eighteenth century: to be found in mosques and religious schools, as well as in the private and endowed libraries of Ottoman dignitaries, there were some twenty-four libraries in Istanbul in 1730. The Muslim religious authorities, however, tried to make sure that only religious literature, but not works of history, philosophy, or sciences, were available in those libraries that were open to the public.[68]

In any event, making books available to a wide reading public became a concern of increasing importance for the vernacular rabbis. Consistent with the widening of their intended reading public, they began to think about the need of public access to printed knowledge. In this context it is worth noting Judah Papo's recommendations for the maximum distribution of musar literature, both in Hebrew and Judeo-Spanish, through the establishment of private collections and the lending of books:

> To buy books for studying is very necessary, for as the craftsman cannot work if he has no tools, so it is for the *hakham* without books. How good it is if one makes a *yeshivah* in his house and buys all [kinds of] books. The door should be open and everyone who wants to read should come and read. . . . And also, how good it is to buy books which are necessary for *baʿale batim* to read. . . . And if there are books for everyone, more and more people will come to read. . . . He should buy books of *dinim* and musar, and if he does not know the holy tongue he should buy books in Ladino.

He then praises "the one who buys books and lends them so that another may read them, how good this is. But he should request a signature or a pledge as a reminder and set a deadline for the number of day for which he gives it."[69]

Papo recommends the establishment of semi-public spaces that will help to realize the ideal of a learning society that is imagined and promoted by the authors of vernacular musar literature. The appeal is directed first of all to the wealthy, of course, who can both afford to buy books—by no means an inexpensive commodity in those days—and may even have space enough to invite people to their home to study. Again, we do not know how successful such appeals were. Itshac Broudo, in his recollections from pre-war Salonika, says that the wealthy in Salonika maintained private yeshivot with their own collections of books, such as the Alhasid family, which had three rabbis come and study every day in a room adjacent to their home.[70] Papo's ideal goes even further, of course, in that he encourages everyone in whose power it is to create a small collection of books in Hebrew or Ladino and share them with others. On the other hand, we continue to hear complaints about the scarcity of books through the end of the nineteenth century as, for example, in *Recontos Morales,* a modernized version of Ladino musar published in Salonika in 1880: "One of the reasons that hamper the progress of our coreligionists in the Orient, in particular among the needy class, is the total lack of books in Judeo-Spanish language."[71]

Conclusion

This chapter has shown that the rabbis understood the "translation" of Hebrew rabbinic literature into the vernacular as rewriting. Both the content (e.g., the exclusion of certain areas of knowledge) and the literary form (e.g., the prominence of *ma'asiyot*) of these rewritings were determined by the rabbis' image of the intended reader. The rabbis themselves usually did not understand translation as being necessarily faithful, either linguistically or discursively, to their sources, but deliberately undertook a paternalistic rewriting for their popular public. We have further seen how collective learning and individual reading coexisted as options for communicating musar. A general tendency away from musar literature as manuals for teachers and toward individual reading can be observed, though this was not a unidirectional development. The rabbis reflected on these different modes of reception; in their advice to the teacher as well as to the individual reader, they tended to stress the mediating function of the *talmid hakham* and did not see vernacular literature rendering this function superfluous. It was very important that the rabbis increasingly widened the intended reading public of vernacular musar to include women. At first, women were supposed to be reached indirectly through their husbands, who "amplified" the musar message learned in the study house; only later did musar literature begin to address women directly. It has further been shown how the reading practice as intended by the rabbis was a ritual and affirmative one, intertwined with the ritual reaffirmation of the symbolic universe in *teshuvah,* and that this expectation went largely uncontested, as far as the textual evidence allows us to say, until we find reactions in the late nineteenth century to the unwanted practice of critical reading, which was perceived as a danger to the integrity of tradition.

"Pasar la Hora" or "*Meldar*"? Forms of Sociability

4

In a recent publication on Ottoman history, François Georgeon has made the case for a study of informal ways of sociability in the Ottoman Empire, examining patterns of socializing in the sphere between the extended family household and the established settings of social interaction provided by the various communities or the state.[1] Following the suggestions of that study, we can learn a great deal about forms of sociability in Ottoman Sephardic society from a close reading of Judeo-Spanish musar literature.

For a long time, accounts of Ottoman (and Ottoman Jewish) history have assumed that a binary opposition existed between "private" and "public" domains in traditional society. At the risk of belaboring the obvious, I argue in this chapter that such a conceptual contrast between "public" and "private" is unsatisfactory for a study of Ottoman Jewish society. Notions of private as opposed to public places are relevant when we speak of the rabbinic *gendering* of space, but these gendering mechanisms cannot be subsumed under a binary opposition between "the public" and "the private" as preexistent entities. As far as sociability in general is concerned, the distinction made in our sources is between the *sacred* and the *profane;* the places, times, and forms of sociability are distinguished and valued according to which side of this dividing line they fall on.[2]

The authors of musar tend to depict *hitbodedut* (loneliness) for the sake of undisturbed study as an ideal. Abraham Palachi dedicates an entire chapter to the praise of *hitbodedut.* Although it is also a kabbalistic value and technique,[3] in this context the term expresses chiefly a social ideal according to which socializing for its own sake is to be avoided and company is to be sought only for the performance of *mitsvot* and the study of Torah. "Man should make sure to be alone because there is nothing better than to be alone," says Abraham Palachi, "except for the sake of *mitsvot* and studying Torah, which it is good to do in company."[4] Sociability is evaluated by the rabbis in terms of whether it serves a higher religious purpose. On this basis, the musar authors draw a binary opposition between legitimate places, times, and forms of sociability and illegitimate, profane sociability. In this chapter, I trace this opposition between socializing for the sake of divine service and the secular notion of leisure, well expressed in a typical statement by Isaac Farhi chastising those who prefer to spend their time at the coffeehouse rather than studying Torah: if someone tries to convince such a person to study, "he will say mockingly: I will gain nothing by studying except for anxiety and distress of the heart. It is better to go amuse oneself in the coffeehouse or the comedy, for there one finds amusement, laughter and pleasure."[5]

The Topography of Sociability

The righteous and the wicked and their "right" and "wrong" patterns of social interaction can be distinguished by the places they frequent. Secular places of sociability are associated with sinfulness and transgression; there is no neutral ground between the sanctified sociability of the synagogue or *bet midrash* and the sinfulness of profane socializing:

> The wicked one is always found in impure places, in the house of prostitution, the coffeehouse or gambling with blasphemers. And not even by chance does he enter synagogues or study houses which are the palaces of the King. The reason is that the synagogue and the study house are like paradise [*gan ʿeden*] for the righteous, and to the wicked they seem like hell [*gehinam*]. What is worse, the wicked one is idle all day and night, speaking vainly, and if someone opens a book in front of him to study, he immediately runs away.[6]

Note that the binary opposition between sacred and profane space, righteous and wicked sociabilities, is expressed here in the rhetoric of so fundamental a binary classification of the symbolic universe as paradise and hell, *gan ʿeden* versus *gehinam*.

Certain places are associated a priori with certain practices of socializing; synagogue and *bet midrash* are sacred points in the coordinates of the community's topography. But these privileged places of prayer and study must also be sanctified through proper behavior and scrupulous performance of the religious duties, and like all other places they are always in danger of being profaned by improper, secular sociability for its own sake. "There are people who go to a study session," says Isaac Farhi, "to smoke the pipe and to drink coffee and talk whatever triviality there is in the world. And when they are tired, they lie down to sleep there with a *minyan*. It were better if they remained in their homes! . . . And even if they do not know how to read, they should be listening and pay attention."[7]

The same is true of the synagogue, where many people prefer to socialize and talk rather than pray and study—surely a timeless complaint of rabbinic musar. Idle talk and gossip delegitimize the socializing in the synagogue and profane it. "Now that the synagogue has replaced the Temple," insists the *Pele Yoʿets*, " . . . if we have no respect in the synagogue, how will [God] rebuild the Temple for us. And how much suffers the heart from seeing that at times quarrels erupt in the synagogue, and this is worse than when they quarrel in the coffeehouse."[8] While it is not surprising for the rabbis to defend the decorum of the community's spiritual centers—synagogue and *bet ha-midrash*—we can say that their defense of appropriate behavior in these spaces is intended to mark the boundaries of legitimate social behavior.

Such complaints about lack of respect in the synagogue or arriving there late are frequent in Judeo-Spanish musar.[9] Isaac Farhi contrasts sociability for the sake of prayer with profane socializing and remarks ironically that, instead of trying to be among the first ten to arrive at services, people vie to be the first to leave: "Who will have the merit of leaving the synagogue first and depart from the light of the *shekhinah*. . . . And mostly this hurry upon leaving the synagogue is in order to participate in the gatherings of blasphemers."[10] A typical literary device for the moral admonition of such people is to point to the example of the gentiles, "for every nation gets up early for its divine service":[11] "The proof is that all the nations show much respect and correct behavior [*derekh erets*] in their houses of worship";[12] "one should learn from the gentile nations who, when they enter their houses of assembly, are full of fear and no voice is heard."[13]

Thus, the topography of the Jewish community is divided into sacred and profane spaces which set the boundaries of what is considered legitimate socializing. The synagogue and the study house are the central points in this topography of the Jewish community, but they are not the only ones. The authors of musar also encourage the establishment of study groups—*compañas de meldar* or *meldados*—in individual homes, inviting neighbors and ideally a *talmid hakham* in order to read together from vernacular musar literature. The *Pele Yoʿets* encourages everyone who builds a new house to include "a separate room for all kinds of gatherings of [community] societies and [for the sake of] *mitsvot* and study sessions [*meldados*] which they want to do in town, so they may do them in that room. Certainly the *shekhinah* will reside in his home."[14] These *meldados* were the most important forum of the new Judeo-Spanish reading public, study groups in which lay people met and read the *Meʿam Loʿez* and other works of Ladino musar together.

The Institution of *Meldados*

> How good it is if they establish a place in every town designated for meeting in order to study, and establish study groups [*compañas de meldar*], on the Sabbath and festivals and some evenings during the week and at dawn, and during winter nights which are long . . . they can meet for many hours to study. And they should invite a *talmid hakham* to teach them books of musar and laws [*dinim*] and the like. And everyone who offers his house for this has great merit.[15]

Musar literature encourages socializing and the construction of an (informal or formal) social framework for studying, the *meldados*. "And he should not only join a study group [*compaña de meldar*]," adds the *Pele Yoʿets*, "but he should join all kinds of groups for [the performance of] *mitsvot*, such as visiting the sick, washing and burying the dead, and the like."[16] Socializing with others in order to study or pray or for charity is not only legitimate, but imperative. Writes Isaac Farhi: "The one who withdraws from the public and does not go to the synagogue and says his prayer alone in his house, even if his prayer is very good it does not find favor before God," and the same is true for other commandments which are better performed collectively than individually.[17] Groups established for some charitable or other religious purpose, known as *hevrot*, were ubiquitous in Ottoman Jewish communities and a central part of their social landscape,[18] and the authors of Ladino musar supported this form of sociability as the only legitimate form of socializing.

What interests us here is the social condition of reading, the *meldado* as a forum for the dissemination of knowledge and, by extension, for social control. Such *meldados* could be tied to the synagogue or to other social institutions such as the guilds and *hevrot*, while others could be held in someone's private home. Abraham Palachi, for example, writes:

> During the winter nights he should take care that they do not make *semlada*,[19] men and women together. . . . How good it is if he brings them together in a home and takes a book and teaches them musar. . . . Particularly on the eve of the first day [of the week, i.e., Saturday night], it is appropriate to listen to [musar] being read [*sentir meldar*] in summer and winter. The one who can bring a *talmid hakham* home to have him read every Saturday night and does not do so should know that the good he has will not endure and his house will disappear. . . . Rabbi Elijah ha-Kohen established that on Sabbath morning every guild [*esnaf*] has its own study [*midrash*], and also in the afternoon on the Sabbath, after lunch, study should be held and the one who does not attend should not be admitted to the profession. . . . It is found in most communities that they read musar [publicly], but to what avail if only few people attend, and even in the morning they do not attend though there is a study [*midrash*] but rather take a walk to places where there is not even an *ʿeruv*.[20]

Palachi speaks of two different social settings for the reading of musar and the study of Torah: institutionalized frameworks such as the synagogues and guilds; and the collective study of family, friends, and neighbors in their private homes, with or without the participation of a *talmid hakham*. With regard to institutionalized forms of study, Palachi cites the *meldados* held at the synagogue which, as he points out, are widespread but poorly attended, and the practice propagated by Elijah ha-Kohen: the members of each *esnaf*, or guild, are encouraged to have their own *midrash* and study groups, and attending these *meldados* is to be obligatory for admission to the guild.

It is difficult to know how widespread this practice was in Elijah ha-Kohen's own time and at later times, or whether it was common beyond Izmir.[21] But we do have some evidence that this practice was still in existence in mid-nineteenth century Izmir, when Abraham Palachi wrote his book: in an agreement dating from 1847, the members of a *hevrah* in Izmir committed themselves to "come every Sabbath . . . in order to study Bible and musar, and if an individual does not come, he will pay a fine of 10 *paras*."[22]

In general, however, we still know little about how widespread the *meldados* of which Ladino musar literature speaks so frequently were at any given time and place. In part, this is precisely why the evidence of this literature is important and can help to fill some of the gaps in our knowledge of traditional Ottoman Jewish society. There is some anecdotal testimony to the continued existence of *meldados* still from the twentieth century, to be sure. Itshac Broudo, for example, writes in his memories of pre-war Salonika about the widespread practice to invite to one's home once a week or month a *talmid hakham* who would read Psalms and teach some musar to the assembled family and guests. People of higher social status would have an accomplished rabbi rather than a student come to their house, and the wealthy maintained a regular private yeshivah with its own library.[23] Others speak of *meldados* being held in private homes after the end of the Sabbath or in honor of a deceased family member or neighbor, likewise held in the family's home rather than in the synagogue.[24]

The Judeo-Spanish *meldado* was not an entirely new social institution, nor was it unique to Ottoman Jewry. Azriel Shohat has studied the establishment of study groups (*limudim*) in the Ashkenazic world. He points out that, while *limudim* may have been more common in the mishnaic or talmudic periods, they were not so during the Middle Ages. Public study of traditional texts—that is, learning among common people as opposed to the study in rabbinic academies and esoteric kabbalistic circles—was largely limited to sermons delivered by the rabbis in the synagogue.[25] In the case of the Ottoman communities, teaching the public was one of the responsibilities of the congregation's rabbi who typically gave a sermon—in Ladino—on the afternoon of the Sabbath.[26]

According to Shohat, there is evidence of study groups first in Jerusalem during the fifteenth century and then in Safed during the sixteenth century, in the latter case clearly a practice encouraged by Lurianic Kabbalah. For the Ashkenazic world, he relates the establishment of regular study circles for lay people (*ba'ale batim*) to Rabbi Judah Loew of Prague, a central figure in the renaissance of musar in sixteenth- and seventeenth-century central Europe.[27] To the best of my knowledge, no such study has been published on the origins of the Ottoman Sephardic *meldado*. It would seem, however, that the establishment of study groups as a widespread practice is owed to the Lurianic idea of the ritual significance of study as a performative act.[28] We know that, in the seventeenth century, societies (*hevrot*) that were formed for various charitable purposes and professional organizations, the "guilds," established the practice of inviting a rabbi to teach them and lead regular study sessions. Typically after concluding the community prayer on the Sabbath, the members of the *hevrah* would gather to study together and to socialize.[29]

In addition to serving the dissemination of knowledge and occupying its place in the Lurianic mentality of *tiqun* through ritual, the *meldados* also were a rabbinic response to the appearance of secular forms of sociability. Here, the emergence and flourishing of the coffeehouses since the sixteenth century provided the first major challenge as a forum for secular socializing and was countered by the promotion of a religiously legitimate alternative. The coffeehouses appeared in the imperial capital of Constantinople with the arrival of coffee in 1555. Tobacco came a half-century later (about 1609). "From its introduction until the second half of the twentieth century, the coffeehouse functioned as the very center of male public life in the Ottoman and post-Ottoman world."[30] The rabbis constructed the ideal of *meldado* as a legitimate alternative to such secular social spaces. In this framework, notions of private as opposed to public space are misleading categories as the rabbis distinguish between legitimate and illegitimate, that is, religiously sanctioned as opposed to secular, forms of sociability. It is this division into sacred or "sanctified" space—the synagogue as much as a private gathering for the sake of study—on the one hand and profane or profaned space on the other.

In the text cited above, Abraham Palachi does not only speak of institutionalized forms of *meldado,* but also of spontaneous gatherings of family, friends, and neighbors in one's private home. If collective study tied to the synagogue, to charitable societies and guilds, was not an altogether new phenomenon in the social landscape of Ottoman Jewry, there was something new in the ideas expressed by the authors of Ladino musar in the nineteenth century: they dissociated the *meldado* from the established institutions of traditional society. The synagogue, for example, was the public forum of the congregation and as such subject to the social, political, and religious hierarchy of the congregation guided by its lay and rabbinic leaderships. The societies, or *hevrot,* were a form of social organization with their own bylaws and rules of conduct. It is true that membership in a society became less selective and elitist in the eighteenth century than before, when membership dues still were prohibitive for many individuals.[31] But not everyone was, or could be, a member of such a *hevrah,* and women were clearly not part of the male world of institutionalized sociability in the form of *hevrot.*

The *meldado* of the vernacular rabbis was socially more open and inclusive. Not necessarily tied to institutionalized forms of sociability, it could be an ad hoc gathering of family or neighbors, on occasion of a certain life-cycle event or with no particular purpose at all. Most important, the vernacular rabbis addressed a female public alongside the male public that dominated the institutions of the traditional community. By providing a popular readership with literature in the vernacular, the rabbis made sociability in a *meldado* less dependent on the direct intervention of a rabbi who did not necessarily have to be present at such gatherings. Social control was decentralized.

Indeed, the vernacular rabbis envisioned that socializing itself should always be "sanctified" through learning, even if not in the form of a *meldado.* Judah Papo, for example, recommended that

> when women meet in one place, instead of passing the time with evil talk . . . or criticizing another [woman] and ridiculing her and similar bad conversations, they should talk among themselves about things that are good for them in this and the other world: how they must behave towards their husbands, with love, not get angry, take care of the expenses . . . not curse their children . . . not swear, not tell lies, not to use the name of the Creator in vain . . . how they must behave when they are separated [from their husbands in the period of impurity], how they must behave with regard to salting and desalting [of meat], look for worms [in the legumes], keep the Sabbath, in the matter of *halah* [separating the dough; cf. Num. 15]. They should study one with another the laws pertaining to these things.[32]

This may well represent wishful thinking on the part of the author, to be sure, but what is important is the fact that the vernacular rabbis ascribe agency to their lay readership, including women, in the enterprise of education and maintaining the traditional order. They trust the educational power of their books so that the Sephardic public will be able to educate each other, popularizing rabbinic knowledge as a medium of indirect social control. Another case in point is Isaac Farhi, who gives the following advice: if one finds that someone is constantly committing a fault and wants to correct his ways, "it is conceivable to invite him to his home to pass the time on the nights of *Tevet* and *Shevat* [during the winter months] which are quite long, and as they are talking, he should take a musar book and read to him about what the other has been doing."[33]

The vernacular rabbis thus express an ideal in which sociability is legitimized as the social realization of a distinction between the sacred and the profane. If dedicated to *meldar* and an exchange of knowledge about religious duties, gatherings with friends, family, and neighbors are instruments for social control, but the agents of control are no longer exclusively the rabbis but also the larger public itself, educated by their books. An evening gathering of friends can be an occasion used for reading from musar literature and thus for moral admonition in an informal setting. Women are advised not to be too talkative; rather than gossip about others, they should discuss their duties as mothers and wives. The list of issues that Papo considers appropriate for women is revealing of the rabbis' view of the role of women, an issue to which we return later. Here it is important to note that informal oral means of communicating knowledge are thought to be desirable modes of social control in addition to, or along with, reading and listening to musar, used to amplify the impact of printed musar literature. Women are supposed to learn from and teach each other what to do and what values to follow.

Judeo-Spanish rabbinic literature thus promoted a forum for sociability in addition to the traditional settings, the synagogue, study house, or *hevrah*. The social practice of collective study was a major feature of vernacular print culture, and the *meldado* in private homes came to complete the topography of the Jewish community as imagined in musar literature, decentralizing a structure previously defined by the central sacred places of the community topography, such as the synagogue, the *bet midrash*, and the *yeshivah*, all dominated by the learned male elite.

Times for Socializing

The rabbis condemn the notion of leisure, of "pasar la hora," and insist that every moment is precious. Time is a divine loan that must be used to study and fulfill the divine commandments, a capital that, invested in *meldar* and *mitsvot*, will be duly profitable.

> I am amazed by many people who say: let us go to such-and-such a place to pass the time [*pasar la hora*]. To say "to pass the time" seems very wrong, given that the Creator, blessed be He . . . has established the time with its minutes and seconds and has allotted to [each] person the time he has to live, how many hours and how many minutes, and he gives him neither more nor less. Man was created

to use his life for serving God and His commandments. How comes man to say: I will play [games] and go for a stroll and will be with people in order to pass the time. Was that time given to you from the heavens as a burden so that it is oppressive for you and you want to pass it? If you took a book to study [*meldar*] you would demand that time be prolonged.[34]

This is, first of all, an unequivocal rejection of the (modern) notion of leisure. For these rabbis, there is no such thing as free time. Quite the contrary, time is assigned to every person in order to be employed for the sake of Torah. Time needed for other activities—earning money, eating, sleeping, and the like—must be sanctified in preparation for or as part of divine service. Unpurposeful, profane activities are thus ultimately sinful and a waste of the precious time allocated by God, just as profane places are dangerous and lead to secular socializing. The implications of this in the context of vernacular, popular rabbinic literature are important: the ideal of the *talmid hakham* is extended to everyone and there is no distinction between a learned elite specializing in traditional knowledge and "ordinary people" in terms of sociability. Social interaction must take place among righteous people and for the purpose of Torah, and its space and time must be sanctified. All other activities are subordinate to the study of Torah, and there is no place for anything like leisure, or "pasar la hora," in the rabbis' universe.[35] The social utopia expressed in Judeo-Spanish musar is a society of learning: "In the evening and when night falls, man should not go to the coffeehouse or to his neighbor's home in order to engage in idle talk to enjoy himself, but he should return home and take his book [and study] till the hour of the evening prayer. He should say the evening prayer with a *minyan* and before or after supper, he should fix hours for studying at night, because he was created only for the sake of studying."[36]

Just as the synagogue and study house mark sacred spaces in the topography of the Jewish community, the Sabbath (and festivals) are sacred moments in time. While every single moment is best used for *meldar*, these days in particular are meant for study. Predictably, the musar authors are concerned that people misinterpret the Sabbath and the festivals as free time. Here is what Isaac Badhab of Jerusalem has to say in his *Nehemadim mi-Zahav:*

How much pain must we feel and how much weariness for what we see nowadays. Even on the Sabbath bad companies of young people meet and go out to stroll and leave behind the exhaustion of the entire week. Apart from carrying *pipitas, trespiles,*[37] drinks and the like, and employing most of the day with these transgressions into the late hours of the afternoon, they finish the day in the tavern [*birería*]. They find justification because they have credit with the owner of the tavern and will not pay on the Sabbath day itself. After filling their wicked bellies with beer and intoxicating beverages, they order bread (it is forbidden to eat gentile bread . . .), and when they are at the point of being drunk, they do not shy away from eating [non-kosher] food (which is forbidden . . .) and when they are on the point of total insensibility, they get up to play billiards and do so for the rest of the night.[38]

Once again, the inadmissibility of profane socializing and the inevitability of sin as its result are pointed out. Shabbat and the festivals are not "free days" of leisure, to rest from the week's labor, to socialize with one's friends, to play billiards, drink, and talk in the tavern, or to go for a stroll. What begins in idleness ultimately leads to the transgression of religious law. The true purpose of the Sabbath and festivals is the study of Torah, not leisure and socializing for its own sake. Sacred space and time do not allow for profane sociability but must be sanctified through study and divine service.[39]

Synagogue and *bet midrash*, Sabbath and holidays, represent the symbolic universe of traditional Judaism in the dimensions of space and time. Sanctifying them is a reaffirmation of the symbolic universe and translates its values into social practice. But other places—private homes, for example—must also be sanctified through *meldar*, and every single moment when one is not working must be used responsibly for the sake of study: "How good and how pleasant it is if he keeps books in his shop, psalms, *mishnayot, ma'amadot*, musar books, for studying whenever he is free."[40] Secular forms of sociability challenge the sacredness of these spatial and temporal symbols of the universe of rabbinic Judaism; they therefore present a danger and are identified as (or are outlawed as being) sinful in themselves or leading to sinfulness. *Meldar* establishes and reaffirms the symbolic universe. Sociability is legitimate only if it serves a religious purpose; it is "dangerous" to the integrity of the universe when it becomes an end in itself, when it becomes leisure and "pasar la hora."

The Dangers of Leisure

The flip side of sociability as social control—the danger of profane sociability—is patent in many pronouncements of Judeo-Spanish musar literature.[41] Virtually all the musar books I have consulted deal at considerable length with the challenges posed to the rabbinic social ideal of learning by the secular concept of "leisure." In the following, I discuss three examples of such illegitimate secular sociability: idle talk, gossip, and joking; drinking wine and improper socializing; and gambling.

IDLE TALK, GOSSIP, AND JOKING

The authors of musar are consistently worried about what they perceive as "idle talk": "this quality is found particularly among old people who sit at their front doors and many simple people assemble around them, and they begin to tell [of the times] when the city walls were built and of the pashas of old times, and their mouths do not get tired from talking. The reason that old people talk a lot is that their sexual desire is dead, and when they eat [their food] has no flavor to them anymore."[42]

What is the problem with apparently inoffensive pastimes like old people telling about earlier times? Obviously, the rabbis are concerned about the possibility of sinful talk—such as indecent jokes, defamation of others, gossip—that is prohibited by rabbinic law.[43] But they go beyond this: very conscious of the power of speech,[44] the rabbis see purposeless profane talk as leading to a breakdown of the boundaries defining legitimate discourse within the traditional symbolic universe. Discussion of Torah is intended to affirm and strengthen the hold of the symbolic universe over those who participate in the discourse, but profane sociability holds the danger of violating the rules of the "speakable," of the legitimate in traditional discourse. Profane talk not only takes up time ideally used for studying Torah, and it is not only a profanation of time and space: it threatens to transgress the boundaries of the legitimate discourse affirming the traditional symbolic universe.

ALCOHOL AND LEISURE

While the association of old people's idle talk with sexual desire seems an unlikely conclusion, it is significant as it illustrates a dominant theme of Ladino musar: the danger of sexual desire and sexual transgressions. This can be seen in the following passage from the eighteenth-century *Shevet Musar:*

> There are people who invite each other and gather to go out to the gardens [outside the city], to sit down under a pear tree or a fig tree or any green tree near springs of water or ponds or rivers, saying: We will have plenty of joy and friendship, with good cold white wine, and will enjoy ourselves with love. How do we know that we are brethren and friends if we do not sit down in joy and pleasure, for the wine makes the heart joyful. . . . They sing and dance and carouse and praise themselves, saying: Who can drink as much wine as I can? So much that they vomit on the table and produce bad smell. Then, woe to them, one falls down as if dead and another fights with his friend and another curses and [is] rude. And what they drank with love and joy turns into grief and sighing. . . . They will end in poverty and depend on charity. . . . Moreover, the drunkard desires wrongdoing, for with the wine his member becomes erect and he desires illicit sex [*zenut*]. They throw their souls behind their bodies [*echan la alma detrás de el guf*] and teach each other with idle talk.[45]

Leisure, the drinking of alcohol, and the danger of sexual desire are closely linked in this passage, and one is portrayed as inevitably leading to the next. These texts testify to the fact that sociability, to the rabbis, is a potentially dangerous situation if not contained and controlled by the rules set by the discourse of the traditional universe and its affirmation in social practice. The influence of alcohol and the casualness of leisure again are seen as leading to the breakdown of important boundaries between sacred and profane, pure and impure, right and wrong behavior. The rabbis fear that sociability for its own sake, as it breaks down these boundaries, will escape the control of their authority.

The progression from purposeless talk to sexual transgressions is somewhat forced, of course; it is a literary construction intended to dissuade people from socializing for any reason other than religious duty. In the rabbis' vision of a life devoted entirely to study and divine service in which the profane and the sacred are separated—or, more precisely, in which the profane is sanctified out of existence—

there is no place for the notion of leisure. Profane socializing had of course always existed in social reality, in traditional no less than in post-traditional society. As the particularly modern notion of leisure made deep inroads into Sephardic society in the nineteenth century, the rabbinic response to new practices of leisure became all the more urgent.

GAMBLING

A final example is the case of gambling, mentioned with certain frequency in Judeo-Spanish musar literature.[46] Since the rabbis do not differentiate between occasional card playing as a pastime and compulsive gambling—they see one as necessarily leading to the other—it is difficult to assess whether they are speaking of gambling as a widespread or isolated problem. The following is a good example of how the rabbis approach this ethical and social problem and what kind of solution they envision:

> With regard to playing all kinds of games, like cards, *table,* dominoes, dice and the like, this is something very evil. It is as the *hakhamim* said: such is the custom of the evil inclination. Today it says "do thus" and he listens, tomorrow it tells him to do something else and worse, and he listens, until it says to him "go and serve idolatry" and he goes and serves [it]. . . . Even if the victim of the evil inclination is a man of honor, he lets his honor be lost and associates with groups of wicked people and vagabonds who have this profession [of gambling]. They become like brothers and do not separate; they gather in hidden places, houses of poor people, coffeehouses, and in the open field under the sun. They make the nights into days, they do not eat or sleep because of the desire to gamble. The one who loses, his desire inflates, because he thinks that he will win and regain what he has lost. The one who wins, his desire inflates because he wants to win more. . . . And when they do not find any more [places] where to borrow from, they sell things from the house for half their price or put in pawn something from the house in order to borrow [money] at high interest. . . . Mostly they do not have supper in their homes for they use the entire nights for gambling. They sleep from one hour before dawn until two hours after morning services. [But] they are not distressed by the prayer they miss but because of the money they lose. . . . Thus the one who is captured by this evil must make haste to escape from it. . . . He should change his ways from evil to good: instead of losing the nights with evil, he should employ them for studying [*meldar*] what he understands; instead of not wanting to know the doors of the synagogue and study house, he should get up early to go to synagogue and to say his prayers with a *minyan,* word for word. Wherever they meet to study in a group, he should be one of them. Each day, he should move forward in the ways of repentance. And if he knows a place where gamblers and blasphemers gather, he should not enter into that street. . . . In a town where there are such evil persons who are involved in gambling, the elders of the town should be careful not to allow this fire in the town, they should dedicate their efforts to considering how to remedy this defect, either kindly or by punishment [*sea con las buenas, sea con las malas*]. They do a favor to the gamblers and to the town, for evil affects everyone, and good affects everyone.[47]

Gambling as a reprehensible form of sociability is described with its economic and social consequences and contrasted to legitimate forms of sociability (*meldar*, prayer). Legitimate socializing serves to enhance the validity of the traditional symbolic and social orders; gambling disrupts both, as it takes away precious time for studying and challenges social peace. Both *meldar* and gambling, legitimate and illegitimate forms of sociability, are identified with certain places in the topography of the community—the synagogue and study house versus the gatherings of evil people in places like the coffeehouse or tavern. The solution is seen in restoring the symbolic order through study and restoring the social order by avoiding the wrong company, practices identified with the sanctified spaces of the community. Repentance, *teshuvah,* is thus meant to reaffirm the values of the traditional universe through study and restore the social order through social interaction with the right people in the right places.

The closing sentence of the passage cited is indicative of the politics of musar: the author calls upon the leaders of the community to actively fight gambling because its social consequences affect everyone, not only the people involved directly: *"de lo negro les toca a todos y de lo bueno les toca a todos."* Judeo-Spanish musar literature conveys a clear sense of the interrelated symbolic and social orders. Practices of sociability are of prime importance for the authors of musar because any disruptions are understood to carry implications for the traditional order at large.

Leisure—wine, men and women dancing together, unpurposeful talk, or gambling—is perceived as a danger to the traditional universe and its symbolic and social orders. *Meldar* is recommended as therapy to restore the integrity of the symbolic universe by re-enacting its constitutive discourse and as a practice to mend fractures in the social order.

Conclusion

I argued earlier that Judeo-Spanish musar literature created a vernacular reading public which was the basis for the secularization of this reading public in the nineteenth century. In this chapter I have suggested that the rabbinic vernacular literature also laid the groundwork for the transformation of socializing practices. The rabbis' complaints about the dangers of leisure are not surprising, and their complaints about idle talk, alcohol, or gambling are hardly unexpected features in such a genre and in a traditional society. Yet more significant is that Judeo-Spanish musar literature offers a legitimate alternative to profane sociability outside the setting of community institutions controlled by the rabbinic elite. The *meldado,* not without precedence but now vernacularized and socially becoming more inclusive, provided the forum for the new Judeo-Spanish reading public. Vernacular musar created new avenues of legitimate sociability beyond the established institutions: formal and informal study groups decentralized the communication of rabbinic knowledge, removing it from community and elite-controlled institutions like the synagogue and *bet midrash.*[48] The ideal of *meldar* and the occasional institutionalization of *meldados* gave legitimacy to socializing outside these community institutions, however central they remained for musar ideology.

Meldar as sociability was contrasted to leisure. Leisure was understood as a danger to the traditional symbolic and social order, but *meldar* ritually reaffirmed and thus stabilized this order, reconstituting the order as a ritual of repentance. Places and times of socializing had to be sanctified through the study of Torah. While there were privileged places for socializing in the topography of the community—the synagogue and *bet midrash*—and particular occasions that invited collective study—Shabbat and festivals—the *meldado* became the universal framework for legitimate sociability and the forum for the dissemination of vernacular musar and for the new Judeo-Spanish reading public.

Part III

Musar Literature and the Social Order

The Construction of
the Social Order

5

"The *Me*ᶜ*am Lo*ᶜ*ez* appealed to the masses," one scholar has maintained, "because it was sympathetic to the poor and downtrodden."[1] And, indeed, Jacob Huli and the authors of Judeo-Spanish musar literature show empathy for the poor and insist on the importance of social solidarity and charity. But this general impression of the rabbis' empathy for the masses—arguably, their intended readers—does not, as I argue in this and the following chapter, represent their vision of the political and social order. I offer a reading of Judeo-Spanish musar literature guided by the question of how the rabbis responded to social inequality and what it teaches us about the relation between knowledge and power.[2]

Two key concepts of Judeo-Spanish musar help us understand how the rabbis constructed social and political order: first, the human body as a metaphor for the Jewish community with its two most important implications, unity and social differentiation; and second, "*yishuv ha-*ᶜ*olam*," or stability of the world, a response to social inequality. In the next chapter, I describe three social ideal types—the rich, the poor, and the *talmid hakham*—as they are represented in the musar literature.

The Community as Human Organism
and the Stability of the World

The metaphor which sets the tone for musar's understanding of the Jewish community is the human body. Every individual is a part of this "body" and is related to the other individuals by virtue of being part of the same organism.

> All the sages of old said that each community [*hevrah*] of human beings is like one human being, and, as man is made up of many [different] members and nerves and everything is part of one body, so all humankind [together] are called one body, and each [individual] person is like one member. As the nerves and members of the human [body] cannot sustain themselves without one another, so persons cannot live without one another. Each of the members and nerves has its own function in sustaining the body, and they help each other; so too each person has his function and together they sustain the world.[3]

The representation of the Jewish community as a human organism has several implications. Two of these are the quest for unity and peace within the community and solidarity among the members. Palachi, for example, affirms that "the reception of guests shows that we, the Jewish nation, are one body," and "charity and loving-kindness show that we, the Jewish nation, are like one body."[4]

A third implication is that the individual members are responsible for each other, "because we, all Israel, are responsible one for another, for if someone else

sins, he has a responsibility in this, and in order to free himself of that responsibility, he must chastise the other from his soul and heart." Unfortunately, the text
continues, times have changed and people do not easily accept the rebuke of their
fellow Jew: "Because of our sins, if someone observes a transgression in someone
else and chastises him, the other dishonors him and says: 'Who are you to chastise me?'"[5]

The fourth implication of the body metaphor is the functional differentiation
and hierarchy of the interdependent members. By fulfilling the commandment to
"love thy neighbor," "he engages in the stability of the world: one is a carpenter, one
is a gardener, one ploughs the fields, one sows, one is a merchant, one weaves
cloth."[6] Human society is described as a body which is maintained by the functional differentiation of its members.

The maintenance and stability of the world (*yishuv ha-ʿolam*) joins the imagery of society as human organism in Judeo-Spanish musar's social outlook. The
quest for unity, solidarity, mutual responsibility, functional differentiation: all this
is not meant as a description of social reality as the rabbis understood it but as a
sine qua non for its continued existence. The image of *yishuv ha-ʿolam* is an important device for legitimizing the social order and political control of the symbolic
universe, and the "world" to be maintained is both the social world of the Jewish
community and the symbolic world of rabbinic tradition.

The Quest for Unity and the Politics of Musar

The quest for unity and peace is a dominant feature of Judeo-Spanish musar
literature—and musar literature in general, for that matter. The lack of national
unity and the appearance of hatred among the Jews are identified as prime causes
of the destruction of the Second Temple and the ensuing exile; the authors lament
the fact that their contemporaries wait impatiently for salvation but do nothing to
remove these ultimate causes of the punishment in exile and do not care to achieve
unity and solidarity.[7] Love of one's neighbor (*ahavat reʿim*; cf. Lev. 19:18) and
peace are key values of musar.

Various definitions are offered for *reʿh*, "neighbor." Amarachi and Sason quote
the eighteenth-century *Sefer ha-Berit* and argue that the broad term "neighbor" is
meant to include the gentiles—if the Torah were speaking only of Jews, it would
have used the term "brothers"; *reʿim*, being more inclusive, refers to gentiles and
Jews alike.[8] Abraham Palachi offers a very different reading, arguing that the word
kamokha (in the verse "*ve-ahavta le-reʿakha kamokha*" [Love thy neighbor as your-
self], Lev. 19:18) refers to the one who is "*kamokha*" (like you) in a far more narrow
sense: one who has the same profession. For Palachi, "love thy neighbor" is a corrective against strong competition among the members of a guild or profession.[9]

Between these two extremes—"love thy neighbor" as meant for humanity in
general or for members of the same profession—the reference group for Judeo-
Spanish musar literature is usually the Jewish community. What interests us here

is the way in which the vernacular rabbis translate the quest for unity and peace into a politics of consensus. The following passage is instructive:

> We are obliged to affirm and sustain all the regulations [*haskamot*] which each one has in his city. The one who transgresses them is subject to great punishment. The leaders of the cities in each generation have the obligation to be attentive and look for those things that are necessary for the well-being of the city, the good things that need to be done, and with regard to defects that require correction, they should unite in order to correct and rectify the matter, so that the town may be perfect and praised among all cities.

The author goes on to insist that the community leaders should not only occupy themselves with general administration but are also responsible for organizing and regulating matters relevant for the well-being of the community, "like visiting the sick, washing and honoring the dead, administration of accommodations for guests, services for the poor in town, support of the *hakhamim*, actions to save on the costs of weddings and celebrations, for because of our sins there is now much poverty in the world."[10] The basic rules for community politics are expressed here: to begin with, the obligation of the community leaders to assure community welfare by creating *haskamot* according to the specific needs of their time and place, and the obligation to respect these *haskamot*. Such community laws must be promulgated to ensure the well-being and functioning of the community and its institutions, but also to promote social peace. The specific example discussed by Papo has to do with controlling the often excessive spending for wedding celebrations. Interestingly, Papo expresses an idea of community leadership that goes well beyond administrative and budgetary concerns and formulates the need for political actions, the need to work for the welfare of the community.

Many people cannot afford the exorbitant costs of weddings, and Papo suggests that the community's leadership should set a limit on such expenses. The honor of the wealthier members would be preserved, because they would be simply complying with a community ordinance; the poor and middle-class members would be relieved of an unbearable financial burden. The chapter goes on to say that community regulations should be realistic and not overly demanding and difficult. As for non-compliance,

> if there is someone who transgresses [a community regulation] in secret and there is a risk that he will transgress it openly when they chastise him, they should turn a blind eye. . . . In each regulation [*haskamah*] that they make, they should invest the leaders of the town with the power to add or subtract according to the needs of the hour. We have said in the chapter on "*galut*" that all nations are united in seeking the benefit and well-being of their people and their own lands, and we should do the same for well-being in this world and the world to come.[11]

Carrying out the *haskamot* is to be entrusted to the community leaders, who must have the prerogative to act according to the needs of each case. It is significant that Papo invokes here (as he does elsewhere in his book) the "nations of the world" whose example the Jews should follow—clearly a new idea of the nineteenth century that entered the traditional discourse of musar. If someone has transgressed a regulation secretly and is unlikely to accept rebuke, the leaders should turn a blind eye lest he openly challenge their authority—a good example of Sephardic rabbis' pragmatic approach to religious practice. Again showing his pragmatic approach, Papo gives advice about the decision-making process: "It is true that the elders want to see the best for the town, but they hesitate to act because there are many opponents, each with his own ideas, obstructing the matter and not letting it be achieved, and if it is achieved, they transgress it. And because there is freedom [*y como es la libertitad*] they cannot be punished. . . . How should it be done? With the consent of all, for the meaning of the word *haskamah* is 'consent.'"[12] Papo then explains how the leaders of the community and the initiators of a new community regulation should proceed: they must try to establish a consensus by convincing the community one by one and only then convene a general assembly to have the matter accepted by a majority. No less important, Judah Papo encourages not only the leaders of the community but every individual member to think of ways to improve matters in the community or one of its institutions and to take the political initiative to get his idea approved by a consensus.[13] The democratization of the eastern Sephardic communities in the nineteenth century is evident from Papo's approach.

As elsewhere, the Judeo-Spanish *Pele Yo'ets* goes beyond most Ladino musar works, but it is nonetheless indicative of a general tendency among the vernacular rabbis who—like other groups within the Sephardic community—have developed a sense of politics going beyond the administration of the community's financial affairs. In the *Pele Yo'ets*, community politics means more than administrative matters; it means identifying the community's problems and things that might be improved and then advancing its welfare by building as broad a consensus as possible and trying to implement ideas pragmatically. While "politics" basically remains the task of the community leaders—notables and rabbis alike—Papo explicitly encourages ordinary members to contribute to the process.

Papo formulates a vision of musar politics which is remarkably pragmatic and built on community consensus and unity. He anticipates dealing with deviant practice tolerantly as long as no one *openly* defies the authority of community leaders. Politics, understood as more than mere administration, is intended to advance the well-being of the community and enhance the stability of the traditional order.

Solidarity and Charity

"*Por mil godra que sea la gallina, tiene menester de la vecina. Una mano lava la otra y dos lavan la cara.*"[14] Here Judah Papo quotes two popular sayings to illustrate his point that mutual solidarity among the members of the Jewish community is a universal value and is not limited to charity. The fat hen in the popular adage stands, of course, for the rich in the community. However wealthy they may be, they still need the other community members. And as one hand washes the other, one member of the community depends on the other, and all must collaborate in the higher task of securing the well-being of the community ("*y dos lavan la cara*"). Musar values are expressed here through folk sayings familiar to their Ladino-speaking audience, a literary technique employed by some musar authors to present ideas in terms of "popular knowledge."

Charity (*tsedaqah*) is still the most conspicuous example of community solidarity, and, as a divine commandment, predictably occupies an important place in Judeo-Spanish musar literature. A typical example in the *Pele Yo'ets*[15] is the story of a wealthy but stingy woman who arrives in the "other world" after her death and sees all the righteous Jews having a festive meal. When she asks why she is not being served anything, she is told that the people eat of the provisions which they have brought from their earthly life. The woman is allowed back to this world to get her own provisions and loads carriages full of white bread. On her way back, the poor ask her for food, but she stubbornly refuses, except for one loaf of bread which falls off the carriage and which she gives to a hungry person by the wayside. When the wealthy woman arrives again in the "other world," her provisions are taken away; she joins the feast, but is served nothing more than the loaf of bread which had fallen off the carriage. When she complains, she is told that "all she has brought is not worth anything, except this loaf of bread which she gave to the poor." Wealth is entrusted to the rich not for their own good and not as payment for their own merit, but to be administered responsibly, and their responsibility is to assist the poor financially and otherwise.[16]

The Ottoman rabbis faced widespread poverty and there were many who depended entirely on the welfare institutions of the communities and on individual charity. A review of Judeo-Spanish musar literature allows us to point out five aspects of the rabbinic politics of charity and how they contribute to the construction of society and the maintenance of the social order.

(1) Lest the rich get tired of supporting an undiminished number of poor people, Judeo-Spanish musar makes sure to point out that charity, *tsedaqah*, as a commandment, sustains the world and might very well serve as a divinely designed atonement in order to spare the community a greater catastrophe.

> Lucky is Israel for they are compassionate and like to do the *mitsvot* and give charity. But because of our sins there are so many poor and they come from everywhere, moving from one town to the next, and thus [the rich] get tired, saying: the house of the wealthy is emptied, but the house of the poor does not become full. But rather they should think and say: surely God wants our best; some fire was about to happen or some plague or another kind of evil, and God wanted to spare us. That is why he sends us poor people [and] *talmide hakhamim*, so we can do good for them, and thus we are spared all evil.[17]

Charity is seen as atonement, averting punishment from the community. It is thus closely related to the notion of *yishuv ha-'olam*, sustaining the world.

(2) The politics of charity is meant to represent and thus sustain social hierarchy: Judeo-Spanish musar clearly distinguishes between a poor *talmid hakham* and a poor ignoramus; the hierarchy of learning is translated into social status:

> If two poor people come to a rich man and ask for charity, and one is a *hakham* and the other an ignoramus, the rich man should not say: I have ten *grush*, so I will give five to each of them. This is not right; rather, he should make a distinction. He should give seven to the *hakham* and three to the ignoramus. . . . The proof [that this is the right thing to do] is that the fingers of one hand are not all equal, there are small [fingers] and larger ones.[18]

The image of the fingers of a hand is related to the use of the human body as a metaphor for human society. The fingers must work together and only together do they form a hand or a fist—but they are not equal. The image is also employed by another author in order to show "that the rank of all Jews is not equal, nor are all the fingers of the hand equal. The more the person studies Torah and affirms the commandments, the more he is loved by the Creator, and it is not easy to reach the level of a good Jew."[19] Learnedness and piety—the qualities represented by the *talmid hakham* and constituting the social ideal of musar—make a person more worthy in the eyes of God *and* socially privileged. The reward in this world and the next should depend on the learnedness of each person. Social difference thus is assumed to be natural, as is expressed by the metaphor of the human organism and its parts.

(3) An important feature of the politics of charity is the rabbis' realistic, pragmatic approach. While Judeo-Spanish musar urges solidarity, this value is pragmatically qualified when it comes to money: "If we say that we are all one body, this does not mean that we put the purse right in the middle [of the road] and everyone who is hungry comes and eats, for this is against nature and Torah," Judah Papo assures us; "the main point is to do things in moderation."[20] Charity must be given in proportion to one's ability to give; one must not go too far and harm oneself. "With regard to money, it is right to give a bit of money to benefit one's fellow . . . and this varies according to whom God has given more [or less] possibilities."[21]

Such a pragmatic approach is also expressed by Amarachi and Sason: the talk of solidarity and "one body" should not be taken as impeding economic competition. The musar authors assure their readers that solidarity must not damage business and that it is right to pursue the better bargain. The example they give—the textile merchant—is representative of the occupations of many Ottoman Jews at the time. There is nothing bad about trying to earn money, as long as one plays fairly: "May everyone move to be faster than his fellow [*cada uno puede meterse con sus vente uñas para ir más presto de su haver*] in order to gain money, but he is not allowed to trip the other up in order to arrive first."[22]

(4) Judeo-Spanish musar encourages people to support others in a way that will enable them to help themselves in the future. What is most important in charity, says one author, is "to create employment for the one who has no work, so that he can maintain himself with honor by his own work and does not have to depend on public welfare."[23] Jewish tradition recognized the problem that charity "all too often fosters permanent helplessness and dependency," and Maimonides' *Mishneh Torah* maintains that "the highest degree [of charity], exceeded by none,

is that of the person who assists a poor Jew by providing him with a gift or a loan or by accepting him into a business partnership or by helping him find employment—in a word, by putting him where he can dispense with other people's aid."[24]

(5) Another idea promoted in the *Pele Yoʿets* is that the community should establish a fund to assist those who have fallen into financial difficulties and have lost credit. The rich members of the community should pay money into the fund, from which loans will be granted to those who need them—without interest, of course, but in exchange for a deposit. If a person is unable to pay back his debt, the community fund will sell the object given in security.[25]

These points show that charity, for Judeo-Spanish musar authors, is a pragmatic measure for relief of the poor and world stability—both theologically, in that it serves as atonement, and socially, in that it promotes social peace. The ideal of charity in musar is not part of a utopia of universal social justice but is a pragmatic response to social inequality, which is understood as inevitable and divinely ordained.

Responsibility and "*Castiguerio*"

If charity means caring for the material needs of one's fellow, to chastise others morally (*castiguerio*) means to care for their souls:

> It is very surprising if a person who is compassionate and takes pity on the poor gives charity, a little bit or much, when he sees them suffering, but when he sees someone committing a sin and transgressing a divine commandment, he does not chastise him or teach him or even think of it. What sort of compassion is this to have pity on the body of one's fellow and not to try to have pity on his soul?[26]

The image of community unity is used in this context as well. If someone traveling in a boat begins to cut a hole in its bottom, his fellow travelers will of course try to prevent him from doing so lest they all drown.[27] Any individual who transgresses a divine commandment, so goes the reasoning of musar, endangers the whole community and, indeed, the entire world, as each individual transgression strengthens the power of evil (following Lurianic thought). It is the responsibility of the community authorities, both lay and rabbinic, to ensure compliance with traditional religious law and community regulations,[28] but social control is by no means restricted to the enforcement of religious law by the community institutions and officials.

A prime instrument of social control, assuring the stability of social order and warding off challenges against the integrity of the traditional symbolic universe, is *castiguerio*—chastising others, teaching and admonishing one's fellow Jews, and showing people where they fail and what to do to mend their ways. Obviously, this is also the function of musar literature and sermons, and a great deal of the educational responsibility lies with the *talmide hakhamim*. In fact, a prime function of vernacular musar literature is not only to chastise its readers, but also to provide them with the knowledge to go out and teach others. Musar wants its readers and listeners to be not only recipients but also carriers of its educational message. It teaches not only to instruct, but also to empower its readers to continue the educational effort on their own and spread the word of musar where the rabbis themselves are not being heard.

Those who read a musar book or attend study groups should repeat what they learn to their families, households, and neighbors. *Castiguerio* is meant to penetrate to all sectors of society and to reach those who do not read musar works by themselves or do not attend the rabbis' studies; the reader is meant to serve as a broadcaster of musar teaching. Papo encourages *castiguerio* as universal social practice and urges sociability for the sake of education. He makes sure to point out the usefulness of his own book:

> If this obligation to chastise applies even to strangers, how much more so to one's family and household, for it is in his hands to defend them and lead them onto the right path with kind and sweet words. He should not leave them, day by day his chastisement should drop down upon them like rain, and as the rain penetrates the stone . . . so does his chastisement penetrate their heart even if it is hard as stone. And how good it is if there are in every town individuals who join to put into practice good things together, like establishing societies for studying [*hevrot de meldar*] on Sabbath and festivals and early in the morning. . . . How advantageous it will be if they determine to read a bit in this book, the *Pele Yoʿets*, for to read from it continuously with a group is enough to benefit others. . . . Everything is achieved by good Jews who talk with each other and spreads by word of mouth, until it is also accepted by the leaders of the town.[29]

The project of vernacular musar is expressed clearly here. The teachings of musar are spread throughout society in a manner best described with the image of concentric circles. Many Hebrew musar books such as the Hebrew *Pele Yoʿets*, but also certain vernacular books such as Palachi's *Ve-hokhiah Avraham*, are directed toward the limited readership of those who can be expected to understand them. They serve as the basis for disseminating musar orally, either in sermons or in study groups. Another route for dissemination is the translation of musar into the vernacular. These vernacular musar books are intended to be read in study groups, the *meldados*. Then, as the authors of musar imagine it, the readers of this literature and the participants in the *meldados* carry the message further, educating those—family, friends, and neighbors—who have had access to the musar books neither as readers nor as listeners in a *meldado*. The vernacular rabbis teach their readers and listeners in order to correct their faults and instruct them to serve as teachers of musar themselves, to admonish their fellows and to think of ways to enhance standards of observance and piety within the community at large.[30] Social control through teaching musar is thus decentralized through the spread of vernacular rabbinic literature.

Yishuv ha-ʿOlam and Social Inequality

The notion of social inequality, the unequal distribution of economic and cultural capital in society and of political power in the community, is perhaps most clearly expressed by Elijah ha-Kohen in the *Shevet Musar* in a passage which combines the idea of *yishuv ha-ᶜolam* and the use of the human body as a metaphor for society:

> The Creator of the world created heads [*terminos*] for the sake of the stability of the world. Know that everywhere there are heads: the lion is the king of the beasts, the ox is the king of the ruminants, the eagle is the king of the birds, and man is the king over all of them. And everywhere there are rulers and those who are ruled over, and God is the lord of all. . . . The same in man himself: in his body there are parts which are primary and stand at the head, one above the other. Some of them serve, and some of them are served. . . . So it must be in the society of people: it is necessary that some of them are lords and some of them servants, some of them rulers and some of them ruled over. Otherwise the world could not be sustained. And as Qorah wanted to do the opposite of this, that everyone should be equal, saying: "for all the congregation are holy" [Num. 16:3], wanting that all should be lords, he, his possessions and everything he had were removed from the world.[31]

This clearly testifies to the conservative attitude of the Sephardic musar authors. For all their sympathy with the ordinary people and the poor, their musar literature clearly serves the additional cause of legitimizing the socioeconomic status quo of eastern Sephardic society. If we ask ourselves how the vernacular rabbis themselves fit into that picture, the following hermeneutical exercise by Isaac Farhi in the 1860s is interesting evidence.

> This is the intention of the Sages according to my humble understanding when they say of the verse from the Psalms, "May he dwell in God's presence forever," that David petitioned God that the whole world be rich. A heavenly voice sounded and said: "Appoint steadfast love to guard him" [Ps. 61:8], which is to say: If everyone were rich, how would the commandments of charity and loving-kindness be affirmed? One wonders how King David could have asked such a thing for if there is stability in the world, it is because there are poor and rich, and with only poor or only rich the world could not exist. If everyone were rich, who would be a mason and who a tailor?[32]

Again, the functional differentiation of society is seen as legitimizing for the existence of social inequality. Amarachi and Sason argue in a similar vein, on the basis of the Ashkenazic *Sefer ha-Berit,* that everyday life teaches the interdependence of different people fulfilling different tasks within the social fabric. In their view, a society is differentiated into specialized and necessarily unequal members, and it is precisely this differentiation that produces the need for verbal communication which distinguishes man from animals.[33] To show the reality and necessity of a functionally differentiated society, Amarachi and Sason cite the innumerable people involved in the process of making the bread we eat or building the cities we live in.[34] Farhi uses this functional understanding of society to present his argument: Why should there be rich and poor people? Because who would work as a tailor or mason if there were no poor? And how could the commandment of charity be fulfilled without poverty? But Farhi does not tell us why a tailor or mason should necessarily be poor. His point is that social inequality is not only a justifiable reality but that it sustains the world. This "world" is the world of rabbinic tradition. The traditional symbolic universe is sustained by the existing socioeconomic order with its social differentiation, with its rich, its poor, and its scholars (three social types which I study in more detail below). The traditional world is grounded in social difference, and the rabbis could not be further from presenting anything like an egalitarian utopia.

But then how could David—according to Farhi's reading—have asked for "the whole world" to be rich if this question is so out of place?

> One has to know that King David was a great sage and his understanding was very great and he knew what he was asking, and he asked it with much understanding. It is well known that "the whole world" refers to the *hakhamim,* for we live by their speech, and without them we are not human beings and do not know where we come from nor where we are going. . . . King David saw by virtue of the holy spirit that these generations, because of our sins, would be very deficient and would not receive the teaching and chastisement of the *talmide hakhamim* because they are poor; just as King Solomon said: "A poor man's wisdom is scorned, and his words are not heeded" [Eccl. 9:16]. Therefore he asked God that the "entire world"—that is, the *hakhamim* who are the entire world—be rich. For thus they could chastise and order the world according to the Law and the commandments. . . . A heavenly voice answered him, saying: Your demand is good, but you must know that one of the foundations that sustain the world is loving-kindness. And as the *hakhamim* sustain the foundation of the Law, so the rest of the people who are not *hakhamim* sustain the foundation of loving-kindness, and thus are in charge of providing the *hakhamim* with a living so that they can concentrate on the Torah and divine service. And thus, if the *hakhamim* were rich, how would the foundation of loving-kindness be affirmed? And this is why it says "appoint steadfast love to guard him."[35]

Farhi develops the rabbinic interpretation of Psalm 61:8 further. Who represents "the world"? No one less than the *talmide hakhamim.* There hardly could be a clearer expression of the rabbinic claim to the interpretive monopoly of the symbolic universe. The *talmide hakhamim* embody the "world" of tradition, and human existence would be meaningless without the *talmide hakhamim* as guides to past, present, and future. Thus David is actually asking: why could not all *scholars* be rich, giving them more authority within society? Again, it is for *yishuv ha-ʿolam* that this is not possible and *hakhamim* cannot be rich, that knowledge and wealth do not, as a rule, fall on the same side. While the rabbis sustain one foundation of the world—the study of Torah—it is the rest of society that sustains the second foundation—*gemilut hasadim* (loving-kindness), financial support for the scholars.

The social order envisioned by the rabbis thus crystallizes around the *talmide hakhamim* of whom the authors of Judeo-Spanish musar are themselves representative. As they depend—both *de facto* and according to their understanding of a differentiated society—on the contributions of those who have money, the alliance between knowledge and wealth is reaffirmed even in these pages which are so replete with sympathy for the poor and insist so firmly on the social responsibility of the rich. The musar idea of charity to sustain the poor and to maintain the *talmide hakhamim* alike does not by any means seek to redistribute economic capital. Quite the contrary, charity as a world-sustaining commandment presupposes social inequality, and the rabbinic social ideal perpetuates and legitimizes the existing inequalities in the communities for which they write. The rabbis legitimize social inequality as necessary for the proper functioning of a diversified society and for the stability of the divinely ordained symbolic order. Their own position as administrators and teachers of the traditional symbolic universe is strengthened along the way: in a differentiated society, the rabbis claim for themselves the position as specialists in knowledge and the cultural capital of authoritative interpretation of tradition, and establish a strategic alliance with the wealthy dignitaries of the community, on whom they rely financially in order to dedicate themselves to the study of Torah.

Conclusion

The rabbis represented human society in general and the Jewish community in particular as a human organism. The parts of this organism depend on each other and are functionally diversified and socially unequal. The rabbis acknowledged and, indeed, legitimized the unequal distribution of economic capital in society by maintaining that the social status quo ensured the stability of the world order (i.e., the social order *and* the integrity of the traditional symbolic universe). They solicited solidarity from the rich in the form of charity and sustenance for the *talmide hakhamim*, but they never challenged the distribution of economic capital as such. The *hakhamim* in turn held the cultural capital, the monopoly over interpretation. Society, as viewed by the vernacular rabbis, was grounded on the distinction and the inequality between the rich and the poor, and between scholars and the non-learned. Socially as well, vernacular musar literature was a stabilizing factor in eastern Sephardic communities.

At the same time, the vernacular rabbis sought to reach out beyond their immediate readership; through the vernacular literature that they produced and the social practices of *meldados* that they recommended, they tried to promote new and indirect forms of social control in society. Everybody was responsible for doing whatever he could "so that Judaism and good Jews may advance."[36]

If, as Joseph Nehama has maintained, "artistocratic and paternalistic tendencies became stronger over time" since the early eighteenth century, and "the simple mortals owed obedience to the rabbis and notables,"[37] the emergence of a vernacular rabbinic literature also produced a decentralization of social control. The vernacular rabbis addressed themselves directly to the people, but they also urged that their musar be carried into evening gatherings in the family and among neighbors and that compliance with the social and religious norms set out in musar be jointly controlled. Knowledge and social control were decentralized by transferring *castiguerio* and the communication of knowledge into a social setting not directly controlled by the rabbis. Vernacular print culture encouraged the emergence of legitimate sociability outside the educational center of the community—synagogue, *bet midrash, yeshivah*—and beyond the social group of the *talmide hakhamim* themselves.

The social consequences of musar literature are thus ambiguous: on the one hand it must be seen as intended to stabilize the social status quo by enhancing the authority of the *hakhamim* in society and strengthening the alliance between the rabbis and the wealthy; on the other hand, by disseminating rabbinic knowledge in vernacular print, in *meldados,* and indirectly through orally circulated propaganda, it decentralized social control, which was always a prerogative of the rabbinic and community lay leadership.

Three Social Types: The Wealthy, the Poor, the Learned

6

The rabbis represented Jewish society as a human organism composed of functionally different and hierarchically related members. Another way to read the rabbinic construction of society is to study three major social types constituting the social order of musar: the wealthy, the poor, and the *talmide hakhamim*. As we have seen, the vernacular rabbis were convinced that this social differentiation and stratification was necessary and God-given, and they never challenged the legitimacy of the social fabric they described. This stabilizing affirmation of social inequality recurs throughout Judeo-Spanish musar and is well expressed in a statement in Elijah ha-Kohen's *Shevet Musar:* "Even those whom [God] made poor have not really lost anything, for their poverty will not lead them to *gehinam.*"[1] Social and divine order depend, we are told, on social differentiation and inequality. The work done by the poor is indispensable in the anti-egalitarian worldview of the vernacular rabbis. And what is no less important: the key values of musar culture—humility, honor, charity—depend, in social practice, on the condition of social inequality—that is, they presuppose a social hierarchy.[2]

The Wealthy

It often seems that the vernacular rabbis side clearly with the poor and against the wealthy. Thus Amarachi and Sason write, "We see with our own eyes that among a hundred poor people, ninety-nine endure poverty and walk in the way of God and one turns out wicked; with wealth, it is the contrary, for among a hundred rich people, ninety-nine leave the way of God and one of their sons walks the right path."[3] As I will try to show, however, the picture is far more complex and the rabbis' attitude far more ambiguous.

The authors of Judeo-Spanish musar attack the desire for wealth as immoral and the insatiable pursuit of material affluence as pointless and dangerous. While the existence of socioeconomic differences is not questioned and it is not considered inherently bad to be rich, the active accumulation of wealth is thought to lead to immoral business practices and sinful conduct. The desire to make more money encourages competitiveness and leads to dishonest behavior by unscrupulous businessmen, who cheat others and cause them financial hardship.[4] Merchants who are always busy risk their health and lives in extensive traveling instead of using their time to study Torah; they are tempted to work with non-Jewish authorities, which always holds the danger of downfall. The one who always is in pursuit of a good bargain, in the words of Amarachi and Sason in their *Darkhe ha-Adam,* does not take care of his body and disregards his health and travels across oceans and highways and deserts and puts himself in great dangers, from drought during the day, from cold during the nights. And how many people get near the authorities, which is dangerous, as the Mishnah states: "Do not make yourself known to the authorities" [Avot 1:10], which is to say that it is not good to get near the authorities. . . . And all this evil because of desire and envy, the wish to have a large palace and kitchenware of silver and silk and filigree clothes for one's wife.[5]

Amarachi and Sason adduce an additional argument from Jewish history. Citing the famous sixteenth-century chronicle *Shevet Yehudah* by Salomon ibn Verga, they warn against the ostentation of wealth and luxury. Ibn Verga had the Christian theologian Thomas argue that wealthy Jews exhibiting their affluence had caused anti-Jewish feelings among ordinary people and had given rise to the repeated blood libels against Jews in medieval Spain.[6] One reason that Amarachi and Sason included extensive material from the *Shevet Yehudah* in their two Judeo-Spanish musar books (*Darkhe ha-Adam* and *Musar Haskel*) was to convey to the wealthy the moral message that they should not provoke the envy of non-Jews. This should perhaps be read in the context of the recurrent (though not widespread) blood libels against Jews originating in the Greek communities of various Ottoman cities.[7]

A critical attitude toward those who abuse their wealth in order to influence community affairs is presented by Abraham Palachi:

> I am very displeased with some people who seek to spread division and strife in the holy community. And even some who are fearful of God and do not fight or yell in the synagogue . . . but are nevertheless dissatisfied with the treasurer or the *hazan* or the caretaker of the synagogue and do not make the payments for *mitsvot* which they owe to the community, or they remain silent and do not buy a *mitsvah* [in the auction of synagogue honors], or they go up to the Torah but do not volunteer [a donation]. . . . Similarly, there are some prominent persons who are discontented for some reason and do not give to charity as they used to. We would like to know what kind of foolishness and insanity this is, for what is the fault of the unfortunate poor?[8]

Palachi condemns the rich within the community who use their financial power to exercise political pressure, always to the detriment of the weakest community members, though he does not give names or cite cases. He rebukes those "who think they have the messiah in the cash box [*que tienen a el mashiah en la caja*]."[9] Here Palachi sides unequivocally with the poor, who depended on the resources of the well-to-do (especially as they were already shouldering a great part of the community's expenses through indirect taxes). The rich abuse their power, says Palachi, when they take the community and its institutions hostage in order to press for their personal interests. But this clear statement is then followed by a surprising qualification in a passage at the end of the chapter:

> Of all we have said in this chapter ["*hamdan be-mamon*"], this chastisement does not apply to the people in our city of Izmir . . . who are all generous and righ-

teous, and seek God, and there are many who have no capital but have good income inexplicable by nature, and they give charity and money out of loving kindness. . . . And I, young and with little understanding, attribute this to the virtue granted us by God, to the fact that the *shehitah* [ritual slaughtering of kosher animals] in our city . . . of Izmir is most praised among all places, whether for checking and investigating [animals for kosher use], in which they are outstanding experts, or whether for learning in Torah, of which they are masters and worthy teachers. Also with regard to the stringencies which we have in many laws and which they do not have in other places: all this brings much abundance to the city. . . . The main reason for the scarcity of income is nothing else than those *shohatim* who are unworthy.[10]

Palachi goes on to explain that the worthy *shohet*, by liberating human souls that might have been reincarnated in animals, sustains the Jewish community, but that a bad *shohet* causes pain to these souls, failing to redeem them from their *gilgul* (incarnation), and thus brings poverty over his community. He then concludes: "As long as the Jews make sure not to eat unkosher meat [*nevelot u-terefot*], they will have a living."[11]

This passage must be seen in the context of the fierce class struggle between rich and poor community members in Izmir over the *gabela*, or meat tax, levied on kosher meat, which was used to pay most of the community's expenses and affected primarily the poor members. Avner Levi has made a detailed study of the 1847 Ladino pamphlet "*Shavat ʿaniyim*," which denounced the desperate situation of the ordinary community members who faced an ever-increasing tax burden while the wealthy elite tried to decrease their own contribution through direct community taxes. Abraham Palachi's father, Hayim, was head of the *bet din* during the *Shavat ʿaniyim* crisis of 1847 and defended the legitimacy of the meat *gabela*, siding—as did all the rabbis, with the exception of David Hazan—with the rich.[12] When nothing else helped, the poor decided to split from the *qehilah* and form their own congregation under the leadership of Rabbi Hazan. The poor were forced to eat meat from butchers without paying the *gabela*—which was, in turn, declared non-kosher by the rabbis. There was later a struggle between Hayim Palachi and the rich *gabaleros* who sold themselves the right to levy the meat tax (worth 90,000 *arayot*) for the sum of 10,000 *arayot*. But when the rich again appeased Rabbi Palachi, he once more sided with them.[13] In the years between 1865 and 1869, another severe conflict erupted over the question of taxation, which was only resolved once Abraham Palachi had been elected his late father's successor as chief rabbi.[14]

In his remark on the wealthy of his hometown Izmir, Abraham Palachi clearly takes a biased position: notwithstanding the abuses by the rich—they lent money to the community (which was having difficulties in meeting its financial obligations) and refused to pay more direct taxes to sustain the community, yet called for an increase in the *gabela*—and the grievances this created among other members of society, the author claims that the rich of Izmir are pious, just, and righteous. One wonders who the moral chastisement against the abuses of the rich was meant for if not the wealthy elite of Izmir.

But Palachi also states that certain *shohatim* are in fact those to blame for the impoverishment of parts of the community. There is evidence that in the 1860s (when Palachi's book appeared) butchers were still selling meat without the *gabela*—meat declared non-kosher by the rabbis—to the poor. Palachi invokes the powerful imagery of Lurianic Kabbalah, holding that human souls could be reincarnated in an animal and would be liberated through ritual slaughter and the appropriate blessing, and bluntly puts the blame for poverty and economic distress on those *shohatim* who provided the poor with tax-free meat. Nowhere is the conservative, socially stabilizing attitude of a vernacular rabbi more clearly expressed than here: rather than blame the political stance of the rich in the community for the widespread poverty (in line with his non-specific allegations earlier in the chapter), Palachi prefers to lay the blame on the poor themselves.

Palachi's text is thus a good example of the ambiguous position taken by the rabbis in the social conflicts of their times. Their abstract musar message is clear: solidarity with the poor, wealth obliges, charity is a prime commandment. But Abraham Palachi's defensive remarks about the rich in his own town of Izmir betray his dependence on the members of the economic elite, the lay leadership of the community. We do not know whether he honestly believed that the rich in Izmir were beyond criticism or whether he was offering excuses for those who would presumably have to finance the publication of his books, and on whom he depended as rabbi (later chief rabbi) of the town. In any event, Palachi's case suggests that the rabbis' empathy for the poor as expressed in their musar books could be (but was not always) far removed from their practice as community leaders or legal authorities.[15]

Avner Levi has observed that the firm alliance between knowledge and wealth was only challenged when community leadership became secularized beginning in the 1860s, and that, when the rabbis began to be marginalized by the rich, they apparently switched sides in community affairs and increasingly supported the interests of the many poor and middle-class members of the community.[16] Whereas Palachi still firmly defended the alliance between knowledge and wealth, more critical voices were heard in later years. A case in point is Judah Papo, who denounced the illegal charging of interest (*ribit*) by the rich:[17]

> The sin of *ribit* is very heavy . . . and because of our sins there is much entanglement in this. . . . How is it that there is no one to investigate or chastise them for this great sin? The answer is obvious, for this practice . . . is found among the banks and businesses of great people. The *hakhamim* and good Jews know about it, but they do not speak up because they are afraid that their words will not be heard. . . . The great merchants and the bankers should look for a remedy. . . . And if it is hard on them to lose the interests, then they should at least issue a cheque [*una camialica*] with someone else's name, even the name of the clerk, stating the sum of the interest he is due to receive, and the other should cash it for him.[18]

In his critique of the practice of *ribit*, Papo clearly reveals what might be suspected from Palachi's remarks cited above: the rabbis, well aware of this illicit practice, fear that their voices will not be heard; one suspects that they also fear for their positions and financial support if they openly confront the rich. Only the economically powerful can do something against the illicit practice, though Papo is quite realistic about the prospects of such a remedy and suggests that people should at least resort to some kind of legal fiction so as not to defy the halakhic prescription openly. The passage testifies to a sense of rabbinic powerlessness against the dominant interests of those holding the economic capital in the community and the community's lay leadership.

While the warnings against illegal interest are also found in the Hebrew version of the *Pele Yoʿets*,[19] a much more outspoken rebuke to the rich is found in the following remarks in the chapter on wealth in Judah Papo's Judeo-Spanish *Pele Yoʿets*. While the Hebrew version only advises the rich on what they should do—give charity, support the *hakhamim*, study Torah, and so on[20]—the Ladino text directly attacks the many sins often associated with wealth and, unlike the Hebrew version, cites assimilation as one problem of the wealthy elite. "The rich person must stand a greater test than the poor," begins the text, because "he has two alternatives before him": either to enter *gan ʿeden* or to enter *gehinam.*

> If the person does not fear God and thinks that he has gained his money by virtue of his strength and resourcefulness, he will be entangled in many sins, for he will cheat in his business and with weight and measures, and speak lies and mislead and swear falsely and in vain in God's name, will try to take away the business from his fellow, and similar entanglements that occur in business. . . . With their wealth they also become arrogant and do not care about anyone and even ignore their poorer relatives. . . . He tries to dig the grave of the one who gets in his way, and if he has the opportunity, he removes him from this world without pity so that the people will be afraid of him and fear of him will be engraved in their hearts. They become angry with anyone who they think does not render them the honor they deserve. They are envious of those who are more wealthy and more honored than themselves. Being rich, they employ their time and money in the vices of this world: good food, good drinking, fine clothes, promenades, evenings of music, dance, and singing with men and women intermingling. . . . But they have no strength nor power to give to the poor and to the *hakhamim*, but rather trample them down and torment them. They speak badly of the *hakhamim* and denigrate them, as if they owe them something and do not pay. They value the words of the philosophers and ridicule the words of our sages. . . . They are lax about Judaism: no studying, no prayers in the synagogue during the entire week. They say a prayer at home which is careless, hasty, and shortened. On the Sabbath or festivals when they go to synagogue, they talk more than pray. Because of wealth they also want to follow the fashions and ways of the [gentile] nations in order to be similar to them. Therefore they come to sin and eat and drink with them and violate Sabbath and festivals, or shave their beards. . . . There is no one who is caught in all the wrongdoings we have mentioned, but there are many who are caught in some of them.[21]

"The rich" can, of course, be virtuous persons provided they give their money generously to charity and support the *talmide hakhamim* and the community

107

institutions—for all of which the reward in the world to come will be great—but the moral traps of wealth are multiple.[22] First, there is the moral concern that the rich will be tempted into forbidden business practices. If someone gets in their way, they will try to remove him, violently if necessary. Out of complacency, they avoid attending to the needs of their poorer relatives. In all this, they challenge the solidarity of the community, either by failing to fulfill their social responsibilities or by embracing criminal behavior in order to achieve their selfish goals.

But there is more: the rich, says the *Pele Yo'ets*, often squander their money on luxury and indecent revelry, which, in turn, leads to sinful socializing with its idle talk, mingling of men and women, drinking, and dancing. The third major accusation is that the rich are negligent in their religious practice and that they assimilate to non-Jewish mores. The neglect of observance must be understood in a context which is still quite firmly traditional. Thus, the rich are chastised for not attending synagogue on weekdays and praying imperfectly and perfunctorily at home. But they do pray, albeit in a manner which is not up to the rabbis' standards, and they certainly go to synagogue on the Sabbath—even if only for the sake of socializing.

The association of wealth and assimilation is an important point. The rich value the words of the "philosophers" more than the wisdom of the rabbis and ridicule the latter; they shave their beards and socialize with non-Jews, even if that means violating the Sabbath and festivals. The latter accusations are not found in earlier texts and refer to the situation of the latter half of the nineteenth century as apprehended by the rabbis. This is the key to the harshness of Papo's (and other nineteenth-century authors') critique of the rich; it goes beyond the more traditional type of moral rebuke, such as the insistence on the importance of community solidarity and compassion for the poor in the *Me'am Lo'ez*.

By the second half of the nineteenth century, the traditional alliance between the rabbis and the wealthy—never openly acknowledged in vernacular musar—is being challenged by a new business elite which increasingly looks to "the West" and questions the rabbis' monopoly on the interpretation of the symbolic universe, and which is in turn accused by the rabbis of setting business interests above community solidarity. While musar literature always had to steer a course between promoting a high moral standard of community solidarity with the poor and placating the rich, the conflict between the rabbinic and economic elites over whether to open the community toward the West catalyzed the critique of the wealthy in musar.

The charge of "westernizing" was not invented out of whole cloth, of course. As students of modern Ottoman Jewry have shown, the establishment of Western institutions such as the Alliance Israélite Universelle's modern schools in the Ottoman Levant would not have been possible without the collaboration (or, indeed, the initiative) of the local wealthy lay leadership. In fact, it was this lay leadership—conspicuously, the merchant elite of European (usually Italian) origin (the "*francos*")—that forged an alliance with local *maskilim* and initiated the move toward a secularization of education, against rabbinic opposition, even before the

Alliance Israélite Universelle arrived on the scene.[23] The authors of Judeo-Spanish musar from the mid-nineteenth century onward also reacted to the new state of affairs in their literature, once the common ideological ground that had sustained the traditional alliance of the economic and learned elites began to erode.

The Poor

In chapter 9 ("*Va-yeshev*") of Elijah ha-Kohen's *Shevet Musar*, we find perhaps the most graphic and impressive description of poverty in Ladino musar. Elijah describes the day of a poor person desperately trying to earn some money and find something to feed his hungry family. What follows is the description of a poor man who is invited to have dinner and spend the night at a rich person's house. The text describes the impossibility of communication between the two and the misunderstandings provoked by the poor man's not knowing how to behave properly and being too ashamed to ask. The context is not a discussion of solidarity and charity or the like; Elijah is advising his readers not to despair and to accept the hardships of repentance, *teshuvah*, because it will certainly be less severe than the suffering of the poor.

The text which I quote here at some length can be read as a representation of poverty as it was perceived by the rabbis. It is clearly a literary construction, but I am convinced that it addresses a social reality of poverty in Ottoman Sephardic communities with which vernacular musar literature had to come to terms. Many hardships await the poor person every day;

> he gets up at dawn and sees his children, who ask for bread, and has no money to buy it for them. So he goes out on the street to search and does not know where to go and where to turn, and looks at everyone who passes by and turns: perhaps someone will recognize his grief, so that they may approach him and have pity on him. But no one turns his face, for those who walk in the street are no prophets [and do not know of his distress]. The poor man wanders around the town until he is tired of walking. He also has not eaten and has no strength to walk. He thinks of his children who are hungry and faint. His poor wife, as she sees the anxiety of her children, stands by the window and looks out, wondering why her husband stays out. She hears footsteps and thinks that her husband is coming, looks and observes the passers-by: some carry bread, some carry meat, some carry fruits and food for their household, and she sighs that there is no one so unfortunate as her husband. . . . [The children] call out: Father, father, bring something to eat, "still there was no sound, and none who responded or heeded" [1 Kings 18:29]. . . . As the evening nears, [the father] becomes anxious for his hands are still empty and seeing the evil in desperation, he takes off the veil of shame . . . and approaches a shopkeeper . . . that he may give him charity or some bread to feed his children. And as he returns home with much anxiety and the bread of affliction, and his wife and children look at his hands as if he brings something because their lives depend on him, and they grab the bread to reanimate their souls. Then they drink water and fill their bellies, for there is no more bread, and they lay down as if ill until they are overcome by sleep.

The account goes on, and finally Elijah ha-Kohen adds:

> As all this happens to the poor man, it is impossible to accuse him, for if he does not know how to behave and does some bad things, it is because he is distraught. Know that the acts of the poor man seem wrong and reprehensible, but they are just nevertheless; the rich man does not understand the grievance of the poor, for he has not experienced it.[24]

Though this dramatic description of poverty is obviously a literary construction, there can be no doubt that many Ottoman Jews lived in extremely difficult conditions and that poverty remained a constant threat to many. Particularly in the second half of the eighteenth century and the early nineteenth century, the economic depression of the Ottoman Empire affected badly the Jewish communities, and poverty and relief for the poor remained among the major concerns of the authors of Judeo-Spanish musar.

The readers of Elijah's book may not have lived in conditions as desperately poor as those described here—but the threat of deep poverty was apparently real enough in the community for Elijah to use it as a rhetorical device in his call for repentance. We often find references to economic instability in Judeo-Spanish musar books: "One does not know how the world goes and there is no security in anything. Money all of the sudden gets wings and flies away. Because of our many sins we see often how many rich people lose all their wealth,"[25] as one author has it. Economic instability, the dangerousness of the overland routes outside the urban centers, the frequent and disastrous fires, epidemics:[26] many readers of Judeo-Spanish musar had plenty of reasons to worry, and, for them, the vantage point of poverty was all too real.

Elijah ha-Kohen also has a list of possible causes of poverty: poverty as retribution for the sins of a preceding reincarnation (*gilgul*), punishment in this world in exchange for a reward in the world to come; poverty to avert sin, because a person would have been led astray if he or she had been blessed with wealth; or poverty borne by the incarnation of a righteous person's soul to atone for the sins of the generation.[27] What these and similar explanations have in common is that poverty is viewed as divinely ordained and serving a superior purpose, and thus is, by definition, just, fair, and deserved. This does not, of course, diminish the importance of community solidarity on the part of the rich, but the social phenomenon of poverty—and of bitter poverty, as the above description from the *Shevet Musar* shows us—is legitimate and by no means contrary to the order of the world. While the community is responsible for supporting the poor, the important social differences within the Ottoman-Sephardic society are divinely ordained and designed, ultimately, for the benefit of the poor himself or that of the entire generation. Musar testifies eloquently to the important social inequalities in eastern Sephardic society. Its message, however, is one of acquiescence to one's fate, unfavorable as it might be.

In addition to empathy for the poor, there is also outright criticism. Two brief
passages illustrate this:

> For all his poverty, he must not let himself be influenced by the evil inclination
> [*yetser ha-ra^c*]: He must not steal, nor cheat, nor defraud, nor speak lies. . . . He
> must not employ the hour when he has nothing to do in gambling, nor spend it in
> the coffeehouse, nor drink wine and raki. Because of our sins there are many poor
> people who have no work and wander the streets; when they are tired of walking,
> they become trapped in the coffeehouse, and out of grief they go to the tavern. . . .
> Thus the poor man who has nothing to do should employ his time in study, he
> should study what he understands.[28]

> Another evil is that there are distressed poor who spend for themselves and eat a
> good breakfast, more than they can permit themselves to pay, and their unfortu-
> nate wives and children can hardly find dry bread. . . . Sometimes too they sit
> down in the evening and get drunk, and at night, when it is dark, they go home
> with empty hands, satiated and drunk, and rather than bring supper to their wives
> and children, they beat them, they beat them instead of giving them food.[29]

Some of the rabbinic critique of secular, profane socializing is invoked here
again. Since poverty is part of the social order sanctioned by the traditional symbolic universe, it cannot be used as an excuse to violate the rules of the traditional
order. It is important to note that the rabbis refer to actual social practice in the
two cases quoted here: formulations like "because of our sins there are many
poor" and "another evil is that . . . " suggest that the rabbis are denouncing real
phenomena of their own time and place. Violating rules against profane socializing, all the more reprehensible as they have hungry families waiting at home, these
people spend their time in the coffeehouses and taverns. Drunk and without
money, they return home only to beat their wives and children. We have no reason
to doubt that such things really happened, though we do not know if the rabbis
were seeing a widespread social problem or only isolated cases. The remedy for all
this is—predictably—the study of Torah: the vernacular rabbis believe that *meldar*
will save the poor from the bad company, alcohol, and domestic violence that the
rabbis associate with poverty. The active reaffirmation of the social and symbolic
order of tradition is meant to explain the social condition of the student of musar,
poor or otherwise, as divinely ordained and keep him or her within the boundaries
of the traditional universe.

The *Talmid Hakham* as Social Ideal

How do the *talmide hakhamim*—a socially diverse group that consisted of those
persuing or having acquired rabbinic learning—fit into Judeo-Spanish musar literature's picture of society?[30] Like the poor, they depend on the good will of those
with economic capital. But their position is quite different from the "ordinary"
poor: they possess, and represent, cultural capital in the sense of traditional knowl-

edge. And, significantly, the authors of musar literature themselves belong to this group.

"The *musar* tradition thus always presented an educational and social ideal for emulation. The ideal that permeated the literature was the *talmid ḥakham*. . . . The *talmid ḥakham* was more than just a master of the law: he was the living embodiment of the law, a 'living Torah.'"[31] This general statement about Jewish ethical literature can be applied to its Judeo-Spanish branch as well. The ideal of the *talmid ḥakham* was always inclusive and meant for society at large.[32]

The inclusiveness of the ideal came under pressure, however, with the educational crisis that worried the group of rabbis who then initiated the vernacularization of rabbinic knowledge. Rabbinic knowledge in Hebrew reached only a small part of the community, but the vernacular literature of the eighteenth and nineteenth centuries translated the social ideal of the *talmid ḥakham* into an educational project of considerably broader appeal.

Still, not everyone could be a *talmid ḥakham*, even given the inclusive social ideal of traditional learning. The *talmide ḥakhamim* did form a distinct social group within the community, albeit a group potentially open to all, entry into which was one way to move up the social hierarchy. How does Judeo-Spanish musar represent this social group within the fabric of the Ottoman Jewish community? And how do they interact with the other social groups in Ottoman Sephardic society?

The *talmide ḥakhamim*, equipped with the cultural capital of traditional knowledge and learning, have an ambiguous relation with those within the community who possess economic capital, the wealthy class in control of the economic resources. We already have insisted on the strategic alliance between the *talmide ḥakhamim* and the notables that predominated community affairs. This alliance, and the equilibrium of power within this alliance, had constantly to be negotiated, and the social ideal expressed in musar literature is part of this jockeying for symbolic capital—social recognition and prestige—and political power between the two elite groups, those possessing cultural capital and those in control of economic capital.

This is why the notion of "honor" figures so prominently in musar literature's description of the *talmid ḥakham* in social interaction with other members of the community. Honor is the expression of social prestige which the rabbis claim for themselves as custodians of the traditional symbolic universe. The claim to social prestige is combined, of course, with a demand for a share in the economic capital (though without moving the general dividing line between wealth and poverty, as we have seen) and for participation in political power:

> The *ḥakhamim* resemble the Sabbath: as the Sabbath is venerated more than the other days of the week, so the *talmid ḥakham* is venerated more than the whole people. And as all the weekdays work for the sake of the Sabbath, so the entire people must work to maintain the *talmid ḥakham*. Our sages have gone to great lengths to describe the rewards for the one who helps the *talmid ḥakham* with his property, and there is no limit to his reward. But the main thing is that when one gives a gift to a *talmid ḥakham*, one honors him and shows him a cheerful

face, and asks him for forgiveness, saying that he deserves more. . . . The one who maintains friendship with a *talmid hakham* will have sons who are *talmide hakhamim*, the one who honors a *talmid hakham* will have sons-in-law who are *talmide hakhamim*, and the one who is fearful of a *talmid hakham* will be a *hakham* himself. And if not a *hakham*, then the people will [at least] revere him and his words will be heard as if he were a *talmid hakham*.[33]

These phrases express at once the rabbis' sense of the distinction of the *talmide hakhamim*, the functional diversification of society, and the potential openness of the group. The *talmid hakham* is a specialist in traditional knowledge, a cultural capital which the rabbis insist must be translated into social prestige. The community must financially maintain *and honor* the *talmide hakhamim* because they dedicate themselves exclusively to the administration and preservation of the symbolic universe, which, in turn, sustains the social order of the community. This financial dependence on the rich is not understood as charity: the other members of the community pay what legitimately belongs to the *talmid hakham*.[34] The social group of the learned is open, however. Whoever treats the scholars as they deserve will be rewarded, and those who honor *talmide hakhamim* can expect themselves (or their sons or sons-in-law) to become *talmide hakhamim* as well.

So far we have discussed the rabbinic ideal. But the authors of Judeo-Spanish musar realized that social reality was far from this ideal. The *talmide hakhamim* were usually poor and depended entirely on the assistance of the community. This problem was particularly serious in Jerusalem and the Land of Israel generally, where the economic situation of the numerous *talmide hakhamim* was desperate and many were forced to travel abroad to raise funds for the maintenance of the *yeshivot* in the Land of Israel and its students.[35] All over the Ottoman Empire, *talmide hakhamim* lived in poverty, and since becoming a teacher of children was often the only way to support a family, "the teachers multiplied more than the pupils."[36] Others left their homes and families in search of a livelihood.[37] Much worse than the prevalent poverty, according to the rabbis, was society's failure to honor the *talmide hakhamim* as they deserved, and Judeo-Spanish musar is full of complaints about the disregard for scholars: "Because of our sin there are blasphemers who make fun and say: The *talmide hakhamim* pursue only their own advantage, and similar and worse words. What we said above, that the one who has friendship with a *talmid hakham* will have sons who are *talmide hakhamim* . . . this is for earlier generations that still venerated and valued the knowledge of the Law."[38] The vernacular rabbis insist that the *talmide hakhamim* do not enjoy the social prestige they deserve and that their economic situation is precarious, depending on the good will of the wealthy of the community.

But now in these generations . . . also the *hakhamim* are despised in our eyes. If they open their mouths to talk, we do not lend our ears to listen to their words, because we think that our understanding [*daʿat*] is very clear and the understanding of the *hakham* is nothing. . . . All this is caused by the fact that, because of our many sins, most *talmide hakhamim* are poor and depend on the wealthy [*gevirim*], and this makes them lose reverence. And if you say that in earlier generations there [also] existed poverty among the *talmide hakhamim* and that they always needed the wealthy, the answer is obvious [*ladina*], for in earlier generations there was much fear of God in the hearts of the rich. . . . Their understanding was: as the wealth is not mine but God's, it is possible that today a *hakham* receives something from me and that tomorrow I will need him. . . . Thus they were very careful about honoring the *talmide hakhamim* and received their words like the Law from Moses on Sinai. . . . But now everyone says . . . : It is with my intelligence, large as the ocean, that I have gathered wealth like the sand on the seashore.[39]

The vernacular rabbis see the division of labor between *hakhamim* and the rich, between cultural and economic capital, as something natural, and the scholars had always depended on the wealthy of the community. To their minds, the one who enables the *talmid hakham* to study is no less worthy than the scholar himself; the image used by many musar authors is that of Issachar studying and being supported by his brother Zebulun.[40] The instrumental role of society is a key issue in Judeo-Spanish musar: in order for the *talmid hakham* to dedicate all his time to the study of the Law, he must be supported—not only financially, but in all his needs—by the rest of society (not only by the rich), and reserves the right to teach and chastise in order to ensure compliance with the standards of tradition.[41]

The problem arises when the rich begin to think they do not need the rabbinic scholars, when they mistakenly assume that they deserve the economic capital they possess because of their brightness. When the rich challenge the division of labor and think they can do without the *talmid hakham*, they endanger the stability of the social order and tradition. Not understanding the nature of this division of labor, they only see the economic capital and denigrate the *talmid hakham* for being poor, not appreciating his symbolic cultural wealth.[42] The exeggerated self-image of the rich who do not understand that they are just administering goods entrusted to them by God challenges the basis of the *talmid hakham*'s social and cultural authority and the basis of the traditional order in general.

Many examples are given of the unworthy treatment of the *talmid hakham*. To begin with, while it was "once" the dream of every father to have at least one son studying to become a *talmid hakham*, now the blessing "*hakham grande que sea*" (may [your son] become a great *hakham*) is understood as an insult, and some even answer by saying: "Better save this blessing for your own sons."[43]

Moreover, many persons prefer an unintelligent but rich person as a son-in-law and desperately try to marry their daughters to someone from a wealthy family.[44] The rich, in turn, do not deign to marry their daughters to a *talmid hakham* and prefer to have someone of their own social group:

How many complaints has God about some rich people who spend thousands of *ducados* to get [a son-in-law] from among rich people like themselves, for with that amount of money they could obtain a good, learned [*meldador*] and accomplished young man. . . . A *hakham* surely will not become so poor as to need to go from door to door asking for charity, for he has his capital inside . . . but the rich person can come to ask for charity at the door, for his capital is superficial.[45]

"And know that this evil and wickedness, that the rich man does not want to marry his daughter to a *talmid hakham*, is due to his wife's counsel," adds Elijah ha-Kohen in the *Shevet Musar*. Not understanding what is really best for their daughters, they prefer a rich *'am ha-arets* (ignoramus) to a decent scholar, ignoring the advice of the sages "who said that everyone who gives his daughter to an *'am ha-arets* is as if he has bound her and laid her before a lion, which seizes her and eats her. Thus is the *'am ha-arets* who beats his wife and then has marital relations with her."[46]

The discrimination against the *talmide hakhamim* does not stop there. Elijah ha-Kohen laments that many people do not want to have a *talmid hakham* as a neighbor and avoid renting to them. Elijah's charge is repeated over a century later by Palachi, who quotes Elijah's book:

> It is appropriate to bring a *hakham* [as a neighbor] into the courtyard, for this is very advantageous. It is known that there is an evil inclination particularly in respect of not wanting to accept a *hakham* [as a neighbor] in one's courtyard, as Rabbi Elijah ha-Kohen has chastised us. . . . The first thing that the evil inclination tells the person is: You will make yourself conspicuous, you will not be able to say or do what you want. Second, being short of money, he will not be able to pay you, and what are you going to do to the *hakham* if he does not pay—have him imprisoned?[47]

In fact, the musar authors insist, there is nothing more advantageous than having a *talmid hakham* as a son, son-in-law, or neighbor. But, one musar author laments, "How much dishonor we cause the *talmide hakhamim*, who seem disgusting . . . in our eyes, and we make blasphemous remarks about them, and we laugh about them. And their only fault is that they study the holy Law. Woe to us if we look at the gentiles, at how much they honor their *hakhamim*!"[48] The use of the first person plural, "*mosotros*," equating the reader and the author, is instructive here. Of course, the author is neither one who ridicules the *talmide hakhamim* nor a neutral observer, but a representative of the *talmide hakhamim* himself, and he uses a literary device that constructs an inclusive community embracing the vernacular rabbis and their public.

Do all these complaints about the mistreatment of the *hakhamim* have any basis in social reality? Does it make sense to assume that the *talmide hakhamim* were humiliated and discriminated against in a society that was still profoundly traditional, and whose values were deeply rooted in the ideal of Torah knowledge which permeated all sectors of social life well into the nineteenth century? One is reminded of the rhetoric of the medieval *Sefer Hasidim*, in which the pietists are described as a persecuted minority among a wicked, malevolent majority. While Judeo-Spanish musar does not share the sectarian outlook in which the pietists are opposed to the wicked[49]—on the contrary, it is directed toward the broad mass of "ordinary" Sephardim—there is no reason to accept its charge at face value any more than the picture of the Ashkenazic Hasidim as an abused and persecuted minority.

But what is the function of the eloquent complaints about the failure to honor the *talmide hakhamim* as they deserve? The symbolic universe requires constant reaffirmation of its central precepts in order to maintain it and in order to translate it into the social order. Rabbinic authority and the social status of the *talmid hakham* need such reaffirmation too, particularly in times of crisis. Whether or not they are reacting to a real crisis of authority may be a secondary issue; what is important is that the rabbis had a *sense of crisis* to which their vernacular musar literature was intended to respond—the crisis of ignorance and insufficient knowledge of Hebrew in the eighteenth century, and the challenge of new, "Western" ideas in the second half of the nineteenth. Musar literature is a reaffirmation of the elements of the traditional universe, and the claim to social prestige, to "honor" for the *hakhamim* as representatives of this traditional universe, is part of the stabilizing function of musar literature. The attack against those who supposedly do not honor the *hakhamim* sufficiently is directed against the—real or imagined—enemies of the *talmid hakham*. Judeo-Spanish musar literature constructs two "Others" vis-à-vis rabbinic knowledge and its representatives: the quintessential Other of eighteenth- and early-nineteenth-century musar is the ignoramus, the ʿ*am ha-arets*, replaced in later works of the second half of the nineteenth century by the *apiqoros*, the heretic, who questions the very legitimacy of the *talmid hakham* (a figure we came across earlier when we discussed the image of the "critical reader" and deviant reading practice).

As for the ʿ*am ha-arets* as the *talmid hakham*'s "Other" in early Judeo-Spanish musar literature, the following remarks by Elijah ha-Kohen are typical:

> The wicked man and the ʿ*am ha-arets*, [like] the camel he opens his mouth and produces bad odor like the impurity of his mouth, and scorns the *talmid hakham* because his animal soul cannot see anything other than the torn cloth that covers him, and he does not see the precious jewel inside him. And so the wicked man sees himself as dressed in fine and precious clothes and the *talmid hakham* in old and torn clothes. . . . His eyes are blind to what lies below his fine and elaborate clothing, that he is a body without any good during his lifetime, like a heap of dirt, and in his death like an evil-smelling dog. . . . Know that the *talmid hakham* cannot be together with the ʿ*am ha-arets* even if they live in the same house, for the nature of one is as far from the other as the difference between light and darkness. . . . As the sages said: The enmity of the ʿ*ame ha-arets* against the *talmid hakham* is worse than the enmity of the nations of the world against Israel.[50]

The prime challenge to the rabbis' authority comes from the ignorant who do not recognize the superiority of the learned elite. The attack on the ʿ*am ha-arets* is old, as the reference to rabbinic tradition shows, and is expressed here in terms that basically reiterate an "othering" of the ignorant that runs throughout the history of rabbinic literature. The contrast could not be clearer: the ʿ*am ha-arets* is identified with darkness, death, and impurity, as against the *talmid hakham,* who is associated with light, life, and purity. The two are pictured as living in different worlds even if they are neighbors, and indeed the musar authors insist that there is no place for the two to socialize, no common ground where they could possibly meet unless, of course, the ʿ*am ha-arets* decides to mend his ways and wants to study. There are even "righteous" ignoramuses who support the *talmide hakhamim* in their labor; their souls happen to be from a higher source.[51] Generally, however, the ignorant person—whether wealthy or poor—is the quintessential antithesis of the scholar, and ignorance the prime enemy of tradition.

From its formative period in the eighteenth century and well into the second half of the nineteenth century, ignorance remained Judeo-Spanish musar literature's arch foe. Only at a relatively late stage, in the last thirty years or so of the nineteenth century, did a new enemy of tradition appear in musar literature: the new openness toward "the West" and the timid secularization of Ottoman Sephardic society, evidenced by the spread of the Alliance schools. New literary formats like the Judeo-Spanish press and new genres like the novel now openly challenged the rabbinic monopoly on the cultural capital of explaining the world. Until the mid-nineteenth century, Judeo-Spanish musar hardly mentioned that people were questioning the legitimizing foundation of the *talmid hakham*'s authority, the integrity of the traditional universe. People were described as lax in observance and the rich in particular as stingy and arrogant, but no one questioned the authority of tradition and its representatives.

It is in Judah Papo's *Pele Yoʿets* (early 1870s) that we find signs of a major change: a growing challenge to the very authority of the rabbis and of rabbinic tradition, a challenge which is aimed at the foundations of the symbolic universe itself and goes far beyond the patterns of deviation known and addressed in earlier musar literature. The *talmid hakham* as a social ideal had been challenged from within traditional society in earlier eras, but a new challenge arose in the last quarter of the nineteenth century from people who placed themselves on the margins of or outside the traditional universe, or at least did not feel themselves bound by its values and rules. The *Pele Yoʿets* outlines this modern challenge well in its definition of the "epicurean," the quintessential heretic:

> The one who disrespects the *hakhamim,* or who says: Of what use are the *hakhamim* to us? If they study, they study for their own advantage; if they are *hakhamim,* so they are for their own advantage. . . . For all these things he is called *apiqoros,* and because of our sins this is frequent. . . . The one who rebels against the words of the *hakhamim* is as one who rebels against the entire Law, and as one who rebels against God, for the words of the *hakhamim* are words of God and are received from generation to generation. . . . These people are worse than idolatry [ʿ*avodah zarah*], for one serves the idol, but the idol does not seduce anyone to serve it. For these people, it is not enough that they themselves are evil,

they even try to convince others of their words. . . . To be in the same place with people like this is evil. . . . Let us distance our ways from them, and we should not come close to the doors of their homes.[52]

"Epicurean" is of course an old talmudic metaphor for anyone placing himself "outside" rabbinic knowledge.[53] The term is applied here to those who represent the modern challenge to rabbinic tradition as perceived by Judah Papo. The Judeo-Spanish version of this chapter is predictably a much expanded version of the rather brief one in the original Hebrew text, which explains only that the "epicurean" is one who disrespects the rabbis, Scripture, and tradition.[54] There is no explicit polemic like that in the Judeo-Spanish text.

According to Papo, the attack on the integrity and authority of the rabbis—even of individual rabbis—is nothing less than a wholesale attack on the traditional religious universe *tout court*. There is no distinction between the abstract body of traditional knowledge and those who represent it. For Papo, it is evident that the breakdown of rabbinic authority cannot but lead to the breakdown of the entire symbolic and social order of tradition. What is worse, the "epicureans" try to educate others in their evil ways and spread their nonconformist ideas (through secular education and secular Ladino literature, one might add). The response of the vernacular rabbis is similar to their response to the *ʿam ha-arets:* strict social segregation, strictures on social interaction between the "righteous" and the "epicureans," and the reaffirmation of tradition through musar.

While ignorance was the foe of tradition in most Judeo-Spanish musar literature and legitimized the translation of Hebrew knowledge into the vernacular in the first place, the exclusiveness of traditional knowledge and the rabbinic monopoly on its administration remained unchallenged. I submit that the rabbinic response to the crisis of ignorance was itself a contributing factor to processes that later led to an individualization of knowledge; this individualization ultimately opened the door to alternative universes of knowledge, and the secularization of the Judeo-Spanish reading public, and the challenge of rabbinic authority.

Thus, the *talmid hakham* is the social ideal representing traditional rabbinic knowledge. The *talmide hakhamim* as a social group consider themselves both as an elite, holding and administering the cultural capital of the traditional universe, and as a social ideal to be emulated. A rather typical expression of the *talmide hakhamim*'s sense of distinction is the talmudic image (employed by Elijah ha-Kohen) of Rabbi Yohanan, "who would sit near the ritual bath, so that the women would see him [upon leaving the ritual bath] and think of him [at the time of having marital relations] and would thus have sons who are *hakhamim* and beautiful like him and as tall as him."[55] The nobility of the *talmid hakham* is translated here into the image of physical beauty. The *talmid hakham* is a social ideal and member of a social group which is distinguished and privileged, but potentially open and inclusive. It is assumed that the rest of society, represented by the social types of "the rich" and "the poor," will take on the instrumental role of supporting the *talmid hakham*, so that he can dedicate himself entirely to his specialized field of Torah study, of administering, interpreting, and perpetuating the traditional symbolic universe.

Conclusion

In the first chapter of the *Shevet Musar*, King Solomon is described as an ideal personality. "He was mightier than all kings and wiser than all the *hakhamim* and wealthier than all the rich."[56] Three types of power and distinction are presented here: "the king," representing the political power now removed from the Jewish community and in the hands of the gentile Ottoman authorities; the scholars, who control the cultural capital; and the wealthy, who possess the economic capital. Judeo-Spanish musar literature is part of the negotiation for social prestige and control among those who hold different types of power, both cultural and economic. It clearly describes its "Others," the ignorant ʿam ha-arets and the westernizing heretic, as the enemies of the *talmid hakham* and of tradition.

What do the social types we have studied here tell us about eastern Sephardic society and the way the vernacular rabbis understood it? What is the function of these social types in musar literature, and what do they tell us about the roles of the authors and readers of Judeo-Spanish musar? Society is clearly described as a stratified system in which both material wealth and knowledge are unequally distributed. Although this social inequality is legitimized and perpetuated in musar literature, individuals must prove themselves worthy of their social status. The rich are reminded of the value of solidarity, and the *hakham*'s responsibility is to teach society. The poor have the right to receive charity, but they only gain the empathy of the musar authors when they accept the social ideal of a learning (*meldando*) society; poverty is no more an excuse for neglecting religious observance than wealth is.

We have seen (in Palachi's case) that the historical circumstances of the musar authors were such that they depended—both financially and in terms of their status—on the good will of the wealthy of the community. Their critique of the rich may have been eloquent, but it remained anonymous; when an author discussed his own community, his criticism was muted and the wealthy were praised—even if, as in the case of Palachi's Izmir, historical circumstances would have led us to expect otherwise.

Vernacular musar literature tries to create an equilibrium within the community and ward off all challenges—poverty with all its disruptive social consequences, the arrogance of the rich, the danger of ignorance, and (at a relatively late stage) the challenge to the traditional ideological foundations presented by the forces of westernization. Meanwhile, the roles of the authors and readers within this social fabric crystallize between the lines. The vernacular rabbis, being dependent on the economic elite, are defending their own interests and the stability of the traditional universe when they create the universal social ideal of the *talmid hakham*. The intended reader seems to live, curiously, somewhere in between the clear-cut social types described here—some closer to absolute poverty, others closer to material well-being; some illiterate, others quite learned. The social types are meant to help these readers understand the society around them and explain reality and its discontents within the parameters of the worldview of musar. The social types also mark the boundaries of traditional society, its social and symbolic order, and help the reader define his or her own place within, and never outside or opposed to, this social and symbolic order.

The Representation of Gender

7

Ambivalent Attitudes

Not surprisingly, the ambivalent attitude toward women that can be found throughout Jewish literature—manifest also in popular culture as expressed in Judeo-Spanish folktales[1]—is evident in the vernacular rabbinic literature in Ladino. Alongside eloquent praise of women we find misogynist remarks. To illustrate this point, it suffices to contrast two passages from Judeo-Spanish musar literature. In the *Shevet Musar,* Elijah ha-Kohen stated clearly that

> it is not possible for a man to achieve perfection of his soul in order to deserve a part in the world to come other than because of a good wife, for the letter with which this world was created forms part of her name [*ishah*]. . . . She leads him onto the right path, because the man listens to the words of his wife, as happened to a wicked person whose wife was righteous and made him into a pious person; and the evil wife of a pious man who made him into a wicked person.[2]

Man attains perfection and cannot gain his share in the world to come without the help of a righteous woman. Just as in Hebrew the letter *heh* is added to the word for "man" (*ish*) in order to form the word for "woman" (*ishah*), the entire world was created with the help of the letter *heh.* Only united as man and woman is the creation of humankind complete, and only in this way can the human soul aspire to reunite with the Creator.[3] Nevertheless, we can already discern the auxiliary role of women, as Elijah ha-Kohen clearly speaks from the perspective of the man, not the woman: "She leads him onto the right path because the man listens to the words of his wife."

Alongside such benevolent statements about women, we also find clearly misogynist passages like the following from the nineteenth-century *Sefer Darkhe ha-Adam:*

> If a woman and a man need clothing or food or must be liberated from captivity, the woman has priority because her temper is weak; but if a man and a woman are in [mortal] danger, because they have fallen into a river or the like, the man has priority [in being saved] . . . because the man has more commandments [to fulfill]. There also is a natural reason, and this reason is valid even for a man who is exempt from the commandments, like the blind one who is exempt from the commandments: it is known that whatever is difficult to find is more valuable and more precious. . . . And it is known that there are more women in this world than men. . . . Every year there are many wars everywhere and males are killed [etc.],

and for these reasons males are more valuable than females, and therefore they have priority over the females in being saved from danger. The reason God made nature thus, that is, the reason there are more females, is that one male is worth many females.[4]

Apart from being misogynist, Amarachi and Sason's argument is circular: after repeating the principle from the Mishnah[5] that it is more important to save a man's life than a woman's because a man has more commandments to observe—shocking enough to the modern reader—the authors also adduce a "natural reason." Men are more precious because there are fewer of them than women; there are fewer of them because they are more precious. While in mishnaic law, women are exempt from certain commandments, and that is why their lives are valued less highly, Amarachi and Sason proclaim their misogynist outlook more directly.

Perhaps more illustrative of the rabbinic imagery of gender than unequivocally misogynist or philogynist remarks in Judeo-Spanish musar literature is what the rabbis have to say when defending women against popular negative attitudes. The *Pele Yoʿets* denounces the deplorable custom that "in some places, they ridicule and debase the one who has a daughter";[6] even worse, there are husbands who are so disappointed and angry when their wives bear daughters that they will not visit them in their lying-in. Huli's *Meʿam Loʿez* presents a "chastisement for those who take it lightly when a daughter of theirs dies."[7] But even in this context, Papo's reasoning in the *Pele Yoʿets* is telling enough: "Better a good daughter than an evil son."[8] The implication, of course, is that a righteous son is still better than a righteous daughter.

While the rabbis are not happy with some manifestations of popular misogyny and do not approve of people making fun of a father to whom a daughter is born—after all, the birth of a daughter is a divine decision—they still rationalize the preference for male children on the grounds that men are privileged to serve God by studying Torah and fulfilling a whole range of commandments from which women are exempt.

The rabbis' ambivalent attitude toward women as the internal Other of the Jewish community is not what interests us here. To quote Natalie Zemon Davis, the historian's goal "is to discover the range in sex roles and in sexual symbolism in different societies and periods, to find out what meaning they had and how they functioned to maintain the social order or to promote its change."[9] What can we expect to find beyond either negative or positive stereotypes about women? As I will try to demonstrate in this chapter, the vernacular rabbis define rather consistent patterns of gender relations along two central axes as a constitutive part of the symbolic and social order of Sephardic tradition: first, the danger of uncontrolled sexuality and its implications for gender relations, the separation of male and female domains; and, second, the instrumental role of women. In a closing section, I will indicate some implications of the discovery of women as a reading public, a development mentioned above.

Purity and Danger

Elijah ha-Kohen gives the following advice to his readers to help them over-come their evil inclinations: when tempted to have sexual relations with a beautiful woman, he should imagine how that woman will be in old age—"she will have many wrinkles and her face will be like that of a monkey, she will be hump-backed . . . like a camel, snot coming out of her nose and slime out of her mouth." And if he has relations with her while she is young, he will certainly regret this later when he sees her old and will ask himself how he could possibly have "intro-duced his member [*berit qodesh*] into a hose full of dirt, an opening full of bad smell."[10] The image of the female body expressed here in the *Shevet Musar* is dis-maying even if we take into account that Elijah ha-Kohen's rhetoric always makes use of rather strong imagery (the description of the male body is sometimes hardly more elevating). In the present context, however, the male and female bodies are described in clearly opposed terms—the *berit qodesh* (literally "holy convenant," an allusion to circumcision) on the one hand, and on the other hand female sexuality, which is denigrated as repellent and impure. Contrast this with Elijah's advice to the one who is tempted to have homosexual relations with a young boy: "When they are both old and find themselves in the same place, they will remember the evil they have done: how much shame and embarrassment and dishonor!"[11] It is telling that Elijah ha-Kohen uses ideas of lost honor and shame in the case of two men, but does not describe the male body as impure or in degrading terms.

At first sight, this could suggest that the rabbis insisted on a separation be-tween the sexes in order to protect men from female impurity. Female impurity would of course be related to the taboo of menstruation, and the issue of purity versus impurity would define the gendering of social space and the boundaries of legitimate interaction between men and women. Furthermore, if we take into account the numerous remarks in musar literature about female seductiveness (Abraham Palachi, for example, transforms Prov. 7:5–20 into a dramatic story of a woman seducing a man),[12] it would seem that the rabbis believe they are protecting men against the unruly and dangerous sexuality of women.

Both arguments—impurity and the danger of female sexuality as the basis for the gendering of social space—have been advanced in two recent studies of women in the Mishnah by Jacob Neusner and Judith Wegner.[13] Their view has been chal-lenged, however, by Judith Hauptman, and a close reading of Judeo-Spanish musar literature provides similar evidence and bears out Hauptman's critique of Neusner and Wegner:

> As for Neusner's assertion that the Mishnah's conception of woman as Other de-rives from the framers' belief that women's unruly sexual potential is always there, just below the surface, a careful reading of the Mishnah suggest that it is men's sexuality—that is, men's easily aroused and then hard-to-control sexual lust—that lies, not below, but on the surface of some of the Mishnah's statements, such as

those concerning the segregation of the sexes in semiprivate settings, like inns or schoolhouses. . . . In the Mishnah, men's uncontrollable sexuality plays a key role in shaping behavioral guidelines for casual social relations between the sexes.[14]

Hauptman also questions Wegner's assumption that women were excluded from the synagogue and the house of study for fear of pollution, claiming that "tractate Niddah in no way suggests that the trajectory of a menstruant's uncleanness extends beyond the private domain."[15]

In a somewhat phallocentric statement, Abraham Palachi explains in his Judeo-Spanish work *Ve-hokhiah Avraham* "that the main thing about Eve's transgression is that Samael came to Eve and defiled her, and from that time a grave defilement has remained, which is the blood of menstruation." By contrast, Adam, in Palachi's interpretation, only defiled his foreskin, "and when man is circumcised, he is [again] pure."[16] Yet it is not female impurity or sexuality which poses the greatest threat to male purity. Men's own unruly sexual desire is perceived as the main danger. Just one page later, Palachi adds that "women are closer to the world to come, more so than men, because there are two great sins among males which do not apply to females: the neglect of [studying] Torah, and the sin of wasting semen."[17] "There is no sanctity akin to the sanctity of the member [*berit*], and there is no defilement akin to the defilement of the member [*berit*],"[18] says another unambiguous statement in the *Pele Yo'ets*.

Circumcision as a symbol of the sanctification of man thus implies a special responsibility, to affirm the covenant by studying Torah (from which women are exempt) and to guard oneself from defiling the *berit qodesh* by wasting semen. While female ritual impurity as a result of menstrual blood determines much of gender relations within matrimony, it is the danger of men's defiling the sanctity of the covenant which defines the limits of gender relations beyond marital relations and the domestic sphere.

Both the male obligation to study Torah and the danger of uncontrolled male sexual desire define the rabbis' approach to gender relations, requiring a separation of the sexes and determining the instrumental role of women. As a result of the functional differentiation of the male and female domains, women run the household in order to enable their husbands and sons to pursue Torah study; they must be decent and preferably stay at home lest they arouse men's sexual desire. It is not female impurity or sexuality that the vernacular rabbis describe as the danger to the traditional order. Rather, two male-centered concepts—Torah study (by men) and male sexual desire—determine the patterns of gender relations.

THE IMPORTANCE OF BEING DECENT

How is this danger of uncontrolled male sexuality translated into the vision of the social order in Judeo-Spanish musar? The following remark in the *Pele Yo'ets* is a valuable summary:

As is well known, the sages said that the one who has an erection through evil thoughts becomes impure [*está en nidui*], and how much more so if he spills semen in vain because of his evil thought. . . . The woman is not free of this sin, for in whatever [sin] the man gets entangled because of her, the sin is her responsibility [*el pecado está en su garganta*]. How much more so if [women] cause men to sin with their pleasantry, laughing, joking and teasing, for they will be punished first. Therefore the woman must be honorable and remain inside her house, so that no man may be entangled [in sin] because of her. . . . Thus the custom of many places in Turkey is to be praised for they are very careful about this.[19]

Papo praises Ottoman society for its comparatively strict gender separation in public spaces. The presence of women in the street and social interaction between men and women must be limited because ultimately women are responsible not only for their own, but also for men's moral integrity. Men must be protected from the *yetser*, their sexual desire, and since they cannot reasonably be expected to conquer it on their own, it is women's responsibility to avoid provoking male lust by keeping contact to a minimum and by following the absolute imperative of decency. As many authors have pointed out, there is nothing negative attached to sexuality as such in rabbinic thought, and the same is true in Judeo-Spanish musar literature.[20] The issue here is the control of male sexuality and the protection of male purity, not from the impurity of women but from the sexual desire of men.

The prime challenge to the gendered order of society is thus female allure; when women are discussed in Judeo-Spanish musar literature (and Jewish musar in general), the rules of female decency, *tseni'ut*, are typically the main issue. Many authors lament that some women "dress themselves like slaves when they are inside their homes, and when they go out to the street, they dress like queens to show their beauty." Rather, according to Elijah ha-Kohen, the righteous woman must adorn herself at home for her husband and must be decent when she goes out, so that other men will not desire her and the envy of gentiles will not be provoked.[21] Incidentally, it would seem that the rabbis are much more pessimistic about the male character than the female: whereas the musar rabbis depict women as willful and active—the wicked woman irresponsibly provokes men's sexual desire and the righteous and decent woman is powerful enough to prevent men from sinning—men appear entirely passive and subject to their uncontrollable desires.

Much worse than the violation of the dress code, of course, is when women take the initiative in leading men astray, flirting with them and bringing sin upon themselves and others. Abraham Palachi denounces what he sees as the hypocrisy of some women who are decent and God-fearing when it suits them, but, if they meet an attractive young man, "she readily wants to put him under her dress and her heart is inflamed for him and she seeks occasions to speak to him even without necessity."[22] The husband who discovers that his wife is irresponsible in this way must, according to Palachi, prevent her from going out more than is absolutely necessary and from attending weddings and other celebrations (except weddings of very close relatives), and should certainly forbid her to drink alcohol or dance at public gatherings.[23]

FEMALE AND MALE SPHERES OF SOCIAL INTERACTION

Whereas female "looseness" is seen as an open challenge to the stability of the social order, the rabbis set some general rules for the gendering of social space and for male and female social interaction. The rabbinic gendering of social space is far more complex than is suggested by the long dominant concept of separate private and public spheres.[24] It is true, however, that the rabbis wish to constrain women's appearance in the public streets and markets: "She should not go out often, for if the woman goes out of the door of her house, she causes others to sin with her, and she [also] harms herself as is proven by what happened to Dina [Gen. 34]. Everyone who sees her will say: She is evildoing . . . she is never home, but you see her in the streets and in the squares, and her children are not by her husband."[25] The same author testifies, however, to the limited success of his moralizing mission: "How many times have I fought and struggled against women sitting at the doors of the courtyards for pastime, and everyone who passes turns and looks at them with the desire of his *yetser*."[26]

The opposition of private and public is misleading nonetheless. Both men and women may partake in public events, but the rabbis very much insist that they do so separately and with "decency." In the *Me'am Lo'ez* on the Book of Esther we read, for example:

> We should learn moral chastisement as we see that the gentiles Ahasuerus and Vashti the wicked, all of whose thoughts were on illicit sex and who wanted to make Israel sin, nevertheless did not seat men and women in the same place. Vashti made a separate feast for the women lest men and women mingle. How much more is it appropriate for us, the holy and blessed Jewish people, not to seat men and women at one table during the celebration of weddings, births and other feasts, and, it goes without saying, not to dance with women and young girls, for this is a great sin.[27]

The Ottoman rabbis want women to stay at home and not frequent public places too often, so that they will not provoke men's desire, and they want women to respect the separation of the sexes; but there is no problem with women going into the public space if they respect the laws of decency. More important, the rabbis talk about a *female* public sphere as well. Social interaction exclusively among women is subject to the same rules and limits as social interaction among men. The rabbis insist that their prescriptions about social interaction among men (not to socialize for its own sake, for "leisure," but only for the sake of *mitsvot* and to exchange words of Torah) applies to the socializing of women as well.[28] The husbands are called upon to ensure that their wives do not meet in the "wrong company." Instead, "when two women or more meet and talk with each other, they should talk about how to chastise their young children and how to lead them onto the right path," they should "teach each other about the rules of [preparing] food and of the housework," "teach each other about the rules of *niddah* [laws pertaining to family purity and menstruation]" and the like.[29]

Female social interaction is thus perfectly legitimate when it respects the boundaries of the speakable in traditional discourse and as long as women respect the rules of decency. What arouses the rabbis' anger is mixed social interaction, which blurs the carefully established gendered order of society. Female social interaction is meant to reaffirm the authority of the traditional order just as male social interaction is meant to do. The vision of male and female spheres of social interaction is determined by the rabbis' understanding of gender roles: while male social interaction centers around the institutions and associations of the community (synagogue and study house, caring for the poor and the burial society), legitimate female discourse is determined by the *instrumental role* of women. Women's conversations, as imagined by the rabbis, should revolve around educating the children, housework, the laws of *niddah,* and honoring their husbands: "with all this they cause their sons to become virtuous."

The Instrumental Role of Women

As women are exempt from Torah study, they are by definition excluded from the social ideal of the *talmid hakham.* Nonetheless, they play a central and decisive role for the social realization of this ideal, encouraging and enabling the men of their households to achieve the status of *talmid hakham.* This instrumental function, in turn, largely determines the ways in which the specific role of women in society and particularly within the family is understood. "Although [women] are exempt from the study of the oral Torah, they are obliged to work with all their strength so that their husbands and sons study, and this counts as if they themselves were studying the Law for they cause others to do so, and the one who causes others to fulfill [a commandment] is greater than the one who does it [himself]."[30]

The instrumental role of women in their relations with men, particularly their husbands, is expressed throughout Judeo-Spanish musar literature. "The main thing about love should be the friendship of the soul," proclaims one rabbi. The woman "should do everything possible to help her husband in Judaism: she should get up early in the night, make the fire and prepare coffee, and then wake up her husband so that he may say *tiqun hatsot.*"[31]

The instrumental role of women parallels the instrumental role of society at large, which is responsible for maintaining and supporting the *talmide hakhamim* and enabling them to fulfill their function as custodians of traditional knowledge. Within the family, this instrumental obligation rests on the women. There is one fundamental difference, however: while the social group of *talmide hakhamim* is potentially open to every male member of the Jewish community, provided he is willing and able to dedicate himself to the study of Torah, women are always—by definition—excluded from the group which controls the symbolic, cultural capital of tradition. While vernacular rabbinic literature is conceived to redress female ignorance of this tradition, the vernacular rabbis never consider challenging the fundamental differentiation of gender roles in society and certainly have no intention of admitting women to the learned elite.

In order to appreciate how the instrumental role of women in home and family is constructed in vernacular rabbinic literature, I give some examples from the list of ten virtues of the perfect woman presented in the *Shevet Musar*.[32] One virtue (the second on Elijah ha-Kohen's list) states the importance of the wife's honoring her husband and having patience with him:

> All the words she speaks to her husband should be spoken with tranquility and kindness and calm, not in a loud voice, and certainly she should not respond to him with rage, because her husband would become angry with her and would dishonor and disdain and beat her. And if he does so once, it will remain a custom and they will lose respect for each other, and he will think of another wife and she of another husband. . . . Even if her husband becomes angry with her, she should endure it, because all his anger is just a moment, for a man, though he becomes angry, is soon appeased, because man was created from the soil and soon gives in and is appeased, but woman is created from the bone and does not give in soon.[33]

The woman is ultimately responsible for the escalation of strife within a marriage; yet this assumption is based on an image of men which is far from flattering. Male ire is easily provoked and men are not expected to control their anger. But since this is the nature of men, according to the rabbis, and since their ire passes as easily as it appears, the wife must be patient and appease her husband. The vernacular rabbis expect women to acquiesce in their lot and calmly accept it, even to the point of tolerating injustice. The rationale behind this, as throughout musar literature, is the primacy of stability (*yishuv ha-ʿolam*), the preservation of the social and symbolic order almost at all cost. The rabbis' attitude toward the inequality of the sexes echoes the way in which they deal with social inequality. The rabbis show a certain empathy for the powerless; but while they employ a rhetoric that can be sympathetic toward women and the poor, ultimately they take the side of the powerful (the husband and the rich) for the sake of stability. Female powerlessness, like poverty, is explained and legitimized as resulting from the divine order. There is thus assumed to be a meaning—whether hidden or obvious—in the universal condition of inequality of which the rabbis are quite aware. This attitude is formulated in the nineteenth-century *Pele Yoʿets* in terms no different from those employed in the *Shevet Musar* a century earlier:

> The wife should bear and endure the anger and resentment of her husband, even if she knows for a certainty that she has not done anything to make him angry, because she should think that someone on the street has angered him, or some difficulty in his work has occurred, and he lets his anger and resentment out at home. . . . The woman who has an evil and violent husband who depreciates and curses her, even if he beats her—God forbid, should receive the punishment from the Creator and should take it as atonement for her sins.

The text goes on to explain that the "good and wise wife" will not reveal her situation to anyone, especially not her parents and family: if they called her husband to account, he would treat his wife even more harshly. Papo concludes: "It is best for the woman if no one knows about her hardship. Rather, whenever she talks with her family, [she should say] that she has it good in her husband's home."[34]

The text betrays a remarkable fatalism. The rabbis are very well aware of problems that nowadays would be called domestic violence, and vernacular musar literature, where it discusses the subject, does not try to gloss over the issue. Nevertheless the rabbis call upon women to accept their lot, to carry their burden as divinely ordained suffering in atonement for her sins. As always with musar's references to social reality, we cannot determine how widespread the evil being denounced actually was in the communities; a future study of the history of Ottoman Sephardic women would have to supplement these texts with other evidence, particularly legal literature. But domestic conflict and violence were obviously an issue important enough to be addressed on several occasions in a number of Judeo-Spanish musar books.[35] The bottom line of all these texts is that concerns like "peace in the house" (*shelom ha-bayit*) or "the stability of the world" (*yishuv ha-ᶜolam*) take precedence over open confrontation of the problem.

After establishing women's stoic role in conflicts (an instrumental function from the perspective of social stability), the *Shevet Musar* presents additional female virtues whose purpose is to make a marriage work. Women are frequently admonished not to make excessive material demands; this is the third point in Elijah's list of ten. Their husbands, so goes the rabbinic argument, would be "obliged . . . to rob people in order to meet her requests, or cross oceans and deserts" for business trips to raise the money.[36] Worst of all, they would not have time to study Torah.

Another point raised in the *Shevet Musar* is the wife's domestic responsibilities in running the household and making the home an agreeable place:

> The woman should not be lazy about her household duties. . . . Laziness causes poverty in the house, because laziness obliterates cleanliness from the house. . . . When the husband returns home, even if he comes from outside with good humor, when he sees the mold and dirt of the house, and so many obstacles in the midst of the house, here some rags . . . there unwashed dishes from the supper of the night before: this leads him to desire his fellow's home, and desiring his home he will also desire his wife.[37]

Elijah's seventh point is particularly interesting:

> To me, it seems a great offense that some women sing lullabies to their children that include love songs and words of desire, for these songs defile the body and the soul. Again because the mind of the woman is light and she interprets all these words of illicit love [*palabras de amores de zenut*] referring to her, she imagines in her mind that what is being described in the story happened to her, and her mind comes to entertain evil thoughts.[38]

Elijah ha-Kohen strongly disapproves of the ballads and love songs which women sing as lullabies to their children. This is a good demonstration of how uncomfortable the rabbis could be with secular folklore which was communicated and transmitted by women. "Idle talk" for the rabbis thus includes not only gossip, but also a rich and ancient part of the Judeo-Spanish oral tradition, the ballads or *romanceros*.[39] The rabbis fear that women will identify with the romantic love described in these ballads and songs, thus presenting a challenge to the framework of traditional matrimony, the instrumental role of the virtuous woman, and indeed to the quietist, stoic stance described above.

This concern would come to prominence in the nineteenth century with the popularity of the secular Ladino novel, and would contribute to changing visions of gender roles and romantic love.[40] Yet the Sephardic musar rabbis expressed this concern with women as carriers of secular traditions as early as the eighteenth century. The rabbis were not in control of this folk knowledge. They disliked its projection of ideas inconsistent with the rules of female decency and were not comfortable with the perpetuation of these oral traditions by women.

MALE OBLIGATIONS

The flip side of the ideal of the "virtuous woman" is an insistence on male obligations. Much as the rabbis legitimize social inequality yet discuss the obligations of the rich in depth, they also legitimize male superiority yet condemn male abuse of power. The husband must respect his wife and treat her with love.

> Let us start with the duties which the husband must fulfill toward the wife. The sages said that the husband must love his wife like his own body and honor her more than his own body, and all this as long as he does not do anything against the will of the Creator out of love for his wife. The essential part of this friendship which he must have with his wife should be the love of the soul. The husband must advise his wife in the ways of Judaism and honesty . . . and how good it is to accustom her to read books of moral chastisement and inform her about all the laws and the severity of the punishment for transgressing them.[41]

For Judeo-Spanish musar, the ideal husband is his wife's teacher of Jewish knowledge and religious observance.[42] The rabbis thus draw two consequences from the exclusion of women from traditional learning: women's role is instrumental, assuring that their husbands and sons dedicate themselves to the study of Torah; but their husbands are required to use this privilege of learning in order to teach their wives. A significant broadening of the husband's duty to teach his family and household is represented by Judah Papo's requirement that the husband "accustom [his wife] to reading books of moral chastisement," that is, musar literature (presumably in the vernacular). This advice is related, of course, to the discovery of women as reading public.

No less important, there exists a male counterpart to the rabbinic request that women suffer an evil husband. A man too must patiently suffer his wife, even if "he has received a violent and evil wife who makes him very angry," for the sake of the "peace of the house":

> He should think of what the sages said, that the mind of women is light, or as the
> women say, the hair of a woman is long and her understanding short [*tiene el cabeo
> largo y el sekhel corto*]. Therefore, understanding always comes from the man. Even
> if she does things against his will he should not get angry . . . and it goes without
> saying that he should not curse or beat her—God forbid, for this is the custom of
> low and lost people. Rather, he should teach and chastise her kindly and with
> sweet words so that she may receive the chastisement of the Creator joyfully.[43]

Again, the rabbis appeal to the husband as a teacher: if his wife does wrong, he should teach her kindly and lead her back onto the path of the musar ideal rather than let himself be carried away by his ire. Both husband and wife must accept each other. Ideally, their roles—the instrumental role of women, the didactic role of men—complement each other; in the worst case, they must think of each other as a divine test in atonement for their sins.[44]

Educating Women

For whom were these texts written? As I have argued above, it seems that during the early stage of Judeo-Spanish musar literature—the eighteenth and early nineteenth centuries—the intended readers were male. Though the *Shevet Musar* presents ample advice on how women should behave (especially in chapter 24, to which I have referred, and chapter 17), this book, which was originally in Hebrew, is not likely to have been intended for a female readership. Rather, the husband was expected to act as his wife's teacher, communicating (orally) what he had learned in his *meldado* or the *bet midrash*. In the nineteenth century, however, the authors of Judeo-Spanish musar literature discovered women as a reading public for their books. The most important case was clearly Judah Papo's *Pele Yoʻets*, which addresses women explicitly among its intended readers.

Earlier in the nineteenth century there were books directed exclusively toward a female public. The most notable example is the *Sefer Dat Yehudit*, by Abraham Laredo and Isaac Halevi, published first in Livorno in 1827 and again in Jerusalem in 1878 and in Vienna in 1881. *Dat Yehudit* is a compendium of *dinim*, or religious laws, not a book of musar; the headings of its six sections are telling evidence of the subjects Judeo-Spanish authors found appropriate for a female public and how gender roles defined their image of women as intended readers: *"Heleq niddah,"* (fifty pages), on the laws of family purity and menstruation; *"Heleq hala"* (two pages), on the laws of baking bread and separating a small part of dough (as described in Num. 15); *"Dinim de los gusanos"* (thirteen pages), on insects found in vegetables and fruit; *"Dinim de carne y manteca"* (one page), on the laws of separating meat and dairy; *"Dinim del salar"* (seven pages), on the laws of salting meat; and *"Heleq hadlaqat ha-ner"* (six and a half pages), on the laws of lighting the Sabbath candles.

Why did the musar authors begin to envision women as potential readers or even write books for an explicitly female public? Eliᶜezer ben Shem Tov Papo (not the author of the *Pele Yoᶜets*, but a different Papo) remarks in his *Dameseq Eliᶜezer*—a Judeo-Spanish compendium of religious law in alphabetical order, based on the *Orah Hayim* section of the *Shulhan ᶜArukh*—that, according to Rabbi Azulai, when Purim falls on the night after Sabbath, the blessings of *havdalah* (the concluding blessing of the Sabbath) should be recited first in the synagogue and later at home by the wife. "But," says Eliᶜezer ben Shem Tov Papo, "this was in his [Azulai's] days when the women were knowledgeable and could say the blessing correctly. But nowadays most women cannot say the blessing [correctly], but say: '*bore more ha-es*' [instead of *bore meʾore ha-esh*] as they also say '*seheyanu vegiyemanu*, etc.' [instead of *she-heheyanu ve-qiyemanu*, etc.]."[45]

This complaint is reiterated in the Ladino *Pele Yoᶜets* in a statement that was added by the translator to the Hebrew original:

> Now there are many women who do not affirm many commandments, like saying the blessings over whatever they eat or drink. . . . And when the blessing over the wine is recited on Sabbath, they do not pay attention to it from beginning to end, and interrupt in the middle by talking. . . . And they are not careful about washing their hands as appropriate. . . . But they do not do all this evil out of wickedness of the heart but because of lack of knowledge. For they affirm the things which they know and which they have taken upon them better than men do. Yet they do not escape sin because they are obliged to seek to know everything they have to do.[46]

Judeo-Spanish musar literature started with the idea that ignorance is the enemy of tradition, and this message is reiterated throughout the various introductions in which the rabbis justify their use of the vernacular to write popular books. The argument is now adduced by Papo in support of his discovery of women as readers of musar literature and to advocate a better traditional education for girls and women. Judah Papo insists that fathers and husbands are responsible for teaching their daughters and wives about their religious obligations, "and they must not look at the time they will lose in teaching them or the money they will spend on employing someone to teach them."[47] Papo invokes an interesting comparison of the Ottoman Empire with Europe in order to advance his argument:

> The women in the lands of Turkey are very lacking in this regard [the recitation of blessings and prayers] because they do not learn to read and write, which is not like this among Ashkenazic women and the women in the lands of Europe who all know to read and write. . . . One should think about this and remedy it: for the sake of honor, lest the people from other lands consider our women like animals; and for the sake of the benefits that result from [saying] the prayers and blessings.[48]

The solution is to provide an adequate education to women and girls. It is worth noting that Judah Papo calls for female education both for reasons of *religious observance*, so that women will correctly recite and understand the blessings and prayers, and for the sake of *honor,* lest people from other countries disdain Ottoman Sephardic women for their ignorance. Papo's comparison with Europe and with Ashkenazic women and his worry about what people in other countries might think are indicative of one important factor in his (and other Sephardic authors') call for change: the new contact with European Jews, representatives of a post-traditional Jewish society, and particularly with a post-traditional education which was open to women (and more secular). Judah Papo, along with many Ottoman intellectuals and *maskilim* and an increasing number of rabbis, was convinced that traditional knowledge could only be perpetuated and secured against challenges from without and from within if it was made accessible to women. What had begun in the eighteenth century as a movement to disseminate knowledge among a broad, non-elite public was now explicitly directed toward women as well.

Conclusion

Women in Judeo-Spanish musar literature, and in traditional Ottoman Sephardic society, are women on the margins. The social ideal promoted in Ladino musar revolves around the study of Torah, but women are functionally excluded from this activity of sustaining and continuously reaffirming the traditional symbolic universe. It is thus inevitable that the rabbis assign them a place on the margins of the sociocultural fabric of the Sephardic community. In this society, women ideally play an instrumental role, making it possible for their husbands and sons to pursue the all-pervasive social ideal of *meldar.*

Another issue that contributes to the definition of gender roles is the rabbis' concern with social stability and the "peace of the house." If marriage is considered a pillar of the social order, both husband and wife are required to sustain it even if domestic problems arise; for musar literature, the question of domestic violence—of which the rabbis are by no means unaware—is also subordinated to the overarching interest of social peace.

Male sexuality, which is perceived as potentially uncontrollable and dangerous, is an even greater challenge to the stability of the social order. This danger—not female impurity or seductiveness—is what lies behind the rules of decency which define the boundaries of legitimate social interaction between the sexes and inform the gendering of social space. This does not mean, of course, that women are confined to their homes; but, as a rule, male and female social interaction must not overlap.

As we have seen, the author of the eighteenth-century *Shevet Musar* was already denouncing the female role in communicating and transmitting secular culture—the ballads or folk songs which are seen as a (potential or real) challenge to the worldview of musar. In the nineteenth century, the rabbis take an increasing interest in combating female illiteracy in traditional matters by addressing women directly as a reading public. Vernacular rabbinic literature had contributed *de facto* to the emergence of a female literary public sphere, even if the rabbis were not aware of this, or at least did not intend it. The nineteenth century, with the proliferation of secular genres and literary forms (the Ladino novel, the Judeo-Spanish newspapers) and their broad acceptance among a female reading public, brought new challenges to the traditional universe. The rabbis then began to address women directly as their intended readers, either by broadening their reading public to include them or by writing for an exclusively female readership. The rabbis understood, in the nineteenth century, that they needed learned, educated women if they wanted to maintain the order of the traditional universe.

Part IV

Exile and History

Understanding Exile, Setting Boundaries

8

In his lucid analysis of *galut*—exile—in Genesis, Arnold Eisen has suggested that "the homelessness of [the Jewish] people which is never at home, even in its own Promised Land, is meant to instruct those who mistakenly believe they *are* at home upon their earth about the true estate of human beings. . . . The rest of the Torah comes as a corrective to the condition of homelessness which Genesis describes. It does so, not by eliminating estrangement entirely, but by containing it within a sacred order."[1] This chapter explores different meanings of exile in Judeo-Spanish musar literature and how this idea set the boundaries for the sacred order of the Torah. The next chapter, on Jerusalem and the Land of Israel, shows that even those Sephardic authors who lived in the Promised Land saw themselves as living in exile; the ideal of homecoming remained a distant hope. In the last three chapters I have concentrated on the literary construction of the social order in Judeo-Spanish musar; I now turn to the construction of the symbolic order of tradition and in particular to the representation of exile and history.

The Meanings of Exile

The chapter on *galut* in the *Pele Yo'ets*, both in its Hebrew and Judeo-Spanish versions,[2] opens with a positive statement about exile: "The sages said that a person should exile himself to a place of Torah [M-Avot 4:14]."[3] According to Papo's explanation, anyone who finds it difficult to earn a living in his hometown should be ready to move to another place where he might fare better. "The person should not think about the separation from his [home] town," Papo writes,

> he should look for a place to earn a living in order to be well established and have the tranquility to serve the Creator. And even though it is very hard for him to leave his town and separate from his people and his relatives, he should take this as atonement for his sins, for this is like exile, and exile atones for sin [BT-Sanhedrin 37b]. And the one who needs to move to another town should exile himself to a town where he finds Torah and Judaism.[4]

Papo argues that the personal "exile" of leaving one's hometown and moving to another place, temporarily and alone or permanently and with one's family, is "like galut." Elsewhere, Papo reflects on how to behave when settling in another town. "The sages said that when one moves to another town, one should follow its rules, and the people say: In the town where you go, you should do as you see [others doing] [*asegún verás ansí harás*]. And the sages also said that a person cannot change the custom of the town lest strife should erupt there. . . . In short, he should do exactly as the majority does, provided no involvement in sin is implied."[5]

The first imperative of life in exile is thus identification with the community (as long as no halakhic transgression is involved). The difficulties and dangers of living in *galut* are countered through identification with the local Jewish community, and the stranger should adapt to the customs of the new place. Papo criticizes the lack of solidarity between Sephardic and Ashkenazic Jews and condemns the widespread attitude that "when an Ashkenazi arrives, they are very annoyed and say: Sephardim should go to Sephardim, and Ashkenazim to Ashkenazim."[6] This imperative of identification is not only valid for the personal exile of the individual living outside his hometown but is a guideline for the survival of the community and its symbolic universe in diaspora.

In Judeo-Spanish musar, *galut* is also a metaphor for the general human condition of estrangement and existential homelessness. Papo's *Pele Yo*ᶜ*ets* reminds its readers, for example, that "we are pilgrims in this world,"

> like passengers, like travelers, and thus we should not pursue vices or abundance . . . like the wayfarer on his way who contents himself with what there is, who says: it is [only] a road, everything passes, and [when we arrive] in the city we will rejoice and look for repose and tranquility. We should dedicate our mind and our thought to accumulating capital and provisions for the world to come, which is the true world and a strong abode.[7]

Exile is the existential condition of human life. Life in this world is likened to a journey, the human being to a wayfarer, and the fulfillment of the divine commandments and the study of Torah is the accumulation of provisions which are necessary both to survive the journey in this world and, more important, to finally "come home" at the end of one's days. The condition of homelessness is invested with meaning by seeing life as a journey with a destination, and the experience of estrangement, of being away from home, opens up the perspective of a future return to home. Musar literature delimits the sacred order for the journey of human life; it sets the rules for that journey and defines the right road to take.

If we look back for a moment to the opening of Papo's chapter on *galut*, a primary function of exile is atonement for sin—"exile atones for sin." The condition of homelessness, both for the individual and for the entire Jewish people, is understood as a tension between punishment for sins and failure and at the same time atonement for these sins. *Galut* is both a consequence of failure and the precondition for undoing it. Musar literature defines the way to achieve this translation of punishment into atonement as the establishment of the sacred order of religious observance and moral perfection. In practice, this creates a special responsibility not only to readily accept exile as divinely ordained, but to translate life in exile into a restoration of divine order.

From this point of view, exile is instrumentalized as promoting the ideal of musar. Exile is not usually understood in political terms and most writers reject an activist stance toward a return to the Land of Israel (a point I revisit in the next chapter). In a dialectical process, the boundaries of the traditional universe must be preserved in order to ensure identity and continuity under the conditions of exile;

and one of the most efficient mechanisms for preserving the traditional universe is the perpetuation of the imagery of estrangement and exile as a unifying force, no matter what the socioeconomic and political conditions might be at a given time and in a given place.

To secure the traditional symbolic and social order, musar is concerned with setting its boundaries; the image of homelessness is employed to define Jewish community and identity and set them apart from the community and identity of the neighboring gentiles. The sense of living in exile is not a reflection of the hardships of Jewish life in the Ottoman Empire—life was no less hard for other Ottoman subjects—but an instrument for preserving the traditional universe, a way to stabilize community and tradition in an "alien" environment.

For the rabbis, coming to terms with life in exile was always an exercise in defining and defending boundaries. Musar literature elaborated "a bounded field, a literary *eruv,*" to adapt Natalie Zemon Davis's phrase, in order to delimit identity in the absence of a homeland.[8] "The rabbis could not reconquer their Land from its foreign invaders," says Arnold Eisen. "But they could and did discriminate the pure from the polluted, holy from profane, we from they, to the degree that circumstances permitted."[9]

Jews and Gentiles: Setting the Boundaries

The preoccupation with the boundaries of the Jewish community and the symbolic universe of rabbinic tradition did not begin with the modernization and the westernization of certain sectors of Ottoman-Sephardic society in the eighteenth century and particularly the nineteenth century. A negotiation between self and other was a prime focus of Jewish literature throughout the ages, and so it was for rabbinic literature, halakhic and meta-halakhic alike.[10]

In the age of Judeo-Spanish literature, the eighteenth and nineteenth centuries of Ottoman Jewry, the boundaries of traditional knowledge and the coherence of the Sephardic community met a new challenge: the growth of an alternative model of the world—that is, the infiltration from "the West," first of European goods, commodities, and fashions, then of representations of European ideas and institutions. These spread throughout the Ottoman Empire, first among an elite (in the Jewish community, particularly the *francos* of Italian origin), then increasingly among all social classes. Although its impact became more pronounced and socially broader in the nineteenth century, the West as a cultural frame of reference emerged in the Ottoman cultural universe no later than the early eighteenth century.[11]

Beginning in the mid-nineteenth century, one of Ladino rabbinic literature's many concerns was to meet this challenge: Judeo-Spanish musar literature responded to the exposure to European and gentile culture by once again employing the time-honored image of exile and homelessness in order to strengthen the boundaries of tradition. In the words of Isaac Farhi, "the divine presence [*la shekhinah*] . . . is away from her palace and spreads tears for her sons who are dispersed among the gentiles because they are learning from the works of the gentiles and are [thus] causing the prolongation of exile."[12] By tearing down the boundaries between Jews and gentiles, the Jews prolong *galut;* by not respecting the sacred order of tradition, they fail to translate punishment into atonement and make exile into suffering rather than a liberating experience. The rhetoric of homelessness thus has clear social and political implications, though it does not suggest a return to a "homeland." Rather, it serves to reiterate the authority of tradition and expresses the rabbinic concern with a blurring of boundaries.

The gentile is the quintessential Other of the traditional universe of rabbinic knowledge;[13] the bounded field of rabbinic knowledge evolves as a continuous realignment of the boundaries between the sacred and the profane and between "them," the gentiles, and "us"—the Jewish community at large, but also the literary "us" of the musar authors and their intended readers. The contrast between gentile and Jewish knowledge is pointedly expressed in the *Shevet Musar,* which proclaims that "all their [the gentile] laws are the opposite of the Law of Moses."[14]

The construction of the gentile as Other, it might be added, does not imply contempt. In fact, there are passages in Judeo-Spanish musar in which the rabbis fight contempt toward gentiles as the misguided popular attitude of "stupid people" and "the women" who say "may all evil be for the gentiles" and the like, who call other Jews "Turk" or "Christian" as an insult, or "who, when a gentile greets them, consider it a *mitsvah* to respond to him with a curse."[15] For the rabbis, exile and the preservation of the rabbinic symbolic universe require the drawing of boundaries between Jews and gentiles, but they condemn expressions of popular xenophobia. On the contrary, they propose that exile be understood as a mission among the gentiles. Expressed in the terms of Lurianic thought, Farhi states that "it is known that we are in exile in order to pick up sparks of holiness that have fallen into impurity because of the sin of the first *Adam,* and how many proselytes have been made therefore! . . . Because of our many sins, however, we now do the contrary and advance and give force to impurity [*tumʾah*]."[16] The boundaries are permeable so that the mission of Judaism will be fulfilled and the fallen sparks brought back into holiness. But Isaac Farhi complains that people do precisely the opposite nowadays (the mid-nineteenth century): they transgress the boundaries in order to approach gentile culture and customs, thus strengthening the forces of contamination (*tumʾah*). Beginning in the mid-nineteenth century, this issue of violating the boundaries between the Jewish community and the gentiles, between the symbolic universe of rabbinic tradition and alternative modes of explaining the world, comes to the forefront in Judeo-Spanish musar literature.

Historians of eastern Sephardic communities have pointed out that

> both the content and the boundaries of Judeo-Spanish ethnicity in the Balkans and Asia Minor were transformed by the vagaries of the process of westernization and state-building practices in the modern period, without, however, any weakening of a distinctive identity. . . . In none of these countries, with the possible exception of Serbia, can one speak of the assimilation or indeed integration of the Judeo-Spanish community except for a few individuals.[17]

If assimilation into their surrounding society was a real (though perhaps some-times exaggerated) threat to Jewish communities in the West, it was not an option for Ottoman Jews. Paula Hyman has distinguished between assimilation as a so-ciological process and as a project. As a sociological process, assimilation "consists of several different stages. The first steps, often called acculturation, include the acquisition of the basic markers of the larger society, such as language, dress, and the more amorphous category of 'values.'" Only then can the minority group be integrated "into the majority institutions," while the "end point of assimilation is the dissolution of the minority by biological merger with the majority through intermarriage."[18]

In the Ottoman context, there was neither an assimilationist ideology nor a process of assimilation, and even the promoters of "Ottomanism" in the early twentieth century had no assimilationist agenda. In terms of social change, we are dealing with acculturation at most (as Hyman defines it) and, after the inception of Ottoman reforms (the *tanzimat*, beginning with the Gülhane Decree of 1839), with a modest integration of Jews into Ottoman majority institutions.[19] Assimila-tion as "merger" became a concern for certain rabbis writing in Judeo-Spanish dur-ing the twentieth century and outside the Ottoman Empire,[20] but even then can hardly be seen as a dominant sociological fact.

There is a problem with the notions of "majority" and "minority," however. Just as, for example, German Jews did not acculturate to an amorphous "majority" cul-ture but rather to a very specific sociological group, the *Bildungsbürger*, Ottoman Jews did not acculturate to the "majority," either the politically dominant Muslims or the economically more successful Greeks or Armenians. Acculturation in the Ottoman Empire was acculturation to an imagined West, to a growing western-ized Levantine bourgeoisie made up of members of many different ethnic and re-ligious groups.[21] (While Ottoman Sephardim acculturated to an "imagined West," the presence of western powers in the Ottoman Levant in economic, cultural, and political terms was of course very real. This is precisely why the imagined West was such a powerful image.)

At first, westernization was about external, "*alafranga*" (European-style) sig-nifiers, to use the Turkish word which was applied to the phenomenon. Commodi-ties imported from Europe—dress, furniture, decoration—became status symbols, going along with a growing interest in everything considered Western. Then, in the nineteenth century, new statements of identification with the sociocultural model of a westernizing bourgeoisie emerged and spread, tentatively, beyond the elites of the community: sending one's children to European schools, learning and reading French, or moving out of the overcrowded traditional areas of the large cities. It is this process of an imagined West serving as a cultural frame of reference for the newly emerging Ottoman bourgeoisie which I call westernization; it is not the same as the more general process (or cluster of related processes) called mod-ernization. As I use the word, westernization was a part of, but not identical with, the general modernizing transformation of Ottoman society.

Far from simply "importing" something from Europe to the Ottoman Empire, the imagined West served as an impetus for the promotion of a new distinctively Ottoman Sephardic sociocultural model by secular Judeo-Spanish journalism and literature in the second half of the nineteenth century and early twentieth century. The authors of Judeo-Spanish musar were quite aware of the fact that this socio-cultural model would endanger the integrity of the traditional universe and weaken the boundaries of the community. They were also quite aware of the fact that what began with the adoption of seemingly meaningless external fashions was bound up with a more complex, and ultimately more challenging, sociocultural process. That is why we find them denouncing the new custom of shaving one's beard as the beginning of all evil:[22]

> The prohibition in the Law "You shall not walk in the customs of the gentiles" [Lev. 20:23] became to them a total permission. . . . How many people cut the edge of their hair and the edge of their beard without any necessity and remove the *tselem* [the image of God] with their hands. And if there is a permission to shave the beard with a paste: this is in those places where the laws of the state require it. But in a place where there is no risk of harm for wearing a beard, with what permission do they do this?[23]

One manifestation of sociocultural change was the transformation of *urban topography*. While the modernization of Ottoman cities and the restructuring of urban space date largely from the last quarter of the nineteenth century,[24] residential changes among the westernizing Ottoman elites can be observed even earlier. Members of the wealthy strata of the great Ottoman cities fled the crampedness of the old districts, moving to newly emerging suburbs. Though residential districts had never been strictly separated along ethnic or religious dividing lines, Jews—like all other groups—tended to live near each other and "cluster" around the institutions of their community. The westernized elite, however, began to give preference to other values, looking for convenience, an ostentatious lifestyle or vistas on the Bosporus or the Gulf of Salonika (a nineteenth-century fashion). This development did not escape the rabbis, as can be seen in Abraham Palachi's *Ve-hokhiah Avraham:*

> A man should avoid living in a gentile quarter, for this will have many bad consequences for his wife and his children. . . . And in our times we have seen that two great wealthy men of Izmir wanted to take a house on the seashore and it did not come out well for them or for their children. . . . How different it is if one gets up every day in the morning and sees the faces of Jews, blessed and circumcised people, rather than the faces of gentiles, who serve idolatry. Especially if one sees the face of a gentile woman, one ignores the prohibition of "Do not turn unto the idols" [Lev. 19:4], which causes him great harm. If the person wants to make a good bargain and a large house and fine vistas, his evil inclination will impel him to take a house among gentiles. And he does not realize that this advance and wideness will thereafter mean constricting his soul.[25]

Members of the new Levantine bourgeoisie, looking for spacious dwellings with a view of the sea, abandoned the older districts with their ethnic intimacy and moved to new quarters where westernized Muslims, Christians, and Jews lived side by side. Unfortunately we do not know to whom Palachi refers and why it "did not come out well for them." In any event, what he does is to denounce the transgression of boundaries. While Jews and non-Jews always lived side by side in Ottoman society and certainly shared many popular beliefs, they never challenged the integrity of each other's religious universes. The rabbis protest now that members of different religious groups are attracted by a unifying westernizing sociocultural model. The common ground of a westernizing culture is threatening to erode the restrictions on social interaction between different ethnic and religious groups and to substitute Western values for traditional ones as points of reference.

Social boundaries between Jews and non-Jews are translated into spatial boundaries between Jewish and non-Jewish spheres of social interaction in the urban topography. As these boundaries are weakened by those who abandon the traditional patterns of urban life, the rabbis fear that the boundaries between the different traditional universes will be next. It is not the suspicion that Jews might assimilate to their non-Jewish environment that leads the "vernacular rabbis" to protest, but the challenge posed by the acculturation of both Jews and non-Jews to a European-inspired culture.

As early as the eighteenth century, Elijah ha-Kohen had declared that "there is no one stupider than the one who studies foreign books, that is, books of the gentiles."[26] In the nineteenth century, hardly any of the authors of musar books could ignore the increasing consumption of foreign literature, both in European languages (chiefly French) or in Judeo-Spanish translation. We have already noted Isaac Farhi's declaration that "many people have, because of our sins, begun to read non-Jewish books of stories and do not put them down day or night."[27] In a particularly interesting twist, Farhi contrasts Torah and gentile literature: "The holy Law delights the hearts, for the person can walk around in it as in a beautiful garden, because he will look at a difficult verse which seems to him like a dead-end street, and he will find many beautiful interpretations of all kinds, more delicious than honey. But in the books of the gentiles, what can he find apart from what is written?"[28] These lines nicely describe the impact of the secularization of literature that was (to repeat) a consequence of the vernacularization inaugurated by the rabbis who wanted to educate the people in their own language, Judeo-Spanish. Curious to read new things, the reader described by Farhi immerses himself or herself in individual reading of secular, foreign literature. Reading gentile literature causes people who were once good Jews to question the words of the rabbis, says Farhi. The "deadly poison" of secular books makes their readers arrogant and leads them to think about rabbinic tradition individually and critically rather than faithfully affirm it. Drawing on what they have read in secular literature, these readers doubt the authority of the rabbis and redefine what is true or false on the basis of foreign, non-rabbinic knowledge. The vernacular rabbis fear that if they lose control over what people read they will lose control over the administration of knowledge and the social and symbolic order that they represent.

It is interesting to see how Farhi compares Torah and secular literature. He pictures the one who reads and studies Torah as being "like one who walks around in a beautiful garden," discovering ever-new interpretations, roaming through a text which, because its possible meanings are infinite, contains everything. By contrast, foreign books offer nothing more than their literal meaning—lacking a divine source, they are necessarily limited and one-dimensional. This can also be read as the construction of a binary opposition between the polysemy of rabbinic tradition's discovery and unpacking of new and unforeseen meanings ("the typical midrashic predilection for multiple interpretations rather than for a single truth behind the text; its irresistible desire to tease out the nuances of Scripture rather than use interpretation to close them off")[29] and modern Western thought of the time which sought, in the optimistic vision of philological positivism, to unveil the "actual" meaning of a text.

Some forty pages later in the *Sefer Imre Binah,* Farhi reiterates his concern:

> Because of our many sins we see in our generations evils that did not exist before. Many young people began to read gentile books in order to learn foreign languages and lose countless hours with this. . . . And they are disgusted to hear words of Torah, still more to study [Torah]. And although I have dwelt on this before in earlier chapters, my heart feels great pain; had I a mouth of fire to chastise and castigate these people who lose themselves in nothing! . . . The proof is that the soul of a person who has stumbled into this sin [and reads foreign books] will not desire any *mitsvah,* either small or great, and when he sees a Jew devote himself to of the Law and Judaism he ridicules him and makes fun of him and considers him like a beast, and holds himself to be very knowledgeable and of unparalleled intelligence. The truth is that there could not be anyone more stupid and foolish than him. . . . In a short time, the evil will bear fruits and he will seek to do as much evil as he can, particularly sexual transgressions. . . . And we have seen that one of the reasons why our fathers were liberated from Egypt was that they did not change their language.[30]

On the pretext of learning foreign languages, young people begin to read European literature and are led to neglect religious observance and Torah study, and begin to ridicule what they perceive as the lack of cultivation among traditional Jews. These westernizers, as they discover a world beyond the traditional universe, are no longer ready to affirm the maxims of Jewish tradition, nor do they respect its representatives, the rabbis. That these young people who read European literature and challenge tradition are particularly prone to sexual transgression is highly debatable, of course, but it is a good illustration of Judeo-Spanish musar's view that the traditional symbolic order, the rules of sexual decency, and the social order are all closely intertwined, and that defiance of an element of that universe challenges the stability of the entire rabbinic world.[31]

It should also be noted that Farhi wrote his critique as early as the mid-1830s (*Sefer Imre Binah* was first published in 1836). While he arguably was not yet observing a widespread social movement of westernization, he considered the matter important enough to return to it several times in this and other books. What is interesting is that it represents a rabbinic response to westernization well before the time when most historiography usually claims that westernization began—before the inauguration of Ottoman reforms and even before the appearance of the first Judeo-Spanish newspapers.[32] Farhi's pronouncements against the consumption of foreign literature suggest that secularizing tendencies had already invaded certain sectors of Ottoman-Sephardic communities in the first half of the nineteenth century, though they would obviously gain momentum and greater social diffusion at a later stage. Farhi's condemnation of studying foreign languages and the claim that "one of the reasons why our fathers were liberated from Egypt was that they did not change their language" reminds one of the emerging Ashkenazic ultra-Orthodoxy and its stance on the use of "non-Jewish" languages. Among Sephardic rabbis in the Ottoman Empire and North Africa, however, opposition to European languages subsided somewhat in later years.[33]

It can be surmised that Farhi was alerted to the consequences of contact with gentile European culture during his fund-raising tour to various European communities in 1828. In his Judeo-Spanish musar book *Zekhut u-Mishor,* he shares with his Ottoman readers some of his impressions from his voyage to Europe. Farhi tells his readers about the breakdown of traditional order that he has observed in various European communities. Obviously, deviant behavior also existed in traditional communities; what scandalizes Farhi is that Jews in Europe transgress the religious law openly and seem to have no sense that they are doing something wrong: "When I was in Europe, because of my sins I had to see . . . many people who defile their mouths and eat meat butchered by non-Jews [ʿarelim] and drink wine of the gentiles. Many open their shop on the Sabbath, openly and without shame, buying and selling, cashing and paying, and writing and rubbing out and smoking cigars."[34]

But Farhi is far from presenting all European Jews as assimilated and neglectful of tradition. He also tells his readers about a wealthy man from Marseille, a certain Abraham Montefiore, whom he praises for his strict observance of the Sabbath even though his business leads him to deal with many gentiles. While Farhi is a guest at his home, a non-Jewish partner comes on the Sabbath. Without timidity, Montefiore sends him away, insisting that he does not receive visitors on business or discuss financial matters on that day. The gentile readily understands that he should return after Sabbath.[35]

Farhi includes his sporadic references to Europe for a pedagogical purpose. Sometimes he expects that his readers will be as scandalized as he is by the open profanation of the Sabbath in European cities or by people eating non-kosher meat and drinking gentile wine. The implicit message is that this is what receptiveness toward foreign (European) knowledge will necessarily lead to: a breakdown of the traditional order. At other times, he invokes the examples of virtuous people like the man from Marseille. The lesson he expects his readers to draw, of course, is that, even in a decadent environment like a European city, traditional observance is possible—and how much more so in the Ottoman Empire.

Thus Farhi cites the European example in order to convince his Ottoman Jewish readers that they should not be imitating gentile fashion—adopting the "external signifiers" of European culture like Western dress or beardlessness is only the first step toward the destruction of the traditional universe:

> There is a very evil trap to catch the person in many sins, and if he thinks about it, he will understand it: it is to dress like the gentiles. Many people in Marseille, fearful of God, are envious of the people in Turkey and say: How lucky are they for one can distinguish the Jews [from the non-Jews], which is not the case there, where you do not know who is a non-Jew and who a Jew. . . . But who forces the people in Turkey to dress in imitation of the gentiles? No one forces them other than their own evil inclination . . . saying to them: Blessed be God, you are a Jew and say *Shema῾ Yisra᾽el*, whether you recite it in a fez or a rabbi's hat.[36]

In Europe, it is impossible to distinguish Jews from Christians by their dress, reports Farhi, but this is due to the assimilatory pressure in Europe. No such pressure exists in the Ottoman Empire, and Farhi claims that God-fearing Jews in the West are envious of their eastern Sephardic brethren because they are not forced to compromise with their gentile surroundings. Pointing out the assimilatory pressure in nineteenth-century France and elsewhere, Farhi idealizes the still rather firmly traditional Ottoman order which allows its different religious groups to be different from each other. To Farhi, the European fashion then spreading among the Ottoman elites, which blurs the distinctions between the different groups, is only the first step toward a decline in religious observance. The example of the fez as head covering is not arbitrary. In 1829, Sultan Mahmut II passed a regulation requiring all officials to wear the fez, and he intended that non-official groups also wear the fez as a sign of Ottoman subjecthood.[37]

This comparison between the West and the Ottoman Empire can also be found in Eli῾ezer Papo's Hebrew *Pele Yo῾ets*. In his chapter on *galut*, he insists that it is preferable for a Jew to live under Turkish rule than "in the cities of Italy and the cities of Edom"[38] for exactly the same reason: the lack of assimilationist pressure in the Muslim East. In the Judeo-Spanish version of the book, published forty-six years after the Hebrew original, this comparison with Europe is omitted. Presumably, the post-*tanzimat* Ottoman Empire of the 1870s no longer offered the advantages of a traditional society which the older Papo praised in the 1820s and Farhi praised in the 1830s.

In the remainder of this chapter, I present a comparative reading of the Hebrew, Ladino, and Judeo-German versions of the chapter on *galut* in the *Pele Yo῾ets*. This will add a diachronic viewpoint—the Hebrew *Pele Yo῾ets* was first published in 1824, the first Judeo-Spanish edition in 1870–72—and add a comparative digression into the neighboring Habsburg Empire where the Judeo-German translation of the *Pele Yo῾ets* appeared in 1886.

A Tale of Three Exiles

As I have indicated, the chapter on *galut* in the *Pele Yo'ets* begins with a discussion of the personal, individual exile of the one who has to leave his hometown. This opening section (roughly one-third of the chapter in the Hebrew and Judeo-German versions, but only a fifth in the Ladino) is basically the same in all three versions of the *Pele Yo'ets* studied here, though there are some minor, but telling, variants. In Eli'ezer Papo's Hebrew *Pele Yo'ets,* the focus was to find a place where one can learn Torah and concentrate on religious perfection, even if this meant leaving one's hometown, while in the Judeo-German version, the issue was the need to send one's children away so that they can study Torah, if they could not do so at home.[39]

Meanwhile, the Judeo-Spanish *Pele Yo'ets* instantly shifts its attention to the one who has to leave his hometown for economic reasons: "If a person has difficulties in his town and cannot earn a living, he should move to another place."[40] Only then, forced into exile because of economic constraints at home, one should make sure to choose a "place of Torah." In a next step, the *Pele Yo'ets* describes *galut* as atonement for one's sin. While the Judeo-Spanish and Judeo-German versions are not literal translations of the Hebrew,[41] there are no important differences between the three texts in terms of contents. "Even to change from the house to the *sukkah* and from the *sukkah* to the house, if he takes it for *galut* it atones [for his sins],"[42] writes the young Papo, and almost literally the same is said in the Judeo-German version.[43]

Where the three versions differ widely is in their assessments of the current exile of the Jewish people. All begin by saying that there is an apparent contradiction between two contrasting sayings of the Sages, one affirming that *galut* is bad for Israel, another proclaiming that it is good for Israel. Only the "original" Hebrew *Pele Yo'ets* takes up this question by explaining that "exile of the soul" is indeed bad for Israel, but "exile of the body" is positive, and then uses the issue as a theme for the remainder of the chapter.[44]

THE HEBREW *PELE YO'ETS:* BETTER
THE OTTOMAN EMPIRE THAN EUROPE

Eli'ezer Papo begins with the "exile of the soul," that is, with conditions in which Jewish religious practice is hindered by state laws, making it obligatory to leave one's home and move elsewhere. The examples he gives are familiar to any student of early modern and modern Jewish history. In some places, in a measure to control their numbers, Jews do not get authorization to marry unless someone else passes away: witness the *"Familiantengesetz"* of the Habsburg emperor Karl VI, which strictly limited the number of Jews in the different areas of the empire, to name just one infamous example.[45] Another problem mentioned by Eli'ezer Papo is the obligation for Jews to enter military service. This too must be considered an "exile of the soul" and one must leave a place where such conditions are imposed.[46] One who fails to flee from these conditions which "oppress the soul" will be held accountable, according to the Hebrew *Pele Yoᶜets*, as it is impossible to remain faithful to Jewish tradition under such unfavorable circumstances.

Exile in the Muslim Ottoman Empire is good, however, especially if compared to life in Italy or other European countries, where Jews' deceptive freedom propels them into sin. "It is problematic for Jews to live in the cities of Italy or other Christian countries," to quote Marc Angel's paraphrase of Papo's Hebrew *Pele Yoᶜets*,

> since no one has the authority to stop sinners there. Jewish judges cannot render justice since everyone goes to the Gentile courts. The Israelites there have grown comfortable and have kicked off the yoke of Torah. These societies are immoral and immodest, and the Jews there are susceptible to the worst influences. Many evils follow in the wake of freedom. Such is not the case in the domain of Islam where the flag of Torah flies high. Jews there live according to the Torah, and rabbis and communal leaders have the power to root out evil and maintain our faith. In Moslem lands, people are modest and moral. They value the appearance of a beard.[47]

Here Eliᶜezer Papo raises three issues which very much determined the Sephardic rabbinic response to modern change: The first issue is that of rabbinic authority, which was severely limited in European countries but still extensive in the Ottoman Empire in the 1820s, when Eliᶜezer Papo wrote his book. The second, modesty and (particularly female) decency, presupposes Papo's identification of the increasing contact with gentiles in the emerging "semi-neutral," bourgeois society and increasing secular social interaction with (the danger of) sexual transgression and/or intermarriage. The final issue is the importance of Western versus traditional signifiers, shaving or not shaving one's beard being the example most frequently used in Judeo-Spanish musar literature. The Ottoman East and the Italian-European West are thus imagined as opposed on three different planes: political power, social interaction, and cultural symbols. The authors of the two later Judeo-Spanish and Judeo-German versions of the *Pele Yoᶜets* rewrite this chapter on *galut* in terms adapted to their contemporary needs; but their response to modernity is also inscribed in this discursive field.

Eliᶜezer Papo is far from idealizing the Jews' situation in Ottoman lands, however. Many hardships afflict the Jews, such as attacks by gentiles, the heavy tax burden, abuses of power by Ottoman officials, and false accusations. But, in the final analysis, this is better than the deceptive freedom in Europe, because the hardships of exile—the exile of the body—in Muslim lands force the people to realize that they *are* in exile, that they are not at home, and, as Papo says, "the Jews won't turn in repentance except at the hand of a firm king."[48] Only suffering in exile will lead the Jews to repentance, Papo argues, and he calls for silent acceptance of the political status quo in the Ottoman Empire. All this amounts, of course, to a rejection of European-style "emancipation." As the Hebrew *Pele Yoᶜets* sees it, the price of such emancipation is too great. It is better to live with the difficulties of the Ottoman exile than to enjoy the opportunities of seductive European emancipation, which ultimately alienates its beneficiaries from tradition.

It is true, concedes Eliᶜezer Papo, that a genuinely pious person can lead a God-fearing life even in a European city. But one should think of one's children: will they be able to escape the seductions of non-Jewish, secular culture? The author bewails the fact that, in Europe, many Jewish youths are educated with "foreign and philosophical knowledge," alienating them from traditional rabbinic knowledge. This should be reason enough, concludes Papo, to move from Europe to Ottoman Turkey where "the flag of Torah flies high."[49]

THE JUDEO-SPANISH *PELE YOᶜETS:* GENTILES THEN AND NOW

When Judah Papo published his Judeo-Spanish version of the *Pele Yoᶜets* in the early 1870s, the situation had changed considerably and he no longer found it appropriate to contrast conditions in Europe and the Ottoman Empire. How did the changes that affected Ottoman Jewry transform Judah Papo's understanding of exile?

In a few sentences, Judah Papo resolves the apparent contradiction between the two statements of the Sages about whether exile is good or bad for Israel: it is both. While the hardships of exile make it difficult to find the tranquility necessary for serving God and fulfilling the commandments, the afflictions of *galut* leave one's heart receptive to chastisement and ready to repent. It is good to serve God with a "repentant heart."[50] Having quickly resolved this issue, Judah Papo dedicates the rest of the chapter to discussing the condition of exile for his contemporaries. He notes from the outset that exile has never been easier to bear, "now that God has shown pity for the Jewish people and has made exile lighter."[51]

Yet despite this considerable easing of the situation, it is appropriate not to forget the condition of exile: "At the thought that our Holy Temple is destroyed, that there are no offerings, nor the [Temple] service of the priests [*kohanim*] and Levites, that our land is in the hands of others, that we have no king, no high priest, no prophets, no Sanhedrin, that we are deprived of all good: for all this it is appropriate to be downhearted."[52] While life in exile is no longer itself an affliction and "exile has become lighter in most parts of the world,"[53] the lack of a "home" must still be bewailed. It is not the present experience of exile which causes grief but the lost past, the loss of a religious and political center (Temple and kingdom) and of legislative and prophetic leadership (prophets and Sanhedrin). While Judah Papo is happy to praise the much improved lot of his people, he warns his readers not to mistake the new freedom for the end of *galut*.

Nevertheless, Papo eloquently praises the numerous improvements in Jewish-gentile relations and the growing respect of the non-Jewish authorities for the Jews. "Now that knowledge is multiplying and the world is approaching the moment of truth," he writes, "the nations consent that our Law is holy and was given to us on Mount Sinai."[54] The "new gentiles" are no longer idol worshipers and the long history of suffering, persecutions, and expulsions has finally given way to a rapprochement between the religions. The key to this change is the "flourishing of science," the advancement of knowledge, which is finally bringing the world to its "moment of truth." For Papo it is clear that antisemitism was religious hatred more than anything else. "In ancient times, the hatred of the Law was engraved on the hearts of the nations against the Jewish people," but this now has finally changed.[55]

Judah Papo makes sure to affirm the Jewish people's indebtedness to the new gentiles and their benevolent policies. In these times, "in which we are very grateful to the states for all the good things they are doing for us," one is certainly obliged to do more than recite a prayer for the peace and welfare of the state in synagogue; in addition, "everyone who knows about something beneficial that comes from the state or the nation in favor of the Jewish people or individual should make it known in public."[56]

This optimistic reading of contemporary Jewish-gentile relations is by no means an exception. In fact, wherever the nineteenth-century vernacular rabbis write about "*goyim*," they make sure to differentiate between the idolaters of ancient times and their own gentile neighbors. Such niceties were not considered necessary by their eighteenth-century predecessors. Elijah ha-Kohen, for example, does not hesitate to write, in terms which are hardly flattering, that "when [a woman] comes out of the ritual bath, she should be careful not to encounter on her way anything impure like a gentile or an impure animal like a dog or an ass or the like."[57] The authors of the nineteenth century, however, find it appropriate to point out the difference between gentiles then and now, and thus an introductory remark in the *Me'am Lo'ez* on Esther reads: "It is advised that wherever it says [in this book] 'gentile' or 'worshipper of the stars and planets' or 'nations,' it refers to the ancient nations which were idolaters and did not believe in God. But the nations of our times are good people and believe in God and honor the Torah and we must live with them and ask for the peace of the city."[58]

But with the advent of the "new gentile," the non-Jewish Other has by no means disappeared. In one rather interesting case, two Sephardic authors, Sason and Amarachi, adapt selections from the eighteenth-century *Sefer ha-Berit* to their purposes. One passage in which they discuss the discoveries of distant continents echoes the Eurocentric discourse on the "savage": now that the "new gentiles" are no longer seen as idolaters, the "savages" of exotic places become the ultimate Other. Since relations with the Muslim and Christian neighbors in the Ottoman Empire are seen in a more favorable light, the geographically distant "savage" people are identified with the chronologically distant idol worshippers of ancient times.

> Human beings must love each other, with the exception of two kinds of persons for whom one should not entertain love, and these are highway robbers and murderers and thieves, and equally those people who live in distant places and are called savages. They are people who have no laws, nor have they houses, but sleep

in the open field, and they walk around naked. They do not plow nor sow, but eat herbs and fruits, and all women are ownerless, and they have no leader nor commander.[59]

A few pages later, Amarachi and Sason continue in terms that not only echo their contemporary concerns but recall the medieval discussions about whether Christians or Muslims should be considered idolaters.

> King David said: "I hate those who hate You" [Ps. 139:21], that is to say: I will abhor those who abhor you. This verse was said about people who claim that there is no God and who are called heretics, but the verse was not said about the gentiles of today. And this verse was said also about the seven nations which lived in the Land of Israel before the Jews entered the land, for these nations were very evil . . . and did not contribute to the stability of the world. . . . This verse is also said about some people who still exist today at the end of the earth, as in China, India and Japan, and worship fire and water.[60]

Unlike the new gentiles, the idol worshippers of old endangered the "stability of the world." Their wickedness is described in terms of their abuse of the weak and unfortunate, their deception of orphans and widows, and in terms of sexual transgression. The vernacular rabbis reach out toward the non-Jews of their own time—repeatedly declaring that these gentiles are different from the idolaters of earlier periods—and at the same time reaffirm the boundary between Jews and gentiles. Amarachi and Sason also take to task those who think that the biblical injunction to kill the seven nations was not really God's word, but was invented by Moses. Amarachi and Sason strongly reject this "humanistic" objection and insist that these peoples endangered the "stability of the world" and thus had to be destroyed.[61]

But let us return to Judah Papo's chapter on *galut*. Even though Papo has a positive and optimistic attitude toward a Jewish-gentile rapprochement, the *Pele Yo'ets* makes a point of reiterating the importance of preserving the boundaries between the different religions. Indeed, for Papo it is the gentiles who are approaching Judaism, not vice versa. When Papo speaks of the new benevolence of the gentiles toward the Jews, he argues that "the proof of this is that, among the good things that the nations do for us, they allow us to follow our laws and give power to the *hakhamim* of every place to enforce the Law."[62] One wonders, of course, what Papo is referring to. It seems that this is a rather wishful reading of the reality of Ottoman Jewry in the age of reform. While there can be no doubt that, together with the wealthy, the rabbis still exercised control over the traditional community, the Ottoman reforms for the first time challenged and limited rabbinic authority and sought to enhance the powers of lay leadership (whether the goals of these reforms were achieved or not is a different question). Curiously, Papo invokes the new gentile "respect" for the *hakhamim* in order to reaffirm their authority within the community.

Beyond this optimistic note, how does the Judeo-Spanish *Pele Yoʿets* address contemporary challenges to tradition? The following passage is a good illustration of the problems the Sephardic rabbis faced during the transformation of Jewish communities in the nineteenth-century Ottoman Empire:

> There are so many who take advantage of the freedom to discharge the yoke of the Law and the commandments and commit transgressions in public, and all their intention is to imitate the [gentile] nations. But they cannot become like them, for they have not received the commandments. . . . But we are commanded [by God], and the one who profanes Shabbat deserves to be stoned [*seqilah*] and the one who eats forbidden fat deserves excision [*karet*]. . . . In all times there were good and bad people, but in past times, the one who did wrong did so covertly and secretly, either out of shame or because he feared punishment. Now they have removed the veil and transgress openly.[63]

The difference between European and Ottoman communities which was still being seen by Farhi has disappeared in these lines from the early 1870s. Judah Papo clearly recognizes that there had always been deviant behavior in traditional society, but now there are people who transgress the religious commandments in public, he claims, and with no sense of shame or awareness of wrongdoing. The examples given are certainly not chosen randomly, and late nineteenth- and twentieth-century musar authors complain on more than one occasion that people desecrate the Sabbath or eat prohibited food in public. The common denominator of these transgressions is that they are often a result of secular social interaction, if not between Jews and gentiles then among young westernized Jews who spend their leisure time together, as we have seen in the chapter on social interaction. What is much worse than the transgression itself, however, is its public character. Publicly defying the traditional order challenges the integrity of the traditional universe itself, as it suggests that there are other universes (the West) which serve as alternative frames of reference and that the power of tradition is far from absolute. Moreover, the authority of those who represent tradition, the rabbis, is openly defied as people begin to publicly disregard what the rabbis have to say.

How widespread were such open challenges to rabbinic authority? I have already cited above Judah Papo's assertion that "there are some people who are heretics against God . . . but the *majority* knows that God is in the heavens and the world is not ownerless."[64] What are the implications for the Judeo-Spanish educational project? Papo clearly imagines that his readers and, indeed, the majority of Ottoman Jews are sufficiently traditional to accept the basic notions of the rabbinic symbolic universe. On this assumption, Judeo-Spanish musar literature can serve as a guide to repentance and a renewed religious practice. In the absence of a consistent ideology of assimilation in the eastern Sephardic communities and with secularization limited to a comparatively small group of westernizers, the Sephardic rabbis believe that their educational project, inherited from their eighteenth-century predecessors, is an adequate response to the challenges of modern change.

THE JUDEO-GERMAN *PELE YO^cETS:*
A TRUE SON OF HIS FATHERLAND

The existence of a Judeo-German version of this classic of Sephardic musar literature gives us an opportunity for a brief, comparative digression into the world of
central European Ashkenazic Jewry, in which we shall be able to appreciate where
Sephardic and Ashkenazic experiences differed and where they coincided. (Incidentally, both the Judeo-Spanish edition of the *Pele Yo^cets* as well as its Judeo-
German version were printed first in the Habsburg Empire: Papo's Judeo-Spanish
version was published in Vienna in 1870–72; sixteen years later, in 1886, a Judeo-
German translation appeared in Paks in western central Hungary. The background
of the two "translators" and the respective audiences were very different, of course.)

The Judeo-German translation by Judah (Julius) Krausz is usually rather close
to the Hebrew *Pele Yo^cets*, but adds a separate commentary, *Tomer Devorah*, at the
bottom of each page. In the case of the chapter on *galut*, however, Krausz preferred
to depart from the original and address what seemed to him the needs of his intended readers in the Habsburg Empire of the late nineteenth century. He explicitly says so at the end of the chapter: "Here we followed a different track of thought
than the author [of the original], who speaks about the differences between Turkey
and other countries; but the overall sense is the same, just more related to our own
time."[65]

The chapter begins, as I have mentioned, with the individual exile of someone
moving to another place or sending his children away so that they may study Torah.
Then, also following the Hebrew *Pele Yo^cets*, Krausz insists that one should leave
those countries where Jews suffer "exile of the soul" and where restrictions apply to
the settlement of Jews—he names Russia, Rumania, and, in the past, Moravia and
Bohemia as examples. While he praises those places where "we can serve God
freely under the protection of the authorities,"[66] he also, very much like Eli^cezer
and Judah Papo, warns of the dangers of freedom. This is the key passage of the
chapter in Judeo-German:

> Freedom is of great value for Judaism, for we can serve God freely under the
> protection of the authorities. But it also has had a negative influence on the Jews.
> . . . One should use one's freedom to serve God, and one should fulfill the Torah,
> which used to be observed with so much pain and suffering, in the bright light of
> freedom. The *majority*, however, thought that the only purpose of freedom was to
> facilitate socializing with gentiles, to sit with them in coffeehouses and taverns . . .
> and to throw off the yoke of the Torah. Driven by ambition and vanity, this went
> on until they were ashamed of Judaism and found insult in being called a Jew. In
> this way they believed to be true patriots. But this is a lie and the authorities are
> wrong if they believe this. Do you find among all the Jewish assassins, socialists,
> anarchists etc. even one Orthodox Jew? Only heretics who abandon Judaism and
> have no religion at all become criminals and traitors. The Orthodox Jew is a true
> son of his fatherland.[67]

At first sight, Krausz is fighting the same battle as Judah Papo: one should seek
freedom, but must not abuse this freedom to abandon tradition and imitate the

gentiles. But there are essential differences between Papo's and Krausz's translations. First, the Judeo-German text says that the majority mistook freedom as an opportunity to cast off the yoke of Torah and to socialize with non-Jews. By contrast, Judah Papo made it clear that he saw the cases of total estrangement from tradition as a minority and that the majority continued in their reverence for the traditional universe.

Second, the difference is not only quantitative: Krausz laments that many Jews, once they taste the fruits of emancipation, begin to actually negate their very Jewishness; they do not just seek to secularize their social practice by interacting more freely with non-Jews and adapting non-Jewish mores, but even go so far as to consider it an insult to be called Jews. The Judeo-German version thus addresses assimilation as a social reality and assimilation as an ideology—both foreign to the reader of the Judeo-Spanish *Pele Yo‘ets* and its author. Whereas the Ottoman-Sephardic *Pele Yo‘ets* censures the opening of shops on the Sabbath, the version that came out in Hungary spoke of people who tried to leave Judaism behind entirely, some of them converting to Christianity.

Judah (Julius) Krausz insists, however, that the ideology of assimilation is based on a double illusion. The gentile governments believe that the assimilated Jew will be a better citizen? They have it backward: all the subversive elements, Jewish anarchists and socialists, are assimilated Jews who have actually betrayed their own people and tradition; the Jew faithful to his Torah is the true patriot— "the Orthodox Jew is a true son of his fatherland," as Krausz puts it. What is more, those Jews who mistakenly believe that they successfully have left behind their Jewishness are readily reminded of their origins by the antisemites, the modern Hamans: "People who . . . did not want to know anything of Judaism, and even baptized Jews, now were insulted as Jews. Those [Jews] who had insulted Judaism were now mocked as Jews themselves. Antisemites, like Haman in ancient times, reminded them of their Jewish origins."[68] In the shadow of the surge in modern antisemitism in the 1870s and 1880s, Krausz also saw his Judeo-German *Pele Yo‘ets* as an Orthodox response to the *desencuentro* between assimilated central European Jewry and the non-Jewish, at best "semi-neutral" society.[69] Both assimilation to surrounding society and intermarriage as well as political antisemitism, so central to the modern experience of European Jewry, were of little importance for Ottoman Jewry. Consequently, the approaches of traditional Sephardic musar literature and of the emerging Askenazic Orthodoxy to the challenges of modernity differed widely.

Conclusion

Judah Krausz and Judah Papo adapted the Hebrew *Pele Yo‘ets* to two entirely different environments. Paks, in post-emancipation Hungary, saw a mid-century split between the Orthodox and Neologue tendencies in the community; the Orthodox were still stronger, but they separated themselves nonetheless and established a "status quo ante" community. Judah Papo, himself living in Jerusalem, wrote for an

Ottoman Sephardic public. It is fascinating to see how one book, translated, rewritten, and transformed, was adapted to the experiences of totally different communities. We have here a good example of how processes of cultural translation and adaptation within rabbinic traditional society worked across linguistic and cultural divides—from one literary system (Hebrew) into two others (Judeo-Spanish and Judeo-German, respectively); from the Ottoman to the Habsburg Empire; from a Sephardic to an Ashkenazic reading public. Musar worked, in this case and throughout its history, as an important vehicle for such processes of cultural translation.

With their intended readers in mind, the authors of Judeo-Spanish musar literature described the sacred order for the Ottoman-Sephardic community, ensuring its continuity in exile. In this chapter, I have focused on the boundaries which were drawn between this sacred order and foreign, Western knowledge, and the boundaries which were drawn between the community and its gentile Others. Musar did more than this, of course: it mapped out the territory of tradition, not just its limits. But particularly in a time of transition and conflict—which the nineteenth century certainly was for Ottoman Sephardim—the preoccupation with and preservation of boundaries gained overwhelming importance. The authors of Judeo-Spanish musar were increasingly concerned with the blurring of boundaries between "us" and "them" as a result of the process of westernization that affected practically all ethnic and religious groups in the Ottoman Empire and created a particular sociocultural group, the westernized Levantine bourgeoisie. An imagined West became the central cultural frame of reference for a growing section of Ottoman and thus also Ottoman Jewish society; the rabbis decided to fight westernization from its most innocent beginnings, the adoption of Western dress or shaving one's beard. They understood that this imagined West could ultimately replace rabbinic tradition as the dominant cultural frame of reference.

The Impossible Homecoming

9

Of the authors discussed in this study, three lived and wrote their Judeo-Spanish musar works in Jerusalem: Isaac Farhi, who was born in Safed in 1779 and died in Jerusalem in 1853; Judah Papo, who moved to the Land of Israel (he is mentioned as a rabbi in Jerusalem in 1856) and died there in 1873, just a year after the appearance of the second volume of his Judeo-Spanish *Pele Yoʿets;* and Isaac Badhab, who was born and died in Jerusalem (1859–1947). Their works allow us to learn more about both the situation in Palestine as seen by these authors and the place of the Holy Land in their respective worldviews, and in Ladino musar in general.

To begin with, exile is more than absence from the Land of Israel. In the *Sefer Darkhe ha-Adam,* Amarachi and Sason quote from a discussion of exile between the king and a Jew in the *Shevet Yehudah.* The passage can be read as illustrating how the "vernacular rabbis" saw their own condition:

> It is a long time since we were exiled, and we have gradually lost our knowledge [*cencia*]. The king said: Your answer is nonsense. Knowledge does not depend on the land, for a man who is a sage does not lose his wisdom by moving to another land. The Jew answered him: I am not saying that it was because of the land, but rather that when we were enslaved, our minds were enslaved as well because of [the difficulties of earning] a living, the levies and poll taxes and everyday difficulties.[1]

The hardships of exile lead to intellectual decline and a loss of knowledge—that ignorance which the vernacular rabbis seek to combat in their Ladino literature. "Knowledge does not depend on the land" (*La cencia no está decolgada en la tiera*): In this chapter I show how the various rabbis related to the Land of Israel as the "center" of the rabbinic traditional universe, yet understood themselves as enduring "exile" even if they lived in the Holy Land, as some of them did.

Return to the Land of Israel: Three Approaches

Though the differences between the chapters on *Erets Yisraʾel* in the Hebrew and Judeo-Spanish versions of the *Pele Yoʿets* are minor at first sight, they betray the different attitudes of Papo father and son toward living in the Land of Israel. Their views appear relatively consistent, however, if we set them against the vision of another rather well-known Sephardic rabbi from the Judeo-Spanish-speaking Balkans, Judah Alkalaʿi, who often is referred to as a forerunner of religious Zionism.

Eliʿezer Papo predictably praises the sanctity of Jerusalem and the Holy Land and readily acknowledges that it is a great *mitsvah* for everyone to settle there, but he immediately adds some cautious remarks that all but discourage emigration to the Land of Israel except by the elderly with adequate economic resources to do so. In fact, Elicezer Papo's stance (and that of most other rabbis) makes it practically impossible for the economic situation to improve in the Palestinian Jewish community, or *yishuv,* as he envisions a community made up essentially of old people who have accumulated savings abroad and *talmide hakhamim* dedicating themselves exclusively to the study of Torah:

> One should not move [to the Land of Israel] except in old age, after his wife . . . will not be having any more children, and he should not take with himself children, neither sons nor daughters. And if God has given him the means, he can take a daughter with him . . . but he cannot take a son with him at all because the son will have many children and he will not know what the day will bring. It is true that "the air of the Land of Israel makes one wise" [BT-Baba Batra 158b], but according to what we see, a person has difficulties making a living in the Land of Israel and most are forced to leave when they seize a *shelihut mitsvah* to travel to cities abroad for ten years or more, and they live dreadful lives, and their wives even more so. . . . Not so those who live outside the Land of Israel and find a living where they reside.[2]

Elicezer's son Judah also warns of the economic difficulties and suggests that it is easier for old people without families to move to Palestine. Nevertheless he does not flatly discourage moving to Jerusalem with one's sons or daughters, nor warn of the difficult fate of young people who cannot make a living in the Land of Israel and are forced to go abroad, or advert to the better economic situation in the diaspora: "Lest one regret it, a move to Jerusalem must be well considered with much wisdom in order to organize one's affairs. When one moves without a family, when an old man and an old woman are alone, they can more easily venture to go, for they have few expenses and do not expect to have expenses. . . . In these circumstances, one must do everything possible to move to Jerusalem."[3] In the Judeo-Spanish version, the warnings of the Hebrew text are toned down. The same tendency can be observed later in the same chapter. Both authors insist on the obligation to support those who live in Jerusalem or want to settle there. The Hebrew text, however, adds that it is inappropriate for poor people to ask others to finance their move to the Land of Israel. The commandment to settle in Israel, says Elicezer Papo, is no more important than, for example, the commandment of *lulav* on the feast of Sukkot, and if someone cannot fulfill such a *mitsvah* because he has no money, his intention is reckoned as tantamount to having performed the act. There are many respectable dignitaries and rabbis outside the Land of Israel—so why should someone who cannot afford to move to Jerusalem do so, asks Elicezer.[4] He makes sure to add that, if someone is distressed and would overcome his grief only by making his way to the Holy Land, one should certainly help him, but the message is clear nonetheless: settling in the Land of Israel is no more important than any other commandment, and one might as well stay where one is in order to assure the well-being of one's family. Of all this, Judah Papo's "translation" retains only the obligation to assist those who want to settle in the Holy Land and then continues with the issue of charity and financial support for the *yishuv*, which also follows in the Hebrew text.

Both the Hebrew and Judeo-Spanish versions quote a passage which is important in understanding "home" and the Land of Israel, namely the rabbinic interpretation of "the poor of your town come first"[5] as referring to the poor of the Land of Israel. In part, this is the logical consequence of the distressing economic situation described by both authors and an expression of solidarity with the Jews living in poverty in the Holy Land. But the phrase also testifies to the special place of Jerusalem and the Land of Israel in the symbolic universe of the rabbis. The sense of geographical distance is replaced by a sense of identification with those who live in the spiritual center, and the poor of Jerusalem are like the poor of one's own city. But one only identifies with those who dwell in the Holy Land; one does not necessarily move there oneself. This identification is expressed through financial support and charity: charity is the symbolic expression of the religious centrality of the Holy Land. Even in the Judeo-Spanish *Pele Yo‘ets* (whose author himself lived in Jerusalem) and certainly in the Hebrew original of the book, it would seem that it is above all the *idea* of the Land of Israel as a center that counts, removed from geography and history. The connection with the Land of Israel is symbolically enacted through financial support and charity, not by settling there.

Judah Papo remarks elsewhere in the *Pele Yo‘ets:*

> Jerusalem is a city revered by all nations, and not because of its abundance or its [beautiful] aspect, for there are many cities that are better favored in terms of abundance and aspect. They esteem [Jerusalem] because of its sanctity. How much more so [should] we [revere it], for it is our true city. . . . All nations spend a great deal of money for those of their people who live in Jerusalem and follow their religion [*guadran sus leys*]; so how much more should the Jewish people do so.[6]

The comparison with other nations is an often-employed rhetorical device, but it also is indicative of how Papo understands the Jewish people's relationship to their spiritual center in the Holy Land. He demands financial support for the small minority of Jews who live in Jerusalem; this support is not only about money, of course, but a symbolic affirmation of the bond between the diaspora and the center. Just as Christians from all over the world support the representatives of various denominations who live in the Holy Land, says Papo, so should the Jews. He never advocates that all or even many Jews should actually move to the land; the bond remains symbolic.

The Hebrew *Pele Yo‘ets* is clearly written by someone living in the diaspora (and both the Hebrew and Judeo-Spanish versions are written *for* an audience living outside the Land of Israel). This is plain when Eli‘ezer Papo insists that one should write to one's relatives who have settled in the Holy Land to keep them from worrying about the fate of their loved ones abroad.[7] The perspective is obvious: it is not that those who live in the diaspora feel like strangers and need to hear from their relatives in Jerusalem, but that those who dwell in the center depend on information from outside. The Land of Israel does not become "here"; it remains the symbolically central, but nonetheless distant "there." The Holy Land is central to the rabbinic symbolic universe—and the rabbis, as we will see later, are ready to defend this centrality when it is challenged—but it remains marginal in terms of social and demographic reality.[8]

This traditional quietist advocacy of waiting for God to restore His people is shared by practically all Ottoman rabbis of the time. This stance affirms the symbolic centrality of the Land of Israel but does not take an activist approach toward enhancing this centrality in real life; the rabbis limit themselves to reaffirming the representation of centrality within the traditional symbolic universe, and make excuses for the declining numbers of people actually settling in the Holy Land in the nineteenth century. Even for the learned elite, the *talmide hakhamim,* the ideal of settling in the Holy Land is clearly secondary. Hayim Palachi of Izmir, for example, writes in his book *Artsot ha-Hayim* (1872) that the home of the *talmid hakham* "is considered to be like the Land of Israel even if he lives outside the Land, and his prayer as though [it were said in] the Land of Israel. . . . Therefore the *talmid hakham* is exempt from [the commandment of] settling in the Land of Israel. . . . In addition, the prayer of the one who supports the students of Torah is being heard as though he prayed in the Land of Israel."[9]

This dominant attitude among Ottoman-Sephardic rabbis contrasts with a new, even revolutionary approach mainly associated with the Bosnian rabbi Judah Alkalaʿi (born in Sarajevo in 1798, died in Jerusalem in 1878), who had been a pupil of Eliʿezer Papo, the author of the Hebrew *Pele Yoʿets.* Marc Angel has compared Papo's and Alkalaʿi's respective approaches: "Whereas Rabbi Eliezer Papo may be taken as a symbol of the policy of accepting one's destiny, Rabbi Alkalai may be taken as a symbol of a policy of activism and rebellion. . . . Rabbi Papo emphasized acceptance of the status quo; Rabbi Alkalai emphasized changing it."[10] Alkalaʿi, though not the first Sephardic rabbi to promote a return to the Land of Israel,[11] is certainly the best-known forerunner of religious Zionism.[12] He shared with others the expectation that redemption would finally occur in the year 5600 (1840), based on the statement of the *Zohar* that "when the sixth millennium comes, in the 600th year of the sixth millennium, the gates of wisdom above and the fonts of wisdom below shall be opened . . . and God will raise up the nation of Israel from the dust of its Exile and will remember it."[13]

When 1840 passed without the coming of the Messiah, Alkalaʿi did not give up hope or abandon his activist ideas (unlike the pupils of the Gaon of Vilna, for example, who had moved to the Land of Israel in expectation of redemption: three rabbis were so disillusioned after 1840 that they even converted to Christianity, and the others returned to the traditional stance that "if God does not build the house, its builders labor in vain").[14] Under the impact of the Damascus affair of that year—which also catalyzed the development of an international Jewish public opinion, the emergence of a Jewish press, and the subsequent foundation of the Alliance Israélite Universelle in Paris—Alkalaʿi reinterpreted 1840 as the beginning of a period favorable to the Jewish people (ʿet ratson) and that redemption would come at the end of this period. In his second Judeo-Spanish book, Alkalaʿi explained that what is written in the *Zohar* and what he himself had believed about the year 5600 (1840) "applies not only to this year for it is not a work of one day. [5]600 are called these one hundred years [that are now beginning]."[15]

Alkalaʿi argued (as Rabbi Bibas of Corfu had done before him) that *teshuvah* should be understood in the double meaning of the Hebrew term: repentance *and* return—return of the Jewish people to the Land of Israel. He advocated a revival of the Hebrew language (his first book was a Hebrew grammar in Judeo-Spanish, *Darkhe Noʿam*, published in 1839) and systematic settlement in the Holy Land. In 1852, he visited various Jewish centers in Europe (Berlin, London, Amsterdam, Vienna, Breslau, Leipzig, and Paris) to promote his ideas. "Seen in the light of the musar tradition that preceded him," Marc Angel remarks, "the thought and work of Rabbi Alkalai represented a revolutionary change of perspective. . . . He was daring enough to challenge the policy of acceptance,"[16] a policy that had always found expression in a preoccupation with the "stability of the world" and the fear that any minor change would endanger the entire traditional universe. While Alkalaʿi had grounded his initial call for a return to the Land of Israel on kabbalistic homiletics, he showed an increasing awareness of modern change. In his *Nehamat ha-Arets* (1866), he wrote, for example:

> As Ezekiel [36:26] has prophesied, "I shall give you a new heart, and a new spirit will I place within you." The spirit of the times does not ask of the individual that he follow the arbitrariness of his heart, but rather that he seek the good of the collective. The spirit of the times has nothing to do with the Torah and divine service, for what the times require is without distinction of religion or people. . . . The spirit of the times demands freedom and liberty for the success of the nation. And thus it demands of us to proclaim liberty to those in captivity. . . . The spirit of the times requires all of the countries to establish their land and to raise up their language. Likewise, it requires of us to establish our living home and to raise up our sacred language and to revive it.[17]

Here Judah Alkalaʿi openly acknowledges the novelty of his approach and advocates following the "spirit of the times," which is of a piece with nineteenth-century nationalist idealism.

Judah Papo was also aware of a "new spirit of the times," and, like Alkalaʿi, was convinced that it was positive. Nevertheless, the young Papo arrived at a different conclusion and, in his Judeo-Spanish version of the *Pele Yoʿets*, engaged in a subtle polemic against Alkalaʿi's activist program. In his chapter on redemption, he repeats his argument that the exile has become much easier to bear in most countries and that the spirit of the times has led to a rapprochement among the religions—that is, the gentiles have gradually approached the teachings of Judaism and can no longer be identified with the evil idolaters of old: "And as this progresses, it may naturally come about [*be-derekh tevaʿ*, i.e., not miraculously] that the kingdoms unite and find it right to confer all the [political] powers upon the Jewish people so that they may have their land and dominion over it. But even this cannot happen if we do not deserve it. . . . But by no means is it possible to say that this is certain, for certainty and truth are known only to the Lord of the world."[18] No less fascinated with current developments than his contemporary Judah Alkalaʿi, the young Papo envisions the gentile nations finally uniting to remedy the suffering of the Jewish people and establish a homeland for the Jews in the Land of Israel. But this will only come about if the Jews deserve it, if they remain faithful to their tradition precisely in these times of accelerated change. The crucial point of difference from Alkalaʿi's vision is that Papo sees the return of the Jews as depending on the good will and action of the non-Jewish countries. While he insists that the time is ripe and that the rapprochement of the religions has laid the ground for gentile action on behalf of the Jews, he denies that the Jews themselves have to play a part in the political process leading to the end of exile. Standing outside history, as it were, they must make sure they deserve redemption by stubbornly following rabbinic tradition and doing repentance, but not by taking the political initiative to settle the land as Alkalaʿi proposes.

Elsewhere, Judah Papo insists that "to make calculations to determine the time when the Messiah will come is to waste one's time, for this is a secret and no one can know the truth." Clearly opposing the messianic speculations and activism of Alkalaʿi and others (but without ever mentioning his adversaries), he insists that "even if we find calculations of the time in the *Gemara* and the holy *Zohar,* we must say that we do not understand their words, just as there are many other things that we still do not understand."[19]

We have thus seen three approaches to settling in the Land of Israel. While Eliʿezer Papo defends the traditional line, symbolically paying reverence to the Land of Israel and committing his readers to solidarity with its inhabitants, his son Judah—himself a resident of Jerusalem—adds an optimistic note to the traditional quietist attitude of his father. Speaking of a "rapprochement of the religions," he imagines a future coalition of gentile political powers which might restore the Jews to their homeland. Judah Alkalaʿi takes a position opposed to the consensus of the Ottoman rabbis. Expecting redemption to begin in the year 5600 (1840), he revolutionizes the traditional attitude of passivity and calls for the active return of the Jews to the Land and the revival of the Hebrew language. While both Judah Papo and Judah Alkalaʿi share an awareness that strong winds of change are blowing throughout the Jewish world (and the world at large), and while both sternly uphold the rabbinic tradition, their visions of the future could not be more different. The young Papo, though hoping for political circumstances that will prove favorable for the Jews, affirms the present order of Jewish existence in the diaspora; against this, Alkalaʿi defends an activist response to modernity, seizing on the ideology of nationalism rocking the Ottoman order at the time. He advocates a departure from that passive, stoic attitude which Judeo-Spanish musar literature demanded for the sake of the "stability of the world."

Under Egyptian Rule

In the 1830s, Rabbi Eliᶜezer Bergmann made reference to the Egyptian rule over Palestine under Muhammad Ali (1831–1840) in a letter from Jerusalem: "The Ishmaelites are greatly humbled, whereas the Jews, especially the Ashkenazi Jews, enjoy impressive status . . . so that it can almost be said that the Redemption has already begun."[20] In their messianic fervor, the group around the disciples of the Gaon of Vilna who had settled in the Holy Land saw in the establishment of Egyptian rule over Palestine an upheaval of theological significance, and paradoxically even considered this change of government to be a defeat of Muslim rule.[21] The legal situation of the religious minorities had in fact improved under Muhammad Ali's rule (though more so for the Christians than for the Jews). In some cases, Jews were permitted to repair old synagogues or to build new ones; they also gained representation in the newly established local councils (*madjlis*). Nevertheless, the years of Egyptian rule were also hard in many ways and witnessed some of the worst anti-Jewish violence in the recent history of Palestine and Syria. In 1834, Egyptian soldiers massacred Jews in Hebron after putting down a local Muslim insurrection. Other incidents of pillaging, killing, and rape occurred in Jerusalem that same year; in Safed, Jews were attacked by Muslim and Druze peasants in 1834 and in 1837, the latter case following the Safed earthquake that left many people dead.[22]

The musar book *Imre Binah* (1837) by Isaac Farhi, one of the Judeo-Spanish musar authors who lived in Jerusalem, includes a detailed account of the violence which erupted in Jerusalem in 1834 in the wake of a local Muslim revolt against the new Egyptian governor. It is interesting to contrast the picture drawn there with the (rather naive) messianic enthusiasm among the group around the disciples of the Gaon of Vilna of the same years.

Farhi's text begins by setting the historical stage. In 1834, when Ibrahim Pasha assumed control over Jerusalem, he created a council to administer the rule of law, composed of eight Muslims and one representative each from among the Jews, the Greeks, the Armenians, and the Europeans. The issue that set the local Muslims against Ibrahim Pasha, we learn from Farhi's explanation, was the order to recruit one out of every five Muslims to serve in the Egyptian army, which was then at war with the Ottomans. A local Muslim, Qasim al-Ahmad of Nablus, began to gather a peasant army to take control of Jerusalem and defy the Egyptian governor, particularly his institution of a military draft.

Farhi's account is a good testimony to the precarious situation in which Jews lived in mid-nineteenth-century Palestine and tells us much about the hardships of the days when Jerusalem was in the hands of the rebels. Jews were always potential victims of pillage, rape, and other violence, and had good reason to fear the local rebels as well as the Egyptian soldiers. In the best case, they could hope to buy off the attackers, as in Farhi's description of armed peasants (*felahim*) who, for exorbitant fees, "protected" Jewish homes against attacks.[23]

פרק שביעי אמרי בינה חנוכה ופורים ס

מירה עוכר ישראל· אי אין· אויינדו איסטוס גזרה· סי
מיזו אה לה אונה קון לום תונגרים גראנדים דילה סיבֿדאד
פֿארה סיר מורד· קון דיזיינדולים ליין סו קאדיר די אקו-
זיר פֿילאחים גבורי חיל כחול הים· אי לו חזימום פֿיויר
מאיל סﬞניּיור אה פֿי דיסקאלסו· אי איסטי לאקירדי
פֿוחי בﬞתר· אי מיזו מעשה חיל חרזר קאחכים אל אחמד·
אי פֿאלﬞייו דילה סיבֿדאד חיל אי סום דום איזﬞום מחנסי-
בﬞום · אי ריבﬞולבﬞיירון חיל מונדו· אי סי אינפֿיסחארון אה
קוֹחרסי חיל נדול· אי מיטיירון מיינטים פֿור בﬞניר סובﬞרי
ירושלם תﬞו אי סוﬞינגואֿרלה· אי אנסי פֿוחי קי אין דיאה
די 16 אייר סי סירו לה סיבֿדאד סיינדו לייה בﬞניּירון
סומﬞה די פֿילאחים אי לה איזﬞיירון מוחסירי· אי נו חבﬞיאה
קין סאלﬞיירה· ני קין אינטרחרﬞה· אי איל קאמינו די יפו
לו סיר/זרון קי נו פֿודיאה בﬞולﬞר פֿאשﬞארו· פֿור קי נו
חובﬞיירה מולדי די דאר חחביר חמיל משנה יר"ך· אי
פֿוחי אין אקיל מיזמו דיאה קי סי סירו לה סיבֿדאד אוﬞ-
רחם די מידיין דיאה· מיזו חון רעש מוי פֿוחירטי קוﬞה
קי חיל קי איסטחבֿה די אונה בﬞאנדה· קאחיאה פֿור לה
אוטרה· אי בﬞימום קון מוחיסטרום חוﬞום קומו לﬞם פֿארי-
דים סי איזﬞאן חקוסטחנדו די חון לונגﬞר אל אוטרו· אי
טורו אין חון הלוך קרוב די סינקו פֿונטוס· אי טודו ירושלם
אין חון פֿידﬞאסו די לייורו אי איסקלﬞמחﬞסיון· אקﬞרﬞר
קי לום פֿילאחים קי איסטחבﬞאן דירידור דילה קﬞלי· ליים
פֿאריסייו קי איזﬞיירון לﬞמנום די חדיינטרו· אי דיירון פֿולבﬞורה·
אי

One key to understanding Farhi's testimony is its inclusion in the chapter entitled "Hanukkah and Purim," holidays that commemorate deliverance from oppression and danger through divine intervention. In the same way that the rabbinic readings of the stories of Hanukkah and Purim feature divine intervention at certain crucial points, Isaac Farhi wishes to demonstrate that—in spite of all the unpleasant incidents—the Jews of Jerusalem in general and he himself in particular had been saved from much worse evil through a series of divinely ordained, miraculous events. For example, when the peasant rebels have massacred fifty Egyptian soldiers sent by the governor in Jaffa and are firmly in control of Jerusalem and the roads linking the Holy City with the coastal plain, the situation of the Jews is precarious. In particular, the general insecurity leaves the Jewish poor without the assistance that they desperately need; there is concern that they will starve, as no one dares to leave his home to give food to those in need. Three *talmide hakhamim* approach Farhi and ask what they should do. The author himself and many others generously provide them with the money necessary to buy flour for the poor. Farhi explains that, as the community has proven worthy of divine help because it heard the cries of its poor, God has taken notice of the suffering of the Jews in the besieged Jerusalem. Miraculously, the Egyptian governor is informed about the situation in Jerusalem and immediately takes the necessary measures.

> That Monday [when the first 50 Egyptian soldiers were killed] . . . when the Jews were in great distress, the governor received notice, and it is unknown whether it was in a dream or whether a fortune-teller told him—in any event, it did not happen in a natural way. . . . He sat down and wrote a letter to his father, the great ruler Muhammad Ali Pasha, that he should send him soldiers and armament. And it was a divine miracle that he sent the letter on Tuesday morning and the great ruler received it in twenty-four hours. In just two hours he filled eighteen ships with soldiers and armament, and they arrived in Jaffa at noon on Wednesday, something which has not been seen or heard in the world: how great are Your deeds, oh Lord![24]

Farhi is thus suggesting that the Egyptian authorities could not possibly have received information about the situation in Jerusalem and reacted so forcefully without divine intervention. Though we may suspect that improved standards of communication—particularly on the Egyptian side—played a role in that "miracle," for Farhi relief came as a divine response to the prayers of the Jews in Jerusalem and in recognition of the consideration shown for the Jewish poor in a time of crisis. The Egyptian army thus successfully put down the revolt in Jerusalem, the situation eased, and the danger for the Jewish inhabitants of the city passed. Two Jews had been killed during the siege and much material damage had been caused to the Jewish community.

But the suppression of the revolt was not the end of the story for the author. Six *felahim* from the Hebron area who were still in the city entered the abandoned house next to Farhi's and could easily have come into the Farhi family's courtyard.

But "God covered the eyes of these *felahim*,"[25] and, after a long, fearful night for the Farhis, the intruders left the house without doing them any harm.

Isaac Farhi's long, detailed accounts of this rebellion in Jerusalem and other upheavals in Hebron and Safed which also had dire consequences for the local Jewish communities are a far cry from the redemptive optimism advocated by the pupils of the Gaon of Vilna or the messianic activism of a Judah Alkalaʿi. Farhi clearly sees himself and the Jews of Jerusalem as still living in a condition of exile. Farhi's account of the 1830s in the Land of Israel only reinforces the conclusion that, in the traditional rabbinic view, a redemptive "return" from exile was impossible, not least because a return to the geographical area called Palestine was not all that was involved. The centrality of Jerusalem and the Land of Israel is an important idea in their worldview, but the spiritual center—the Temple—has been destroyed. *Galut* is a condition, a human and specifically Jewish condition, which affects Isaac Farhi writing in Jerusalem no less than his readers in the diaspora. For Sephardic rabbis (except Judah Alkalaʿi), "home" is not a geographical term but rather a concept of time (memory of the biblical past, hope for future redemption), and "exile" is a theological concept (punishment and atonement).

In Defense of Jerusalem

In the eighteenth century, most of the pilgrims who visited the Land of Israel and those who decided to settle there came from communities in the Ottoman Empire, as did the greater part of the financial contributions to the well-being of the *yishuv*. However, this situation changed considerably in the nineteenth century. The numbers of pilgrims, settlers, and sponsors diminished, the once all-important institution of the *Peqide Erets Yisraʾel be-Qushta*[26] lost much of its status, and immigrants now came from Europe or North Africa instead of other regions of the Ottoman Empire. Modern European institutions like the Alliance Israélite Universelle (or, in the early twentieth century, the German *Hilfsverein* and the Zionist organizations) took over the initiative. The reasons for this development cannot be sought only in the economic difficulties experienced by the nineteenth-century Ottoman Jewish communities; Jacob Barnai holds that the Land of Israel itself had improved economically and thus should have attracted more immigrants; yet it attracted fewer.[27]

The stance of the Judeo-Spanish rabbis toward the centrality of the Land of Israel in the nineteenth century was dictated by two concerns. On the one hand, as we have seen, the rabbis did not encourage their readers to actually move to the Holy Land. They saw the economic problems as a major obstacle and did not set the *mitsvah* of settling the Holy Land above any other commandment. While they affirmed the centrality of Jerusalem as an idea, and the bond between the diaspora and the center was symbolically reinforced by charity to the inhabitants of the Holy Land, the rabbis did not approve of any activities to "hasten redemption" and the return to *Erets Yisraʾel*.

On the other hand, with the spread of an idealized West as a cultural model and the secularization and transformation of patterns of social practice, the centrality of Israel could no longer be taken for granted. An increasing number of "modernizers" dissociated themselves from the centrality of the Land of Israel as a symbol of a utopian ideal to be realized through the meticulous observance of religious law and the study of Torah. The critics of the traditional order challenged the centrality of Jerusalem by pointing to the dismaying "facts on the ground." The Judeo-Spanish rabbis of the nineteenth century would take up the defense of Jerusalem and the Holy Land. The first reaction is best illustrated by a lengthy passage in Judah Papo's chapter entitled "*Mitsvot*" (added to the Hebrew *Pele Yo͑ets*), in which the author not only depicts the Land of Israel as an idea but now refers to the *real* Jerusalem, presenting the *yishuv* as a social model.

As we learned from the description in Farhi's *Imre Binah*, political conditions were difficult for the Jewish communities in the Land of Israel on more than one occasion around the mid-nineteenth century. The rabbis testify also to the widespread poverty and harsh economic conditions under which Jews were living. All this Jewish suffering in the very heart of the Jewish symbolic geography—how can it be explained? Judah Papo is quick to state that this suffering must not be understood as punishment for the Jerusalemite Jews' own sins. Indeed, he insists, there are very few sins among the Jerusalem Sephardic and Ashkenazic communities, but many merits: "There is no shaving of the beard or the sidelocks. There is no drinking of un-kosher wine. Sexual transgressions, perhaps one in a thousand is found. There is no gambling and no comedies [i.e., a theater]. The great majority pray with a *minyan* and very few pray alone. There is a lot of studying among the *ba͑ale batim*."[28] The examples are not randomly chosen, of course: Papo presents the Jerusalem Jewish community as a model to be followed, as a community still safe from the evils of westernization. All the sins he enumerates as absent from Jerusalem are those identified as signs of secularization throughout the Ottoman diaspora. Shaving one's beard stands for adopting the signifiers of Western culture, drinking non-kosher wine for the dangers of secular socializing, and it will be remembered that Papo attacks the wealthy westernizers for not praying with a *minyan*. While Papo, in the early 1870s, presents the Jerusalem Jewish community as a safe haven from the evils of westernization—surely an idealized view even in his time—things were to change considerably in the subsequent decades. Westernization reached Jerusalem too, eloquently denounced by Isaac Badhab in his *Nehemadim mi-Zahav*. We return to the latter case below.

But why, then, do the inhabitants of Jerusalem suffer poverty and violence? "We must say for certain," reiterates the Judeo-Spanish *Pele Yo͑ets*, citing the eighteenth-century rabbi H. J. D. Azulai, "that this is not because of their sins but for the sins of other places and old sins [of earlier generations]." All misery is caused by the sins of others and "they bear all the evils to atone for the sins of all Jews."[29] Papo uses the notion that Jews living in the center are atoning for the sins of their generation and preceding ones (which is not new in itself) as a way to reinvest the concept of the centrality of the Holy Land with meaning. If they are atoning for the sins of the generations, Jerusalem and its community are not only assured of centrality, but in fact they also guarantee the "stability of the world," the future existence of the Jewish people and the traditional symbolic order. Those who commit sins, particularly the sins enumerated above, and blur the lines between Jewish and foreign culture, between the sacred and the profane, are ultimately responsible for the suffering in the Holy Land (and beyond).

While Jerusalem is called the "capital of Torah" and the "capital of Judaism," it is also the "capital of poverty."[30] Many musar authors deplore the miserable economic situation in the Land of Israel and the poverty in which the Jews live there: "There are no people with great capital who could live off their interest; there are no people with income from real estate; there are no people with large enterprises who would need to employ servants or secretaries. They can only support themselves with trade and crafts."[31] There is some commercial activity in the textile industry, but people in Jerusalem have little capital and, as Papo puts it, "the one who has little capital loses it easily."[32] In textile-related and all other professions, there are too many people and too little demand to keep the local economy going, and most people, whatever their professions, are out of work or underemployed. There are more women than men, most people are poor, and the number of orphans is also distressing.[33] Especially affected by poverty are the many *talmide hakhamim* who dwell in the Land of Israel, as Isaac Farhi points out: "And because of the many sins most poverty is found among the *talmide hakhamim*. . . . And this is found mostly in the Land of Israel. They learn and study Torah without having a shirt to wear. And when the situation becomes intolerable [*cuando ya les toca el cuchillo a-el güeso*] they are obliged to leave and travel the world, over fields and streets, sea and land, passing many hardships in search of God's pity."[34]

The rabbis' response to the situation is to insist on the responsibility of the diaspora communities to support their brethren in the Land of Israel. "Even the [gentile] nations have pity and send support and give much money to sustain their people in Jerusalem," urges Judah Papo; we have seen a similar formulation elsewhere in the *Pele Yoʿets.* "All the more should we do the same, for the true sanctity [of Jerusalem] is ours, and Jerusalem is our land."[35]

Ultimately, Papo's response echoes the accepting stance of the vernacular rabbis when confronted with social inequality. In fact, I would claim that the quietist stance toward exile largely conditions the rabbis' response to social problems. Although they denounce injustice, they always make sure to maintain the status quo, guaranteeing the stability of the traditional order at large. Just as charity emerges as the stabilizing answer to intra-community social inequality and men are reminded of their obligations toward their wives as a response to gender inequality, Papo (and all others musar authors) invoke the instrumental role of the diaspora communities as an answer to the difficulties faced by the *yishuv* in the Land of Israel. In contrast to a radical (though traditional) thinker like Judah Alkalaʿi, they do not envision changing the general situation in Palestine and they do not propose any way of arriving at a long-term improvement of the Jewish condition in the Holy Land, but rather appeal to the time-honored practice of financially supporting a colony of *talmide hakhamim* in the Land of Israel from outside.

Papo is plainly writing these lines for a diaspora public, requesting solidarity with the *yishuv*. While the Judeo-Spanish *Pele Yo'ets* does not promote mass emigration to the Land of Israel any more than the earlier Hebrew text did, it fights off a challenge to the centrality of Jerusalem in the symbolic universe, and of the symbolic universe itself. Papo complains that people speak ill of Jerusalem, which, he asserts, is totally unjustified. Of course, "it is impossible to say that there is no fault in Jerusalem. They are no angels. . . . Poverty does not leave good virtue. . . . Nonetheless the Jews are lucky, for, as we said, much good is found and very little evil."[36]

Papo gives several examples of complaints typically made against the *yishuv* in Jerusalem.[37] One unjust accusation is that the Jews living in the Holy City "want to eat promptly, but they do not want to work and earn [their own living]." Papo rejects this as an unfounded prejudice and points to the difficult economic situation: people in Jerusalem do take pains to earn their living, but circumstances being adverse, they still depend on funding from abroad. Another prejudice is that the Jews in Jerusalem have their children marry at a very early age. Papo claims that this is actually a virtuous thing to do, and that the age of marriageability set by the Mishnah at eighteen should be understood as a maximum rather than a minimum age. A further charge is that Jerusalem destroys peace between husband and wife; but we are told that this is due to the fact that there are people from all over the world in the Holy Land and Jews of different backgrounds marry, causing potential conflicts unknown in more homogeneous communities in the diaspora. Finally, "They have another complaint that the gentlemen from Europe tried hard to open schools in Jerusalem to teach [foreign] languages and writing, which is something that advances employment, and that the rabbis of Jerusalem always refused and did not accept this."[38] Papo rejects this too as a false accusation. Later in the same chapter he comes back to the rabbis' and his own objections to the modern schools:

> We have said that heresy and epicureanism come from reading the books of philosophers, heretics and epicureans. Where do the [westernizers] have this from? Because they dedicated themselves to learning foreign languages and writing. . . . Many rabbis protested . . . saying that this will damage Judaism, and many ridiculed those rabbis, saying that it is an improvement for the nation. . . . But from what we are saying it is clear that the rabbis were right in their protest, for [learning foreign languages and writing] is a dangerous thing that leads the person away from Judaism, and there is nothing to counterweigh this damage done to Judaism.[39]

Papo explains that in particular in Jerusalem, studying foreign languages is just a waste of time, for few people maintain business relations with Europe and therefore they have little use for what the modern schools have to offer. However, he admits, "we cannot deny the truth that it is good, a perfection and an advantage, and necessary to know languages and writing. But one has to be very sure, lest it damage one's faith and Judaism. Sons and daughters should not be sent to [foreign language] schools unless they are first well rooted in faith in our Torah, and they should not be allowed to see books that could damage their faith."[40]

Papo defends himself (and the Jerusalem rabbis) against the claim that they are opposed to giving their children a good education, including knowledge of European languages. Learning foreign languages is called "good," an "advantage," and "necessary." But, Papo contends, to venture beyond the secure confines of traditional knowledge is dangerous, and it is irresponsible to have one's children attend foreign language schools without first making sure that they are firmly rooted in tradition. First comes musar education, and only then foreign languages. European and westernizing literature presents a danger because it opens up new horizons and challenges the self-contained exclusiveness of traditional knowledge. The problem of foreign language schools is not the fact that they teach European languages, but that they open the door to a foreign and disorienting world.

It is very significant that in the second edition of Papo's *Pele Yo'ets*, published in 1900, part of this passage is missing. Instead, the text reads: "We have said that heresy and epicureanism come from reading the books of philosophers, heretics and epicureans. Where do the [westernizers] have this from? Because they dedicated themselves to learning foreign languages and writing. We cannot deny the truth that it is good, a perfection and an advantage, and necessary to know languages and writing."[41] The intermediate part of the original passage, citing the reason of the rabbis' opposition to modern schools, is missing, thus giving more weight to Papo's more pragmatic declaration that the study of foreign languages is agreeable as long as it is preceded by a solid traditional education. Unless the omission is accidental (it is the only such change in the text between its two printings that I have come across), it would seem that the study of foreign languages was so well established by 1900 that it did not make sense to oppose it in principle as authors writing earlier in the century still did.

Papo's approach, both in the original version from 1872 and in its later variant, is a typically defensive response to the challenges of modernity. Papo sees himself as forced to accept the usefulness and necessity of learning foreign languages, but he rejects the "civilizing mission" of the Alliance Israélite Universelle and other European institutions. One might use French for business but should not read French literature; accepting that a certain degree of change is still compatible with tradition, Papo hopes to keep the spirit of modernity out.

It is certainly no coincidence that this attitude of Ottoman Sephardic rabbis to the study of the French language and to Western culture in general is similar to the attitude adopted by many Muslim Ottoman intellectuals and reformers, an ambiguous attitude that informs the entire Ottoman political reform effort in the nineteenth century: not unlike Papo, they try to distinguish between the "good" or useful side of Western civilization (material culture, sciences, technological progress), and a "negative" or corrupt side of Western culture (in particular its secularism). When opening the new imperial medical school in 1838, Sultan Mahmud II declared, for example: "You will study scientific medicine in French. . . . My purpose in having you taught French is not to educate in the French literature; it is to teach you scientific medicine and little by little to take it into our language."[42]

The Holy Land and the West

Judah Papo describes the Jewish community of Jerusalem in somewhat idealistic terms. Another author, Isaac Badhab, draws a very different picture toward the end of the nineteenth century. Now all the westernizing practices which Papo had declared absent from Jerusalem are described as having made inroads into the Sephardic community of Jerusalem. I have quoted passages from Badhab's musar treatise in which he denounces the dangers of leisure and condemns secular socializing.[43] Elsewhere, he complains about the fact that young men shave their beards (Papo had maintained that this could not be found in Jerusalem), and he criticizes the women who, while pretending to follow the rules of female decency, are eager to emulate European fashions. "The women whose hair must not be seen make themselves fancy wigs," he says, and add a plait "no different from those of the young girls," "and thus they take liberties and go out into the streets without a head covering, without even a scarf, and one who does not know them certainly takes them for non-Jewish women."[44]

Badhab does not hesitate to assert that one who shaves his beard is like an idolater. He explains that even if some use scissors to cut their beards, not a knife, this is still forbidden, because the result looks as if they had used a knife.[45] Women openly defy the rules of decency and adopt Western fashion no less than men. But this is not his only complaint. Even in the Holy City, people do not respect the Sabbath, taking strolls and carrying things beyond the city limits:

> They are very careful about their handkerchiefs and tie it to their belts [for it is forbidden on the Sabbath to carry outside the ʿeruv]. . . . But nevertheless they hold a walking stick in their hands. . . . Moreover, now . . . that the post office has been set up outside the city, they not only move from one area to another [which is forbidden on the Sabbath] but also open their letters and read them. If some receive bad news about their business or private difficulties, they are troubled.[46]

Badhab is obviously still writing about a fairly traditional society, certainly if compared to religious observance in turn-of-the-century Europe. From this point of view, even Isaac Badhab's moralizing, lachrymose book testifies to the remarkable hold which tradition still exerts over everyday social practice. Women comply with the rules of decency that forbid exposing their own hair, but they do so by wearing fancy wigs and follow Western fashion. People take care to tie their handkerchiefs to their belts lest they carry on the Sabbath, but then venture beyond the city limits to read their letters in the new post office. Or consider the example cited earlier of young people going to the tavern on the Sabbath, but only after making sure that they will not have to pay on that day. What Badhab describes here is entirely consistent with the mode of response to secularizing trends which Harvey

Goldberg has described for North African Jewry at the time: "In general, patterns of secular life that emerged among the Jews of North Africa did so gradually and selectively. Certain aspects of tradition were abandoned, while others were maintained, but this rarely became a matter of consistent principle or of ideology." He proposes "to view their religious lives not in terms of a systematic reaction to the challenges of modernity, but as the cut-and-paste continuation of traditional patterns."[47] This is also applicable to the Sephardic Jews of Jerusalem as depicted by Isaac Badhab and, indeed, throughout Judeo-Spanish musar literature. For the great majority, westernization and secularization were not a matter of ideology; but as new options emerged with the processes of modernization, new amalgamations of traditional observance and secular social practices were negotiated.

A more serious challenge to the rabbinic universe was perhaps presented by the activities of the Christian missionaries in the Holy Land, arguably of special urgency in Jerusalem, where a great number of missionary schools, hospitals, and other institutions were established as a result of European powers' race to gain a foothold in the Ottoman Levant. Westernization was in most cases promoted by *Jewish* European agents of change (the Alliance Israélite Universelle and others) and not, as in European countries, through a state-imposed program of "regeneration" as a precondition for emancipation. But Badhab describes the challenge as arising from the activities of non-Jewish (Christian) European institutions. He laments that the Christian mission has taken advantage of the needs of the community and opened a hospital and schools for boys and girls, "and they meet all their needs with their tremendous financial power." Moreover, many people are buying Ladino Bible translations published by the mission "because they are cheap." Badhab is ready to forgive those who have recourse to Christian institutions out of need, if they are poor and if there are no alternatives. But no justification is possible now that there are Jewish hospitals and schools in and around Jerusalem, he adds bitterly.[48] It is clear why the rabbis were concerned with people sending their children to non-Jewish schools. The problem was not restricted to Jerusalem, of course, and similar complaints can be found in many other musar books of the nineteenth century.[49] Nevertheless, there is no indication whatsoever that attending foreign, non-Jewish schools or reading the Ladino Bible translations of Protestant missionaries had significant social consequences for the cultural outlook of Ottoman Sephardic communities.

In the *Nehemadim mi-Zahav*, Jerusalem is thus no longer the piously regarded model to be emulated that it was in Papo's work, and Badhab does not hesitate to look for positive models in the diaspora. He approvingly cites a rule of Salonikan rabbis forbidding male musicians at weddings and other celebrations to perform in front of women, or female musicians to play before men, concluding, "I wish our *hakhamim* [in Jerusalem] did the same."[50] With Badhab we return to the traditional rabbinic attitude toward the Land of Israel. Isaac Badhab was born, lived, and wrote his book in Jerusalem, yet exile was the central experience for him. He saw himself as living in exile no less than Eliᶜezer Papo, who wrote in the Ottoman Balkans in the first quarter of the century.

Conclusion

"The combination of memory and neglect which made of the Land [of Israel] both a center of aspiration and a periphery to actual existence"[51] is also evident in Judeo-Spanish musar literature. While the Holy Land is an important part of the topography of the rabbinic symbolic universe, the role of the real Land of Israel is far from central. When Judah Papo defends Jerusalem against those who challenge the validity of the Land of Israel as a cultural point of reference, he wants to reaffirm the traditional symbolic relation of the diaspora to its center, through charity and pilgrimage, but does not encourage active settlement any more than his father did; he polemicizes against those (like Judah Alkalaʿi) who believe that they can hasten redemption by means of a large-scale return to the land. Those who live in the Land of Israel—Farhi in the first half of the nineteenth century, Badhab at the end of the century—still express a feeling of homelessness and exile even though they live in the city of Jerusalem. For Judeo-Spanish musar literature, "homecoming" remains a utopia. Thus, it is not surprising to see that political Zionism does not take root in the large urban centers of the Ottoman Empire (notably Istanbul and Salonika) until a relatively late stage.[52] The Land of Israel always occupies a central place in the imagery of Ottoman Sephardic Jewry and is also promoted in Ladino rabbinic literature. But it is, and remains, peripheral to the actual experience of Ottoman Jewry in the eighteenth century and, even more so, in the nineteenth century.

Reincarnation and the Discovery of History

10

Time can be defined as the difference between past and future,[1] and the experience of time as the difference between the realm of experience (memory) and the horizon of expectation (hope).[2] Time, for Judeo-Spanish musar, is experienced as the tension or difference between the mythic past of biblical times and the suffering throughout the history of exile, and as the difference between the memory of exile and the expectation of redemption. For the rabbis, it is ultimately the difference and tension between the imperfection of humanity and the perfection of the divine order.

I explore here how Judeo-Spanish musar literature approaches time. In a first step, I show how history is traditionally understood as suffering, and how suffering is explained and legitimized within the parameters of the traditional symbolic universe. I then present the new approach to the representation of history in Amarachi and Sason's musar books published in the 1840s, which incorporate passages from the sixteenth-century *Shevet Yehudah* in Judeo-Spanish translation. Finally I discuss how messianic expectation and the future are depicted in vernacular Sephardic musar literature.

The Earthquake of Safed (1837): History as Suffering

In the preceding chapter, we saw Isaac Farhi's account of the violence in Jerusalem in 1834. This is not the only reference to the difficulties of the Jewish community in the Land of Israel at the time. In the chapter entitled "*Tishʿah be-Av*," we find (after a brief description of the violent attacks on the Jews of Hebron committed by the Egyptian soldiers who had put down a local revolt, also in 1834) the following account of the 1837 earthquake in Safed and Tiberias.

> An even greater evil happened in the year 5597 [1837]: On the 24th of *Tevet*, in the afternoon of the first day of the week, there was a heavy earthquake in the Land of Israel, and because of our many sins, the wrath [of God] seized Safed and Tiberias. In one moment, all of Safed was destroyed and not one wall remained as a sign. And because of our many sins, two thousand people died in Safed and four hundred in Tiberias. Woe to us that this great evil has happened in our time. One day after the event became known, people from Jerusalem, Hebron, and Damascus went there to bury the dead. Many *talmide hakhamim* went there and when they approached, they saw the city destroyed and raised their voice in lamentation, moaning, and wailing, and moaned for the holy city of Safed and all the beautiful synagogues that had been there, and the beautiful *yeshivot* . . . and for so many Jewish souls that perished, and began their work digging [graves] to bury [the dead]. They found so many kinds of affliction as to make heaven and

earth wail. They found women who had been breast-feeding their children, and still the mothers were united with their babies, the breast in their mouth. They found young boys still with a piece of bread in their mouth, for they had finished their study and they were eating. They had no time to swallow the bite they had taken when the evil decree overwhelmed them. They found a great Ashkenazic rabbi in his tallit and tefillin and the *Midrash Rabah* in his hands, and such things as one trembles to hear of. . . . It is appropriate to wail day and night, for this evil cannot be forgotten. Our sins have certainly caused all this, particularly the sin of neglecting [the study of] Torah, for because of our many sins we are very weak and lose our time without taking a book to study. . . . Therefore it is time to turn in complete repentance.[3]

The outstanding feature of Farhi's description is the complete incomprehensibility of the suffering in Safed. For the reader of Farhi's text, it is difficult to take refuge in a simple theory of divine retribution. Innocent children and righteous sages lost their lives; women feeding their children and a rabbi wearing *talit* and *tefilin*, reading the *Midrash Rabah*, are among the victims of the earthquake which destroyed the city of Safed, one of the most important Jewish centers in the Ottoman Empire. All this culminates in a passionate call for repentance, because "our sins have . . . caused all this." The catastrophe in Safed in 1837, like Jewish suffering in exile generally, seems to be a breach in the scheme of divine justice and seems to call into question the integrity of divine order. But this is only apparent, explains Farhi; "we," the author and his readers, have caused the fracture in the divine order "because of our sins."

The rabbis explain the suffering of innocent and righteous people as representative suffering: the suffering soul of the righteous atones for the sins of either earlier generations, the sins of the contemporary generation, or else its own sins in an earlier reincarnation (*gilgul*).[4] This suffering for the atonement of the sins of the generations invests it with heroic meaning. The cause of suffering is the corruption of the world order as a result of human sin generally, and Farhi encourages his readers to acknowledge their responsibility for the agony of those innocent people in Safed and to repent. Significantly, the main reason given for the catastrophe is identified with the neglect of Torah study—precisely the ill that Judeo-Spanish musar seeks to remedy.

Every symbolic universe has to explain, or legitimize, suffering and death as "the marginal situation *par excellence.*" The "legitimation of death is . . . one of the most important fruits of symbolic universes."[5] Suffering appears to be a breach in the symbolic universe. But in truth, the rabbis explain, it is precisely those who disrespect and challenge the laws governing the universe who are responsible for the corruption of the ideal order. It is thus only appropriate that the quintessential activity to preserve the universe—devoted ritual study, *meldar*—is invested with so much importance. Only continuous reaffirmation of the traditional universe through study can remedy such existential disruptions of order. Farhi does not look for a "natural" explanation of earthquakes or political reasons for the violence in Egyptian-occupied Palestine. He understands history as a function of the symbolic universe; suffering is thus given meaning, and a remedy—however utopian—is provided by the image of a studious (*meldando*) and repentant society.

In consequence, Farhi and most Judeo-Spanish rabbis see no point in seeking to improve the situation of the Jews in the Holy Land or elsewhere by transforming and changing the traditional universe. European-inspired programs of modernizing the *yishuv* remain irrelevant and insufficient. Change is actually dangerous if it means casting off the yoke of Torah and taking the commandments lightly, because only full immersion in the traditional symbolic universe and its social order can explain and (eventually, in a utopian future) remedy pain, poverty, and powerlessness: in short, the condition of exile.[6]

Farhi's assertion that the righteous and innocent are suffering for the sins of their generation allows him to appeal to his readers to repent and to immerse themselves in traditional study. Often, suffering is discussed in terms linking it to the past (it is retribution for past sins or even a past *gilgul*) or the future (it earns the sufferer a place in the world to come). Abraham Palachi enumerates these explanations in his chapter on suffering:

> [1] . . . When suffering afflicts him or the people of his household physically or financially, then he must consider carefully what sin caused the suffering, for it is certainly not without purpose. . . . It is to atone for sins. . . . [2] Sometimes a person suffers even though he is a righteous man, because of a past *gilgul,* or because of the sins of his parents. . . . [3] It is known that the righteous man endures suffering out [of] love [*yisurin shel ahavah*] . . . for God's love for him brings suffering upon him in order to benefit him, so that he will end well and his sons will live well, and also to make him merit the world to come and give him a greater reward.[7]

The first type of suffering—suffering for one's own sins—does not pose an ethical problem for a worldview based on the notion of divine justice as reward and punishment; what really tests the traditional divine order is seemingly senseless and undeserved suffering. The only solution here is to project the causes of suffering back into an unknown past (one does not know the origins and wanderings of one's soul) or forward into an unknowable future (the hope of having a share in the world to come). The implication is that the causes of suffering are beyond historical time. The notion of metempsychosis also demonstrates the musar rabbis' understanding of time. "History" is not merely the course of chronological time; "the true history of the world would seem to be that of the migrations and interrelations of the souls," as Gershom Scholem remarked on the notion of metempsychosis in Lurianic thought.[8]

The pervasiveness of the concept of *gilgul* has been pointed out for Lurianic Kabbalah, but it also permeated Judeo-Spanish musar's approach to suffering. Earlier kabbalists "knew nothing of a universal law of transmigration considered as a system of moral causality";[9] the old Kabbalah associated the transmigration of souls above all with sexual trangressions. Lurianic Kabbalah developed a far more inclusive concept of metempsychosis. An example is Elijah ha-Kohen's *Shevet*

Musar, which presents a long list of transgressions and the corresponding *gilgul* for each of them:

> I will give you many examples [of] how the soul of the wicked returns in *gilgul,* so that the person may remember it and will not sin and will thus escape this agony. The *Kavanot ha-Ar"i* writes that the one who has marital relations in candlelight returns in *gilgul* of a goat. The one who is haughty against other people returns in *gilgul* of a wasp. The one who has killed a person returns in *gilgul* of water, and the proof is "[Only ye shall not eat the blood;] thou shalt pour it out upon the earth as water" [Deut. 12:16]. The one who has illicit sexual relations with a married or engaged woman returns in *gilgul* of a water mill, and there both, man and woman, are judged. The one who speaks slander returns in *gilgul* of a stone.[10]

The list goes on for another two pages. The transmigration of souls represents the experience of homelessness in exile: the loss of home—a powerful metaphor for the homelessness of the Jewish people—and the loss of historical time in exile. Every person's fate is determined at least as much by prior *gilgulim* as it is by contemporary, external conditions and by the psychological struggle between the good and evil inclinations.

Let us return to Isaac Farhi's explanation for the suffering of the righteous in Safed. It is significant that Farhi includes this passage in his chapter on the day commemorating the destruction of the Temple, the ninth of Av. The destruction of Jerusalem is the *ur*-catastrophe for the musar rabbis, determining the pattern for understanding and legitimizing suffering in exile within the parameters of the symbolic universe of rabbinic tradition. The clear challenge to the order of this universe posed by the destruction of the Temple and the ensuing exile call for a reconciliation with the symbolic order. Once it is established that man's sinful acts are responsible for the suffering, which is understood in terms of punishment, musar literature sets out to establish a system of values for the community to prevent individual and general punishment from recurring. Many musar authors encourage their readers to "learn from history," as Isaac Badhab expresses it in what is perhaps the best example of this attitude in our textual corpus:

> From all this [his description of the sins that led to the destructions of the First and Second Temples] comes the great obligation for us to wake up from this evil sleep which obscures the brightness of our soul. All this comes to us . . . because we do not endeavor to know the stories of our [past] [*muestros cuentos*], for only by studying them is there enough strength in them to awaken our consciousness by putting to use everything that happened to our forefathers.[11]

Badhab's musar treatise *Nehemadim mi-Zahav* is built around the "causes of the destruction" of the First and Second Temples, and individual transgressions are identified as the causes of the first and second exiles.[12] Badhab is not interested in the historical circumstances of the destruction of Jerusalem, but in the symbolic figure of destruction and exile as deserved divine punishment.

The passage from Farhi's *Imre Binah* on the Safed earthquake clearly expresses the pain felt by the author. One suspects that it was not easy for him to accept this suffering as a just and ordered thing. But it is precisely the goal of musar literature—and Judeo-Spanish musar is no exception—to reaffirm the traditional universe in the face of the liminality of Jewish historical experience in exile. Time is understood as a tension between remembered suffering and hoped-for redemption.

Amarachi and Sason and the Discovery of History

Isaac Amarachi and Joseph Sason present a new approach to history. There can be no doubt that one purpose of their two Judeo-Spanish musar books, *Sefer Darkhe ha-Adam* and *Sefer Musar Haskel,* first published in the early 1840s, is to entertain. They also try to communicate knowledge, as all vernacular musar authors do. Nevertheless, their books are rather atypical of mid-nineteenth-century Judeo-Spanish musar in that they include secular (though not "foreign") knowledge in their educational enterprise. In a number of chapters, Amarachi and Sason present Judeo-Spanish translations of selected passages from Solomon ibn Verga's *Shevet Yehudah* (ed. princ. Adrianople 1554), "a precociously sociological analysis of Jewish historical suffering generally, and of the Spanish Expulsion in particular."[13]

I discuss the important question of Amarachi and Sason's integration of rabbinic and secular knowledge in the next chapter. Here, however, I mention the "historiographical" chapters taken from the *Shevet Yehudah.* The inclusion of historical subjects for their own sake (though arguably with a pedagogical purpose as well) alongside more predictable musar material is remarkable in itself. Amarachi and Sason's choice of source is also a novelty. For all its encyclopedic inclusiveness and the great number of sources used by Jacob Huli in his *Me'am Lo'ez* on Genesis, the *Shevet Yehudah* is not among the sources identified by Luis Landau in his study of Huli's work.[14] Elijah ha-Kohen refers twice to Ibn Verga's book, once quoting a *ma'aseh* which is related there[15] and a second time to support his argument that pride and presumption cause the envy of gentiles.[16] It seems that only Amarachi and Sason decided to include historiographical material from the *Shevet Yehudah* within the framework of vernacularized rabbinic literature.

The passages to be treated below revolve around episodes of blood libel against the Jews and discuss a chapter of *Musar Haskel* dedicated to the history of false messianic movements among the Jews. Both are announced in the introductions to the two books: the texts presented "are entertaining things which remove anxiety and sadness from the heart by telling of what happened in the times of Spain";[17] they are "entertaining" (*graciosas*) because all the cases of false accusations against the Jews that are described end happily with the Jews convincing the king of their innocence and with the disgrace of their persecutors. As for the messianic movements, "many evils have happened to Israel because of the false messiahs that have arisen. . . . Therefore, in the end [of our book] we will write about the messiah."[18]

Why did Amarachi and Sason include these readings from the *Shevet Yehudah?*

The answer is rather obvious in the blood libel case; they published their books in 1842, only two years after the Damascus affair. As will be remembered, a number of Jews in the city of Damascus were accused of ritual murder after an Italian monk and his servant had disappeared. The affair also caused much polemical and diplomatic activity in Europe and brought the fate of eastern Sephardic Jews to the attention of an emerging European Jewish public sphere. Only after the intervention of a delegation of European Jews (led by Sir Moses Montefiore of England and Adolphe Crémieux of France) and an unprecedented political campaign on behalf of the innocent Jewish prisoners in then Egyptian-controlled Damascus did the local authorities drop the charges. It is not within the scope of the present work to discuss the 1840 Damascus affair and its extremely important implications for European Jewish politics and the emergence of a secular, trans-national Jewish public sphere.[19] What interests us here is how two Ottoman Sephardic authors responded to the affair—without ever mentioning it explicitly—in their Judeo-Spanish musar books.

Chapter 6 of *Sefer Darkhe ha-Adam* is a translation from Ibn Verga's *Shevet Yehudah*.[20] The author-translators' preliminary remark suggests its purpose:

> The Temple was destroyed because of the senseless hatred that existed between one and another. Therefore, I wanted to present a story written by the [author of the] *Shevet Yehudah*, for in this story we learn that the Temple was destroyed because of senseless hatred, and we also learn from this story how to respond to those uncircumcised persons who claim that we Jews put blood into the *matsah* [the unleavened bread eaten during Passover].[21]

Again we find that the destruction of the Temple and its causes are the principal figure of collective memory thought to provide lessons for contemporary times. Ibn Verga recounts a discussion between King Alfonso and the Catholic scholar Thomas in which Thomas identifies the "natural causes" of the downfall of the Jews and the enduring exile. Strife and hatred brought down the Jewish commonwealth and led to the destruction of Jerusalem, but the hatred of the Jews is explained as the reaction of the ignorant "masses"—not of the learned elite (*ba'ale sekhel*)—against the economic success and the arrogance and pride ("*enseñoramiento*") of the Jews. Interwoven into the lengthy dispute between the king and Thomas is an account of some Christians who, at the instigation of a fanatical priest, accuse the Jews of having killed a child because they needed his blood. The accusation is proven false by following Thomas's counsel and the Christians admit that they tried to rid themselves of the Jews in order to get back lands which they had lost to pay off debts to Jewish money lenders. The king decides that the Jews should give back the land, but the blood libel is successfully disproven. Amarachi and Sason's second book, *Sefer Musar Haskel*, again takes up the issue, borrowing from the *Shevet Yehudah* another case of blood libel and the case of a frustrated plan to expel the Jews from the Papal state.[22]

Yosef Hayim Yerushalmi has remarked that in Ibn Verga's *Shevet Yehudah*

there is . . . not a trace of messianism, and in several respects its boldness and originality are impressive. Ibn Verga alone transfers the concept of "natural cause" . . .
from the sphere of philosophy and science to history, and it is he who went
farthest in exploring the real mundane causes of the Spanish expulsion. . . . The
truth is [however] that his use of "natural cause" by no means precludes or contradicts the notion of divine providence.[23]

But whereas the *Shevet Yehudah* was the most popular of the Jewish historiographical works written in the wake of the Spanish expulsion—Yerushalmi speaks of
seventeen different editions—its readers clearly were not so interested in the novelty of Ibn Verga's historiographical imagination. "By the time we come to the
third edition," writes Yerushalmi, "a Yiddish translation printed in Cracow in 1591
'for ordinary householders, men and women' [*far gemayne baale-batim, man un
vayber*], we can see from the title page that the *Shebet Yehudah* has been transmuted
perceptually into a standard piece of edifying folk literature."[24]

Although it is a reasonable assumption that Amarachi and Sason included
chapters from the *Shevet Yehudah* partly for their entertaining value, the book was
by no means a standard item in the popular library in the Judeo-Spanish world. Or
at least this is what the translator-authors suggest when they write in their introduction to the *Darkhe ha-Adam*, "These are things taken from some precious books
which are not available to everyone, like the *Sefer ha-Berit* and the *Shevet Yehudah*.
. . . We have translated it into Ladino, so that everyone can understand it."[25] I
believe that we cannot dismiss the appearance of the *Shevet Yehudah* in Judeo-
Spanish musar literature as a mere literary gimmick to keep the readers entertained
with Jewish rather than foreign literature (though this undoubtedly was one purpose). Rather, it seems appropriate to see the inclusion of Ibn Verga's "natural cause"
explanation for suffering in Jewish history as part of an effort by authors like
Amarachi and Sason (and Judah Papo) to broaden perspectives beyond the confines of the Sephardic rabbinic knowledge of their time. Although they continued
to affirm the traditional understanding of things (divine providence, suffering as
caused by sins), these authors wanted to include secular knowledge in their representations of the traditional universe. This was by no means a universal trend
among mid-nineteenth-century Ottoman rabbis. Rafael Pontremoli, for example,
had the declared goal to describe the miraculous divine intervention in his *Me^cam
Lo^cez* on the Book of Esther (1864), eloquently rejecting the notion of "natural" or
"rational" explanations in his commentary on the story of how the Jews were saved
from Haman's persecution.

Amarachi and Sason's decision to present selected passages from the *Shevet
Yehudah* in their Judeo-Spanish musar books was intended to put events like the
Damascus affair, and contemporary experience in general, into a historical perspective. Never questioning, still less altering theological or kabbalistic explanations of
Jewish existence in exile, they invested historical time with new importance. If it
was usually the distant biblical past or the paradigmatic *Erinnerungsfigur* of the
destruction of the Temple that guided rabbinic visions of history and was set

against the utopian expectations of a messianic future, Amarachi and Sason, by using the sixteenth-century chronicle by Ibn Verga, upgraded historical memory so that it would be worthy of inclusion in the educational enterprise of vernacular musar literature. Later on we will see how the young Papo ventured toward a new understanding of the future; Amarachi and Sason, meanwhile, established a precedent for new approaches to the past.

Sixteen years after Amarachi and Sason's musar books, a Judeo-Spanish translation of the *Shevet Yehudah* appeared (Belgrade 1859);[26] only Moses Almosnino in the sixteenth century (*Crónica de los reyes otomanos*) and Abraham Asa's translation of the brief *Sipure malkhe 'Otmanlis* (Istanbul 1767 and 1863) had previously presented secular history in Judeo-Spanish.[27] It was not until the late 1880s that Ottoman Jewish authors began to produce secular histories of the Sephardic, Jewish, and Ottoman world, a new literary genre that gained momentum in the early years of the twentieth century.[28] In their use of the pre-modern historiography of Ibn Verga (and the eighteenth-century Ashkenazic *Sefer ha-Berit*, to which we return in the next chapter), Amarachi and Sason can be seen as pioneers in exposing Judeo-Spanish readers to "secular" historiography and putting contemporary events like the Damascus and Rhodes blood libels into the perspective of post- biblical, diaspora history. In a manner quite representative of the genre, they broadened the educational perspective of musar literature, but made sure to choose material that would not fail to entertain its readers. Their works could consequently be read as edifying entertainment.

Messianic Expectations

In the last chapter of their *Sefer Musar Haskel*, Amarachi and Sason give an account of the various messianic movements that have disrupted Jewish history. Their choice of source on the Sabbatean crisis of the late seventeenth century[29] (a topic which was perhaps of particular interest to an Ottoman reading public, although they do not treat the issue very differently from events more remote in time and place) is no less noteworthy than their inclusion of the *Shevet Yehudah*: the *Ma'ase Tuviyah* by Tobias Cohen, first printed in Venice in 1707, and called "the most influential early modern Hebrew textbook of the sciences, especially medicine."[30] David Ruderman has argued that Tobias Cohen "believed that the image of Jews was degraded in the Gentile world by his coreligionists' pathetic obsession with false messiahs," and he

> felt acutely the crisis of Jewish communal life in his era and the sense of despair and insecurity it had engendered. His response was to direct his energies to restoring the intellectual image of the Jews by writing a sophisticated and updated scientific and medical textbook. . . . Tobias believed that a knowledge of contemporary science could profitably be employed to bolster and rehabilitate Jewish culture in an age of intellectual and religious turmoil exacerbated by frenetic messianic enthusiasm.[31]

As with Ibn Verga's *Shevet Musar,* the fact that Amarachi and Sason used this source is no proof that they understood or shared a belief in the larger implications of such new openness toward scientific knowledge (again, an issue to which I return in the next chapter). But the use of these sources hardly seems a mere coincidence either. I suggest that Amarachi and Sason did indeed seek to broaden the perspective of the pedagogic enterprise of Judeo-Spanish musar. They wanted to "enlighten" their readers in the manner of rabbinic moralizing literature; yet they did open the door to secular knowledge too (albeit communicated through translated Hebrew literature).

These implications aside, the chapter on messianic expectations in the *Musar Haskel* is a good representation of the consensus of vernacular Judeo-Spanish musar literature on the question (and thus must be contrasted with the activist style of Judah Alkala꜀i). Not even the *Shevet Musar* of Elijah ha-Kohen, an author whose Sabbatean leanings have been demonstrated by Scholem,[32] is an exception to this consensus.

The consensus involves a number of assumptions held by the rabbis, which determine Judeo-Spanish musar's vision of the future and are all firmly grounded in the maxims of Maimonides.

1. Predictably, the belief in the messiah is affirmed; he will eventually come, even if there is no sign of redemption yet. "Even if the Messiah does not appear until the year 5999 [the world is supposed to exist for 6,000 years], I will not lose hope in the Messiah."[33]
2. If the Messiah comes, the authenticity of his claim will be proven by the reconstruction of the Temple and the gathering of the exiles. "Even if all the Jews say that he is certainly the Messiah and even if he performs great and supernatural signs and miracles in the heavens and the earth, I will not believe in him if he does not fulfill [the promise] and remedy Israel's exile . . . and build the walls of Jerusalem and the Temple . . . and if the divine presence does not descend."[34]
3. False expectations only give power to the gentiles and make the Jews the laughingstock of the nations; they can even threaten the safety of the Jewish people if a messianic movement threatens to antagonize the gentile authorities. Thus, "the false messiahs have given power to the nations of the world, so that they ridicule and mock us";[35] "because of our many sins, these false messiahs put the sword into the hands of the gentiles to kill us, and the nations of the world have an excuse, saying: The Lord has abandoned you and your hope is void."[36]
4. Even if the present generation does not seem to deserve redemption, the Messiah has already been born and is only waiting to redeem Israel. "Nachmanides says he lives in *Gan ꜀eden* to be sent here the very day when Israel turns in repentance."[37] Everything depends on the Jews' repenting and pursuing spiritual perfection (as Papo also argues). To achieve this is the goal of the educational enterprise of vernacular musar literature.

The distant, utopian future is thus clearly prefigured. While for Judeo-Spanish musar there can be no doubt about what to expect from the messianic future—the restoration of the old, divine order, the reconstruction of Jerusalem and the Temple, the gathering of the exiles—the immediate historical future cannot be foreseen and planned. Likewise, it is impossible and senseless to speculate about when redemption will come, and thus it is all the more important to guide one's life according to the meta-temporal rules of halakhah and musar. Obviously, such an ahistorical vision of law and musar does not represent the halakhic process as it actually unfolds over the centuries; but it represents the worldview of the Judeo-Spanish rabbis, who did not seek to change the world, but rather to stabilize it and its traditional order.

Conclusion

Judeo-Spanish musar's vision of time between the experience of suffering and the hope for redemption can be readily seen in another story told by Isaac Farhi in the concluding chapter of *Imre Binah*, the work with which I began this chapter, and which I quote at some length here:

> *Ma'aseh* that happened in the praiseworthy city of Salonika . . . in the time of the great Rabbi Joseph David. . . . There was a Jew who committed every possible sin and satisfied very well his evil inclination, especially sexually, so much so that he came to have sexual relations with a gentile woman. And as they were having relations, two or three Turks caught them, seized him and brought him directly to a [Muslim] judge. The judge investigated and analyzed the matter and knew that [the accusation] was true and certain. He sentenced him to hanging, and instantly they put the rope around his neck to lead him around the streets and squares and then to hang him. And as they were leading him around, some Turkish dignitaries approached him and urged him to convert [to Islam], and his sin would be pardoned. . . . The young man did not respond. At that moment, a good old Jewish woman passed by on the street and heard the Turks urging that he should convert and thus escape death. In order to test the young man, the old woman said to him: "Why do you not listen to what they are saying and escape death?" The young man answered with the bitterness of his soul and said to her: "My mother, when will I find a better hour than this to satisfy God, blessed be He, for all the evil I did for all that time? What better moment to give life [to sanctify] his unity?" The old woman said: "Blessed be you, my son, in the world to come. May this death be an atonement for all your sins!" And the young man answered: "Amen." They led him to the site of the gallows. . . . Before they tore the rope, he cried: "Have patience until I praise my God." And they waited, and he said the confession of sins with a voice of wailing and then raised his voice and said, "Hear o Israel, the Lord your God the Lord is One." And he died with the word "One." In that moment, the old woman declared in front of all the people in a loud voice: "Lord of the universe! . . . You knew well the holy people you have chosen, a people that give their souls and lives for your great name. . . . This young man, after not having left out one sin and having satisfied his evil inclination, when it came to betraying Judaism, he did not value his life at nothing." . . . That night,

they [?] appeared to Rabbi Joseph David in a dream and told him: "Know that when the old woman spoke all those holy words, the gates of heaven opened and all the heavenly company were terrified and began to praise Israel. . . . Immediately, many evil decrees which had been ordered were torn. And with the old woman's words, all prosecutors of the young man disappeared and he was led directly into *Gan ʿeden.* . . . " From this we learn how great is God's love for his people Israel, and how much God, blessed be He, rejoices when Israel goes to the synagogues and the study houses to declare the unity of his holy name with intention [*kavanah*] . . . and especially when they gather in order to listen to words of Torah and words of musar, He is happy and pleased and tries to bring redemption soon.[38]

Reality is explained and invested with a superior meaning in a manner typical of Judeo-Spanish musar's understanding of historical time, though in the dramatic form of a *maʿaseh.* The young man in the story who is going to be executed by the Ottoman Turkish authorities fully deserves his punishment for the many sins he has committed. As so often, sexual transgressions serve as the paradigm for deviant behavior. The punishment is going to be meted out by the non-Jewish authorities, and this too is part of a general pattern in which suffering at the hands of gentiles is explained as divinely ordained retribution rather than senseless pain.

The suffering inflicted on the young person leads him to finally recognize his sins, and in his moment of greatest pain, he not only rejects the ultimate seduction of the evil *yetser* to abandon his Jewish faith but recognizes the justness of God's sentence and confesses his sins. This again is a common figure: the suffering sent by God is not cruel but leads the individual to recognize his wrongdoings, and the right thing to do is to accept the yoke of Torah, confess, and repent. The old woman's prayer on behalf of the young man is heard. Though he cannot expect to escape death, and suffering cannot always be expected to cease, the story assures its reader that there is hope for the future. The young, repentant sinner enters into *Gan ʿeden* and the people of Israel await redemption. Between suffering and hope lies the drama of human existence; time is invested with meaning beyond the immediate past and the immediate future, extending back to a reassuring biblical past and forward to a hoped-for utopian future.

What follows in the story is no less important. It is no coincidence that it is a great rabbi who is told, in his dream, that the old woman's prayer has indeed been heard. The rabbi is the authority through whom it is possible to understand the meaning of events, and it is he who achieves knowledge of the divine order.

What does the story teach, according to Farhi? That God will not abandon His people, and that He rejoices to see the Jews gathering in the synagogue and study house, and especially "when they gather to listen to words of Torah and words of musar." This is where musar literature itself enters the picture. Providing reassurance of the justness of divine order, explaining suffering in terms of the traditional symbolic universe, communicating the certainty of redemption (though perhaps not in the immediate future), and teaching the way of piety and repentance, musar literature recommends itself as a guide through the troubled times of history.

Part V

The Challenge of Modernity

Scientific and Rabbinic Knowledge and the Notion of Change

11

Secular Knowledge and Rabbinic Authority

In November 1873, the Judeo-Spanish newspaper *El Tiempo,* published in Istanbul, carried a series of popular scientific articles explaining the astronomical phenomenon of eclipses. The first article began: "Among the phenomena that caused exaggerated bewilderment and provoked terrible fear among the ignorant people of the past is the eclipse of the moon and sun, which they considered a bad omen."[1] In the traditional universe, eclipses were ominous harbingers of disaster, divinely ordained signs warning of imminent punishment. The anonymous author in *El Tiempo* continues his article by praising modern science as having liberated people from such superstitions.[2]

In the typical rhetoric of the *maskilim,* he affirms: "[Science] liberates the people from the darkness, it illuminates them by sending out the rays of its light and makes them feel the weight of their cloak of ignorance and the pleasure of throwing it off. Thus, the scientists do themselves honor for knowing the map of the heavens as they know that of the earth."[3] Newspapers, the article goes on to say, are the ideal vehicle for educating the people and spreading scientific knowledge among the masses. The popular scientific account then begins with an exposition of the Copernican-Newtonian system, which, by ousting the Earth from its position at the center of the universe, had also challenged the geocentric vision of rabbinic Judaism. It is worth noting that even the spelling of Copernicus in the Judeo-Spanish text—"*Copernic*"—testifies to the heavy French influence on the Sephardic *haskalah* in the nineteenth-century Ottoman Empire. It was from European, and particularly French, literature that Ottoman Sephardic intellectuals acquired their secular knowledge and subsequently adapted it for the Judeo-Spanish newspapers and other modern literary formats in order to educate the "masses."

At first sight, it hardly seems remarkable that the Copernican-Newtonian system had made it into the columns of Ottoman Ladino press by the 1870s. As I argue in the first part of this chapter, however, this Enlightenment discourse in the secular newspapers represented an important departure from Ladino rabbinic literature and illustrates the challenge to the rabbinic monopoly on explaining the world.

If we turn back to Jacob Huli's *Me^cam Lo^cez* on Genesis, we find only the classical astronomy of the Talmud restated in Judeo-Spanish terms. The sun moves around the earth; it is in the north during summer and in the south during the winter, which allows the earth to cool. Elsewhere, Huli cites the slightly divergent opinions of two talmudic rabbis and explains that the sun moves below the sky during the day and above the sky at night.[4] Writing in 1730, Huli is by no means defensive in his approach to talmudic authority in scientific issues. While (for example) the Maharal of Prague, in the seventeenth century, seems to have been fully aware of Copernicus's alternative account of astronomical motion,[5] Jacob Huli is either oblivious of contemporary astronomy (although it is discussed in Hebrew literature of the time) or has decided to ignore it in his popular encyclopedic Bible commentary. It is clear that Huli's imagined public would need no argument to take talmudic pronouncements on science for truth; this readership would have no symbolic universe as an available alternative to rabbinic knowledge.

It is true, of course, that Huli is completely uninterested in communicating abstract knowledge. His work is based on the assumption that knowledge is closely related to religious observance and piety. Therefore, asking whether the account of eclipses in the *Me'am Lo'ez* is consistent with the scientific knowledge of the time—which it obviously is not—misses the point. To Huli, eclipses really are a divine warning and their intent is to teach something. Thus, he asserts that an eclipse of the sun is a bad sign for the entire world and an eclipse of the moon a bad sign for Israel.[6] He also gives a rather bizarre list of four causes of eclipses of the sun: a great sage has not been buried according to his rank; a virgin has been raped and no one heard her cries for help; homosexual activity; or the simultaneous murder of two brothers because of hatred between them.[7] In other words, Jacob Huli does not discuss astronomy for its own sake. Natural phenomena interest him insofar as they carry a divine message (such as a call for repentance), but not as enigmas requiring explanation. It is nonetheless indicative of the understanding of rabbinic knowledge as all-encompassing that references to astronomy (and medicine, geography, and much more) are included in the material presented by the *Me'am Lo'ez*.

It would distort the image of Ladino literature in the eighteenth century to convey a picture of a homogeneously traditional outlook totally without alternative, secular modes of explaining the world. Witness David Atias's Judeo-Spanish book *Güerta de Oro*, published in Livorno in 1778, the first Judeo-Spanish book of secular contents. Though directed toward Ladino-reading Jews in the Ottoman Empire,[8] *La Güerta de Oro* is clearly a product of Italian Jewish culture. Most Sephardic Jews in Ottoman lands lived in a traditional society whose ideological foundations were still unchallenged by secular scientific knowledge, but Atias—a businessman from Livorno—propagated the importance of secular, scientific knowledge: "Nowadays, everyone needs to be like a King Solomon of science"[9] in order to socialize with others. He laments the absence of secular learning in the Jewish curriculum and the lack of books by Jewish authors on secular subjects, particularly in the vernacular. He writes, explaining the verse from Deuteronomy, *"for this is your wisdom and your understanding in the sight of the peoples"* (Deut. 4:6):

> [In order for the Jewish people to] be taken by the gentiles for wise and erudite people, [God] wanted to provide His people with wise and sacred doctrines and laws. But for our sins, the gentiles take us for the most stupid and evil people in

the world. . . . Even though there are also stupid and traitorous people among them, they respond that there are also many sages of astrology, and of mathematics, and algebra, and geometry, and of philosophy, and many other virtuous things. And good teachings that help to open and enlighten people's minds, about both this world and the next. However, among us there is no one who writes nor enlightens us about the painful path through this world. Much less is there anyone to be envious to follow the example of the gentiles who, the further they go, the more refined they are and more enlightened in the sciences.[10]

An enlightened Judeo-Spanish rhetoric favoring the study of secular subjects thus predates the Ottoman Sephardic *maskilim* and their writings by one century, although it was a product of the Italian-Jewish experience and arguably did not have too much of an echo in the Ottoman Empire. It is not until the mid-nineteenth century that secular knowledge made its first inroads as a legitimate subject into Ladino rabbinic literature of the Ottoman Empire, not least of all thanks to authors such as Isaac Amarachi and Joseph Sason.

We have pointed out the importance of Amarachi and Sason's inclusion of passages from Judah ibn Verga's historiographical book *Shevet Yehudah* in their two musar books, *Darkhe ha-Adam* and *Musar Haskel*. If their adaptation of Ibn Verga's "natural cause" explanation of the Jewish exile represents an important broadening of perspectives, their integration of scientific knowledge—from the fields of geography, astronomy, and hygiene/medicine—into their writings certainly goes beyond what had been permissible in Judeo-Spanish musar literature up to the mid-nineteenth century. I begin with some remarks on two chapters of the *Musar Haskel*. In the second part of this chapter, I turn to chapter 3 of *Darkhe ha-Adam* and discuss rabbinic responses to contemporary discoveries and technological progress.

It is important to understand that Amarachi and Sason have an educating, "enlightening" agenda. In the first chapter of *Musar Haskel*, for example, they describe the importance of smallpox vaccinations after the deaths from smallpox of "more than a thousand children" in Salonika the year before.[11] This would not have happened, say the authors, if everyone had listened to the rabbis who had called for the smallpox vaccination of all children. The authors oppose popular misconceptions and ignorance; for example, "crazy people and the majority of the ʿam ha-arets mock and say: We have seen children who were vaccinated and had pox," not understanding that vaccination is important nonetheless.[12] In the same chapter, they clearly identify folk knowledge as female knowledge when they declare: "Do not listen to the words of old women" who administer wine and raki to the sick and give other bad advice.[13] Elsewhere, popular superstitions are condemned as "old women's talk."[14]

This first chapter of *Musar Haskel* is an important departure from other models for explaining the world in vernacular musar literature. We must be aware of the plagues and epidemics common in all Ottoman cities well into the second half of the nineteenth century[15] in order to appreciate how important it was for

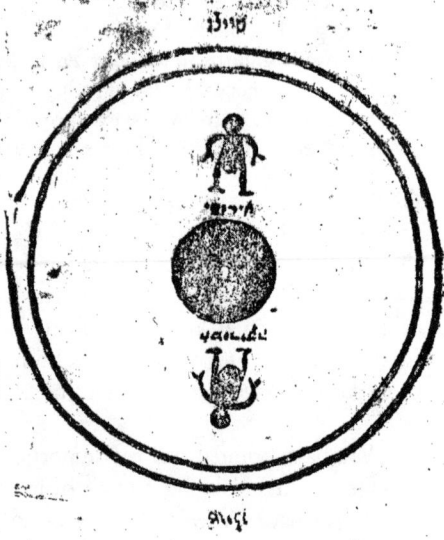

Illustration from chapter 3, which speaks about the "new world," or the Americas, in *Sefer Darkhe ha-Adam* (Salonika, 1843). The caption reads "Europe" and "America" and, above and below the outer circle, "heaven."

Amarachi and Sason's potential readers to make sense of these afflictions. It will be recalled how Isaac Farhi explained the suffering of Jews in the Safed earthquake as divine punishment. Amarachi and Sason do not draw such theological conclusions from the epidemic a year earlier, but look for rational explanations and remedies. It is clear that their reference to the rational mode of explanation for historical events in the *Shevet Yehudah* is no coincidence. The two Salonikan authors seek to include secular knowledge in their educational musar project in order to explain the world.

However, secular knowledge does not compete with the authority of the rabbis. This becomes patently clear in chapter 10 of Amarachi and Sason's *Musar Haskel*, which discusses geography and astronomy and also gives an explanation of eclipses, including several illustrations. Twice quoting the phrase to which David Atias had alluded in his *Güerta de Oro*, Amarachi and Sason declare that the talmudic sages had explained Deut. 4:6—*"for this is your wisdom and your understanding in the sight of the peoples"*—as referring to astronomy.[16] Thus, they undertake to teach their Ladino-reading public some basic astronomy. In so doing, they confidently proclaim the traditional pre-Copernican, geocentric view which we have also found in the *Meᶜam Loᶜez:* "It is well known that the sun moves around the earth in twenty-four hours. When the sun is where we are, it is night for those who are in America, and when the sun is on America's side, it is night for us as is said in the *Zohar,* in *Va-yiqra.*"[17] They claim that the talmudic sages and the *Zohar* had made it quite clear that the earth is round—"*una pelota*"—and proudly conclude: "Behold how great was the science of our ancient sages. They had already told us about something that appears to have been discovered by the scientists through their studies, and there is nothing which is not written or hinted at in our holy Law."[18]

Amarachi and Sason, unlike Jacob Huli in the eighteenth-century *Meᶜam Loᶜez,* admit that there are important things to be learned from science; they recognize that there is something beyond the confines of the rabbinic universe, called scientific knowledge. But, they claim, there is no conflict between these two universes of knowledge. If science gets it right, it only confirms what tradition already knew. It might help us better understand Scripture or the rabbinic classics, but science will never contradict the sacred texts.

Were Amarachi and Sason unaware of the fact that they based their reading of scientific knowledge as confirming rabbinic knowledge (as if it needed such confirmation) on scientific models long outdated when they wrote their book? The answer is clearly no. They cite as their main source for geography and astronomy the eighteenth-century *Sefer ha-Berit* by Pinhas Horowitz (a pupil of the Gaon of Vilna), first published in Brünn in 1797. This book, ostensibly written as an introduction to Hayim Vital's *Shaᶜare Qedushah,* is an attempt to reconcile modern science with Jewish tradition. Isaac Amarachi's own press published the first Ladino translation of the book, by Abraham Benveniste, in Salonika in 1847; it was later reprinted several times.[19]

The author of the Hebrew *Sefer ha-Berit* presents material from many different areas of modern science—astronomy, geography, physics, biology, zoology, philosophy, etc.—in order to familiarize his readers with this knowledge, frequently introducing specific scientific terms or geographic proper names in German (transliterated in Hebrew characters, of course). Where modern science apparently contradicts rabbinic knowledge, Horowitz either tries to reconcile the two or else (after presenting it) refutes the scientific view on the basis of rabbinic literature, as in his discussion of the Copernican system. By contrast, Amarachi and Sason's adaptation of the *Sefer ha-Berit*'s passage on astronomy to the needs of their brief chapter entirely omits any reference to the fact that the Copernican-Newtonian system conflicts with the traditional rabbinic geocentric view and flatly denies any contradiction between the universes of secular, scientific, and rabbinic knowledge.

What does this tell us about the authors' intended readers and educational project? Obviously, Amarachi and Sason see no need to tell their readers that Copernicus was wrong and the rabbis were always right. On the one hand, they do not seem to expect their readers to even be aware of an alternative model contradicting the rabbinic view. And for them, there really is no conflict between rabbinic and scientific knowledge. Rather than attributing this to the authors' own ignorance, one might see this as a difficult negotiation between two symbolic universes which Amarachi and Sason try to integrate and to communicate to a broad popular audience. In adapting the *Sefer ha-Berit* for their intended readers, they omit all controversy.

The original *Sefer ha-Berit* presents the opinion of a (fictitious) Jewish defender of Copernicus who argues that those biblical verses or rabbinic adages that speak of the movement of the sun and suggest a stationary earth only "spoke in the language of the people of the time," but that the truth is obviously that the earth moves around the sun. The author of *Sefer ha-Berit* understands that this way of reconciling rabbinic with scientific knowledge is dangerous because it ultimately gives the last word to science and reinterprets rabbinic traditions so as to fall into line with modern science. Such an approach is rejected in the *Sefer ha-Berit,* and Pinhas Horowitz undertakes to refute Copernicus's theory rather than adapt rabbinic knowledge so as to be consistent with it.[20] He thus follows the attitude of the Maharal of Prague and Moses Isserles, both of whom had rejected Maimonides' idea that the rabbis of the Talmud enjoy absolute authority in terms of religious law but only represent the standards of their time with regard to scientific knowledge. (This view was forcefully restated by the Italian author Azariah de' Rossi and broadened to include history. By contrast, those Ashkenazic rabbis of the seventeenth and eighteenth centuries with an interest in the sciences—and our Sephardic authors in the nineteenth century—reaffirm the absolute authority of the Talmud in all matters, including science.)[21]

Amarachi and Sason want to open new scientific horizons to their readers but avoid conflict with received rabbinic traditions. Their intended reader in the mid-nineteenth-century Ottoman Empire would apparently not have been intrigued to read the straightforward assertion, "As is well known, the sun moves around the earth in twenty-four hours."

Amarachi's and Sason's unapologetically traditional view should not obscure the novelty of their approach. While they avoid contrasting rabbinic and scientific knowledge (which they describe as ultimately leading to identical conclusions), they do contrast expert—rabbinic and scientific—knowledge with popular folk knowledge. They seek to include rational scientific explanations into the canon of knowledge to be communicated through vernacular musar literature in order to go beyond the confines of rabbinic tradition proper. Thus, unlike Jacob Huli in the *Me'am Lo'ez,* Amarachi and Sason strip the phenomenon of the eclipse of its ominous character and tell their readers not to be terrified, adding a rational, scientific explanation based on *Sefer ha-Berit*'s geocentric astronomy. While the authors rely only on Hebrew literature for their scientific information and do not care whether their view reflects contemporary scientific knowledge, the important novelty of their approach is that they include this secular, scientific knowledge into vernacular Judeo-Spanish musar at all.

Astronomy had long played a role in rabbinic literature as a byproduct of tal-mudic study, and the laws of astronomy were studied for halakhic reasons originat-ing in Maimonides' treatise on the laws of the sanctification of the new moon.[22] Nonetheless, the appearance of astronomy and other sciences for their own sake and as rational models of the world in vernacular, non-legal musar literature di-rected toward a broad public is a remarkable development in Ladino rabbinic lit-erature.

The scene changes significantly once we turn to Judah Papo's *Pele Yo'ets*, first published, as will be recalled, in 1870–72. In the chapter on *mitsvot* which is added to the Ladino version of the book, numerous references are made to technological innovations of the time. Before we turn to this issue in the second part of this chapter, it is worthwhile comparing what Papo has to say about astronomy with what we have seen in the *Me'am Lo'ez* and in Amarachi and Sason's *Musar Haskel*. At first sight, Papo continues in the course set by his predecessors. He also affirms the geocentric vision of a stationary earth and the sun moving around it, and like Amarachi and Sason uses the *Sefer ha-Berit* as his main source. The decisive dif-ference is that Judah Papo, writing less than thirty years after the first publication of *Musar Haskel*, finds it necessary to defend his view. What was taken as a truth self-evident to the intended reader in the 1840s needs to be explained and justified in the 1870s.

It is this awareness and the acknowledgment of the existence of an alternative symbolic universe which distinguish the *Pele Yo'ets* from the earlier works. The "others" of Papo's discourse, the "philosophers" and "epicureans" who are identified as deniers of rabbinic authority, are those Sephardic intellectuals, the so-called westernizers, who champion the introduction of the sciences into a canon of knowledge which will no longer be controlled by the rabbis. As illustrated by the series of articles quoted at the beginning of this chapter, in the 1870s there were two conflicting universes of knowledge, each with its representatives in the eastern Sephardic public sphere (rabbis and intellectuals), and new amalgamations of these two universes were being negotiated.

Presenting the alternative view of the sun as the immovable center of the uni-verse and the earth as moving around it, Judah Papo ultimately arrives at this con-clusion: "Whoever converses with the philosophers of the [gentile] nations will see that they insist very much on this opinion. But in the *Sefer ha-Berit* . . . [its author] went to great lengths to rationally refute this opinion. And what we have known since old times, namely that the sun moves around the earth, is the truth."[23] Papo says that it is sufficient to believe what one sees with one's own eyes. "They," how-ever, argue that one should not believe what one sees with one's physical eye but rather with one's intellectual "eye" or *ratio*. Thus, according to the "philosophers," while it appears to man's eye that the sun moves around the earth, the contrary is true. He then goes on to tell a parable in order to deconstruct the rationalists' reasoning.[24]

In this story two travelers, one from Aleppo and one from Damascus, meet in Baghdad. Together they buy bread to eat. While the Aleppan has to go out into the street, the other eats all the bread; when his companion returns, he accuses the man from Damascus of stealing his part of the food they had purchased together. In front of the judges of the city, however, the man from Damascus explains his behavior: When they arrived in town, the Aleppan entered first through the door of their inn even though he was the younger one, claiming that not age but knowledge (*cencia*) privileged him. He, the Aleppan, was a "*hakham en la filosofía.*" The Damascene responded that he too was a *hakham* in his profession, a painter who made beautiful paintings which pleased the eye. He was rebuked by the "philosopher," who explained to him that it does not count what one sees with one's (physical) eyes. Thus, for example, though with his eyes he sees only the one loaf that they bought, in a deeper sense it is two loaves: "Everything which one sees in reality [*be-fo'al*] implies another one in potential [*be-koah*], which is not seen by the physical eye but rather by the eye of intellect" (the object and its idea). Thus, when the Aleppan went out to the market and the Damascene was hungry, he decided to eat all of the (physical) bread—the "philosopher" would be satiated by the second bread which he sees by virtue of his intellect.

The point of the story is, of course, to ridicule the "philosopher" and to prove his speculative knowledge to be absurd or, at best, irrelevant to human reality. Judah Papo clearly faces the challenge of an alternative symbolic universe and its representatives, and he must assume that his intended readers are familiar with this alternative approach to explaining the world.

Why is this point so important to Papo? The first reason is the context in which Papo introduces his remarks with regard to the sun and the earth. He discusses at length the elevated and central status of the people of Israel and later goes on to praise the centrality of the holy city of Jerusalem and the Land of Israel. It is clear that, in his religious universe, all this is related. The centrality of the earth in the divine creation, the centrality of the people of Israel in history, and the centrality of Jerusalem both for the Jewish people and universally: all these elements are intertwined symbols of the religious tradition's universe of knowledge. Whoever claims that the earth is not the center of the cosmos by the same token challenges the whole symbolic universe. Second, rabbinic authority over knowledge is at stake. Papo, like the author of the *Sefer ha-Berit* or the Maharal before him, rejects Maimonides' view that the rabbis might be wrong about science because this would provide an opportunity to damage the integrity of rabbinic tradition just when rabbinic authority has come under assault, as the Ladino *Pele Yo'ets* constantly asserts.

In his attack on secular challenges to the rabbinic universe, Papo returns to the issue of astronomy. Though he is clearly fascinated with scientific discoveries and technological innovations, he wants to make sure that his readers understand the relativity of all non-religious knowledge. Because only the rabbis can claim to possess definite knowledge, he warns the intellectuals of his own time not to be too sure of themselves:

According to the theory of the ancients, the sun moved around the earth and the earth was stationary. In later generations, other philosophers discovered that the sun is stationary and the earth moves around the sun. In later generations, yet other philosophers claimed that the sun is moving and the earth also. . . . And as it happened to the philosophers of earlier times, so it can happen to the philosophers of our day. This is to say, in the science of philosophy there is no basis and nothing is certain.[25]

Papo then produces a remarkable witness for his claim: "In the year 5541, which is the year 1781 according to [the Christian] calendar, there was a great philosopher in Prussia, in the city of Königsberg." Again relying on the *Sefer ha-Berit*,[26] Immanuel Kant (not identified by name in the Judeo-Spanish text) is produced as a witness to testify to the uncertainty of philosophical knowledge. Kant is cited as claiming in his writing that he could refute the proofs of all prior and contemporary philosophers, "and this is sufficient," infers Judah Papo, "[to teach us] not to waste time studying the knowledge of philosophy. The right thing is to stay with the tradition of our fathers and our sages and not to waiver from it either to the right or to the left."[27]

It is clear that Papo is still arguing in terms of the medieval controversies between rationalists and anti-rationalists, identifying "science" and "philosophy." He apparently ignores the contribution of the Rabbi Judah Loew of Prague (d. 1609), "whose most important clarification was to disentangle natural philosophy from the assumptions and restraints of Jewish theology and Aristotelian metaphysics, and in so doing to provide an autonomous realm in which scientific pursuit could legitimately flourish."[28] Thus Papo can express his fascination with technological inventions but has no conceptual place for scientific thought in its own right, since he perceives it as an intrinsic part of "philosophy" which, for him, is antithetical to the rabbinic universe.

Nevertheless, Judah Papo is ambivalent about secular knowledge, and as will become clear below, he has an acute awareness of contemporary change compared to other "vernacular rabbis," even optimistically interpreting it as progress. So far we have seen the difference between Jacob Huli's refusal to confront the alternative scientific universe at all; Amarachi's and Sason's assertion that there is no contradiction between rabbinic and scientific knowledge; and finally Papo's polemical response to the science of the "philosophers."

Rabbinic Responses to the Ottoman Communications Revolution

In the book of Ecclesiastes, King Solomon said: "*There is nothing new under the sun*" [Eccl. 1:9]. . . . Whenever we see something that seems to be new, know that it existed already beforehand. And if someone asks: We have seen so many new things that are invented every day, how could King Solomon say that "*there is nothing new under the sun*"? The answer is simple: King Solomon says that there cannot be anything new, as, for example, there are seven types of metal in the world and it is impossible that an eighth type will appear, because when God created the world, He created seven [metals]. . . . But Solomon was not referring to man-made things that are invented every day, like the steamship, since no new type of metal other than iron is needed to construct a steamship.[29]

Thus opens the chapter on the discovery of the Americas in Amarachi and Sason's *Sefer Darkhe ha-Adam.* They also insist that this allegedly "new world" (*mundo muevo*) is not really new and assure their readers that the creation of the world included the American continent.[30]

This remark on technological innovations, such as the steamship, is among the references to the nineteenth-century revolution in communications in the Ottoman lands which are scattered throughout Ladino musar books of the time. Though they do not form a continuous discourse, I will try to gather some of these references and argue that it is possible to discern two different attitudes: one well expressed by the frequently quoted phrase that "there is nothing new under the sun," and the other marked by an acute and enthusiastic awareness of change (here exemplified by Judah Papo, though it was shared by other Sephardic rabbinic figures like Judah Alkalaꜥi).

The Judeo-Spanish rabbis' reaction to the communications revolution is part of a general process culminating at the turn of the nineteenth century: "From around 1880 to the outbreak of World War I, a series of sweeping changes in technology and culture created distinctive modes of thinking about and experiencing time and space."[31] People everywhere were fascinated with the new experience of simultaneity, the nearly instantaneous bridging of space, the shortening of distances through telegraphs and railways. "The wireless and telephone, . . . simultaneity and the spatially expanded present, . . . the temporally thickened 'spacious present,' and finally . . . the positive evaluation of the present . . . outline the distinctive experience of the present in this period."[32] This experience also affected the Ottoman Empire[33] and is present in Judeo-Spanish rabbinic literature. In my view, the responses to the nineteenth-century communications revolution represent two different rabbinic responses to modernity.

RODITI: HEZEKIAH AND THE TELEGRAPH

In the second part of Ben-Tsion Roditi's book *Ki Ze Kol ha-Adam* (Izmir 1884), which deals with the issues of illness and death, Roditi discusses in elaborate detail the biblical story of the illness and cure of King Hezekiah (Isaiah 38:1–39:8).[34] Hezekiah prays for healing; when he receives the promise of recovery, he asks for a sign of confirmation and gets the following response: "And this is the sign for you from the Lord that the Lord will do what He has promised: I am going to make the shadow on the steps, which has descended on the dial of Ahaz because of the sun, recede ten steps" (Isaiah 38:7–8). This prompts Roditi to quote the midrashic commentary on the episode in which the Babylonian king Merodakh heard of King Hezekiah's recovery and sent him his regards:[35]

> The day of the miracle of Hezekiah['s recovery], Baladan went to sleep as he did every day, and when he woke up, he saw that the sun stood in the East and thought he had slept till morning of the next day and wanted to have his servants

executed because they let him sleep so much, [through] the day and the night. The servants answered him: "Our lord, the king, the day was made longer and the sun was returned to the morning [hour], and God did this miracle for Hezekiah, whom he cured of his illness." The king exclaimed: "A man so esteemed as [Hezekiah], and I do not send him regards?" [So] he wrote him [Hezekiah] a letter as follows: "Peace upon king Hezekiah, peace upon the city of Jerusalem, peace upon the great God."

At the end of the story, Roditi adds a surprising twist, making a certainly unexpected point about the contemporary significance of the midrashic account: "From this story about Merodakh it can be proven that the telegraph was already in existence; there is nothing new [*en kol hadash*]: Hezekiah was in Jerusalem and Merodakh in Babylonia . . . but he knew at this very hour [about Hezekiah's recovery], as the verse says: 'At this time [*ba-ʿet ha-hi*] [Isaiah 39:1] sent Merodakh etc.' "[36]

The passage from Isaiah and the midrashic commentary represent a play on the notion and perception of time. The point is, of course, that time is always subservient to God's will and command and the course of time itself is subject to divine intervention: Hezekiah's life is prolonged by fifteen years; the sun miraculously regresses by ten steps, making the day longer (note that here again it is the sun that moves around the earth). The implication of Roditi's own addition, then, is to reassure his readers that contemporary change, technological innovations, and the fascination with new modes of communication that seem to change perceptions of time and space are not, in fact, anything new. Everything that needs to be known is already inscribed in the canon of traditional knowledge represented by the classical texts of Judaism.

The shortening of distances by the telegraph and the ensuing "disembedment" of time and space (Giddens) has apparently left an impression on Roditi; he assumes that it will also fascinate his intended reader, so he includes his aside on the telegraph. He assures his reader that the late nineteenth-century revolution in communications has no effect on the divine control over time. In fact, he goes further than other authors and simply denies that the telegraph is new at all. The experience of simultaneity, says Roditi, has nothing to do with modern technology, but is already described in the Bible.

Roditi's vision of modernity is probably the subtext of a story which he tells in his *Sefer Ki Ze Kol ha-Adam*,[37] although the immediate context is not modern change, but individual illness. In the story, a ship is caught in a dangerous storm on the open sea. The passengers decide to throw all ballast overboard in order to avoid shipwreck. One of them goes out of his way and discards his prayer shawl (*talit*). "Could there be a worse folly," asks Roditi rhetorically—not only is the *talit* so light that it can hardly be considered ballast, but its owner should have used it for prayer and thus could have saved the ship from disaster. The author explains that in troubled times, in times of illness, one does well in praying and studying the biblical and rabbinic texts that he includes at the end of the chapter. The story could also be read as metaphor for the uneasy times of modernization in which

Roditi's readers live: one certainly should not jettison rabbinic tradition, throwing it overboard as if it were ballast. Quite to the contrary: one will find the response to all contemporary challenges, and an explanation even for the most modern of innovations, the telegraph, in the canon of traditional knowledge.

PAPO AND THE "SPIRITUAL TELEGRAPH"

Whereas Roditi, like Amarachi and Sason forty years earlier, invokes the phrase "*en kol hadash tahat ha-shemesh*" in his response to modernity, flatly denying change, Judah Papo presents a more complex, and certainly more ambiguous, view.

On the one hand, Papo is fascinated by the new technologies of communication and transportation appearing in the Ottoman Empire beginning in the mid-nineteenth century. He is aware of the novelty of these inventions, and proposes that they be seen as expressions or symbols of a more general progress:

> In the beginning, the different parts of the world were the distance of a long voyage from one another. In ancient times, one feared to travel by crossing the open sea, [people] traveled close to the seashore, and traveling took a lot of time. Then the sciences of navigation were invented, [making it possible] to travel by crossing the open sea and the routes became shorter and less risky. Subsequently, the science of the steamship was invented and the entire world could be traversed in a short time. On the mainland, the railway was invented and traverses the world in a few days. The telegraph was invented and traverses the entire world in a few hours. It is clear that spiritually it is the same, that is, the faiths approach each other, which has already begun to show its point. . . . [But] we should not subtract anything from our Law, for thus we have been commanded, as it is said: "[You shall not add to the word that I command you,] nor shall you subtract from it." . . . Therefore the coming closer of faiths must occur through the gentile nations' becoming more and more aware of the holiness of our Law and the holiness of Israel.[38]

Invoking two generic symbols of modern technological progress, the steamship and the telegraph (which also featured prominently in the Ottoman press of the time),[39] Papo presents a narrative to counter the proponents of the modernization or westernization of Ottoman Sephardic society. As I have shown in the chapter on the impossibility of homecoming to the Land of Israel, Papo's interpretation of the rapprochement of religions is that the gentiles would gradually approach the Jews; in a decidedly optimistic reading, he presents the revolution of communications as symbols of the dawn of a new age that might even see the gentile nations unite and restore the Jews to their land. The same idea is reiterated in the second volume of the *Pele Yo'ets*, where Papo praises God who "wants to lead all the [gentile] nations closer to the true beliefs and is revealing the secrets of nature" in order to teach certain spiritual insights. Again, the "science of the telegraph" is interpreted as a sign for a "spiritual," or religious truth: "The Law and the commandments are the *spiritual* telegraph, whereby one understands how powerful [the Law] is. It is this spiritual telegraph which is mentioned in the verse [Gen. 28:12], when our father Jacob, on his way to Haran and sleeping at the site of the Holy

Temple, saw in his dream 'a stairway set in the ground and its top reached to the sky': this is the spiritual telegraph."[40]

There can be little doubt that Judah Papo is determined to interpret scientific and technological progress *as progress,* as something positive that fits into a divine scheme leading to the redemption of the Jews. Papo is convinced that his generation lives in a privileged time and that there are a lot of positive and encouraging developments that affect nineteenth-century Ottoman Jewry and mark progress toward redemption. He praises even the activities of the Alliance Israélite Universelle (although he calls on its leaders to promote the restoration of Jewish legal autonomy in the Ottoman Empire and the post-Ottoman states in the Balkans, clearly misunderstanding the Alliance's westernizing agenda). He points to the flourishing of Hebrew and Ladino printing which, he hopes, will help spread rabbinic knowledge. The appearance of the *Pele Yo^cets* itself is quoted as one of the great achievements of the generation, and he envisions it as a universally read Jewish textbook.[41] All this is cast into a picture in which the time is ripe for an end to exile,[42] whose conditions have already improved considerably: "It might appear that, if there were no repentance and good deeds in earlier times, they are still less to be expected in the present time. But in reality it is not like this, the time is propitious for our becoming good Jews."[43]

But there are limits to Papo's optimism about science and technology. We already have seen his stance against the "philosophers" and their inflated view of themselves. In the same vein, he also warns of the dangers inherent in scientific-technological progress and the perceived rapprochement of the nations. According to Papo, some people invoke the advances in the sciences in order to argue that "everyone should understand and know things by his own intellect," rejecting everything that they cannot explain rationally and by the laws of nature, rather than accepting the authority of the divine revelation and its rabbinic interpreters. Such people, Papo argues, strive to assimilate and imitate the values and norms of non-Jewish culture (*"hacer igualanza," "asemejarmos a ellos"*), even at the price of transgressing Jewish law. "This," he claims, "they have from reading philosophers' books," a term, as we have seen, denoting various kinds of "foreign" knowledge.[44]

Papo's strategy for regaining the rabbinic hold over the Judeo-Spanish public sphere is certainly something new in Ladino rabbinic literature: in an attempt to neutralize the contemporary discourse on progress which was spearheaded by the intellectuals dominating secular mass communication, he integrates important elements of it. Thus, he emphatically embraces the talk of novelty in science and technology and even adopts the modern vision of progress; but at the same time, he reaffirms the certainty of religious tradition which must be defended and affirmed now that a new age is dawning. Despite all the inventions and scientific and technological progress, "we cannot claim that the *hakhamim* of today are greater than the *hakhamim* of earlier generations, particularly in knowledge of Torah."[45]

In a time of accelerated change and technological innovation, Papo is also aware of the insecurity that all this new technology creates. When pointing to the progress he observes all around, he also reaffirms the comforting continuity of divine providence. His argument goes as follows: when the first steamships appeared, one had to assume that all sailors would lose their jobs; the advent of the railway necessarily threatened the future of people making a living with animal transport. However, there is no reason to be afraid of modernity, says Papo, precisely because it does not affect the certainties of the traditional universe. Thanks to God's wisdom and providence, sailing vessels still operate, animal transport is still needed, and people have not lost their source of income.[46]

Papo's observation is correct, to be sure. Although the transition to steamships was almost complete by the end of the century and only five percent of the ships calling on the port of Istanbul were sailing vessels, the overall increase in shipping was such that "this 5 percent represented more sailing vessels than had visited Istanbul in any preceding year during the nineteenth century." The same is true of animal transport; it gained in importance because it still was needed to bring the goods to the major lines of the Ottoman railroad.[47] Papo's *Pele Yo‘ets* thus makes a quite well-informed observation about Ottoman economic realities, which then is fitted into a larger narrative of divine providence, continuity of traditional knowledge, and progress toward redemption.

Conclusion

Though it is always tempting to work historical material into one linear narrative, the result is too often a tunnel vision of history, describing everything as the outcome or precedent of something else and weaving the data together into one thread whose course appears inevitable to the historian. The uneasy coexistence of the "modern" and the "traditional" in Judah Papo's *Pele Yo‘ets*—it is clear that these labels explain little or nothing here—might help in appreciating the complexity of the social and cultural transformation of eastern Sephardic Jewry. Huli's *Me‘am Lo‘ez*, Amarachi and Sason's *Darkhe ha-Adam / Musar Haskel*, and Papo's *Pele Yo‘ets* could be seen as three stages in the slow advance of secular knowledge in the Judeo-Spanish public sphere. But they could also be read as showing the continuity of traditional concepts in changing circumstances and contexts. Each stage contains both the disruptive force of the new and the stabilizing force of tradition.

The *Me‘am Lo‘ez* is on the one hand an entirely parochial enterprise that does not look beyond the textual tradition of rabbinic Judaism. On the other hand, it brings into being a vernacular Judeo-Spanish reading public, which ultimately destroys the rabbinic monopoly over printed communication and makes the subsequent secularization of communication possible. Amarachi and Sason, as we have seen both in chapter 10 and in this chapter, open the pages of vernacular musar to historiography (Judah ibn Verga's *Shevet Yehudah*) and the sciences (particularly on the basis of the *Sefer ha-Berit*), a further step toward the legitimization of secular subjects. But they refuse to admit that there can be a conflict between rabbinic and scientific/historiographic knowledge and thus fail to provide a model with which their readers can reconcile the two universes on their own. The Ladino *Pele Yo‘ets*, finally, is firm and unconditional in its opposition against the "philosophers" and secular knowledge—a polemical stance entirely absent from the Hebrew "original," by the way. At the same time, the author shares the current enthusiasm for technological innovations and produces a rabbinic response to modernity by integrating elements of the discourse of "modernity" and "progress" itself. In this sense, the evidence of Ladino musar confirms what historians have observed as the major difference between modern Sephardic and Ashkenazic halakhah: confronting the onslaught of modernity, the emerging Ashkenazic Ultra-Orthodoxy tended to redraw the boundaries of tradition in terms of an increased stringency and rigidity, arguing "that a weak, sick body needs more care and protection than a healthy body" and that therefore "it is proper to make a fence around the Torah, to be stringent and not add lenient ruling."[48] In contrast, Sephardic rabbis "felt free to continue to apply traditional canons of halakhic decision-making processes which enabled, and sometimes even encouraged, intrahalakhic novelty."[49] Sephardic rabbis such as Amarachi, Sason, and Papo widened the boundaries around musar discourse to include secular knowledge and the notion of progress in order to reaffirm the continuity of tradition.

Vernacular rabbinic literature thus must be seen as a cultural factor contributing to the process of transformation of Ottoman-Sephardic society. It lays the ground for a Judeo-Spanish public sphere; it legitimizes this public sphere's new openness toward secular, non-rabbinic knowledge; and it becomes part of the late-nineteenth-century discourse of modernity by embracing its notion of progress. But vernacular rabbinic literature is also a response to outside factors. Huli, for example, perceives an educational crisis and tries to remedy it; Papo responds to the challenges to rabbinic authority resulting from the dissemination of secular knowledge to a public sphere that was already escaping rabbinic control.

Conclusion

As we have seen, the eighteenth century marked a cultural juncture in the history of the Sephardic communities in the eastern Mediterranean. Jacob Huli's encyclopedic Bible commentary *Me'am Lo'ez*, which would become the classic of Ladino literature; Abraham Asa's popular library of rabbinic knowledge in Judeo-Spanish; the flourishing of the Ladino *coplas:* the eighteenth century witnessed unprecedented literary creativity in the Ladino vernacular and gave birth to Judeo-Spanish print culture and thus provided the basis for the emergence of a Judeo-Spanish public sphere in the nineteenth century. Rabbinic literature in Ladino would play a key role in establishing the lineaments of this Judeo-Spanish literary public sphere, the emergence, transformation, and tentative secularization of which defined much of Ottoman Jewish history in these two centuries of continuity and change.

Beginning in the first half of the eighteenth century, a group of rabbis—with few exceptions, marginal figures in the Ottoman rabbinic establishment—embarked upon an innovative enterprise of educating the masses to combat what they had identified as the prime foe of tradition: ignorance. In a paternalistic, popularizing way, they translated rabbinic knowledge into a vernacular discourse. They were guided both by an image of their intended readers and by an inclusive educational ideal which was arguably based on the Lurianic idea that every single act of every single Jew played an important part in mending the world and preparing for redemption. Envisioning a readership which was unlearned but loyal to tradition, the Ladino authors embarked on an educational enterprise which involved selecting and translating material. They selected what they deemed fit and necessary for their intended public—moral chastisement and practical halakhic guidance—but excluded other material, such as kabbalistic theosophy (although isolated kabbalistic ideas appear throughout musar). They translated this material into a language that they believed would be easily understood by a large public, so that the works would educate and entertain at the same time. The prominence of illustrative and instructive stories (*ma'asiyot*) is perhaps the best example of how the authors of vernacular musar literature intended to communicate knowledge to their imagined public.

As the masses were supplied with printed reading material in the vernacular, a new forum for the dissemination of rabbinic knowledge in Ladino was being promulgated: the *meldado*, or study session, in which relatives, friends, or neighbors gathered and listened to musar books (or the *Me'am Lo'ez*, or books of halakhah) being read aloud and explained by a scholar, a *talmid hakham*, who was invited for the occasion. Our exploration of the Judeo-Spanish musar literature and our inquiry into how the authors represented evolving reading practices and how they responded to them have found that collective learning in *meldados* and individual reading of Ladino books coexisted throughout the two centuries under review and arguably supplanted sermons in synagogues as the prime vehicle of rabbinic instruction of "the people." Conscious of the potential dangers of individual reading, and concerned that vernacular literature would undermine the mediating authority of the community rabbis, the musar authors reaffirmed the importance of seeking the guidance of a *talmid hakham*, whether as an advisor for the individual reader or as a leader of a *meldado*.

The creation of a rabbinic literature in the vernacular includes from the outset groups that had been all but excluded from rabbinic knowledge, either because of insufficient learning and proficiency in Hebrew or due to the gender taboo making women exempt from Torah study. Vernacular rabbinic literature broadens the social spectrum of popularized rabbinic learning, first to include the unlearned masses and soon reaching out to women as well. While authors in the eighteenth century still imagine the husband who attends a *meldado* or the *bet midrash* as an amplifier of the musar message, telling his wife and daughters what he has learned, later authors increasingly come to expect female readers and actually encourage the establishment of women's *meldados* alongside those for men. A female reading public emerges as a consequence of the vernacularization of rabbinic literature.

The *meldado* thus becomes the universal framework for legitimate socializing. In the rabbis' view of social interaction, notions of private and public appear to be obsolete: the Judeo-Spanish rabbinic literature suggests a juxtaposition of sacred and profane spaces, times, and forms of social interaction and contrasts legitimate socializing for the purpose of religious study with the notion of leisure. From the rabbis' perspective, leisure and idleness necessarily lead to sinfulness and are a waste of the time allocated for study, reaffirming the symbolic universe of tradition. Significantly, however, legitimate social interaction is now disengaged from the community institutions. Synagogue and *bet midrash* retain their privileged positions, but domestic spaces and *meldados* become legitimate zones of social interaction beyond the confines of the community institutions.

Ladino musar literature represents the community as a human organism, implying a functional differentiation among its members and their inherent inequality. The key terms of the social vision of musar are unity and stability, which points to the essentially conservative function of this literature. The authors of Judeo-Spanish ethical literature set out to reaffirm the stability of the symbolic order of rabbinic tradition. This preoccupation with stability and the continuity of tradition also implies the preservation and legitimization of the prevalent social status quo. While musar tries to soften the consequences of social inequality, it is built upon an alliance, both ideological and practical, between the learned elite of the *talmide hakhamim* and the wealthy of the community. The wealthy become subject to criticism only when they begin to be perceived as westernizers, when they question the integrity of the traditional symbolic universe. But even then, the complaints remain anonymous; since the rabbis depend on financial support by local wealthy persons, their social critique remains cautious and is always muted as a result of their concern for social stability. A great deal of empathy for the poor is expressed throughout musar literature. As we have seen, however, no socially transformative message is implied, and the social inequality and poverty of many in the Ottoman Jewish communities of the time is legitimized by being interpreted as divinely willed.

The metaphor of the human organism to describe the Jewish community has other consequences. Because all the members are functionally differentiated, they also depend on each other. This creates a mutual responsibility among all Jews in the community; all must be concerned with moral chastisement and the dissemination of musar teachings, regardless of their socioeconomic position. Social control thus is increasingly decentralized. *Castiguerio* was once the prerogative of the learned; now—with musar available to everyone in its vernacular form—it becomes a universal obligation. Thus, while Judeo-Spanish ethical literature legitimizes and perpetuates the social status quo despite the numerous conflicts that rocked Ottoman Jewish communities throughout the period, it also decentralizes social control.

Clearly, in the stratified society of Ottoman Jewry, the *talmid hakham*—and thus the author of Judeo-Spanish musar literature himself—is assigned a privileged role. He controls and administers the cultural capital of the community—its traditional learning—and thus serves as a social ideal. But the rabbis are realistic enough to recognize that poverty often accompanies learnedness, and though they perpetuate the alliance between wealth and learning, the wealthy and the learned are clearly differentiated. The social group of the *talmide hakhamim*, although privileged by its learning, is always understood as a potentially open group. Indeed, Ladino ethical literature advocates the emulation of the *talmid hakham* as a social ideal. The *talmid hakham* is contrasted with the ʿam ha-arets, the ignoramus, who is the learned person's all-purpose "other." To remedy the condition of ignorance is precisely what vernacular rabbinic literature seeks to do. Later, in the second half of the nineteenth century, ignorance is replaced by "heresy" and the ignoramus by the "westernizer" as the prime foes of tradition, and of the *talmid hakham*.

Women remain on the margins of musar literature and are assigned an instrumental role. In a view of men which is far from flattering, uncontrollable male sexual desire poses a constant threat to the stability of the social order. The strict rules of female decency—which are believed by the rabbis to make life in the Ottoman Empire superior to that in European lands until the mid-nineteenth century—thus have nothing to do with the alleged danger of female impurity or female sexuality, but is a consequence of women's instrumental role, in guarding men from the dangers of their sexual desire. The assignment of gender roles (the definition of domestic tasks and child rearing as belonging to the female sphere) and the exclusion of women from formalized social interaction in the community are also a consequence of the instrumental role of women.

This role results from the exemption of women from studying. Because men are obliged to study and women are not, it is only logical to assign women a secondary, instrumental role, helping men to comply with their religious obligations. But Ladino rabbinic literature also contains the seeds of transformation of these gender roles, in that it discovers women as a reading public. Though women are exempt from the study of Torah, the rabbis understand—increasingly in the nineteenth century—that they need to include women in their educational ideal if they want to reaffirm tradition and defend it against the onslaught of modern change. Study of Torah, of rabbinic knowledge, in Judeo-Spanish becomes an ideal including women, thus tentatively redrawing the patterns of gender roles.

A comparison of three different versions of the *Pele Yoʿets* in three different languages, from different times and places, shows that the rabbis are preoccupied with drawing boundaries to assure the continuity of Jewish identity and tradition in exile, and demonstrates how these boundaries vary across time and space. Judeo-Spanish musar literature tries to limit social contact beyond the boundaries of the Jewish community, and it defines the boundaries of legitimate knowledge (rabbinic as opposed to foreign literature). The boundaries are drawn and redrawn, and the nineteenth century witnesses a new challenge: not full-fledged assimilation into gentile society as a project, or even a social option, but the trend of westernization, the emergence of a (fictitious) image of the West as the dominant cultural reference point for the emerging Ottoman bourgeoisie, Jewish and non-Jewish alike. Westernization and the exposure to foreign literature—in foreign languages learned by an increasing number of people, and later in Judeo-Spanish adaptations—become major concerns of Ladino musar beginning in the mid-nineteenth century; if it set out to fight ignorance in the eighteenth century, it now embarks upon a struggle against the forces of modern change and the adoption of the West as a cultural model.

If exile is understood geographically, one can contrast it with the notion of home—the center of Jewish existence, the Land of Israel. It then becomes clear that exile, in Ladino musar literature, is not a geographical term but a condition of existential homelessness—and a condition felt by authors living and writing in Jerusalem no less than by those in the diaspora. Jerusalem is still adduced as a model for diaspora communities around the mid-nineteenth century; by the turn of the twentieth century, westernization has also made inroads into the Holy Land. Though the Land of Israel remains the centerpiece of the symbolic universe of rabbinic tradition and is defended as such, it also remains marginal to the real life of Ottoman Jews. The authors of Judeo-Spanish ethical literature strongly defend a passive, quietist waiting for redemption, urging moral and halakhic perfection as a precondition, and deny the alternative activist attitude of Judah Alkalaʿi and later the Zionists (though they do not explicitly refer to them).

History in exile is understood primarily as suffering; and suffering is an eternal dynamic of punishment and atonement for sins—one's own sins, the sins of one's generation, the sins of earlier generations. It is this complex of punishment/ atonement, together with a somewhat inflated use of the Lurianic concept of metempsychosis in some works, that determines the rabbis' understanding of history. History is not teleological, nor does it represent a constant decline, but unfolds as a tension between the experience of suffering and the expectation of redemption, a tension resolved by the imagery of punishment and atonement.

It is only in the works of Amarachi and Sason that another dimension of history is opened up to the readers of Ladino musar literature. The authors begin to explain the "natural causes" of history (based on Judah ibn Verga's *Shevet Yehudah*); their references to blood libels and deceptive messianic movements—which were not unknown to the modern Ottoman Jewish experience—do not rely on the dynamic of punishment and atonement, but tentatively present rational, divinely inspired, yet "natural" historical causes.

These two authors do not speak only of history; they include scientific knowledge (e.g., geography, astronomy) in their musar books, perhaps for the first time in Judeo-Spanish rabbinic literature. Jacob Huli simply ignores non-rabbinic, scientific knowledge in his *Me'am Lo'ez*. Amarachi and Sason present rabbinic and scientific knowledge as complementary. And Judah Papo, in the 1870s, openly takes up the challenge to tradition posed by the spread of a conflicting secular knowledge in the Judeo-Spanish literary public sphere. But Papo is no less fascinated with technological progress and the revolution in communications in the contemporary Ottoman world than his westernizing counterparts, and he joins their modern discourse of history as progress. However conservative his message, the novelty of this approach becomes clear when compared to the "nothing new under the sun" response to modern change which we have also seen.

Until the mid-nineteenth century, Ladino rabbinic literature was a cultural factor, an agent of change that impelled the transformation of Ottoman Jewish culture by creating and dominating a new Judeo-Spanish literary public sphere. Beginning in the latter half of the nineteenth century, this vernacular rabbinic literature became more and more responsive and defensive toward the winds of change that blew through the Ottoman Jewish communities of the time: the state reforms, *tanzimat*, that would undo the century-long institutional structures of the Ottoman Sephardic communities based on an alliance between the wealthy and the rabbis; the "civilizing mission" and educational efforts of the Alliance Israélite Universelle and other European organizations; and the emerging predominance of the West as a cultural reference in the Judeo-Spanish public sphere.

Ladino rabbinic literature set many of the parameters of the Judeo-Spanish literary public sphere, which would define the absorption of external change in the late nineteenth and early twentieth centuries. Ottoman *maskilim* rewrote European literary classics into a popular Judeo-Spanish discourse, trying to educate and to entertain: they were following a model that had been evolving since the early eighteenth century. Women became a highly receptive reading public for modern genres of Judeo-Spanish literature: they had been discovered and first addressed as a reading public by vernacular rabbinic literature. People gathered to read the newspaper together and others spent hours reading and satisfying their intellectual curiosity: these patterns of vernacular reading culture had begun to develop as the forum for Judeo-Spanish rabbinic books. Secular knowledge gained legitimacy alongside rabbinic knowledge: it had been first integrated into certain musar books.

Until now, Ottoman Jewish historiography has perceived vernacular rabbinic literature only as a response; there is ample evidence that it should also be appreciated as a cultural factor in the transformation of Ottoman Sephardic Jewry in the modern age. Its role should not be exaggerated, of course, but it set the contours of the Judeo-Spanish literary public sphere and helps us better understand the eighteenth and nineteenth centuries as a period of transformation.

Notes

Introduction

1. Sarah Abrevaya Stein, *Making Jews Modern: The Yiddish and Ladino Press in the Russian and Ottoman Empires* (Bloomington, 2004), 4, and the sources cited therein on Ottoman Sephardic literacy in the Ladino vernacular.

2. A similar point has been made by Robert Bonfil regarding Jewish sermons as a mediating genre: Robert Bonfil, "Preaching as Mediation between Elite and Popular Cultures: The Case of Judah Del Bene," in *Preachers of the Italian Ghetto*, ed. David Ruderman (Berkeley, 1992), 67–88.

3. Cf. the remarks by Sarah Abrevaya Stein, "Sephardi and Middle Eastern Jewries since 1492," in *The Oxford Handbook of Jewish Studies*, ed. Martin Goodman (Oxford, 2002), 327–362.

4. Not to mention the modern Sephardic experience in western Europe or the Americas, which followed a very different path. On the growing difference between western and eastern Sephardim, cf. Daniel Schroeter, "Orientalism and the Jews of the Mediterranean," *Journal of Mediterranean Studies* 4 (1994), 183–196. On the Sephardic experience in western Europe, see, for example, Yosef Kaplan, *An Alternative Path to Modernity: The Sephardi Diaspora in Western Europe* (Leiden, 2000); idem, *Ha-pezurah ha-sefaradit ha-maʿaravit* (Tel Aviv, 1994).

5. One could argue, in fact, that those works published in the sixteenth or seventeenth centuries were written in Castilian Spanish rather than a distinctive Judeo-Spanish or Ladino.

6. Yaron Ben-Naʾeh, "Hebrew printing houses in the Ottoman Empire," in *Jewish Journalism and Printing Houses in the Ottoman Empire and Modern Turkey*, ed. Gad Nassi (Istanbul, 2001), 73–96, mentions that throughout the entire sixteenth century only twenty books were printed in Ladino, "mainly for the benefit of the *Marranos* returning to Judaism in the Ottoman Empire" (76).

7. Isaiah Tishby and Joseph Dan, *Mivhar sifrut ha-musar* (Jerusalem, 1970), 12. Elsewhere, Joseph Dan discusses the problematic determination of "musar" as "ethics": "ʿAl ha-musar ve-ʿal sifrut ha-musar," in Joseph Dan, *On Sanctity: Religion, Ethics and Mysticism in Judaism and Other Religions*, 2nd ed. (Jerusalem, 1998), 322–354.

8. Cf. Joseph Dan, s.v. "Ethical literature," *Encyclopedia Judaica*.

9. Joseph Dan, *Jewish Mysticism and Jewish Ethics* (Seattle, 1986), 1, 104.

10. Data from Vinograd's *Otsar ha-Sefer ha-ʿIvri*, cited in Zeʾev Gries, *The Book as an Agent of Culture, 1700–1900* (Tel Aviv, 2002), 58 (Hebrew).

11. E.g., Aryeh Shmuelevitz, *The Jews of the Ottoman Empire in the Late Fifteenth and Sixteenth Centuries* (Leiden, 1984); Joseph Hacker, "The Jewish Society of Salonika in the Fifteenth and Sixteenth Centuries: A Chapter in the History of Jewish Society in the Ottoman Empire" (Ph.D. dissertation, Jerusalem, 1978) (Heb.), and other studies published by Hacker on Ottoman Jewry; Yaron Ben-Naʾeh, "The Jewish Society in the Urban Centers of the Ottoman Empire During the Seventeenth Century (Istanbul, Salonica, Izmir)" (Ph.D. dissertation, Jerusalem, 1999) (Heb.); and a few others. Cf. Marc D. Angel, "The Responsa Literature in the Ottoman Empire as a Source for the Study of Ottoman Jewry," in *The Jews of the Ottoman Empire,* ed. Avigdor Levy (Princeton, 1994), 669–685.

12. Isadore Twersky, "Religion and Law," in *Religion in a Religious Age,* ed. S. D. Goitein (Cambridge, 1974), 69–82.

13. Peter L. Berger and Thomas Luckmann, *The Social Construction of Reality: A Treatise in the Sociology of Knowledge* (Harmondsworth, 1971 [1966]), 113f.

14. Ibid., 120.

15. For a discussion of the problematic assumption that literature "documents" (and much less "reflects") a reality beyond itself, cf. Dominique Maingueneau, *Le contexte de l'œuvre littéraire: Énonciation, écrivain, société* (Paris, 1993).

16. Olga Borovaya, "The Role of Translation in Shaping the Ladino Novel at the Time of Westernization in the Ottoman Empire," *Jewish History* 16 (2002), 263–282; idem, "The Serialized Novel as Rewriting: The Case of Ladino Belles Lettres," *Jewish Social Studies* 10 (2003), 30–68; idem, "Translation and Westernization: *Gulliver's Travels* in Ladino," *Jewish Social Studies* 7 (2001), 149–168.

17. Michael Molho, *Literatura sefardita de Oriente* (Madrid, 1960), 227–241; Elena Romero, *La creación literaria en lengua sefardí* (Madrid, 1992), 107–140.

18. Romero, *Creación literaria,* 107–118. I did not include what Romero calls "moral para niños" and "narrativa patrimonial" (118f. and 120–132, respectively). She lists forty-three titles in the category of "dinim" and "musar." The numbers are meant only to give a general idea of the representativeness of my textual corpus; obviously, Romero's bibliographical list is not necessarily complete and I do not always agree with her categorization.

19. Henceforth cited as ShM; all page numbers refer to the edition of Izmir 1860. In most cases, I have used first editions; since this study focuses on the nineteenth century and the impact of musar literature on social and cultural developments during that period, I have chosen to cite the *Shevet Musar* according to the Izmir 1860 edition that was available to me in the library of the CSIC, the text of which is identical with the first Ladino version published in 1748.

20. Dan, *Sifrut ha-musar,* 243.

21. Gershom Scholem, "Eliyahu ha-Kohen ha-Itamari ve-ha-Shabtaʾut," in Gershom Scholem, *Mehqare Shabtaʾut* (Tel Aviv, 1991), 453–477; English quotation follows Marc Saperstein, *Jewish Preaching 1200–1800: An Anthology* (New Haven, 1989), 301.

22. For more on Abraham Asa, see chapter 2.

23. Henceforth cited as DA; all page numbers refer to the Salonika edition of 1843.

24. Henceforth cited as MH; all page numbers refer to the Salonika edition of 1843.

25. Yitshaq Emanuel, "Bate defus u-madpisim," in *Zikhron Saloniqi,* ed. David Recanati, vol. 2 (Tel Aviv, 1986), 242.

26. Romero, *Creación literaria,* 136.

27. Henceforth cited as IB; all page numbers refer to the edition of Belgrade, 1836.

28. Henceforth cited as ZM; all page numbers refer to the edition of Izmir, 1868,

published by Sa'adi Ha-Levi. This is the second edition, which is largely identical with the first edition published in 1850, with the exception discussed below.

29. Different years are mentioned by Ga'on and Ya'ari; see Moshe Ga'on, *Yehude ha-mizrah be-erets Yisra'el* (reprint, Jerusalem, 1999), 574; Abraham Ya'ari, *Sheluhe Erets Yisra'el: Toldot ha-shelihut meha-arets la-golah* (reprint, Jerusalem, 1997), 716–718.

30. Henceforth cited as HA; all page numbers refer to the edition of Salonika, 1853 (vol. 1), Izmir, 1862 (vol. 2).

31. Aron Rodrigue, *French Jews, Turkish Jews* (Bloomington, 1990), 53. Cf. also Abraham Galante, *Histoire des Juifs de Turquie*, 9 vols. (reprint, Istanbul, 1985), vol. 3, 19–22.

32. Esther Benbassa and Aron Rodrigue, *A Sephardi Life in Southeastern Europe: The Autobiography and Journal of Gabriel Arié, 1863–1939* (Seattle, 1998), 125.

33. Henceforth cited as PY; all page numbers, unless otherwise noted, refer to the first edition (Vienna, 1870/1872). The Hebrew *Pele Yo'ets* is cited as PY (Hebr.).

34. Ga'on, *Yehude ha-mizrah*, 537.

35. Marc Angel, ed., *Eliezer Papo: The Essential Pele Yoetz—An Encyclopaedia of Ethical Jewish Living* (New York, 1991), xv f.; Ga'on, *Yehude ha-mizrah*, 535.

36. Henceforth cited as KA.

37. Abraham Ya'ari, "Hebrew Printing at Izmir," *Aresheth* 1 (1958), 110 (Hebr.).

38. Henceforth cited as NZ.

39. Ana Riaño, ed., *Isaac Mikael Badhab: Un tratado sefardí de moral* (Barcelona, 1979), 24f.; Ga'on, *Yehude ha-mizrah*, 128f.; *Encyclopedia Judaica*, s.v. Badhav; *Rabbi Isaac Badhav (1859–1947): His Life's Work and Environs*, ed. Joseph Levy (Jerusalem, 1977) (Hebr.).

40. Jacob Huli, *Me'am Lo'ez* on Genesis (Istanbul, 1730), introduction, iv b. Cf. Romero, *Creación literaria*, 91. Cited henceforth as MLGen.

41. PY (Vienna, 1870), 1:8–9, 337.

42. Ben-Na'eh, "Hebrew Printing Houses," 77–78. Ben-Na'eh cites as an example the Istanbul edition of the Talmud from 1583, in the introduction of which it says: "Every Sabbath we shall publish sections from the Talmud and distribute them among those who wish to buy them. They will receive these booklets each Sabbath and pay their price so that with God's help the Talmud will be in the hands of everyone in a short while."

43. PY (Salonika, 1899), 1:11.

44. Sevket Pamuk, "Money in the Ottoman Empire, 1326–1914," in *An Economic and Social History of the Ottoman Empire*, ed. Halil Inalcik, with Donald Quataert (Cambridge, 1994), 968, 971.

45. Amelia Barquín López, *Edición y estudio de doce novelas aljamiadas sefardíes de principios del siglo xx* (Vitoria, 1997), 143–147.

46. Rodrigue, *French Jews, Turkish Jews*, 112.

47. ShM 2:167a–169a.

48. IB 4a.

49. Roger Chartier, *Culture écrite et société: L'ordre des livres (xive–xviiie siècle)* (Paris, 1996), 217: "Il faut donc récuser toute approche qui considère que le répertoire des littératures de colportage exprime la 'mentalité' ou la 'vision du monde' des lecteurs populaires qu'on leur suppose. Une telle mise en relation, ordinaire dans les travaux sur la *Bibliothèque bleue* française, les *chapbooks* anglais ou les *pliegos de cordel* castillans et catalans, n'est plus recevable." For a critical discussion of "the popular," cf. Stuart Hall, "Notes on Deconstructing 'the Popular,'" in *People's History and Socialist Theory*, ed. Raphael Samuel (London, 1981), 227–240; John Frow, *Cultural Studies and Cultural Value* (Oxford, 1995). On the

concept of "popular literature," cf. Roger Chartier, "Lecturas y lectores 'populares' desde el Renacimiento hasta la época clásica," in *Historia de la lectura en el mundo occidental*, ed. Guglielmo Cavallo and Roger Chartier (Madrid, 1997), 413–434.

1. Historical Background

1. Morris Goodblatt, *Jewish Life in Turkey in the XVIth Century as Reflected in the Legal Writings of Samuel De Medina* (New York, 1952), 139–143.

2. There is a growing literature on Ottoman history; for the beginnings and classical age of the empire, see the following recent publications: Daniel Goffman, *The Ottoman Empire and Early Modern Europe* (Cambridge, 2002); Halil Inalcik, *The Ottoman Empire: The Classical Age, 1300–1600* (London, 1973); Halil Inalcik with Donald Quataert, eds., *An Economic and Social History of the Ottoman Empire, 1300–1914* (Cambridge, 1994); Robert Mantran, ed., *Histoire de l'Empire ottoman* (Paris, 1989); Suraiya Faroqhi, *Subjects of the Sultan: Culture and Daily Life in the Ottoman Empire* (London, 2000); Cemal Kafadar, *Between Two Worlds: The Construction of the Ottoman State* (Berkeley, 1995); see also Andrew Hess, "The Ottoman Conquest of Egypt (1517) and the Beginning of the Sixteenth-Century World War," *International Journal of Middle East Studies* 4 (1973), 55–76.

3. This was not the last forced transfer; in 1523, for example, numerous Jewish families were transferred from Salonika to the island of Rhodes.

4. Joseph Hacker, "The *Sürgün* System and Jewish Society in the Ottoman Empire During the Fifteenth to the Sixteenth Centuries," in *Ottoman and Turkish Jewry*, ed. Aron Rodrigue (Bloomington, 1992), 1–65.

5. Quoted by Bernard Lewis, *The Jews of Islam* (Princeton, 1984), 136.

6. On the Jews in medieval Spain, see Elijah Ashtor, *The Jews of Muslim Spain*, 3 vols. (Philadelphia, 1992), and Yitshak Baer, *A History of the Jews in Christian Spain*, 2 vols. (Philadelphia, 1992); on the expulsion, see also Henry Kamen, "The Expulsion: Purpose and Consequence," in *Spain and the Jews*, ed. Elie Kedourie (London, 1992), 74–91.

7. Esther Benbassa and Aron Rodrigue, *Sephardi Jewry: A History of the Judeo-Spanish Community, 14th–20th Centuries* (Berkeley, 2000), xxxvii, discuss the various numbers that have been advanced by historians of the expulsion.

8. The expulsion from Spain in 1492 and the forced conversion in Portugal in 1497 were followed by expulsions from Navarra in 1498, from Provence and other French regions in the 1490s; from Sicily in 1492; and from Naples in 1510–11. On the Sephardic immigration to the Ottoman Empire, see Minna Rozen, *A History of the Jewish Community in Istanbul: The Formative Years, 1453–1566* (Leiden, 2002), 47–49.

9. Rozen, *Jewish Community in Istanbul*, 38; Benbassa and Rodrigue, *Sephardi Jewry*, 7–8.

10. Cited by Rozen, *Jewish Community in Istanbul*, 43.

11. Rozen, *Jewish Community in Istanbul*; Yaron Ben-Na'eh, "The Jewish Society in the Urban Centers of the Ottoman Empire During the Seventeenth Century (Istanbul, Salonica, Izmir)" (Ph.D. dissertation, Jerusalem, 1999) (Hebr.).

12. Joseph Néhama, *Histoire des Israelites de Salonique* (Salonika, 1978); Joseph Hacker, "The Jewish Society of Salonika in the Fifteenth and Sixteenth Centuries: A Chapter in the History of Jewish Society in the Ottoman Empire" (Ph.D. dissertation, Jerusalem, 1978) (Hebr.); *Saloniqi: 'Ir va-em be-Yisra'el*, ed. Center for Research into Salonikan Jewry (Jerusalem and Tel Aviv, 1967); Minna Rozen, "Individual and Community in the Jewish Society

of the Ottoman Empire: Salonica in the Sixteenth Century," in *The Jews of the Ottoman Empire,* ed. Avigdor Levy (Princeton, 1994), 215–273.

13. Abraham David, *To Come to the Land: Immigration and Settlement in Sixteenth-Century Eretz-Israel* (Tuscaloosa, 1999), 100–137; Lawrence Fine, *Physician of the Soul, Healer of the Cosmos: Isaac Luria and His Kabbalistic Fellowship* (Stanford, 2003), 41–77.

14. Jacob Barnai, "The Origins of the Jewish Community of Izmir in the Ottoman Period," *Peʿamim* 12 (1982), 47–58 (Hebr.).

15. Rozen, *Jewish Community in Istanbul,* 87–92. In Istanbul, Sephardim were a minority as late as 1623: Avigdor Levy, *The Sephardim in the Ottoman Empire* (Princeton, 1992), 60.

16. This was not the case in the Arabic-speaking regions which the Ottomans conquered in the course of the sixteenth century; cf. Norman A. Stillman, *The Jews of Arab Lands* (Philadelphia, 1979), and idem, *The Jews of Arab Lands in Modern Times* (Philadelphia, 1991).

17. Daniel Goffman, "Jews in Early Modern Ottoman Commerce," in *Jews, Turks, Ottomans,* ed. Avigdor Levy (Syracuse, 2002), 15–34; Jonathan Israel, *Diasporas within a Diaspora: Jews, Crypto-Jews and the World Maritime Empires (1540–1740)* (Leiden, 2002), in particular 1–96; Benbassa and Rodrigue, *Sephardi Jewry,* 36–44; Rozen, *Jewish Community in Istanbul,* 222–243; Ben-Naʾeh, "Jewish Society in the Urban Centers," 297–320; Shmuelevitz, *The Jews of the Ottoman Empire,* 128–178; Stanford Shaw, *The Jews of the Ottoman Empire and the Turkish Republic* (New York, 1991), 86–97.

18. Azriel Shohat, "The King's Cloth in Salonika," *Sefunot* 12 (1971–78) (Hebr.), 168–188; Benjamin Braude, "The Rise and Fall of Salonica Woollens, 1500–1650," *Mediterranean History Review* 4 (1991), 216–236.

19. Translation of the responsum in Goodblatt, *Jewish Life in Turkey,* 188.

20. Winfried Busse, "Zur Problematik des Judenspanischen," *Neue Romania* 12 (1991), 37–84, and the literature cited there; Almuth Münch, "Die Hebräisch-aramäische Sprachtradition der Sepharden in ihrem Verhältnis zum Spanischen der Juden in Sepharad I sowie zum *Djudeo-Espanyol* in Sepharad II und die Rolle des *Ladino,*" *Neue Romania* 12 (1991), 171–239; Ralph Penny, *Variation and Change in Spanish* (Cambridge, 2000), 174–193.

21. Yosef Hayim Yerushalmi includes some remarks comparing Ladino with Yiddish in his "Kastilianit, portugezit, ladino: ha-sifruyot ha-loʿaziyotʾ shel ha-yahadut ha-sefaradit," in *Meʾaz ve-ʿad ʿatah,* ed. Tsvi Ankori (Tel Aviv, 1984), 35–53. On late medieval and early modern Poland, cf. Moshe Rosman, "Innovative Tradition: Jewish Culture in the Polish-Lithuanian Commonwealth," in *Cultures of the Jews,* ed. David Biale (New York, 2002), 519–570; Gershon Hundert, *Jews in Poland-Lithuania in the Eighteenth Century* (Berkeley, 2004).

22. On the *dhimma* regime in the Islamic world, cf. Bernard Lewis, *The Jews of Islam* (Princeton, 1984); Mark Cohen, *Under Crescent and Cross* (Princeton, 1994); Antoine Fattal, *Le status légal des non-musulmans en pays d'Islam* (Beirut, 1958); Youssef Courbage and Philippe Fargues, *Chrétiens et Juifs dans l'Islam arabe et turc* (Paris, 1992); Adel Th. Khoury, *Christen unterm Halbmond: Religiöse Minderheiten unter der Herrschaft des Islams* (Freiburg i. Br., 1994); on the status of non-Muslims in the Ottoman Empire, cf. Karl Binswanger, *Untersuchungen zum Status der Nicht-Muslime im Osmanischen Reich des 16. Jahrhunderts, mit einer Neudefinition des Begriffes 'Dhimma'* (Munich, 1977); Benjamin Braude, "Foundation Myths of the Millet System," in *Christians and Jews in the Ottoman Empire,* ed. Benjamin Braude and Bernard Lewis, 2 vols. (New York, 1982), vol. 1, 69–88; and Michael Ursinus, "Zur Diskussion um *'millet'* im Osmanischen Reich," *Südostforschungen* 48 (1989), 195–207.

23. In 1613, they are said to have represented more than 68 percent of the total population in Salonika (Benbassa and Rodrigue, *Sephardi Jewry,* 9); through the end of the nineteenth century, they still represented somewhere between 50 and 55 percent (Rena Molho, "Le renouveau . . . ," in *Salonique 1850–1918: La "ville des Juifs" et le réveil des Balkans,* ed. Gilles Veinstein [Paris, 1993], 65).

24. On the structure of the traditional Jewish community in the Ottoman Empire, see Ben-Naʾeh, "Jewish Society in the Urban Centers," 137–295; Rozen, *Jewish Community in Istanbul,* 62–86, 197–221; Shmuelevitz, *Jews of the Ottoman Empire,* 15–30; Benbassa and Rodrigue, *Sephardi Jewry,* 16–35; Shaw, *Jews of the Ottoman Empire,* 37–77; Levy, *Sephardim,* 42–70; Rozen, "Individual and Community."

25. Cf. Ben-Naʾeh, "Jewish Society in the Urban Centers," 189–203; also "*hakham ha-qahal,*" cf. Rozen, *Jewish Community in Istanbul,* 78; on the terminology associated with rabbinic learning and office in the eighteenth and nineteenth centuries, cf. Dov Cohen, "Maʿamadam ha-hevrati shel talmide hakhamim be Izmir ba-meʾot 18–19" (M.A. thesis, Jerusalem, 2002), 95–114; Meir Benayahu, *Marbits Torah: Samkhuyotav tafqidav ve-helqo be-mosdot ha-qehilah bi-Sefarad be-Turqiyah uve-artsot ha-mizrah* (Jerusalem, 1953).

26. On the synagogue in Ottoman cities, see Ben-Naʾeh, "Jewish Society in the Urban Centers," 215–233. If there were congregational and private synagogues in the Ottoman Empire, the private *qahal* was the dominant type of synagogue in other Sephardic communities, namely in Morocco. Cf. Shlomo Deshen, *The Mellah Society: Jewish Community Life in Sherifian Morocco* (Chicago, 1989), 86–103.

27. Baer, *Jews in Christian Spain.*

28. Joseph Hacker, "Jewish Autonomy in the Ottoman Empire: Its Scope and Limits. Jewish Courts from the Sixteenth to the Eighteenth Centuries," in *The Jews of the Ottoman Empire,* ed. Avigdor Levy (Princeton, 1994), 153–202.

29. On the traditional *qehilah* in Ashkenazic lands, cf. Jacob Katz, *Tradition and Crisis: Jewish Society at the End of the Middle Ages* (New York, 1993), 63–179.

30. Quoted according to Goodblatt, *Jewish Life in Turkey,* 137.

31. On the Ottoman chief rabbinate, see Avigdor Levy, "*Millet* Politics: The Appointment of a Chief Rabbi in 1835," in *The Jews of the Ottoman Empire,* ed. Avigdor Levy (Princeton, 1994), 425–438; Esther Benbassa, *Un Grand Rabbin sépharade en politique, 1892–1923* (Paris, 1990).

32. Joseph Hacker, "The Intellectual Activity of the Jews of the Ottoman Empire during the Sixteenth and Seventeenth Centuries," in *Jewish Thought in the Seventeenth Century,* ed. Isadore Twersky and Bernard Septimus (Cambridge, 1987), 95–135; Rozen, *Jewish Community in Istanbul,* 244–277.

33. Abraham Yaʿari, *Hebrew Printing in Constantinople* (Jerusalem, 1967) (Hebr.).

34. On Joseph Caro, see Zvi Werblowsky, *Joseph Karo: Lawyer and Mystic* (Oxford, 1962). The *Shulhan Arukh* was first printed in Venice in 1565. On the controversy generated by the *Shulhan Arukh* in the Ashkenazic world and its ultimate acceptance (with a supra-commentary by Moses Isserles clarifying Ashkenazic customs), see Moshe Rosman, "Innovative Tradition: Jewish Culture in the Polish-Lithuanian Commonwealth," in *Cultures of the Jews,* ed. David Biale (New York, 2002), 519–570.

35. Lawrence Fine, *Physician of the Soul, Healer of the Cosmos: Isaac Luria and His Kabbalistic Fellowship* (Stanford, 2003); Gershom Scholem, *Major Trends in Jewish Mysticism,* 3rd ed. (New York, 1954), chapter 7; Moshe Idel, "'One from a Town, Two from a Clan': The Diffusion of Lurianic Kabbala and Sabbateanism: A Re-examination," *Jewish History* 7 (1993), 79–104; Yehudah Liebes and Rachel Elior, eds., *Lurianic Kabbalah: Pro-*

ceedings of the Fourth International Conference on the History of Jewish Mysticism, Jerusalem Studies in Jewish Thought 10 (Jerusalem, 1992) (Hebr.).

36. Hayim Vital, introduction to his *Shaʿar ha-mitsvot,* quoted according to Fine, *Physician of the Soul,* 193–194.

37. Huri Islamoglu-Inan, ed., *The Ottoman Empire and the World Economy* (Cambridge and Paris, 1987); Charles Issawi, ed., *The Economic History of Turkey, 1800–1914* (Chicago, 1980); Sevket Pamuk, *The Ottoman Empire and European Capitalism* (Cambridge, 1987); Israel, *Diasporas within a Diaspora.*

38. Quoted in Bernard Lewis, *The Emergence of Modern Turkey,* 3rd ed. (Oxford, 2002), 28.

39. Richard Clogg, "The Greek Millet in the Ottoman Empire," in *Christians and Jews in the Ottoman Empire,* ed. Benjamin Braude and Bernard Lewis (New York, 1982), vol. 1, 185–208; Charles Issawi, "The Transformation of the Economic Position of the *Millets* in the Nineteenth Century," in *Christians and Jews in the Ottoman Empire,* ed. Benjamin Braude and Bernard Lewis (New York, 1982), vol. 1, 261–286.

40. On Izmir, see Daniel Goffman, *Izmir and the Levantine World, 1550–1650* (Seattle, 1990); the data cited ibid., 57.

41. Henri Nahum, *Juifs de Smyrne, XIXe–XXe siècle* (Paris, 1997), 18.

42. On the Jews of Izmir, see Nahum, *Juifs de Smyrne.*

43. Their role is acknowledged but usually not elaborated on in most of the literature on Ottoman Jewry in modern times; cf. Attilio Milano, *Storia degli ebrei italiani nel Levante* (Florence, 1949); Aron Rodrigue, "The Beginnings of Westernization and Community Reform Among Istanbul's Jewry, 1854–65," in *The Jews of the Ottoman Empire,* ed. Avigdor Levy (Princeton, 1994), 439–456; idem, "Abraham de Camondo of Istanbul: The Transformation of Jewish Philanthropy," in *From East to West: Jews in a Changing Europe, 1750–1870,* ed. Frances Malino and David Sorkin (Oxford, 1990), 46–56; Anthony Molho, "Ebrei e marrani fra Italia e Levante ottomano," in *Storia d'Italia, Annali 11: Gli ebrei in Italia,* ed. Corrado Vivanti, vol. 2 (Torino, 1996), 1009–1043; Minna Rozen, "Contest and Rivalry in Mediterranean Maritime Commerce in the First Half of the Eighteenth Century: The Jews of Salonika and the European Presence," *Revue des Études Juives* 147 (1988), 309–352; idem, "Strangers in a Strange Land: The Extraterritorial Status of Jews in Italy and the Ottoman Empire in the Sixteenth to the Eighteenth Centuries," in *Ottoman and Turkish Jewry: Community and Leadership,* ed. Aron Rodrigue (Bloomington, 1992), 123–166.

44. Gershom Scholem, *Sabbatai Sevi* (Princeton, 1973, enl. trans. from the Hebr. orig., Jerusalem, 1957); Jacob Barnai, *Sabbateanism: Social Perspectives* (Jerusalem, 2000) (Hebr.); idem, "Messianism and Leadership: The Sabbatean Movement and the Leadership of the Jewish Communities in the Ottoman Empire," in *Ottoman and Turkish Jewry: Community and Leadership,* ed. Aron Rodrigue (Bloomington, 1992), 167–182; idem, "Organization and Leadership in the Jewish Community of Izmir in the Seventeenth Century," in *The Jews of the Ottoman Empire,* ed. Avigdor Levy (Princeton, 1994), 275–284; idem, "On the History of the Sabbatean Movement and Its Place in the Life of the Jews in the Ottoman Empire," *Peʿamim* 3 (1979), 59–72 (Hebr.); Meir Benayahu, "The Sabbatean Movement in Greece," *Sefunot* 14 (1971–77) (Hebr.), 79–108; Matt Goldish, *The Sabbatean Prophets* (Cambridge, 2004).

45. Jacob Barnai, "The Spread of the Sabbatean Movement in the Seventeenth and Eighteenth Centuries," in *Communication in the Jewish Diaspora: The Pre-modern World,* ed. Sophia Menashe (Leiden, 1996), 323f.

46. Levy, *Sephardim*, 88. Yaron Ben-Naʾeh ("Jewish Society in the Urban Centers") does not discuss Sabbateanism at all in his study of seventeenth-century Ottoman Jewry, questioning its overall importance.

47. Also in general Ottoman historiography, the simplified view of a "decline" through-out the eighteenth and early nineteenth centuries has been abandoned in favor of a careful differentiation of military, economic, cultural, and political trends. Cf. Suraiya Faroqhi, *Kultur und Alltag im Osmanischen Reich* (Munich, 1995), 273; Jonathan Grant, "Rethinking the Ottoman 'Decline': Military Technology Diffusion in the Ottoman Empire, Fifteenth to Eighteenth Centuries," *Journal of World History* 10 (1999), 179–201; Bernard Lewis, "Ottoman Observers of Ottoman Decline," in idem, *Islam in History* (La Salle, Ill., 1972); cf. also the attempt to define an "Islamic enlightenment" in the eighteenth century by Reinhard Schulze, "Das islamische achtzehnte Jahrhundert: Versuch einer historiographischen Kritik," *Die Welt des Islams* 30 (1990), 140–159, and the critique by Rudolph Peters in the same volume, 160–162.

48. S. N. Eisenstadt, *Revolution and the Transformation of Societies: A Comparative Study of Civilizations* (New York, 1978), 52.

49. Jacob Barnai, "From Sabbateanism to Modernization: Ottoman Jewry on the Eve of the Ottoman Reforms and the Haskala," in *Sephardi and Middle Eastern Jewries: History and Culture in the Modern Era*, ed. Harvey E. Goldberg (Bloomington, 1996), 78. A good alternative model to understand modern transformation of non-European Jewish communities (though not for the Ottoman Empire) which luckily departs from the dichotomy of "tradition" versus "modernity" is Daniel Schroeter and Joseph Chetrit, "The Transformation of the Jewish Community of Essaouria (Mogador) in the Nineteenth and Twentieth Centuries," in *Sephardi and Middle Eastern Jewries: History and Culture in the Modern Era*, ed. Harvey E. Goldberg (Bloomington, 1996), 99–116.

50. Paul Dumont, "La période des *Tanzîmât* (1839–1878)," in *Histoire de l'Empire ottoman*, ed. Robert Mantran (Paris, 1989), 459–522; Donald Quataert, "The Age of Reforms, 1812–1914," in *An Economic and Social History of the Ottoman Empire*, ed. Halil Inalcik (with Donald Quataert) (Cambridge, 1994), 759–943; Roderic F. Davison, *Reform in the Ottoman Empire, 1856–1876* (New York, 1973); Carter V. Findley, *Bureaucratic Reform in the Ottoman Empire: The Sublime Porte, 1789–1922* (Princeton, 1980); Halil Inalcik, "Application of the Tanzimat and Its Social Effects," *Archivum Ottomanicum* 4 (1972), 97–127; Lewis, *Emergence of Modern Turkey;* Niyazi Berkes, *The Development of Secularism in Turkey* (1964; reprint, New York, 1998); Sherif Mardin, s.v. "Tanzimat," and Gudrun Krämer, s.v. "Minorities in Muslim Societies," in *Encyclopaedia of the Modern Islamic World*, ed. John L. Esposito (Oxford, 1995); Feroz Ahmad, *The Making of Modern Turkey* (London, 1993).

51. Butrus Abu-Manneh, "The Islamic Roots of the Gülhane Rescript," *Die Welt des Islams* 34 (1994), 173–203.

52. Lewis, *Emergence of Modern Turkey,* chapters 5–6.

53. Sarah Abrevaya Stein, *Making Jews Modern* (Bloomington, 2004), chapter 2. On the ideology of Ottomanism, see Lewis, *Emergence of Modern Turkey,* and Berkes, *Development of Secularism;* see also Hasan Kayali, *Arabs and Young Turks: Ottomanism, Arabism and Islamism in the Ottoman Empire, 1908–1918* (Berkeley, 1997).

54. Count Stanislas de Clermont-Tonnerre in the French National Assembly, 1789, quoted in Paula Hyman, *The Jews of Modern France* (Berkeley, 1998), 27.

55. Nancy Reynolds, "'Difference and Tolerance in the Ottoman Empire,' interview with Aron Rodrigue," *Stanford Humanities Review* 5 (1995), 81–90.

56. Rodrigue, *French Jews, Turkish Jews;* idem, *De l'instruction à l'émancipation: Les enseignants de l'Alliance Israélite Universelle et les Juifs d'Orient 1860–1939* (Paris, 1989); idem, "Réformer ou supplanter: l'éducation juive traditionnelle en Turquie à l'épreuve de la modernité," in *Transmission et passages en monde juif,* ed. Esther Benbassa (Paris, 1997), 501–522; Paul Dumont, "Jewish Communities in Turkey during the Last Decades of the Nineteenth Century in the Light of the Archives of the Alliance Israelite Universelle," in *Christians and Jews in the Ottoman Empire: The Functioning of a Plural Society,* ed. Benjamin Braude and Bernard Lewis (New York, 1982), vol. 1: *The Central Lands,* 209–242; Simon Schwarzfuchs, *L'"Alliance" dans les communautés du bassin méditerranéen à la fin du 19ème siècle et son influence sur la situation sociale et culturelle* (Jerusalem, 1987) (French and Hebr.).

57. Quoted by Rodrigue, *French Jews, Turkish Jews,* 71.

58. This seems to be true even though the Alliance schools only reached around 20 percent of the Jewish school age population in cities such as Istanbul and Izmir, being more successful in smaller communities and in Edirne where the Alliance school merged with the existing traditional talmud torah. A discussion of the available data in Rodrigue, *French Jews, Turkish Jews,* 90–95.

59. Esther Benbassa, *Una diaspora sépharade en transition: Istanbul, xixe–xxe siècles* (Paris, 1993); idem, "Zionism in the Ottoman Empire at the End of the 19th and the Beginnings of the 20th Century," *Studies in Zionism* 11 (1990), 127–140; idem, "Presse d'Istanbul et de Salonique au service du sionisme (1908–1914): les motifs d'une allégeance," *Revue Historique* 276 (1986), 337–365; Benbassa and Rodrigue, *Sephardi Jewry,* chapter 4; Isaiah Friedman, *Germany, Turkey, and Zionism 1897–1918* (Oxford, 1977).

60. On traditional education in the Ottoman Sephardic communities, see Ben-Naʾeh, "Jewish Society in the Urban Centers," 247–256; Cohen, "Maʿamadam ha-hevrati," 13–54 (Hebr.); Rodrigue, *French Jews, Turkish Jews,* 35–38; idem, "Réformer ou supplanter. L'éducation juive traditionnelle en Turquie à l'épreuve de la modernité," in *Transmission et passages en monde juif,* ed. Esther Benbassa (Paris, 1997), 501–522.

61. For the distinction between the terms "talmud torah" and "*meldar,*" cf. Cohen, "Maʿamadam ha-hevrati," 20; Rodrigue, *French Jews, Turkish Jews,* 36.

62. Yitshaq Emanuel, "Toldot yehude Saloniqi," in *Zikhron Saloniqi,* ed. David Recanati, vol. 1 (Tel Aviv, 1972), 129, 166. On Salonika's Great Talmud Torah, see Abraham Amarillo, "The Great Talmud Torah Society in Salonika," *Sefunot* 13 (1971–78), 275–308 (Hebr.).

63. Cf. Cohen, "Maʿamadam ha-hevrati," 13–54, and Rodrigue, *French Jews, Turkish Jews,* 35–38.

64. Alexander Ben-Guiat, *Suvenires del meldar* (Izmir, 1920).

65. MLGen, introduction [iii b–iv a].

66. Cohen, "Maʿamadam ha-hevrati," 29.

67. Rodrigue, "Beginnings of Westernization," 453.

2. Print and the Vernacular

1. Frank Kermode, *The Classic* (London, 1975), 43–44.

2. In fact, Iacob Hassán has argued that this classic of Ladino literature transformed the Judeo-Spanish language into "un sistema lingüístico autónomo diferenciado del castellano." Iacob M. Hassán, "La literatura sefardí culta: sus principales escritores, obras y géneros," in *Judíos. Sefardíes. Conversos,* ed. Angel Alcalá (Valladolid, 1995), 320; he also refers to the eighteenth century as "edad de oro" (323).

3. Benbassa and Rodrigue, *Sephardi Jewry,* 64. It is true, of course, that the *Me'am Lo'ez* as a tool for popular education does not necessarily "represent" the mentality of its readers. Cf. Roger Chartier, *Culture écrite et société: L'ordre des livres (xiv²–xviii² siècle)* (Paris, 1996), 217: "Il faut donc récuser toute approche qui considère que le répertoire des littératures de colportage exprime la 'mentalité' ou la 'vision du monde' des lecteurs populaires qu'on leur suppose. Une telle mise en relation, ordinaire dans les travaux sur la *Bibliothèque bleue* française, les *chapbooks* anglais ou les *pliegos de cordel* castillans et catalans, n'est plus recevable."

4. Moshe David Ga²on, *Maskiyot levav 'al Me'am Lo'ez* (Jerusalem, 1933), 48; Michael Molho, *Le Meam-Loez: Encyclopédie populaire du séphardisme levantin* (Salonika, 1945); Michael Molho, *Literatura sefardita de Oriente* (Madrid, 1960), 242.

5. Arnold Goldberg, *Me'am Lo'ez: Diskurs und Erzählung in der Komposition. Hayye Sara, Kapitel 1* (Frankfurt a.M., 1984), 24.

6. MLGen, introduction [iii b].

7. Barnai, "From Sabbateanism to Modernization," 78.

8. Iacob M. Hassán, "Visión panorámica de la literatura sefardí," *Hispania Judaica* 2 (Barcelona, 1982), 34–35; Romero, *Creación literaria,* 86–102.

9. Molho, *Literatura,* 261.

10. The story of the *Me'am Lo'ez* continues in our own day. Because the Judeo-Spanish text has become less accessible with the destruction of Judeo-Spanish culture in the Holocaust and the disappearance of Ladino as a living language in Israel and elsewhere, an extraordinarily popular Hebrew translation of the *Me'am Lo'ez* (by S. Yerushalmi, 20 vols., Jerusalem 1967–81) has appeared. An English translation exists, apparently based on the Hebrew version, and is now also being followed by French and Spanish translations. This classic of vernacular Judeo-Spanish literature still disseminates traditional, rabbinic knowledge among a broad audience, now in Hebrew (and English, French, and Spanish). It is not at all limited to Sephardic Jews but is at least as widely read among Ashkenazic Jews in Israel and elsewhere.

11. PY (Hebr.) 21–22; PY 1:42.

12. Steven D. Fraade, *From Tradition to Commentary: Torah and Its Interpretations in the Midrash Sifre to Deuteronomy* (Albany, 1991), 1f., gives the following definition of "commentary," which seems perfectly applicable to the case of the *Me'am Lo'ez:* "They begin with an extended base-text, of which they designate successive subunits for exegetical attention, to each of which they attach a comment or chain of comments, which nevertheless remain distinct from the base-text, to which the commentary sooner or later returns (that is, advances) to take up the next selected subunit in sequence. Thus, the overall movement of the commentary follows to some degree, depending on how much of the base-text it comments upon, the progression of the base-text to which it attends. Herein lies what might be viewed as commentary's paradoxical nature: of necessity it fragmentizes its base-text in order to consider its parts in isolated detail, even as that base-text provides the overall structural framework in relation to which a collection of otherwise discrete and sometimes discordant comments acquire a *degree* of progressive continuity and at least external coherence."

13. This is at least my impression from a close reading of *Va-yeshev,* chapter 4 of the *Me'am Lo'ez,* which I undertook in preparation for this work but whose inclusion would have gone far beyond its scope. The excursive texts in the chapter studied by Goldberg (*Haye Sara,* chapter 1) also confirm the impression of an overarching theme. My remark is tentative, however, because, as Goldberg, *Me'am Lo'ez,* 176, mentions, it is still difficult to make

definite statements about the general structure of Huli's *Me'am Lo'ez* as a whole because only selected parts of non-halakhic sections have been studied so far.

14. Clearly the best analysis of the literary structure of Huli's *Me'am Lo'ez* is Goldberg's study cited above.

15. *Sefer Ki Ze Eliyahu,* 15a–15b, quoted in Romero, *Creación literaria,* 94.

16. Jacob Elbaum, "*Yalqut Shim'oni* and the Medieval Midrashic Anthology," *Prooftexts* 17 (1997), 146–147.

17. MLGen, introduction [iv a].

18. Iacob M. Hassán, ed., *Introducción a la Biblia de Ferrara* (Madrid, 1994).

19. Harm den Boer, *La literatura sefardí de Amsterdam* (Alcalá de Henares, 1996).

20. Following Salomon A. Rosanes, *Qorot ha-yehudim be-Turqiyah ve-artsot ha-qedem,* vol. 5 (Sofia, 1937–38), 93f.

21. The Constantinople translation of 1547 contained only the books of the Pentateuch; the Bible of Ferrara was written in Latin characters and thus basically inaccessible to the average Sephardic Jew in the Ottoman Empire.

22. David Qimhi (ca. 1160–ca. 1235), grammarian and biblical exegete of Narbonne (Provence).

23. Isaac Abrabanel (1437–1508), biblical exegete, philosopher, and one of the leaders of Spanish Jewry at the time of the expulsion in 1492.

24. Abraham Asa in his introduction to the translation of the "minor prophets," i b, cited by Romero, *Creación literaria,* 40.

25. On the *coplas,* see Romero, *Creación literaria,* 141–176, and the literature cited there; a good first approach to the genre is provided by Elena Romero, *Coplas sefardíes: Primera selección* (Córdoba, 1988). On *coplas* as a medium of popular rabbinic education, see Elena Romero, *Seis coplas sefardíes de 'castiguerio' de Hayim Yom-Tob Magula* (Madrid, 2003).

26. Romero, *Creación literaria,* 157.

27. MLGen, introduction [iii b–iv a].

28. Menachem Kellner, *Maimonides on the "Decline of Generations" and the Nature of Rabbinic Authority* (Albany, 1996), 24–25.

29. Joseph Hacker, "The Intellectual Activity of the Jews of the Ottoman Empire During the Sixteenth and Seventeenth Centuries," in *Jewish Thought in the Seventeenth Century,* ed. Isadore Twersky and Bernard Septimus (Cambridge, 1987), 95–135.

30. Maimonides, introduction to *Mishneh Torah;* English quotation from Isadore Twersky, *A Maimonides Reader* (New York, 1972), 39–40.

31. MLGen, introduction [v a].

32. PY (Hebr.) 373–374.

33. Marc D. Angel, *Voices in Exile: A Study in Sephardic Intellectual History* (Hoboken, N.J., 1991), 119.

34. Dan, *Jewish Ethics and Jewish Mysticism,* 100f.

35. Scholem, *Major Trends,* 274.

36. Moshe Idel, *Kabbalah: New Perspectives* (New Haven, 1988), 260.

37. Cf. Romero, *Creación literaria,* 81. On Sabbateanism, cf. above, chapter 1.

38. Barnai, "From Sabbateanism to Modernization," 77f.

39. Fine, *Physician of the Soul,* 3.

40. Ze'ev Gries likewise has observed that the massive influence of Lurianic musar literature is to be dated only to the second half of the seventeenth and the early eighteenth century and that the diffusion of the popular Lurianic writings may be the result, rather

than the cause, of Sabbateanism. Ze'ev Gries, "The Fashioning of Hanhagot (Regimen Vitae) Literature at the End of the Sixteenth Century and during the Seventeenth Century and Its Historical Importance," *Tarbiz* 56 (1987), 527–581. Cf. also Gries, *The Book as an Agent of Culture.*

41. Elizabeth Eisenstein, *The Printing Press as an Agent of Change,* 2 vols. (London and New York, 1979), vol. 1, 29.

42. Hacker, "Intellectual Activity," 102–104.

43. Ben-Na'eh, "Hebrew Printing Houses": printing in Istanbul ceased from 1598 to 1639, when Solomon Franco started his printing press. In the entire period between 1639 and 1695, only twenty-eight books were printed in Istanbul. In Salonika, a printing house was founded by Eliezer Toledano, who arrived from Lisbon. Printing flourished in the sixteenth century but declined seriously through the seventeenth century and resumed only in the early eighteenth century. In Izmir, no Hebrew books were published from 1675 to 1728, when Jonah Ashkenazi established a printing house in Izmir as a branch of his Istanbul business.

44. Ben-Na'eh, "Hebrew Printing Houses," 82. More of Asa's translations, though not all, as well as his *Sefer Tsorkhe Tsibur,* were published by Jonah Ashkenazi and later by his sons Reuben and Nisim. Jonah Ashkenazi's sons also published the second edition of *Me'am Lo'ez* Genesis. Cf. Abraham Ya'ari, *Reshimat sifre ladino ha-nimtsa'im be-vet ha-sefarim ha-le'umi ve-ha-univerista'i bi-Yerushalayim,* Jerusalem, 1934.

45. Romero, *Creación literaria,* 92f.

46. Franz Babinger, *Stambuler Buchwesen im 18. Jahrhundert* (Leipzig, 1919).

47. Likewise in the early eighteenth century, printing was established in Persia; Egypt followed in the early nineteenth century.

48. Babinger, *Stambuler Buchwesen,* 11; Levy, *Sephardim,* 90.

49. Quoted in Fatma Müge Göçek, *East Encounters West: France and the Ottoman Empire in the Eighteenth Century* (New York, 1987), 115.

50. Göçek, *East Encounters West,* 115.

51. Ibrahim Müteferrika states, in a letter to De Saussure, that "the religious dignitaries, who possess influence in this country, insistently did not give permission for this new invention [the printing press]. . . . They have mentioned that the aforesaid invention would be dangerous to public order and to the conduct of religion; it would place more than the necessary amount of books into circulation." Quoted in Göçek, *East Encounters West,* 113.

52. Faroqhi, *Kultur und Alltag,* 111–113; Berkes, *Development of Secularism,* 39–41; Louis Bazin, "La vie intellectuelle et culturelle dans l'Empire ottoman," in Robert Mantran, ed., *Histoire de l'Empire ottoman* (Paris, 1989), 715. Before 1840, only an average of eleven books a year were published in Istanbul: Donald Quataert, *The Ottoman Empire, 1700–1922* (Cambridge, 2000), 167f.

53. Göçek, *East Encounters West,* 111.

54. Klaus Roth, "Populare Lesestoffe in Südosteuropa," in *Südosteuropäische Popularliteratur im 19. und 20. Jahrhundert,* ed. Klaus Roth (Munich, 1993), 21; on popular Bulgarian literature, Ines Köhler-Zülich, "Von der Handschrift zum Buch und zur Heftchenliteratur: Bulgarische Geschichten über Alexander den Großen im 19. und 20. Jahrhundert," in *Südosteuropäische Popularliteratur,* 188.

55. Quoted in Lewis, *Emergence of Modern Turkey,* 66.

56. Romero, *Creación literaria,* 20.

57. Natalie Zemon Davis, "Printing and the People," in idem, *Society and Culture in Early Modern France* (Cambridge, 1987), 189–226.

58. Romero, *Creación literaria*, 141–176; Paloma Díaz-Mas, *Los Sefardíes: Historia, lengua y cultura*, 3rd ed. (Barcelona, 1997), 137–144.

59. Elchanan Reicher, "The Ashkenazi Elite at the Beginning of the Modern Era: Manuscript versus Printed Book," *Polin* 10 (1997), 85–98; Moshe Rosman, "Innovative Tradition," 530–547.

60. Levy, *The Sephardim*, 82.

61. On Judeo-Spanish folktales, see Tamar Alexander-Frizer, *The Beloved Friend-and-a-Half: Studies in Sephardic Folk Literature* (Jerusalem, 1999).

62. Cf. the study by Pilar Romeu Ferré, *Las llaves del Meam loez* (Barcelona, 2000).

63. Jacob ben Isaac in his *Melits Yosher*, quoted in Israel Zinberg, *A History of Jewish Literature*, vol. VII: *Old Yiddish Literature from Its Origins to the Haskalah Period* (Cincinnati and New York, 1975), 131.

64. The most notable exception among the works studied here is Abraham Palachi, who followed his father, Hayim Palachi, as chief rabbi of Izmir. Notably, most of his extraordinarily numerous publications are in Hebrew, and even his Judeo-Spanish *Ve-Hokhiah Avraham* is among the most difficult works of Ladino rabbinic literature.

65. Goldberg, *Me'am Lo'ez*, 11; I. R. Molho, "El humanista R. Yaakob Kuli," *Tesoro de los judíos sefardíes* 5 (1962), 80–94 (Hebr.).

66. So says, at least, Molho, *Le Meam-Loez*, 15.

67. Rabbi Raphel Isaac Yerushalmi of Istanbul writes in his approbation for the second volume of Huli's *Me'am Lo'ez* (on Exodus, published 1733 in Istanbul): "Let there not be any dispute, and let the sages of Israel not argue, as did Rabbi Hanina and Rabbi Hiya, regarding logic and scrolls." This alludes to the Babylonian Talmud, *Ketubbot* 103b and *Baba Metzia* 85b, which speaks about a debate between Rabbi Hanina and Rabbi Hiya. Hanina wants to restore the Torah through scholarly disputation, while Hiya says he would write scrolls of Torah and teach it to young children. Huli agrees with Hiya's approach: knowledge of Torah should be taught to the "masses," while many other rabbis, criticizing Huli, adopted Hanina's approach, arguing that the maintenance or restoration of Torah depended on scholarly debate. Cf. Arye Kaplan's English translation of the *Me'am Lo'ez*, published as *The Torah Anthology* (New York, 1978), vol. 4, vi–vii.

68. Cohen, "Ma'amadam ha-hevrati," 40–41.

69. Emanuel, "Bate defus u-madpisim," 242.

70. Ya'ari, "Hebrew Printing at Izmir," 110. There are other examples: one of the most productive publishers in Salonika, printing many Ladino books, was Sa'adi ha-Levi, who was a *hazan*. At the end of his *Nehemadim mi-Zahav*, the Jerusalem rabbi Isaac Badhab announces that he also sells books, including "books printed in Livorno, for a good price" (NZ 128); in 1899, Badhab tried to open an import business for books from Livorno but did not succeed: Ga'on, *Yehude ha-mizrah*, 128.

71. Cf. Romero, *Creación literaria*, 86–99 (*Me'am Lo'ez*) and 115f. (musar).

72. Ben-Na'eh, "Hebrew printing houses."

73. Romero, *Creación literaria*, 180f.

74. *Sha'are Mizrah*, 17 Sivan 5606 [1846], 1.

75. Emanuel, "Bate defus," 242–243; idem, "Toldot yehude Saloniqi," 183–184.

76. The best recent study of this emerging secular Judeo-Spanish literature is Sarah Abrevaya Stein's *Making Jews Modern;* cf. Borovaya, "The Role of Translation in Shaping the Ladino Novel"; idem, "Translation and Westernization"; Aron Rodrigue, "The Ottoman Diaspora: The Rise and Fall of Ladino Literary Culture," in *Cultures of the Jews*, ed. David Biale (New York, 2002), 863–886.

77. On Saʿadi Halevi, cf. Ben-Naʾeh, "Hebrew printing houses," 91.

78. Fatma Müge Göçek, *Rise of the Bourgeoisie, Demise of Empire: Ottoman Westernization and Social Change* (New York and Oxford 1996), 126.

3. The Translation and Reception of Musar

1. Olga V. Borovaya, "Translation and Westernization: *Gulliver's Travels* in Ladino," *Jewish Social Studies* 7 (2001), 156.

2. PY 1:4.

3. Hassán, "Dos introducciones," 26. Séphiha has somewhat arbitrarily defined Ladino as the *"judéo-espagnol calque,"* the "calque" translations of the Hebrew Bible and other texts into Judeo-Spanish, as opposed to *Djudezmo,* the *"judéo-espagnol vernaculaire."* For a brief summary of this position, which has been repeated in innumerable publications, cf. Haïm Vidal Séphiha, "Ladino et Djudezmo," in *Salonique 1850–1918: La "ville des Juifs" et le réveil des Balkans* (Paris, 1993), 79–95. For a position against Séphiha cf. Hassán, "La literatura sefardí culta," 324. In the present work, I use "Ladino" and "Judeo-Spanish" interchangeably; "Ladino" is the term used in the sources themselves.

4. PY 2:97.

5. PY 1:49.

6. PY 1:82–85.

7. PY 2:225.

8. PY (Hebr.) 449.

9. PY (Hebr.) 449–450.

10. PY 1:46.

11. PY 1:238.

12. PY 2:163.

13. Romero, *Creación literaria,* 126f., 132f. Cf. the study of the image of Luria in the *Meʿam Loʿez* by Tamar Alexander, "The Character of R. Isaac Luria in the Judeo-Spanish Story: The Story of 'The Converso and the Shewbread' in Meʿam Loʿez," *Peʿamim* 26 (1986), 87–107 (Hebr.).

14. As a matter of fact, the title page of *Leqet ha-Zohar* (Belgrade, 1877) clearly announces that it presents *"divre musarim"* from the *Zohar* in Ladino.

15. Dov Cohen, "Maʿamadam ha-hevrati," 43, has noted that, on the one hand, there was almost no systematic study of Kabbalah as a field of esoteric knowledge in the rabbinic institutions of Izmir in the eighteenth and nineteenth century but that, on the other hand, kabbalistic practices were pervasive in the Izmir community.

16. PY 2:195.

17. PY 2:196.

18. PY 2:197–200.

19. PY (Hebr.) 401.

20. PY (Hebr.) 401–402.

21. PY (Hebr.) 403–407.

22. PY (Hebr.) 403.

23. PY 1:93–94; cf. ZM 54b where Farhi cites Rabenu Bahye as the source for this *maʿase.* Other examples can be found in PY 1:109–111, 1:255–258, 1:260–263, 1:265, 1:270–271, chapters in which the Ladino version includes a significant number of *maʿasiyot* not found in the Hebrew original, and elsewhere.

24. PY (Hebr.) 12. The reference is to BT-Nedarim 66b.

25. PY 1:27.

26. HA 1, front page.

27. This must not be confused with the "calque" translations of Hebrew texts into Ladino, precisely because Palachi very often does not translate in imitation of the Hebrew original, but incorporates Hebrew elements as is into a new Judeo-Spanish text.

28. The 1868 Salonika edition from the *Estampería de la Qupah de Gemilut Hasadim* was announced in the June 1999 issue of *Judaica Jerusalem,* catalogue # 55, as "an important bibliographic discovery! Not listed by Ya'ari." I am very grateful to Dov Cohen of the Ben-Zvi Institute in Jerusalem, who called my attention to this edition.

29. PY (Hebr.), ed. princ. (Istanbul, 1824), 2b.

30. HA 1:20a.

31. PY 1:2.

32. MLGen, introduction [v a].

33. IB 23b–24a.

34. Cf. Dan, *Sifrut ha-musar,* 223f.

35. Incidentally, it is Elijah ha-Kohen in the *Shevet Musar* who presents a different position, encouraging his readers to study "whatever your heart enjoys most: if *Gemara,* then *Gemara;* if *derush* [homily], then *derush;* if *remez* [implied meaning, referring to one of the four levels of biblical exegesis], then *remez;* if *kabbalah,* then *kabbalah*" (ShM 1:4b). The reason is that, if one prefers to study a given aspect of rabbinic knowledge, one's soul has certainly transmigrated and come back because in an earlier life one had not adequately studied this area of knowledge. Elijah does not speak of a hierarchy, however, but of different domains of rabbinic knowledge, without distinguishing between easier and more difficult matters or learned and unlearned readers.

36. HA 1:33a.

37. HA 1:32b.

38. Cf. PY 2:63.

39. Still the best study of the *yetser* is Frank Chamberlin Porter, "The Yeçer Hara: A Study in the Jewish Doctrine of Sin," in *Biblical and Semitic Studies* (New York, 1901), 91–156; cf. Daniel Boyarin, *Carnal Israel: Reading Sex in Talmudic Culture* (Berkeley, 1993), 61–76.

40. PY 2:75–76.

41. Water being, of course, a metaphor for the Torah.

42. BT-Sukkah 52b; cf. BT-Qiddushin 30b. Quote from the Soncino translation.

43. DA 65b.

44. On the Enlightenment "mythe de l'Éducation" through books, cf. Michel de Certeau, *L'invention du quotidien: Arts de faire* (Paris, 1990), 241.

45. MLGen, introduction [v b].

46. MLGen, introduction [viii b].

47. PY 1:5.

48. Quoted in Romero, *Creación literaria,* 94f.

49. Davis, "Printing and the People," 192f.

50. For a comparative perspective, see Shaul Stampfer, "Gender Differentiation and Education of the Jewish Woman in Nineteenth-Century Eastern Europe," *Polin* 7 (1992), 63–87.

51. ShM 1:72a.

52. PY 1:202–203.

53. PY 1:202.

54. MH 25b.

55. PY 1:203–204.

56. PY 1:151.

57. Robert Bonfil, "La lectura en las comunidades hebreas de Europa occidental en la época medieval," in *Historia de la lectura en el mundo occidental,* ed. Guglielmo Cavallo and Roger Chartier (Madrid, 1997), 263f.; Harvey E. Goldberg, "The Zohar in Southern Morocco: A Study in the Ethnography of Texts," *History of Religions* 29 (1990), 233–258.

58. Fine, *Physician of the Soul,* 207–219.

59. Cf. Gries, *The Book as an Agent of Culture,* 82.

60. *Zekhut u-Mishor* (Izmir, 1850).

61. The chapters of the second part of *Kol Ze ha-Adam* are titled *"holeh," "holeh ha-guf,"* and *"holeh ha-nefesh."*

62. Tim Dant, *Knowledge, Ideology and Discourse: A Sociological Perspective* (London, 1991), 170.

63. PY 1:65.

64. PY 1:122–123.

65. IB 21a–21b.

66. PY 1:177–179.

67. Simha Assaf, "Sifriyot bate ha-midrash," *Yad la-Qore* 1 (1947), 170–172.

68. Göçek, *East Encounters West,* 110.

69. PY 2:227–228.

70. Itshac Broudo, "Masoret u-minhagim ʿamamiyim," in *Zikhron Saloniqi,* ed. David Recanati, vol. 2 (Tel Aviv, 1986), 368.

71. *Recontos Morales,* ed. "Società El Avenir" (Salonika, 1880), v.

4. "Pasar la Hora" or *"Meldar"*?

1. François Georgeon, "Présentation," in François Georgeon, Paul Dumont, eds., *Vivre dans l'Empire ottoman: Sociabilités et relations intercommunautaires (xviiiᵉ–xxᵉ siècles)* (Paris, 1997), 5–20: 6, 7: "Nous pouvons retenir de Max Weber que la sociabilité se déploie dans l'espace qui se situe entre la famille et l'État mais sans nous limiter aux seules 'structures'; les formes organisées, telles que les associations, sont loin d'épuiser le champ de la sociabilité. Nous devons chercher celle-ci aussi dans le domaine informel, spontané, intermédiaire des relations sociales, en deçà du fait associatif: par exemple, dans les conversations et les visites, dans les jeux et les divertissements, dans les échanges intellectuels et les relations commerciales, etc."

2. Minna Rozen, "Public Space and Private Space among the Jews of Istanbul in the Sixteenth and Seventeenth Centuries," *Turcica* 30 (1998), 331–346.

3. Moshe Idel, "'Hitbodedut' as Concentration in Ecstatic Kabbalah," in *Jewish Spirituality I,* ed. Arthur Green (New York, 1986), 405–438.

4. HA 1:15a.

5. IB 77b.

6. ShM 1:54b.

7. IB 56a–56b.

8. PY 1:82–84.

9. Cf. IB 28a–29b.

10. ZM 68b–69a.

11. IB 28a.

12. PY 1:84.

13. KA 46a.

14. PY 1:98.

15. PY 1:85.

16. PY 1:86.

17. IB 27b.

18. Ben-Naʾeh, "Jewish Society in the Urban Centers," 274–295; idem, "Ben gildah le-qahal: ha-hevrot ha-yehudiyot ba-imperiyah ha-othmanit ba-meʾot ha-17–18," *Zion* 63 (1998), 277–318.

19. Pascual Pascual Recuero, *Diccionario básico Ladino-Español* (Barcelona, 1977), explains "semolada" as a kind of warm drink prepared in the winter time.

20. I.e., beyond the confines of the territory within which one is permitted to carry objects on the Sabbath. HA 1:15b.

21. Jacob Barnai, "Gildot yehudiot be-Turkiyah ba-meʾot ha-16–19," in *Yehudim ba-kalkalah*, ed. Nahum Gross (Jerusalem, 1985), 133–147; Barnai mentions guild's synagogues and *midrashim*, 139.

22. The agreement is now in the Central Archives for the History of the Jewish People in Jerusalem; cited in Cohen, "Maʿamadam ha-hevrati," 84.

23. Broudo, "Masoret u-minhagim ʿamamiyim," 368.

24. Emanuel, "Toldot yehude Saloniqi," 169–170; Isaac Jerusalmi, "El ladino, lengua del judaísmo y habla diaria," in Ángel Alcalá, ed., *Judíos. Sefarditas. Conversos* (Valladolid, 1995), 314: "Sea que estos *limmudim* se aplicaran a un pariente, en cuyo caso se realizaban en casa, o que los amigos invitaran a las suyas para sus *meldados*, o incluso a las de los vecinos para una *minyan* . . . la mayor parte de las personas asistían a estas reuniones al menos una vez o más cada mes. . . . Según los recursos de la familia se invitaba a cuatro o cinco rabinos, los cuales llegaban a la casa al menos una hora antes del servicio con sus libros de *Musar* . . . en ladino y se turnaban leyéndolos y explicándoles su contenido a todos los miembros de la familia y a sus amigos, mujeres y hombres, reunidos para la ocasión. Para subrayar ciertos puntos citaban numerosos *maʿasim* y *aggadot* así como refranes populares, resumiendo sus lecciones en máximas fácilmente recordables." Jerusalmi also points to a parallel of the *meldado* in memory of the defunct among Muslim Turks, the *mevlût nebevi*, during which a lengthy poem on the birth of the prophet Muhammad was recited (314).

25. Azriel Shohat, "Hevrot limud ba-meʾot ha-16–18 be-erets Yisraʾel, be-Folin-Lita uve-Germanyah," in idem, *Mehqarim*, part 1 (Haifa, 1978), 214–240.

26. Ben-Naʾeh, "Jewish Society in the Urban Centers," 195.

27. Shohat, "Hevrot limud." On Rabbi Loew (the Maharal) and his significance for the initiation of a modernization process of central European Jewry, see Dan, *Sifrut ha-Musar*, 230–237; David Sorkin, *The Transformation of German Jewry* (Detroit, 1999), 47. On the practice in Safed, see also David, *To Come to the Land*, 131–134.

28. See above, chapter 3.

29. Ben-Naʾeh, "Jewish Society in the Urban Centers," 274–295.

30. Quataert, *Ottoman Empire*, 158.

31. Ben-Naʾeh, "Jewish Society in the Urban Centers," 274–295.

32. PY 1:199–200.

33. ZM 37b.

34. HA 14b–15a. Cf. also PY 1:94–95.

35. Cf. PY 1:273; ZM 24b–25a.

36. HA 1:31b.

37. Defined by Nehama as "chapelet à grains d'ambre que l'Oriental des classes aisées tient volontiers constamment à la main et qu'il égrène avec nonchalance pour tromper son ennui."

38. NZ 42–43. Cf. NZ 57–58. Cf. HA 1:15b–16a, IB 55a–55b, NZ 26.

39. According to Isaac Emanuel, "Toldot yehude Saloniqi," 272–273, even in the eighteenth century it was a widespread practice among the Jews of Salonika, including *talmide hakhamim,* to spend Sabbath afternoon socializing in gentile coffee houses. Rabbi Hayim Abulafia of Izmir likewise complained about the practice in his book *Hanan Elohim* (published 1737): Shmuel Ettinger, *Toldot ha-yehudim ba-artsot ha-Islam* (Jerusalem, 1981), vol. 1, 261. In the nineteenth century, Rabbi Joseph Hayim b. Elijah al-Hakam (Ben Ish Hay) of Baghdad ruled leniently on the question of frequenting gentile coffeehouses on the Sabbath and did "not protest vociferously for a number of reasons": Norman Stillman, *Sephardi Religious Responses to Modernity* (Luxembourg, 1995), 21.

40. PY 2:80.

41. Cf. Farhi, ZM 19b–20a.

42. MH 42a.

43. Cf. PY 2:64: "To ridicule and slander people carries great punishment.... This sin is more often found among women because they do not know its seriousness. The evil inclination lets this slanderous talk seem delectable and funny, and how much more so if obscenities are involved, the joy is great and they cannot stop laughing. The one who talks, as he sees that they like his talk, imagines and thinks about what other jokes and obscene remarks to make.... The one who talks and those who listen and enjoy it, like it and laugh: all of them will have to burn in *gehinam.*"

44. Cf. the extensive chapter on "dibur" in the *Pele Yoʿets:* PY 1:150–175.

45. ShM 1:11a–11b.

46. Cf. KA 1b.

47. PY 2:301–304.

48. One can even argue that the establishment of *meldados* predates and prepares the ground for the later (nineteenth century) associational life in Ottoman Sephardic communities. On associations in the nineteenth century, cf. Esther Benbassa, "Associational Strategies in Ottoman Jewish Society in the Nineteenth and Twentieth Centuries," in Avigdor Levi, ed., *The Jews of the Ottoman Empire* (Princeton, 1992), 457–484.

5. The Construction of the Social Order

1. Angel, *Voices in Exile,* 106.

2. "Discourse is the form in which knowledge appears as a social phenomenon, as something that can be shared," as Tim Dant has argued. "At the same time, the process of discourse has ideological effects in that as lived relations are rendered into representations in language, those relations are simplified and transformed. Most importantly, the representation of lived relations in language-like processes obscures or smooths over contradictions.... If the contents of knowledge are treated as present in discourse, rather than present in 'thought' as in the traditional sociology of knowledge, then the relations between knowledge and its context can be analysed through studying discourse. Accounts in discourse are not simply 'accounts' of the world; they are also among those human practices that constitute the world." Dant, *Knowledge, Ideology and Discourse,* 207.

3. DA 41b–42a.

4. HA 2:8a, 8b.

5. ZM 35b, 36a.

6. DA 29b.

7. PY 1:33. Cf. Isaac Badhab's musar treatise that serves as introduction to his history of the Jews and where he likewise names the strife and lack of unity as one reason that brought down the Temple and caused the sufferings of the present exile (NZ 56).

8. DA 33b ff.

9. HA 1:35b.

10. PY 1:197.

11. PY 1:198.

12. PY 1:198.

13. PY 1:198–199.

14. PY 1:35. "However fat the hen, she needs her neighbor. One hand washes the other, and together they wash the face."

15. PY 2:269–270.

16. Cf. another popular story (*ma'ase*) à propos the right use of wealth (for charity and *mitsvot*) which is found in more than one musar book, e.g., in PY 2:272–273 or ShM 1:5b–6a.

17. IB 73a.

18. IB 71a.

19. PY 1:1.

20. PY 1:35.

21. PY 1:35.

22. DA 44a–44b.

23. PY 2:96.

24. David Hartman and Tzvi Marx, "Charity," in *Contemporary Jewish Religious Thought*, ed. Arthur A. Cohen and Paul Mendes-Flohr (New York, 1987), 52, quoting *Mishneh Torah, Hilkhot Matenot 'Aniyim* 10:7.

25. PY 1:210–217.

26. IB 20a–20b.

27. PY 2:70–71.

28. PY 2:251–252.

29. PY 2:73–74.

30. To chastise and educate others is not an easy task, as the rabbis are well aware, and requires a certain degree of resourcefulness. Cf. HA 1:19a–b.

31. ShM 1:72b. Cf. PY 1:136. Farhi (IB 70a) explains that it is "la regla de el mundo": if someone has another person writing a letter for him, he has to pay according to the latter's social status, depending on whether he is a student, a rabbi, the head of a *yeshivah*, and so on.

32. ZM 48a.

33. DA 32a.

34. DA 30b–31b.

35. ZM 48b–49a.

36. PY 1:36–37.

37. Joseph Néhama, *Histoire des Israélites de Salonique*, vol. 6 (Salonika, 1978), 102.

6. Three Social Types

1. ShM 1:22a.

2. In fact, Elijah ha-Kohen argues that the central task of musar, moral chastisement,

itself depends upon this social differentiation, for people only accept it if it comes from above and is backed by the authority of political-economic power or expertise in traditional knowledge (ShM 22a–22b).

3. DA 58a.

4. HA 2:56b–57a.

5. DA 3b.

6. DA 76a; cf. Shelomo ibn Verga, *Sefer Shevet Yehudah,* ed. Isaac Baer (Jerusalem, 1977), 26ff.

7. On blood libels in the Ottoman Empire, see Jacob Barnai, "Blood Libels in the Ottoman Empire of the Fifteenth to Nineteenth Centuries," in *Antisemitism through the Ages,* ed. Shmuel Almog (New York, 1988), 189–194. The presumptive exhibition of wealth was often cited as a reason for popular anti-Jewish feelings in the Muslim world as well; cf. Cohen, *Under Crescent and Cross.*

8. HA 2:76a–b.

9. HA 1:38b.

10. HA 2:61b.

11. Ibid.

12. Hayim Palachi published a book on taxes and community finances in 1849 under the title *Masa Hayim.* Cf. Leah Bornstein-Makovetsky, "Halakhic and Rabbinic Literature in Turkey, Greece, and the Balkans," *Pe'amim* 86 (2001), 144.

13. Avner Levi, "*Shavat Aniim:* Social Cleavage, Class War and Leadership in the Sephardic Community—The Case of Izmir 1847," in *Ottoman and Turkish Jewry: Community and Leadership,* ed. Aron Rodrigue (Bloomington, 1992), 183–202. Levi points out Hayim Palachi's role: "In 1847, Hayim Palachi was president of the *Beit Din,* and he fought for the meat *gabela* [siding with the rich party]. Later, the rich party prevented him from dealing with financial matters. Immediately after that he declared the meat *gabela* was null and void. When the rich appeased him, he regained his authority and forgot completely about the annulment" (197). Also see Avner Levi, "Changes in the Leadership of the Main Spanish Communities in the Nineteenth-Century Ottoman Empire," in *The Days of the Crescent: Chapters in the History of the Jews in the Ottoman Empire,* ed. Minna Rozen (Tel Aviv, 1996), 237–271 (Hebr.). Paul Dumont describes the transformation of Sephardic society in Salonika at the turn of the twentieth century in his "The Social Structure of the Jewish Community of Salonica at the End of the Nineteenth Century," *Southeastern Europe* 5 (1978), 33–72.

14. Rodrigue, *French Jews, Turkish Jews,* 52; Abraham Galanté, *Histoire de Juifs d'Anatolie,* 2 vols. (Istanbul, 1937–39), vol. 1, 58–66; Shaw, *Jews of the Ottoman Empire and the Turkish Republic,* 173–175; Jacob Barnai, "Organization and Leadership in the Jewish Community of Izmir in the Seventeenth Century," in *The Jews of the Ottoman Empire,* ed. Avigdor Levy (Princeton, 1994), 278–279. This was not the last conflict involving the Palachi family: on the problems after Abraham Palachi's death in 1899, cf. Gabriel Arié's autobiography (Benbassa and Rodrigue, *A Sephardi Life in Southeastern Europe,* 125).

15. Similarly ambiguous was the attitude of the Salonikan rabbis of the time before the nineteenth century, usually siding with the wealthy notables in their decisions but requesting the solildarity of the rich: Eli'ezer Bashan, "The Attitude of the Sages of Salonika in the Sixteenth to the Eighteenth Centuries, in the Confrontation over Oligarchic Rule," *Mi–mizrah umi-ma'arav* 2 (1980), 27–52 (Hebr.).

16. Levi, "Changes in the Leadership."

17. On Jewish money lending in the Ottoman Empire, cf. Hayim Gerber, "Jews and Money-Lending in the Ottoman Empire," *Jewish Quarterly Review* 72 (1981), 100–118.

18. PY 2:82–84.

19. PY (Hebr.) 555–556.

20. PY (Hebr.) 470–471.

21. PY 2:246–247.

22. Incidentally, many of these charges were also those of Zionist activists in the early twentieth century who "couched their language and action within the context of class struggle" and called to "combat the rich, the 'assimilationists,' Frenchified, occidentalized, exploiters of the community's rank and file." Benbassa, "Zionism in the Ottoman Empire," 136.

23. Cf. Rodrigue, "Beginnings of Westernization," and references on the Italian Jews in the Ottoman Empire given in the introduction.

24. ShM 1:55a–56a.

25. PY 1:66.

26. The pessimistic description offered by Shaw, *History*, is unfortunately too determined by his opposition of a golden age in the sixteenth century, the catastrophic decline in the eighteenth and the revival of the nineteenth century. A very good description of the precariousness of pre-modern life in an Ottoman urban center is provided in Abraham Marcus's study *The Middle East on the Eve of Modernity: Aleppo in the Eighteenth Century* (New York, 1989).

27. ShM 1:21b–22a.

28. PY 2:241–242.

29. HA 1:29b.

30. Very helpful is Dov Cohen's recent study "MaꜤamadam ha-hevrati shel talmide hakhamim be-Izmir."

31. Sorkin, *Transformation*, 45.

32. Cf. the remarks on rabbis, the ethos of the *yeshivah*, and society in Robert Bonfil, "Le savoir et le pouvoir: Pour une histoire du rabbinat à l'époque pré-moderne," in *La société juive à travers l'histoire*, ed. Shmuel Trigano, 4 vols. (Paris, 1992), vol. 1, 115–195.

33. ZM 53a–b.

34. PY 1:266–267.

35. I expand on this in the chapter on the Land of Israel.

36. "Se muchiguaron los rubisim más de los talmidim."

37. MH 24a–b.

38. ZM 54a.

39. ZM 47a–b.

40. PY 1:258; see also the quotation from ShM 14a cited above. Cf. *Bereshit Rabah* 72:5.

41. PY 1:31–32; PY 1:268–269.

42. This is a recurrent theme throughout Judeo-Spanish musar; cf. for example ZM 4a–b.

43. ZM 54a.

44. ShM 1:24b, 25b.

45. PY 1:93.

46. ShM 1:26a.

47. HA 2:9b. The reference to Elijah ha-Kohen is ShM 2:126a–127b.

48. IB 85b.
49. For the *Sefer Hasidim,* cf. Yitzhak F. Baer, "The Socioreligious Orientation of 'Sefer Hasidim,'" *Binah: Studies in Jewish Thought,* ed. Joseph Dan, vol. 2 (New York, 1989), 57–95; Ivan G. Marcus, *Piety and Society: The Jewish Pietists of Medieval Germany* (Leiden, 1981).
50. ShM 64b–66a.
51. ShM 67a.
52. PY 1:64–66.
53. Encyclopedia Judaica, s.v. "Apikoros."
54. PY (Hebr.) 39.
55. ShM 1:14a. Cf. BT-Berakhot 20a.
56. ShM 1:6b.

7. The Representation of Gender

1. Reginetta Haboucha, "Misogyny or Philogyny: The Case of the Judeo-Spanish Folktale," in *New Horizons in Sephardic Studies,* ed. Yedida K. Stillman and George K. Zucker (Albany, 1993), 239–251; idem, "Women in the Judeo-Spanish Folktales," in *The Sephardic Scholar,* series 4 (1979–1982) (New York, 1982), 32–47. On the status of Sephardic women in traditional society, cf. Renée Levine Melammed, "Sephardi Women in the Medieval and Early Modern Periods," in *Jewish Women in Historical Perspective,* ed. Judith R. Baskin (Detroit, 1991), 115–134. For a comparative perspective on Ottoman women in general, cf. Madeline C. Zilfi, ed., *Women in the Ottoman Empire: Middle Eastern Women in the Early Modern Era* (Leiden, 1997).
2. ShM 2:8a. The parable of the righteous woman converting her wicked husband to righteousness, and the wicked woman who makes her husband into a villain, is used more often. Cf. PY 1:202.
3. Charles Mopsik, *Lettre sur la sainteté: Le secret de la relation entre l'homme et la femme dans la cabale* (Paris, 1986); Elliot R. Wolfson, *Circle in the Square: Studies in the Use of Gender in Kabbalistic Symbolism* (Albany, 1995).
4. DA 61a–b.
5. Cf. M-Horayot 3:7. Judith Romney Wegner, *Chattel or Person? The Status of Women in the Mishnah* (New York, 1988), 166f.
6. PY 1:90.
7. MLGen 228a.
8. PY 1:91.
9. Quoted by Joan Scott Wallach, "Gender: A Useful Category of Historical Analysis," *American Historical Review* 91 (1986), 1054.
10. ShM 1:18b–19a.
11. ShM 1:19a.
12. HA 1:159a–b.
13. Jacob Neusner, *Judaism: The Evidence of the Mishnah* (Chicago, 1982); Wegner, *Chattle or Person.*
14. Judith Hauptman, "Feminist Perspectives on Rabbinic Texts," in *Feminist Perspectives on Jewish Studies,* ed. Lynn Davidman and Shelly Tenenbaum (New Haven, 1994), 45.
15. Hauptman, "Feminist Perspectives," 53.
16. HA 1:120a.
17. HA 1:120b.

18. PY 1:227.

19. PY 1:230–232.

20. Cf. PY 1:234–235.

21. ShM 1:103a–b.

22. HA 1:160b.

23. HA 1:160b–161a.

24. Gunilla-Friederike Budde, "Das Geschlecht der Geschichte," in *Geschichte zwischen Kultur und Gesellschaft: Beiträge zur Theoriedebatte,* ed. Thomas Mergel and Thomas Welskopp (Munich, 1997), 125–150.

25. ShM 2:10b. Palachi expresses the same idea: HA 1:17a.

26. ShM 2:27b.

27. MLEst 34a.

28. HA 1:17a.

29. ShM 2:13b–14a.

30. ShM 1:62a.

31. PY 1:25. *Tiqun hatsot,* the studying of certain texts at midnight, is a practice informed by Lurianic Kabbalah.

32. A counterpart to this list of ten virtues in the *Shevet Musar* is Farhi's list of the ten faults that one can find in women: "There are many bad qualities among women, and if she does not have all of them, then at least some. The first bad quality is insincerity and hypocrisy, demonstrating love for her husband while her heart is evil. The second bad quality is that she talks without thinking, causing anxiety and sadness to the one who listens to her. The third bad quality is that she is [like a] thief, for whenever she sees her husband having some money, he must pay her her share (*maʿaser*). The fourth bad quality is that she is stupid and though one gives her advice, she does not overcome her stupidness. The fifth bad quality is that she does not even know how to fry an egg, when it is right, when over-salted, when burned. The sixth bad quality is that she is furious and her anger is resented by all who enter her house. The seventh bad quality is that she is stingy and does not want to share with anyone the light of her candle. The eighth bad quality is that she is very dirty and filthy, so that it is disgusting to look at her. The ninth bad quality is that she destroys everything, and when she puts on a new dress, she soon enough will have destroyed it. The tenth bad quality is her falsehood and that she is a liar and one cannot believe anything she says" (ZM 29a–b).

33. ShM 2:8a–b.

34. PY 1:28–29.

35. Cf. ShM 1:102a; HA 1:37a; DA 46a–b.

36. ShM 2:8b.

37. ShM 2:8b–9a.

38. ShM 9b.

39. The Judeo-Spanish *romancero* is arguably the best-studied aspect of Judeo-Spanish tradition. Cf. the ground-breaking works by Samuel Armistead and Joseph Silverman.

40. Barquín López, *Doce novelas,* 176–182.

41. PY 1:22–23.

42. The husband as his wife's teacher is also invoked in the following: "The bridegroom must take care during the first night to talk with his bride about [the laws of] Judaism, about *halah* and how to light the candles of the Sabbath . . . and he also must admonish her well about the laws of decency, so that she be strictly decent" (HA 1:160a).

43. PY 1:23.

44. The rabbis also have practical advice to encourage the husband to preserve domestic peace. A husband should meet his wife's wishes as much as he can, "for it is the nature of most women that they desire whatever they see" (PY 1:24). Another piece of practical advice is to avoid long business trips, and if he has to travel, "he should at least content her with frequent letters and gifts" (PY 1:24).

45. Eliᶜezer ben Shem Tov Papo, *Sefer Dameseq Eliᶜezer,* part *Orah Hayim* (Belgrade, 1860), 128b.

46. PY 2:219.

47. PY 1:77.

48. PY 1:201.

8. Understanding Exile, Setting Boundaries

1. Arnold M. Eisen, *Galut: Modern Jewish Reflection on Homelessness and Homecoming* (Bloomington, 1986), 14, 17.

2. For a comparison between the Hebrew, Judeo-Spanish, and Judeo-German version of the chapter, see *infra,* "A Tale of Three Exiles."

3. PY 1:117. PY (Hebr.) 91.

4. PY 1:117.

5. PY 1:218. For references, cf. *Shemot Rabah* 47:5, BT-Pesahim 50b, BT-Ketubot 17a. The same is said in the beginning of the chapter on *"minhag"*—PY 2:186.

6. PY 1:134.

7. PY 1:132.

8. Natalie Zemon Davis, *Women on the Margins: Three Seventeenth-Century Lives* (Cambridge, Mass., 1995), 211.

9. Eisen, *Galut,* 36f.

10. Shaye J. D. Cohen, *The Beginnings of Jewishness: Boundaries, Varieties, Uncertainties* (Berkeley and Los Angeles, 1999).

11. This is true not only for the Jewish community but for Ottoman elites at large. Cf. Berkes, *Secularism,* 23–50.

12. IB 41a.

13. Cf. the contributions in Laurence J. Silberstein and Robert L. Cohn, eds., *The Other in Jewish Thought and History: Constructions of Jewish Culture and Identity* (New York, 1994).

14. ShM 1:64b.

15. DA 38a.

16. IB 17b.

17. Aron Rodrigue, "Eastern Sephardi Jewry and New Nation-States in the Balkans in the Nineteenth and Twentieth Centuries," in *Sephardi and Middle Eastern Jewries,* ed. Harvey E. Goldberg (Bloomington, 1996), 81, 87.

18. Paula E. Hyman, *Gender and Assimilation in Modern Jewish History: The Roles and Representation of Women* (Seattle, 1995), 13.

19. Carter V. Findley, "The Acid Test of Ottomanism: The Acceptance of Non-Muslims in the Late Ottoman Bureaucracy," in *Christians and Jews in the Ottoman Empire: The Functioning of a Plural Society,* ed. Benjamin Braude and Bernard Lewis (New York, 1982), vol. 1: *The Central Lands,* 339–368.

20. E.g., Zemach Rabbiner, *Las Madres Judías de la Epoca Biblica* (Constantinople, 1913).

21. Göçek, *Rise of the Bourgeoisie, Demise of Empire;* Faroqhi, *Kultur und Alltag;* cf. Paul Dumont, "Le français d'abord," in *Salonique, 1850–1918: La 'ville des Juifs' et le réveil des Balkans,* ed. Gilles Veinstein (Paris, 1993), 208–225.

22. E.g., HA 2:55b.

23. IB 22a.

24. The contributions in Paul Dumont and François Georgeon, *Villes ottomanes à la fin de l'empire* (Paris, 1992), are instructive; cf. also Faroqhi, *Kultur und Alltag,* 166–182, 281–285.

25. HA 2:8b–9a.

26. ShM 1:30a.

27. IB 21a.

28. IB 21a–b.

29. David Stern, *Midrash and Theory: Ancient Jewish Exegesis and Contemporary Literary Studies* (Evanston, 1996), 3 and 15–38 ("Midrash and Hermeneutics: Polysemy vs. Indeterminacy").

30. IB 66a–67a. Cf. also IB 80b–81a.

31. The responsa literature of the eighteenth and nineteenth centuries also deals with a growing number of sexual transgressions (and testifies to other shortcomings denounced in musar, such as neglect of prayers, going to the coffeehouse on the Sabbath, and the like). Cf. Bornstein, "Halakhic and Rabbinic Literature," 124.

32. *La Buena Esperanza* (1842) and four years later *Sha'are Mizrah (Puertas de Oriente);* see above, chapter 2.

33. Michael Silber, "The Emergence of Ultra-Orthodoxy: The Invention of a Tradition," in *The Uses of Tradition: Jewish Continuity in the Modern Era,* ed. Jack Wertheimer (New York, 1992), 23–84; on the language issue, cf. David Bunis, Joseph Chetrit, and Haideh Sahim, "Jewish Languages Enter the Modern Era," in Reeva Spector Simon, Michael Menachem Laskier, and Sara Reguer, eds., *The Jews of the Middle East and North Africa in Modern Times* (New York, 2003), 113–141 (Ladino, 116–128; Judeo-Arabic, 128–133); David Bunis, "Modernization and the Language Question among Judezmo-Speaking Sephardim of the Ottoman Empire," in *Sephardi and Middle Eastern Jewries: History and Culture in the Modern Era,* ed. Harvey E. Goldberg (Bloomington, 1996), 226–239.

34. ZM 32b.

35. ZM 12b–13a.

36. ZM 18b.

37. Quartaert, *The Ottoman Empire,* 146; cf. Stein, *Making Jews Modern,* 185.

38. PY (Hebr.) 93.

39. PY (Judeo-Ger.) 1:50.

40. PY 1:117.

41. PY (Hebr.) 92.

42. PY 1:117–118.

43. PY (Judeo-Ger.) 1:50.

44. PY (Hebr.) 92f. (*galut ha-nefesh*) and 93–95 (*devarim ha-nog'im el ha-guf*).

45. Mordechai Breuer, "Frühe Neuzeit und Beginn der Moderne," in *Deutsch-jüdische Geschichte in der Neuzeit,* vol. 1: *Tradition und Aufklärung 1600–1780,* ed. Michael A. Meyer (Munich, 1996), 148f.

46. PY (Hebr.) 93.

47. Angel, *The Essential Pele Yoetz,* 45; PY (Hebr.) 93.

48. PY (Hebr.) 93–94: "*Yisra'el en hozrin bi-teshuvah ela 'al-yede melekh qasheh.*"

49. PY (Hebr.) 94.
50. PY 1:118–119.
51. PY 1:118.
52. PY 1:118–119.
53. PY 1:119.
54. Ibid.
55. Ibid.
56. PY 1:121.
57. ShM 2:10b.
58. MLEst, note before page 1a.
59. DA 29b–30a. On colonialism and the representation of non-European "indigenous people" in the Judeo-Spanish press, see Stein, *Making Jews Modern*, 136f.
60. DA 34a–35b.
61. DA 35b.
62. PY 1:120.
63. PY 1:121.
64. PY 1:122–123.
65. PY (Judeo-Ger.) 1:52.
66. PY (Judeo-Ger.) 1:50.
67. PY (Judeo-Ger.) 1:50–51.
68. PY (Judeo-Ger.) 1:51.
69. Cf. the important article on the origins of ultra-orthodoxy in Hungary by Silber, "The Emergence of Ultra-Orthodoxy."

9. The Impossible Homecoming

1. DA 17a.
2. PY (Hebr.) 31. This was a rather common attitude, informed by the precarious economic situation in Palestine. In the eighteenth century, the Istanbul Committee of Officials for Palestine, acting as intermediaries between the communities in Israel and the Diaspora, limited the number of immigrants to Palestine and, in the case of Jerusalem, established a prohibition of bachelors under the age of sixty settling in the city. Jacob Barnai, *The Jews in Palestine in the Eigtheenth Century* (Tuscaloosa, 1992), 47. On positive, typically messianic attitudes in favor of immigration in the same period, see, in the same volume, 41–46.
3. PY 1:57.
4. PY (Hebr.) 32.
5. Cf. BT-Baba Metsia 71a; *Shulhan ʿArukh: Yore Deʿah* 251:3.
6. PY 1:267–268.
7. PY (Hebr.) 32–33.
8. Jean-Christophe Attias and Esther Benbassa, *Israël Imaginaire* (Paris, 1998), 63: "Le thème de la centralité de Jérusalem et de son sanctuaire," in the words of a recent study of representations of the Land of Israel, "devait connaître une fortune remarquable au Moyen Age. Mais alors la *représentation* de la centralité prendra largement le pas sur sa *réalité*—elle se sera substituée à elle, elle en fera pour ainsi dire fonction."
9. Quoted in Jacob Barnai, "Ha-yehudim ba-imperiyah ha-ʿOthmanit," in *History of the Jews in the Islamic Countries,* part 2: *From the Middle of the Nineteenth to the Middle of the Twentieth Century,* ed. Shmuel Ettinger (Jerusalem, 1986), 292 (Hebr.).

10. Angel, *Voices in Exile*, 138.

11. R. Judah Bibas, born in Gibraltar 1870 and rabbi in Corfu after 1832, reinterpreted *teshuvah* to its literal meaning of "return" to the Land. Bibas and Alkalaʿi met in 1839. Cf. Norman Stillman, "'My Heart's in the East': Sephardi Zionism," in Stillman, *Sephardi Religious Responses to Modernity*, 54f.

12. Cf. Arthur Hertzberg, ed., *The Zionist Idea* (New York, 1960), 103–107; Jennie Lebel, "'Longing for Jerusalem': Rabbi Yehudah Alkalay, the Political and Communal Context of His Activity," *Peʿamim* 40 (1989), 21–48 (Hebr.); Zvi Loker, "Le rabbin Juda ben Salomon Hay Alcalay et l'Alliance Israélite Universelle à propos de ses lettres inédites," *Revue des études juives* 144 (1985), 127–144.

13. *Zohar, Va-yera* 1:117, quoted in Arie Morgenstern, "Messianic Concepts and Settlement in the Land of Israel," in *Essential Papers on Messianic Movements and Personalities in Jewish History*, ed. Marc Saperstein (New York, 1992), 435f.

14. Morgenstern, "Messianic Concepts and Settlement," 444–451.

15. Judah Alkalaʿi, *Sefer Shelom Yerushalayim* (Ofen, 1840), 5.

16. Angel, *Voices in Exile*, 139.

17. Quoted in Stillman, "Sephardi Zionism," 57.

18. PY 1:129.

19. PY 1:124. Elsewhere, the PY (1:95) has: "It is because of our tears that God delivers us from exile," that is to say, wailing because of the destruction of the Temple and the fate of exile, not political activism and settling the land, will bring "galut" to an end.

20. Quoted in Morgenstern, "Messianic Consepts and Settlement," 442.

21. This way of interpreting the replacement of one Islamic power by another is not new: the Ottomans' conquests of the Mamluk empire also had been drawn in messianic colors, for example in Elijah Capsali's chronicle *Seder Eliyahu Zuta* (ed. Aryeh Shmuelevitz and Shlomo Simonsohn, 2 vols. [Jerusalem, 1975–77]).

22. Moshe Maʿoz, "Changes in the Position of the Jewish Communities of Palestine and Syria in Mid-Nineteenth Century," in *Studies on Palestine during the Ottoman Period*, ed. Moshe Maʿoz (Jerusalem, 1975), 147f.

23. IB 59a–65b.

24. IB 64a.

25. IB 65a.

26. Barnai, *Jews in Palestine*.

27. Barnai, *Ha-yehudim*, 290f.

28. PY 2:105. The passage is taken from the book *Yosef Omets* by the eighteenth-century rabbi Hayim Joseph David Azulai, but Papo apparently still thinks the praise of the Jerusalem community is appropriate enough in his own time.

29. PY 2:105–106.

30. PY 2:105, 106.

31. PY 2:106.

32. PY 2:107.

33. Ibid.

34. IB 72a–b.

35. PY 2:108.

36. Ibid.

37. PY 2:109.

38. Ibid.

39. PY 2:166.

40. PY 2:167.

41. *Pele Yoꞌets,* vol. 2 (Salonika, 1900), 195.

42. Quoted in Lewis, *Emergence of Modern Turkey,* 85.

43. See references above, chapter 4; cf. also NZ 63–64.

44. NZ 46.

45. NZ 43.

46. NZ 58. Various violations of the laws of Sabbath are involved in the latter case. Badhab seems troubled by their reading business correspondence, profaning the Sabbath, and the possible receipt of bad news which will distract them from the celebration of the Sabbath.

47. Harvey E. Goldberg, "Religious Responses among North African Jews in the Nineteenth and Twentieth Centuries," in *The Uses of Tradition: Jewish Continuity in the Modern Era,* ed. Jack Wertheimer (New York, 1992), 132f.

48. NZ 28–30.

49. Cf. Rafael Pontremoli, *Meꞌam Loꞌez* on Esther (Izmir, 1864), 181b–182a: the Jews were saved from Haman's plan to annihilate them because of "the merit of the 22,000 children [assembled by] Mordecai, who were studying (*estaban meldando*) and crying out to God: This is why God saved them [the Jews]. . . . Therefore, it says: '*And the memory of them shall never perish among their descendants*' [Est 9:28]. It remained as a remembrance for them forever, that in every affliction that comes upon the Jewish people, they must bring the children from the *meldar* [traditional school] so that they may say prayers. . . . And thus the Jewish nation should make sure to continue to send their children to the *meldar* and not to remove them from the *meldar* in order to teach them polite behavior (*cunplimientos de ꞌolam ha-ze*) in non-Jewish schools, because if they do so, there will not remain anyone who knows how to study (*meldar*) and how to cry out to God and thus cancel the evil decrees."

50. NZ 74.

51. Eisen, *Galut,* 51.

52. With the notable exception of Bulgaria; cf. Benbassa and Rodrigue, *Sephardi Jewry,* 116–143; Benbassa, "Zionism in the Ottoman Empire," 127–140; idem, *Une diaspora sépharade;* idem, "Zionism and the Politics of Coalitions in the Ottoman Jewish Communities in the Early Twentieth Century," in *Ottoman and Turkish Jewry: Community and Leadership,* ed. Aron Rodrigue (Bloomington, 1992), 225–251; idem, "Les relais nationalistes juifs dans les Balkans au xixᵉ siècle," in *Transmission et passages en monde juif,* ed. Esther Benbassa (Paris, 1997), 403–434.

10. Reincarnation and the Discovery of History

1. Luhmann, *Soziale Systeme,* 377–487; idem, "The Future Cannot Begin: Temporal Structures in Modern Society," *Social Research* 43 (1976), 130–152.

2. Reinhart Koselleck, "'Erfahrungsraum' und 'Erwartungshorizont,'" in idem, *Vergangene Zukunft: Zur Semantik geschichtlicher Zeiten,* 3rd ed. (Frankfurt, 1995), 349–375.

3. IB 88a–89b.

4. Cf. HA 2:28b; cf. also the similar explanations given for poverty (above, chapter 6).

5. Berger and Luckmann, *The Social Construction of Reality,* 119.

6. IB 35b–36a.

7. HA 2:28a–29a.

8. Scholem, *Major Trends,* 283.

9. Ibid., 281.

10. ShM 1:87b.

11. NZ 18.

12. Jan Assmann, *Das kulturelle Gedächtnis: Schrift, Erinnerung und politische Identität in frühen Hochkulturen* (Munich, 1999), 52, speaking of the "cultural memory" of premodern societies: "Das *kulturelle* Gedächtnis richtet sich auf Fixpunkte in der Vergangenheit. Auch in ihm vermag sich Vergangenheit nicht als solche zu erhalten. Vergangenheit gerinnt hier vielmehr zu symbolischen Figuren, an die sich die Erinnerung heftet."

13. Yosef Hayim Yerushalmi, *Zakhor: Jewish History and Jewish Memory* (Seattle, 1982), 57. It is impossible to decide whether they were interested in this work because it appealed to them as *Sephardic* Jews, creating a link with the old *Sefarad.* One might object, however, that the *Shevet Yehudah* was also popular in the Ashkenazic world (the first Yiddish translation appeared centuries before the Ladino one) and that we hardly find any particular reference to Spain throughout Judeo-Spanish musar literature.

14. Landau, *Content and Form,* 34–45.

15. ShM 1:58a.

16. ShM 1:103b.

17. DA i b.

18. MH [i a–i b].

19. These issues are amply discussed in a recent study by Jonathan Frankel, *The Damascus Affair: "Ritual Murder," Politics, and the Jews in 1840* (Cambridge, 1997).

20. DA 72a–91b; Shelomo ibn Verga, *Shevet Yehudah,* ed. Azriʾel Shohat (Jerusalem, 1947), chapter 7, 26–46.

21. DA 72a.

22. MH 27a–33a; *Shevet Yehudah,* chapter 17, 63–66; 161–163.

23. Yerushalmi, *Zakhor,* 65. Robert Bonfil challenges Yerushalmi's interpretation in his "How Golden Was the Age of the Renaissance in Jewish Historiography?," reprinted in *Essential Papers on Jewish Culture in Renaissance and Baroque Italy,* ed. David B. Ruderman (New York, 1992), 219–251, where he remarks, "The fanciful presentation of the persecutions of the Jews, as set out in Solomon Ibn Verga's *Shebet Yehudah* . . . cannot be considered as truly historical, however important this work may be for analyzing the perception of Jewish suffering in the wake of the Spanish Expulsion" (226f.).

24. Yerushalmi, *Zakhor,* 68f.

25. DA [i b].

26. A Judeo-Spanish translation of another sixteenth-century Jewish historiographical work, Joseph ha-Kohen's *ʿEmeq ha-Bakhah,* appeared only in 1935 in Salonika.

27. Pilar Romeu, ed., *Moisés Almosnino: Crónica de los reyes otomanos* (Barcelona, 1998); Romero, *Creación literaria,* 132.

28. Romero, *Creación literaria,* 203–207.

29. MH 86b–88a [wrong pagination in the printed edition = 92b–94a].

30. David B. Ruderman, *Jewish Thought and Scientific Discovery in Early Modern Europe* (New Haven, 1995), 229.

31. Ibid., 242–244.

32. Gershom Scholem, "Eliyahu ha-Kohen ha-Itamari veha-Shabtaʾut."

33. MH 77b [= 79b].

34. MH 79b [= 88b].

35. MH 85b [= 91b].

36. MH 90a [= 96a].

37. MH 92a [= 98a].

38. IB 91a–93a.

11. Scientific and Rabbinic Knowledge and the Notion of Change

1. *El Tiempo*, 10.11.1873, 4.

2. On the representation of scientific knowledge and the project of westernization, see Stein, *Making Jews Modern*, chapter 4.

3. *El Tiempo*, 10.11.1873, 4.

4. MLGen11a.

5. Ruderman, *Jewish Thought and Scientific Discovery*, 78.

6. MLGen 14b.

7. Ibid.

8. So says the title page of David Atias, *La Güerta de Oro* (Livorno, 1778): "To please a friend in the east," and, in a note preceding the table of contents (i a), he adds: "and at the same time in order to be of use for all those Levantine men who are attached to their wealth . . . and to knowing what they do not know." I study Atias's *Güerta de Oro* in more detail in my "A Livornese Port Jew and the Sephardim of the Ottoman Empire," *Jewish Social Studies* (forthcoming).

9. Atias, *Güerta de Oro*, 3a.

10. Ibid., 4a.

11. MH 1a–4a.

12. MH 3a.

13. MH 3b.

14. MH 18a.

15. Cf. the brief overview offered by Quataert, *The Ottoman Empire*, 112f.; cf. Abraham Marcus's discussion of eighteenth-century Ottoman Aleppo in this regard: Marcus, *The Middle East*, 252–276.

16. MH [i a], 73b [wrong pagination; should be 71b].

17. MH 67a [= 69a].

18. MH 67b [= 69b].

19. In 1847, 1881, and 1900, all in Salonika, in the Ladino version of Hayim Abraham Benveniste Gateño and in 1900 in Istanbul as part of the *Berakhah ha-Meshuleshet*. See Romero, *Creación literaria*, 135. Subsequent references to the *Sefer ha-Brit* in Ladino are to the first Salonika edition (1847); for references to the Hebrew text I use the edition published in Vilna 1904.

20. *Sefer ha-Brit* (Hebr.), 45b–47b; (Ladino), 129a–138a.

21. Kellner, *Maimonides*, 55–59; Ruderman, *Jewish Thought and Scientific Discovery*, 80.

22. Ruderman, *Jewish Thought and Scientific Discovery*, 69.

23. PY 2:120.

24. PY 2:120–122.

25. PY 2:155.

26. *Sefer ha-Berit* (Hebr.), 107a.

27. PY 2:155–156.

28. Ruderman, *Jewish Thought and Scientific Discovery*, 77.

29. DA 25a–b.

30. DA 25b.

31. Stephen Kern, *The Culture of Time and Space, 1880–1918* (Cambridge, Mass., 1983), 1.

32. Ibid., 87.

33. Cf. Donald Quataert, "The Age of Reforms, 1812–1914," on transportation, 798–823; Paul Dumont and François Georgeon, eds., *Villes ottomanes à la fin de l'empire* (Paris, 1992); Quataert, *Ottoman Empire*, 117–124; on Ottoman industrialization and the Jewish community, cf. Donald Quataert, "Premières fumées d'usines," in *Salonique, 1850–1918: La 'ville des Juifs' et le réveil des Balkans*, ed. Gilles Veinstein (Paris, 1993), 177–194. Historiography of Ottoman Jewry has so far ignored this important transformation of the experience of time and space, with the major exception of the study on halakhic responses by Zvi Zohar, *Tradition and Change: Halakhic Responses of Middle Eastern Rabbis to Legal and Technological Change (Egypt and Syria, 1880–1920)* (Jerusalem, 1993) (Hebr.).

34. KA 4b–7a.

35. KA 6b–7a. Roditi translates from *Yalqut Shimʿoni*, II Kings, 20, 244. Cf. also *Pesiqta de-Rav Kahana* II.6; *Shir ha-shirim Rabah* III.4.2; *Zohar* II.174b–175a; BT-Sanhedrin 96a; Louis Ginzberg, *The Legends of the Jews*, 7 vols., 5th ed. (Philadelphia, 1947), vol. 4, 275f. and 300.

36. I discuss Roditi's attitude toward technological innovation and change in more detail in my article "Two Perceptions of Change in Judeo-Spanish Rabbinic Literature," *Sefarad* 60 (2000), 95–121.

37. KA 9b–10a.

38. PY 1:128–129.

39. Palmira Brummet, *Image and Imperialism in the Ottoman Revolutionary Press, 1908–1911* (Albany, 2000), 302, 308f.

40. PY 2:134–135.

41. PY 2:172–175.

42. Papo is not the only one to give a messianic interpretation to technological progress. One of the founding fathers of Hungarian ultra-Orthodoxy, Akiva Yosef Schlesinger, would also praise scientific and technological innovation and interpret it as "a sign of Messianic stirrings." Cf. Silber, "The Emergence of Ultra-Orthodoxy," 65.

43. PY 2:171.

44. PY 2:140.

45. PY 2:160.

46. PY 2:156–157.

47. Quataert, *Ottoman Empire*, 118, 123. The reference by Papo is, by the way, the only one I have come across that refers—though only in passing—to the social consequences of Ottoman industrialization (which, to be sure, gains momentum in the years after the period covered in this study). Our sources unfortunately do not permit us to get any further into the matter. Cf. Donald Quataert, *Social Disintegration and Popular Resistance in the Ottoman Empire, 1881–1908* (New York, 1983), and idem, "The Industrial Working Class of Salonika, 1850–1912," in *The Days of the Crescent: Chapters in the History of the Jews in the Ottoman Empire*, ed. Minna Rozen (Tel Aviv, 1996), 311–330 (Hebr.).

48. Silber, "The Emergence of Ultra-Orthodoxy," 47f.

49. Zvi Zohar, "Traditional Flexibility and Modern Strictness: Two Halakhic Positions on Women's Suffrage," in *Sephardi and Middle Eastern Jewries*, ed. Harvey E. Goldberg (Bloomington, 1996), 130. Cf. also Zohar, *Tradition and Change*.

Bibliography

Rabbinic Sources

Alkala‘i, Judah. *Sefer Shelom Yerushalayim.* Ofen, 1840.

Amarachi, Isaac Bekhor, and Joseph ben Meir Sason. *Darkhe ha-Adam.* Salonika, 1843; Salonika, 1849; Salonika, 1892.

———. *Musar Haskel.* Salonika, 1843; Salonika, 1849; Salonika, 1892.

Attias, David. *La Güerta de Oro.* Livorno, 1778.

Badhab, Isaac. *Nehemadim mi-Zahav.* Jerusalem, 1899.

Farhi, Isaac. *Imre Binah.* Belgrade, 1836; Salonika, 1863; Salonika, 1887.

———. *Zekhut u-Mishor.* Izmir, 1850; Salonika, 1868 [Sa‘adi ha-Levi]; Salonika, 1868 [Qupah de gemilut hasadim]; Salonika, 1887.

Ha-Kohen, Elijah. *Shevet Musar.* 1st ed., Istanbul, 1712; modern ed. Jerusalem, 1989 (Hebrew).

———. *Shevet Musar.* Trans. Abraham Asa. Istanbul, 1748; Istanbul, 1766; Salonika, 1800; Izmir, 1860; Izmir, 1889 (Ladino).

Horowitz, Pinhas. *Sefer ha-Berit.* Salonika, 1847 (Ladino).

———. *Sefer ha-Berit.* Vilna, 1909 (Hebrew).

Huli, Jacob. *Me‘am Lo‘ez Bereshit.* 1st ed. Istanbul, 1730.

Laredo, Abraham; Isaac Ha-Levi. *Sefer Dat Yehudit.* Livorno, 1827; Jerusalem, 1878; Vienna, 1881.

Palachi, Abraham. *Ve-hokhiah Avraham.* Salonika, 1853 [vol. 1]; Izmir, 1862 [vol. 2]; Izmir, 1877 [in one volume].

Papo, Eli‘ezer. *Pele Yo‘ets.* 1st ed., Istanbul 1824; modern ed., Jerusalem, 1994 (Hebrew).

———. *Pele Yo‘ets.* Trans. Judah Papo. Vienna, 1870 [vol. 1]; Vienna, 1872 [vol. 2]; Salonika, 1899/1900 [both volumes] (Ladino).

Papo, Eli‘ezer ben Shem Tov. *Sefer Dameseq Eli‘ezer: Orah Hayim.* Belgrade, 1860.

Pontremoli, Rafael Hiya. *Me‘am Lo‘ez Ester.* Izmir, 1864.

Rabbiner, Zemach. *Las madres judías de la epoca bíblica.* Istanbul, 1913.

Roditi, Ben-Tsion. *Ki Ze Kol ha-Adam.* Izmir, 1884.

Secondary Sources

Abu-Manneh, Butrus. "The Islamic Roots of the Gülhane Rescript." *Die Welt des Islams* 34 (1994), 173–203.

Ahmad, Feroz. *The Making of Modern Turkey.* London, 1993.

Alexander, Tamar. *The Beloved Friend-and-a-Half: Studies in Sephardic Folk Literature.* Jerusalem, 1999.

———. "The Character of R. Isaac Luria in the Judeo-Spanish Story: The Story of 'The Converso and the Shewbread' in Meᶜam Loᶜez." *Peᶜamim* 26 (1986), 87–107 (Hebr.).

Alkalaᶜi, Yehudah. *Kitve ha-rav Yehudah Alkalaᶜi.* Ed. Isaac Werfel. Jerusalem, 1944.

Amarillo, Abraham. "The Great Talmud Torah Society in Salonika." *Sefunot* 13 (1971–78), 275–308 (Hebr.).

Angel, Marc. "The Responsa Literature in the Ottoman Empire as a Source for the Study of Ottoman Jewry." In *The Jews of the Ottoman Empire,* ed. Avigdor Levy, 669–685. Princeton, 1994.

———. *Voices in Exile: A Study in Sephardic Intellectual History.* Hoboken, N.J., 1991.

Angel, Marc, ed. *Eliezer Papo: The Essential Pele Yoetz:. An Encyclopaedia of Ethical Jewish Living.* New York, 1991.

Ashtor, Elijahu. *The Jews of Muslim Spain.* 3 vols. Philadelphia, 1992.

Assaf, Simha. "Sifriyot bate ha-midrash." *Yad la-Qore* 1 (1947), 170–172.

Assmann, Jan. *Das kulturelle Gedächtnis.* München, 1999.

Attias, Jean-Christophe, and Esther Benbassa. *Israël Imaginaire.* Paris, 1998.

Babinger, Franz. *Stambuler Buchwesen im 18. Jahrhundert.* Leipzig, 1919.

Baer, Yitshak. *A History of the Jews in Christian Spain.* 2 vols. Philadelphia, 1992.

———. "The Socioreligious Orientation of 'Sefer Hasidim.'" In *Binah: Studies in Jewish Thought,* ed. Joseph Dan, vol. 2, 57–95. New York, 1989.

Baraldi, Claudio, Giancarlo Corsi, and Elena Esposito. *GLU: Glossario dei termini della teoria dei sistemi di Niklas Luhmann.* Urbino, 1989.

Barnai, Jacob. "Blood Libels in the Ottoman Empire of the Fifteenth to Nineteenth Centuries." In *Antisemitism through the Ages,* ed. Shmuel Almog, 189–194. New York, 1988.

———. "From Sabbateanism to Modernization: Ottoman Jewry on the Eve of the Ottoman Reforms and the Haskala." In *Sephardi and Middle Eastern Jewries: History and Culture in the Modern Era,* ed. Harvey E. Goldberg, 73–80. Bloomington, 1996.

———. "Gildot yehudiot be-Turqiyah ba-meʾot ha-16–19." In *Yehudim ba-kalkalah,* ed. Nahum Gross, 133–147. Jerusalem, 1985.

———. "Ha-yehudim ba-imperiyah ha-ᶜOthmanit." In *History of the Jews in the Islamic Countries,* part 2: *From the Middle of the Nineteenth to the Middle of the Twentieth Century,* ed. Shmuel Ettinger, 183–297. Jerusalem, 1986 (Hebr.).

———. *The Jews in Palestine in the Eighteenth Century.* Tuscaloosa, 1992.

———. "Messianism and Leadership: The Sabbatean Movement and the Leadership of the Jewish Communities in the Ottoman Empire." In *Ottoman and Turkish Jewry: Community and Leadership,* ed. Aron Rodrigue, 167–182. Bloomington, 1992.

———. "On the History of the Sabbatean Movement and Its Place in the Life of the Jews in the Ottoman Empire." *Peᶜamim* 3 (1979), 59–72 (Hebr.).

———. "Organization and Leadership in the Jewish Community of Izmir in the Seventeenth Century." In *The Jews of the Ottoman Empire,* ed. Avigdor Levy, 275–284. Princeton, 1994.

———. "The Origins of the Jewish Community of Izmir in the Ottoman Period." *Peᶜamim* 12 (1982), 47–58 (Hebr.).

———. *Sabbateanism: Social Perspectives.* Jerusalem, 2000 (Hebr.).

———. "The Spread of the Sabbatean Movement in the Seventeenth and Eighteenth Centuries." In *Communication in the Jewish Diaspora: The Pre-modern World*, ed. Sophia Menashe, 313–338. Leiden, 1996.

Barquín López, Amelia. *Edición y estudio de doce novelas aljamiadas sefardíes de principios del siglo xx.* Vitoria, 1997.

Bashan, Eliʿezer. "The Attitude of the Sages of Salonika in the Sixteenth to the Eighteenth Centuries, in the Confrontation over Oligarchic Rule." *Mi-mizrah umi-maʿarav* 2 (1980), 27–52 (Hebr.).

Bazin, Louis. "La vie intellectuelle et culturelle dans l'Empire ottoman." In *Histoire de l'Empire ottoman*, ed. Robert Mantran, 695–724. Paris, 1989.

Benayahu, Meir. *Marbits Torah: Samkhuyotav tafqidav ve-helqo be-mosdot ha-qehilah bi-Sefarad be-Turqiyah uve-artsot ha-mizrah.* Jerusalem, 1953.

———. "The Sabbatean Movement in Greece." *Sefunot* 14 (1971–77) (Hebr.).

Benbassa, Esther. "Associational Strategies in Ottoman Jewish Society in the Nineteenth and Twentieth Centuries." In *The Jews of the Ottoman Empire*, ed. Avigdor Levi, 457–484. Princeton, 1992.

———. *Una diaspora sépharade en transition: Istanbul, xixᵉ–xxᵉ siècles.* Paris, 1993.

———. "Education for Jewish Girls in the East: A Portrait of the Galata School in Istanbul, 1872–1912." *Studies in Contemporary Jewry* 9 (1993), 163–173.

———. *Un Grand Rabbin sépharade en politique, 1892–1923.* Paris, 1990.

———. "Presse d'Istanbul et de Salonique au service du sionisme (1908–1914): les motifs d'une allégeance." *Revue Historique* 276 (1986), 337–365.

———. "Processus de modernisation en terre sépharade." In *La société juive á travers l'histoire*, ed. Shmuel Trigano, 4 vols., vol. 1, 565–605. Paris, 1992.

———. "Les relais nationalistes juifs dans les Balkans au xixᵉ siècle." In *Transmission et passages en monde juif*, ed. Esther Benbassa, 403–434. Paris, 1997.

———. "Zionism and the Politics of Coalitions in the Ottoman Jewish Communities in the Early Twentieth Century." In *Ottoman and Turkish Jewry: Community and Leadership*, ed. Aron Rodrigue, 225–251. Bloomington, 1992.

———. "Zionism in the Ottoman Empire at the End of the 19th and the Beginnings of the 20th Century." *Studies in Zionism* 11 (1990), 127–140.

Benbassa, Esther, and Aron Rodrigue. *A Sephardi Life in Southeastern Europe: The Autobiography and Journal of Gabriel Arié, 1863–1939.* Seattle, 1998.

———. *Sephardi Jewry: A History of the Judeo-Spanish Community, 14th–20th Centuries.* Berkeley, 2000.

Ben-Guiat, Alexander. *Suvenires del meldar.* Izmir, 1920.

Ben-Naʾeh, Yaron. "Ben gildah le-qahal: ha-hevrot ha-yehudiyot ba-imperiyah ha-othmanit ba-meʾot ha-17–18." *Zion* 63 (1998), 277–318.

———. "Hebrew Printing Houses in the Ottoman Empire." In *Jewish Journalism and Printing Houses in the Ottoman Empire and Modern Turkey*, ed. Gad Nassi, 73–96. Istanbul, 2001.

———. "The Jewish Society in the Urban Centers of the Ottoman Empire during the Seventeenth Century (Istanbul, Salonica, Izmir)." Ph.D. dissertation. Jerusalem, 1999 (Hebr.).

Berger, Michael. *Rabbinic Authority.* Oxford, 1998.

Berger, Peter L., and Thomas Luckmann. *The Social Construction of Reality: A Treatise in the Sociology of Knowledge.* Harmondsworth, 1971 [1966].

Berkes, Niyazi. *The Development of Secularism in Turkey.* 1964; reprint, New York, 1998.

Binswanger, Karl. *Untersuchungen zum Status der Nicht-Muslime im Osmanischen Reich des 16. Jahrhunderts, mit einer Neudefinition des Begriffes "Dhimma."* Munich, 1977.

Bonfil, Robert. "How Golden Was the Age of the Renaissance in Jewish Historiography?" In *Essential Papers on Jewish Culture in Renaissance and Baroque Italy,* ed. David B. Ruderman, 219–251. New York, 1992.

———. "La lectura en las comunidades hebreas de Europa occidental en la época medieval." In *Historia de la lectura en el mundo occidental,* ed. Guglielmo Cavallo and Roger Chartier, 231–279. Madrid, 1997.

———. "Preaching as Mediation between Elite and Popular Cultures: The Case of Judah Del Bene." In *Preachers of the Italian Ghetto,* ed. David Ruderman, 67–88. Berkeley, 1992.

———. "Le savoir et le pouvoir: Pour une histoire du rabbinat á l'époque pré-moderne." In *La société juive à travers l'histoire,* ed. Shmuel Trigano, 4 vols., vol. 1, 115–195. Paris, 1992.

Bornstein-Makovetsky, Leah. "Halakhic and Rabbinic Literature in Turkey, Greece and the Balkans, 1750–1900)." *Pe'amim* 86–87 (2001), 124–174 (Hebr.).

———. "Jewish Lay Leadership and Ottoman Authorities during the Sixteenth and Seventeenth Centuries." In *Ottoman and Turkish Jewry: Community and Leadership,* ed. Aron Rodrigue, 87–121. Bloomington, 1992.

———. "Rabbinic Scholarship: The Development of Halakhah in Turkey, Greece and the Balkans, 1750–1900." *Jewish Law Association Studies* 9 (1997), 9–18.

Borovaya, Olga. "The Role of Translation in Shaping the Ladino Novel at the Time of Westernization in the Ottoman Empire." *Jewish History* 16 (2002), 263–282.

———. "The Serialized Novel as Rewriting: The Case of Ladino Belles Lettres." *Jewish Social Studies* 10 (2003), 30–68.

———. "Translation and Westernization: *Gulliver's Travels* in Ladino." *Jewish Social Studies* 7 (2001), 149–168.

Boyarin, Daniel. *Carnal Israel: Reading Sex in Talmudic Culture.* Berkeley, 1993.

———. *Intertextuality and the Reading of Midrash.* Bloomington, 1990.

Braude, Benjamin. "Foundation Myths of the Millet System." In *Christians and Jews in the Ottoman Empire,* ed. Benjamin Braude and Bernard Lewis, vol. 1: *The Central Lands,* 69–88. New York, 1982.

———. "The Rise and Fall of Salonica Woollens, 1500–1650." *Mediterranean History Review* 4 (1991), 216–236.

Breuer, Mordechai. "Frühe Neuzeit und Beginn der Moderne." In *Deutsch-jüdische Geschichte in der Neuzeit,* vol. 1: *Tradition und Aufklärung 1600–1780,* ed. Michael A. Meyer, 85–247. Munich, 1996.

Broudo, Itshac. "Masoret u-minhagim 'amamiyim." In *Zikhron Saloniqi,* ed. David Recanati, vol. 2, 364–371. Tel Aviv, 1986.

Brummet, Palmira. *Image and Imperialism in the Ottoman Revolutionary Press, 1908–1911.* Albany, 2000.

Budde, Gunilla-Friederike. "Das Geschlecht der Geschichte." In *Geschichte zwischen Kultur und Gesellschaft: Beiträge zur Theoriedebatte,* ed. Thomas Mergel and Thomas Welskopp, 125–150. Munich, 1997.

Bunis, David. *Judezmo: An Introduction to the Language of the Sephardic Jews of the Ottoman Empire.* Jerusalem, 1999 (Hebr.).

———. *A Lexicon of the Hebrew and Aramaic Elements in Modern Judezmo.* Jerusalem, 1993.

———. "Modernization and the Language Question among Judezmo-Speaking Sephardim of the Ottoman Empire." In *Sephardi and Middle Eastern Jewries: History and Culture in the Modern Era,* ed. Harvey E. Goldberg, 226–239. Bloomington, 1996.

——. *Voices from Jewish Salonika.* Jerusalem, 1999.

Busse, Winfried. "Zur Problematik des Judenspanischen." *Neue Romania* 12 (1991), 37–84.

Capsali, Elijah. *Seder Eliyahu Zuta,* ed. Aryeh Shmuelevitz and Shlomo Simonsohn, 2 vols., Jerusalem, 1975–77.

Chartier, Roger. *Culture écrite et société: L'ordre des livres (xive-xviiie siècle).* Paris, 1996.

——. "Lecturas y lectores 'populares' desde el Renacimiento hasta la época clásica." In *Historia de la lectura en el mundo occidental,* ed. Guglielmo Cavallo and Roger Chartier, 413–434. Madrid, 1997.

Chetrit, Joseph. "Tradition du discours et discours de la tradition dans les communautés juives du Maroc: Étude socio-pragmatique." In *Communication in the Jewish Diaspora: The Pre-Modern World,* ed. Sophia Menashe, 339–407. Leiden, 1996.

Clogg, Richard. "The Greek Millet in the Ottoman Empire." In *Christians and Jews in the Ottoman Empire,* ed. Benjamin Braude and Bernard Lewis, vol. 1: *The Central Lands,* 185–208. New York, 1982.

Cohen, Dov. "Maᶜamadam ha-hevrati shel talmide hakhamim be Izmir ba-meʾot 18–19." M.A. thesis. Jerusalem, 2002.

Cohen, Mark R. *Under Crescent and Cross: The Jews in the Middle Ages.* Princeton, 1994.

Cohen, Shaye J. D. *The Beginnings of Jewishness: Boundaries, Varieties, Uncertainties.* Berkeley and Los Angeles, 1999.

Courbage, Youssef, and Philippe Fargues. *Chrétiens et Juifs dans l'Islam arabe et turc.* Paris, 1992.

Crews, C. M. "Extracts from the *Meam Loez* (Genesis) with a Translation and Glossary." *Proceedings of the Leeds Philosophical and Literary Society* 9 (1960), 13–106.

Dan, Joseph. *Jewish Mysticism and Jewish Ethics.* Seattle, 1986.

——. *On Sanctity: Religion, Ethics and Mysticism in Judaism and other Religions.* 2nd ed. Jerusalem, 1998 (Hebr.).

——. *Sifrut ha-musar veha-derush.* Jerusalem, 1975.

Dant, Tim. *Knowledge, Ideology and Discourse: A Sociological Perspective.* London, 1991.

David, Abraham. *To Come to the Land: Immigration and Settlement in Sixteenth-Century Eretz-Israel.* Tuscaloosa, 1999.

Davis, Natalie Zemon. "Printing and the People." In *Society and Culture in Early Modern France,* 189–226. Cambridge, 1987.

——. *Women on the Margins: Three Seventeenth-Century Lives.* Cambridge, Mass., 1995.

Davison, Roderic. *Reform in the Ottoman Empire, 1856–1876.* New York, 1973.

de Certeau, Michel. *L'invention du quotidien,* vol. 1: *Arts de faire.* Paris, 1990 [1980].

den Boer, Harm. *La literatura sefardí de Amsterdam.* Alcalá de Henares. 1996.

Deshen, Shlomo. *The Mellah Society: Jewish Community Life in Sherifian Morocco.* Chicago, 1989.

Díaz-Mas, Paloma. *Los Sefardíes: Historia, lengua y cultura.* 3rd ed. Barcelona, 1997.

Dubin, Lois C. *The Port Jews of Habsburg Trieste: Absolutist Politics and Enlightenment Culture.* Stanford, 1999.

Dumont, Paul. "Le français d'abord." In *Salonique, 1850–1918: La "ville des Juifs" et le réveil des Balkans* (= Editions Autrement, série Mémoires 12), ed. Gilles Veinstein, 208–225. Paris, 1993.

——. "Jewish Communities in Turkey during the Last Decades of the Nineteenth Century in the Light of the Archives of the Alliance Israélite Universelle." In *Christians and Jews in the Ottoman Empire: The Functioning of a Plural Society*, ed. Benjamin Braude and Bernard Lewis, vol. 1: *The Central Lands*, 209–242. New York, 1982.

——. "Naissance d'un socialisme ottoman." In *Salonique, 1850–1918: La "ville des Juifs" et le réveil des Balkans* (= Editions Autrement, série Mémoires 12), ed. Gilles Veinstein, 195–207. Paris, 1993.

——. "La période des *Tanzîmât* (1839–1878)." In *Histoire de l'Empire ottoman*, ed. Robert Mantran, 459–522. Paris, 1989.

——. "The Social Structure of the Jewish Community of Salonica at the End of the Nineteenth Century." *Southeastern Europe* 5 (1978), 33–72.

Dumont, Paul, and François Georgeon. *Villes ottomanes à la fin de l'empire*. Paris, 1992.

Eisen, Arnold M. *Galut: Modern Jewish Reflection on Homelessness and Homecoming*. Bloomington, 1986.

——. *Rethinking Modern Judaism: Ritual, Commandment, Community*. Chicago, 1998.

Eisenstadt, S. N. *Revolution and the Transformation of Societies: A Comparative Study of Civilizations*. New York, 1978.

Eisenstein, Elizabeth. *The Printing Press as an Agent of Change*. 2 vols. London and New York, 1979.

Elbaum, Jacob. "*Yalqut Shimʿoni* and the Medieval Midrashic Anthology." *Prooftexts* 17 (1997), 133–151.

Emanuel, Yitshaq. "Bate defus u-madpisim." In *Zikhron Saloniqi*, ed. David Recanati, vol. 2, 230–249. Tel Aviv, 1986.

——. "Toldot yehude Saloniqi." In *Zikhron Saloniqi*, ed. David Recanati, vol. 1, 3–272. Tel Aviv, 1972.

Faroqhi, Suraiya. *Kultur und Alltag im Osmanischen Reich*. Munich, 1995.

Fattal, Antoine. *Le status légal des non-musulmans en pays d'Islam*. Beirut, 1958.

Findley, Carter. "The Acid Test of Ottomanism: The Acceptance of Non-Muslims in the Late Ottoman Bureaucracy." In *Christians and Jews in the Ottoman Empire: The Functioning of a Plural Society*, ed. Benjamin Braude and Bernard Lewis, vol. 1: *The Central Lands*, 339–368. New York, 1982.

——. *Bureaucratic Reform in the Ottoman Empire: The Sublime Porte, 1789–1922*. Princeton, 1980.

——. *Ottoman Civil Officialdom: A Social History*. Princeton, 1989.

Fine, Lawrence. *Physician of the Soul, Healer of the Cosmos: Isaac Luria and His Kabbalistic Fellowship*. Stanford, 2003.

Fishbane, Michael, ed. *The Midrashic Imagination: Jewish Exegesis, Thought and History*. Albany, 1993.

Foucault, Michel. *L'archéologie du savoir*. Paris, 1969.

Fraade, Steven. *From Tradition to Commentary: Torah and Its Interpretations in the Midrash Sifre to Deuteronomy*. Albany, 1991.

Frankel, Jonathan. *The Damascus Affair: "Ritual Murder," Politics, and the Jews in 1840*. Cambridge, 1997.

Friedman, Isaiah. *Germany, Turkey, and Zionism 1897–1918*. Oxford, 1977.

Frow, John. *Cultural Studies and Cultural Value*. Oxford, 1995.

Funkenstein, Amos. *Perceptions of Jewish History*. Berkeley and Los Angeles, 1993.

Galanté, Abraham. *Histoire de Juifs d'Anatolie*, 2 vols. Istanbul, 1937–39.

——. *Histoire des Juifs de Turquie*, 9 vols. Reprint, Istanbul, 1985.

Gaʾon, Moshe David. *Maskiyot levav ʿal Meʿam Loʿez*. Jerusalem, 1933.

———. *Yehude ha-mizrah be-Erets Yisra'el.* 1928; reprint, Jerusalem, 1999.

Georgeon, François. "Le dernier sursaut (1878–1908)." In *Histoire de l'Empire ottoman,* ed. Robert Mantran, 523–576. Paris, 1989.

Georgeon, François, and Paul Dumont, eds. *Vivre dans l'Empire ottoman: Sociabilités et relations intercommunautaires (xviiie–xxe siècles).* Paris, 1997.

Gerber, Haim. "Jews and Money-Lending in the Ottoman Empire." *Jewish Quarterly Review* 72 (1981), 100–118.

Giddens, Anthony. *The Consequences of Modernity.* Stanford, 1990.

Ginzberg, Louis. *The Legends of the Jews,* 7 vols. 5th ed. Philadelphia, 1947.

Göçek, Fatma Müge. *East Encounters West: France and the Ottoman Empire in the Eighteenth Century.* New York, 1987.

———. *Rise of the Bourgeoisie, Demise of Empire: Ottoman Westernization and Social Change.* New York and Oxford, 1996.

Goffman, Daniel. *Izmir and the Levantine World, 1550–1650.* Seattle, 1990.

———. "Jews in Early Modern Ottoman Commerce." In *Jews, Turks, Ottomans,* ed. Avigdor Levy. Syracuse, 2002.

———. *The Ottoman Empire and Early Modern Europe.* Cambridge, 2002.

Goldberg, Arnold. "Entwurf einer formanalytischen Methode für die Exegese der rabbinischen Traditionsliteratur." *Frankfurter Judaistische Beiträge* 5 (1977), 1–41.

———. "Form-Analysis of Midrashic Literature as a Method of Description." *Journal of Jewish Studies* 36 (1985), 159–174.

———. *Me'am Lo'ez: Diskurs und Erzählung in der Komposition. Hayye Sara, Kapitel 1.* Frankfurt a.M., 1984.

Goldberg, Harvey E. "Religious Responses among North African Jews in the Nineteenth and Twentieth Centuries." In *The Uses of Tradition: Jewish Continuity in the Modern Era,* ed. Jack Wertheimer, 119–144. New York, 1992.

———. "The Zohar in Southern Morocco: A Study in the Ethnography of Texts." *History of Religions* 29 (1990), 233–258.

Goldish, Matt. *The Sabbatean Prophets.* Cambridge, 2004.

Goodblatt, Morris. *Jewish Life in Turkey in the XVIth Century as Reflected in the Legal Writings of Samuel De Medina.* New York, 1952.

Grant, Jonathan. "Rethinking the Ottoman 'Decline': Military Technology Diffusion in the Ottoman Empire, Fifteenth to Eighteenth Centuries." *Journal of World History* 10 (1999), 179–201.

Gries, Ze'ev. *The Book as an Agent of Culture, 1700–1900.* Tel Aviv, 2002 (Hebr.).

———. "The Fashioning of Hanhagot (Regimen Vitae) Literature at the End of the Sixteenth Century and during the Seventeenth Century and Its Historical Importance." *Tarbiz* 56 (1987), 527–581.

Habermas, Jürgen. *Strukturwandel der Öffentlichkeit.* Frankfurt a.M., 1990 [1962].

Haboucha, Reginetta. "Misogyny or Philogyny: The Case of the Judeo-Spanish Folktale." In *New Horizons in Sephardic Studies,* ed. Yedida K. Stillman and George K. Zucker, 239–251. Albany, 1993.

———. "Women in the Judeo-Spanish Folktales." *The Sephardic Scholar,* series 4 (1979–1982), 32–47. New York, 1982.

Hacker, Joseph. "The Intellectual Activity of the Jews of the Ottoman Empire during the Sixteenth and Seventeenth Centuries." In *Jewish Thought in the Seventeenth Century,* ed. Isadore Twersky and Bernard Septimus, 95–135. Cambridge, 1987.

———. "Jewish Autonomy in the Ottoman Empire: Its Scope and Limits—Jewish Courts from the Sixteenth to the Eighteenth Centuries." In *The Jews of the Ottoman Empire,* ed. Avigdor Levy, 153–202. Princeton, 1994.

———. "The Jewish Society of Salonika in the Fifteenth and Sixteenth Centuries: A Chapter in the History of Jewish Society in the Ottoman Empire." Ph.D. dissertation. Jerusalem, 1978 (Hebr.).

———. "The *Sürgün* System and Jewish Society in the Ottoman Empire during the Fifteenth to the Seventeenth Centuries." In *Ottoman and Turkish Jewry: Community and Leadership,* ed. Aron Rodrigue, 1–65. Bloomington, 1992.

———. "Yots'e Sefarad ba-imperiyah ha-Othmanit ba-me'ah ha-16—qehilah ve-hevrah." In *Moreshet Sefarad,* ed. Hayim Beinart, 460–478. Jerusalem, 1992.

Hall, Stuart. "Notes on Deconstructing 'the Popular.'" In *People's History and Socialist Theory,* ed. Raphael Samuel, 227–240. London, 1981.

Hartman, David, and Tzvi Marx. "Charity." In *Contemporary Jewish Religious Thought,* ed. Arthur A. Cohen and Paul Mendes-Flohr, 47–54. New York, 1987.

Hartman, Geoffrey H., and Sanford Budick, eds. *Midrash and Literature.* New Haven, 1986.

Hassán, Iacob M., ed. *Introducción a la Biblia de Ferrara.* Madrid, 1994.

———. "La literatura sefardí culta: sus principales escritores, obras y géneros." In *Judíos. Sefardíes. Conversos,* ed. Angel Alcalá, 319–330. Valladolid, 1995.

———. "Transcripción normalizada de textos judeoespañoles." *Estudios sefardíes (Anejo de Sefarad)* 1 (1978), 147–150.

———. "Visión panorámica de la literatura sefardí." *Hispania Judaica* 2. Barcelona, 1982.

Hauptman, Judith. "Feminist Perspectives on Rabbinic Texts." In *Feminist Perspectives on Jewish Studies,* ed. Lynn Davidman and Shelly Tenenbaum, 40–61. New Haven, 1994.

Hertzberg, Arthur, ed. *The Zionist Idea.* New York, 1960.

Hess, Andrew. "The Ottoman Conquest of Egypt (1517) and the Beginning of the Sixteenth-Century World War." *International Journal of Middle East Studies* 4 (1973), 55–76.

Hundert, Gershon. *Jews in Poland-Lithuania in the Eighteenth Century.* Berkeley, 2004.

Hyman, Paula E. *Gender and Assimilation in Modern Jewish History: The Roles and Representation of Women.* Seattle, 1995.

———. *The Jews of Modern France.* Berkeley, 1998.

Idel, Moshe. "'Hitbodedut' as Concentration in Ecstatic Kabbalah." In *Jewish Spirituality I,* ed. Arthur Green. New York, 1986.

———. *Kabbalah: New Perspectives.* New Haven, 1988.

———. "'One from a Town, Two from a Clan': The Diffusion of Lurianic Kabbalah and Sabbateanism—A Reexamination." *Jewish History* 7 (1993).

Inalcik, Halil. "Application of the Tanzimat and Its Social Effects." *Archivum Ottomanicum* 4 (1972), 97–127.

Inalcik, Halil, ed., with Donald Quataert. *An Economic and Social History of the Ottoman Empire.* Cambridge, 1994.

Islamoglu-Inan, Huri, ed. *The Ottoman Empire and the World Economy.* Cambridge and Paris, 1987.

Israel, Jonathan. *Diasporas within a Diaspora: Jews, Crypto-Jews and the World Maritime Empires (1540–1740).* Leiden, 2002.

Issawi, Charles, ed. *The Economic History of Turkey, 1800–1914.* Chicago, 1980.

Jerusalmi, Isaac. "El ladino, lengua del judaísmo y habla diaria." In Ángel Alcalá, ed., *Judíos. Sefarditas. Conversos,* 301–318. Valladolid, 1995.

Kafadar, Cemal. *Between Two Worlds: The Construction of the Ottoman State.* Berkeley, 1995.

Kamen, Henry. "The Expulsion: Purpose and Consequence." In *Spain and the Jews,* ed. Elie Kedourie, 74–91. London, 1992.

Kaplan, Yosef. *An Alternative Path to Modernity: The Sephardi Diaspora in Western Europe.* Leiden, 2000.

Karpat, Kemal. "Jewish Population Movements in the Ottoman Empire, 1862–1914." In *The Jews of the Ottoman Empire,* ed. Avigdor Levy, 399–415. Princeton, 1994.

———. *Ottoman Population, 1830–1914: Demographic and Social Characteristics.* Madison, 1985.

Katz, Jacob. *Tradition and Crisis: Jewish Society at the End of the Middle Ages.* New York, 1993 [Hebr., 1958].

———. "Traditional Society and Modern Society." In *Jewish Societies in the Middle East: Community, Culture and Authority,* ed. Shlomo Deshen and Walter P. Zenner, 35–47. Lanham, Md., 1992.

Kayali, Hasan. *Arabs and Young Turks: Ottomanism, Arabism and Islamism in the Ottoman Empire, 1908–1918.* Berkeley, 1997.

Kellner, Menachem. *Maimonides on the "Decline of Generations" and the Nature of Rabbinic Authority.* Albany, 1996.

Kermode, Frank. *The Classic.* London, 1975.

Kern, Stephen. *The Culture of Time and Space, 1880–1918.* Cambridge, Mass., 1983.

Köhler-Zülich, Ines. "Von der Handschrift zum Buch und zur Heftchenliteratur: Bulgarische Geschichten über Alexander den Großen im 19. und 20. Jahrhundert." In *Südosteuropäische Popularliteratur im 19. und 20. Jahrhundert,* ed. Klaus Roth, 187–226. Munich, 1993.

Kohring, Heinrich. "I las noches de invierno ke son muy largas . . . Jakob Kuli und sein Vorwort zum *Me'am Lo'ez.*" *Neue Romania* 19 (1997) (= Judenspanisch ii), 67–167.

Koselleck, Reinhart. *Vergangene Zukunft: Zur Semantik geschichtlicher Zeiten.* 3rd ed. Frankfurt, 1995.

Kraemer, David. "The Intended Reader as a Key to Interpreting the Bavli." *Prooftexts* 13 (1993), 125–140.

———. *Reading the Rabbis: The Talmud as Literature.* Oxford, 1996.

Landau, Louis. "Content and Form in the Me'am Lo'ez of Rabbi Jacob Culi." Ph.D. diss., Jerusalem, 1980 (Hebr.).

———. "*Me'am Lo'ez*—masoret ve-hidushah ba-sifrut ha-sefaradit-yehudit." *Shevet va-'Am,* second series, 5 (1984), 307–321.

———. "R. Jacob Khuli's Attitude towards Shabbateanism." *Pe'amim* 15 (1983), 58–66 (Hebr.).

———. "The Transformation of the Talmudic Story in the 'Me'am Lo'ez'." *Pe'amim* 7 (1981), 35–49 (Hebr.).

Lebel, Jennie. "'Longing for Jerusalem': Rabbi Yehudah Alkalay, the Political and Communal Context of his Activity." *Pe'amim* 40 (1989), 21–48 (Hebr.).

Lehman, Marjorie. "The *'Ein Ya'aqov:* A Collection of Aggadah in Transition." *Prooftexts* 19 (1999), 21–40.

Lehmann, Matthias B. "The Intended Reader of Ladino Rabbinic Literature and Judeo-Spanish Reading Culture." *Jewish History* 16 (2002), 283–307.

———. "A Livornese Port Jew and the Sephardim of the Ottoman Empire." *Jewish Social Studies* (forthcoming).

———. "Representations and Transformation of Knowledge in Judeo-Spanish Ethical Literature: The Case of Eliᶜezer and Judah Papo's *'Pele Yoᶜets'*." In *Jewish Studies between the Disciplines,* ed. Klaus Hermann et al., 299–324. Leiden, 2003.

———. "Two Perceptions of Change in Judeo-Spanish Rabbinic Literature." *Sefarad* 6 (2000), 95–122.

Levi, Avner. "Changes in the Leadership of the Main Spanish Communities in the Nineteenth-Century Ottoman Empire." In *The Days of the Crescent: Chapters in the History of the Jews in the Ottoman Empire,* ed. Minna Rozen, 237–271. Tel Aviv, 1996 (Hebr.).

———. "*Shavat Aniim:* Social Cleavage, Class War and Leadership in the Sephardic Community: The Case of Izmir 1847." In *Ottoman and Turkish Jewry: Community and Leadership,* ed. Aron Rodrigue, 183–202. Bloomington, 1992.

Levine Melammed, Renée. "Sephardi Women in the Medieval and Early Modern Periods." In *Jewish Women in Historical Perspective,* ed. Judith R. Baskin. Detroit, 1991.

Levy, Avigdor. *The Sephardim in the Ottoman Empire.* Princeton, 1992.

Levy, Joseph, ed. *Rabbi Isaac Badhav (1859–1947): His Life's Work and Environs.* Jerusalem, 1977 (Hebr.).

Lewis, Bernard. *The Emergence of Modern Turkey.* 3rd ed. Oxford, 2002.

———. *The Jews of Islam.* Princeton, 1984.

———. "Ottoman Observers of Ottoman Decline." In Lewis Bernard, *Islam in History.* La Salle, Ill., 1972.

Liebes, Yehuda. *On Sabbateanism and Its Kabbalah.* Jerusalem, 1995 (Hebr.).

Liebes, Yehuda, and Rachel Elior, eds. *Lurianic Kabbalah: Proceedings of the Fourth International Conference on the History of Jewish Mysticism.* Jerusalem Studies in Jewish Thought, no. 10. Jerusalem, 1992 (Hebr.).

Loker, Zvi. "Le rabbin Juda ben Salomon Hay Alcalay et l'Alliance Israélite Universelle à propos de ses lettres inédites." *Revue des études juives* 144 (1985), 127–144.

Luhmann, Niklas. "The Future Cannot Begin: Temporal Structures in Modern Society." *Social Research* 43 (1976), 130–152.

———. *Soziale Systeme: Grundriß einer allgemeinen Theorie.* Frankfurt a.M., 1999 [1984].

Maeso Gonzalo, David, and Pascual Pascual Recuero, eds. *Meam Loez: El gran comentario biblico sefardí.* 4 vols. Madrid, 1969–1974.

Mah, Harold. "Phantasies of the Public Sphere: Rethinking the Habermas of Historians." *Journal of Modern History* 72 (2000), 153–182.

Maingueneau, Dominique. *Le contexte de l'œuvre littéraire: Énonciation, écrivain, société.* Paris, 1993.

Mantran, Robert. "Les débuts de la Question d'Orient (1774–1839)." In *Histoire de l'Empire ottoman,* ed. Robert Mantran, 421–458. Paris, 1989.

———. "L'État ottoman au xviiiᵉ siècle: la pression européenne." In *Histoire de l'Empire ottoman,* ed. Robert Mantran, 265–286. Paris, 1989.

Maᶜoz, Moshe. "Changes in the Position of the Jewish Communities of Palestine and Syria in the Mid-Nineteenth Century." In *Studies on Palestine during the Ottoman Period,* ed. Moshe Maᶜoz, 142–163. Jerusalem, 1975.

Marcus Abraham. *The Middle East on the Eve of Modernity: Aleppo in the Eighteenth Century.* New York, 1989.

Marcus, Ivan G. *Piety and Society: The Jewish Pietists of Medieval Germany.* Leiden, 1981.

Mardin, Serif. "Tanzimat." In *Encyclopaedia of the Modern Islamic World*, ed. John L. Esposito. Oxford, 1995.

McCarthy, Justin. "Jewish Population in the Late Ottoman Period." In *The Jews of the Ottoman Empire*, ed. Avigdor Levy, 375–397. Princeton, 1994.

Milano, Attilio. *Storia degli ebrei italiani nel Levante*. Florence, 1949.

Molho, Anthony. "Ebrei e marrani fra Italia e Levante ottomano." In *Storia d'Italia, Annali 11: Gli ebrei in Italia*, ed. Corrado Vivanti, vol. 2, 1009–1043. Torino, 1996.

Molho, I. R. "El humanista R. Yaakob Kuli." *Tesoro de los judíos sefardíes* 5 (1962), 80–94 (Hebr.).

Molho, Michael. *Literatura sefardita de Oriente*. Madrid, 1960.

———. *Le Meam-Loez: Encyclopédie populaire du séphardisme levantin*. Salonika, 1945.

Molho, Rena. "Le renouveau. . . . " In *Salonique, 1850–1918: La "ville des Juifs" et le réveil des Balkans*, ed. Gilles Veinstein, 64–78. Éditions Autrement, série Mémoires 12. Paris, 1993.

Mopsik, Charles. *Lettre sur la sainteté: Le secret de la relation entre l'homme et la femme dans la cabale*. Paris, 1986.

Morgenstern, Arie. "Messianic Concepts and Settlement in the Land of Israel." In *Essential Papers on Messianic Movements and Personalities in Jewish History*, ed. Marc Saperstein, 433–455. New York, 1992.

Münch, Almuth. "Die Hebräisch-aramäische Sprachtradition der Sepharden in ihrem Verhältnis zum Spanischen der Juden in Sepharad I sowie zum *Djudeo-Espanyol* in Sepharad II und die Rolle des Ladino." *Neue Romania* 12 (1991), 171–239.

Nahum, Henri. *Juifs de Smyrne: xixe–xxe siècle*. Paris, 1997.

Nehama, Joseph. *Dictionnaire du Judéo-Espagnol*. Madrid, 1977.

———. *Histoire des Israélites de Salonique*. Salonika, 1978.

Noth, Michael, ed. *Kommunikationsrevolutionen: Die neuen Medien des 16. und 19. Jahrhunderts*. Vienna, 1995.

Oliel-Grausz, Evelyne. "La circulation du personnel rabbinique dans le communautés de la diaspora sépharade au xviiie siècle." In *Transmission et passages en monde juif*, ed. Esther Benbassa, 313–334. Paris, 1997.

Pamuk, Sevket. *The Ottoman Empire and European Capitalism*. Cambridge, 1987.

Panzac, Daniel et al. *Les Balkans à l'époque ottomane*. Revue du monde musulman et de la Méditerranée, no. 66. La Calade [France], 1993.

Penny, Ralph. *Variation and Change in Spanish*. Cambridge, 2000.

Philipp, Thomas. "French Merchants and Jews in the Ottoman Empire during the Eighteenth Century." In *The Jews of the Ottoman Empire*, ed. Avigdor Levy, 315–325. Princeton, 1994.

Pontrémoli, Rafael Hiya. *Meam Loez: Libre d'Esther*. Trans. Albert Benveniste. Paris, 1997.

Porter, Frank Chamberlin. "The Yeçer Hara: A Study in the Jewish Doctrine of Sin." In *Biblical and Semitic Studies*, 91–156. New York, 1901.

Quataert, Donald. "The Industrial Working Class of Salonika, 1850–1912." In *The Days of the Crescent: Chapters in the History of the Jews in the Ottoman Empire*, ed. Minna Rozen, 311–330. Tel Aviv, 1996 (Hebr.).

———. *The Ottoman Empire, 1700–1922*. Cambridge, 2000.

———. "Ottoman Women, Households, and Textile Manufacturing, 1800–1914." In *Women in Middle Eastern History: Shifting Boundaries in Sex and Gender*, ed. Nikki R. Keddie and Beth Baron, 161–176. New Haven, 1991.

———. "Premières fumées d'usines." In *Salonique, 1850–1918: La "ville des Juifs" et le réveil des Balkans,* ed. Gilles Veinstein, 177–194. Editions Autrement, série Mémoires 12. Paris, 1993.

———. *Social Disintegration and Popular Resistance in the Ottoman Empire, 1881–1908.* New York, 1983.

Reicher, Elchanan. "The Ashkenazi Élite at the Beginning of the Modern Era: Manuscript versus Printed Book." *Polin* 10 (1997), 85–98.

Reynolds, Nancy. "'Difference and Tolerance in the Ottoman Empire': Interview with Aron Rodrigue." *Stanford Humanities Review* 5 (1995), 81–90.

Riaño López, Ana María. *Isaac Mikael Badhab: Un tratado sefardí de moral.* Barcelona, 1979.

Rodrigue, Aron. "Abraham de Camondo of Istanbul: The Transformation of Jewish Philanthropy." In *From East to West: Jews in a Changing Europe, 1750–1870,* ed. Frances Malino and David Sorkin, 46–56. Oxford, 1990.

———. "The Beginnings of Westernization and Community Reform among Istanbul's Jewry, 1854–65." In *The Jews of the Ottoman Empire,* ed. Avigdor Levy, 439–456. Princeton, 1994.

———. *De l'instruction à l'émancipation: Les enseignants de l'Alliance Israélite Universelle et les Juifs d'Orient 1860–1939.* Paris, 1989.

———. "Eastern Sephardi Jewry and New Nation-States in the Balkans in the Nineteenth and Twentieth Centuries." In *Sephardi and Middle Eastern Jewries,* ed. Harvey E. Goldberg, 81–88. Bloomington, 1996.

———. *French Jews, Turkish Jews.* Bloomington, 1990.

———. "From *Millet* to Minority: Turkish Jewry." In *Paths of Emancipation: Jews, States, and Citizenship,* ed. Pierre Birnbaum and Ira Katznelson, 238–261. Princeton, 1995.

———. "The Ottoman Diaspora: The Rise and Fall of Ladino Literary Culture." In *Cultures of the Jews,* ed. David Biale, 863–886. New York, 2002.

———. "Réformer ou supplanter. L'éducation juive traditionnelle en Turquie à l'épreuve de la modernité." In *Transmission et passages en monde juif,* ed. Esther Benbassa, 501–522. Paris, 1997.

———. "The Sephardim in the Ottoman Empire." In *Spain and the Jews,* ed. Elie Kedourie, 162–188. London, 1992.

Romero, Elena. *Coplas sefardíes: Primera selección.* Córdoba, 1988.

———. *La creación literaria en lengua sefardí.* Madrid, 1992.

———. *El libro del buen retajar: Textos judeoespañoles de circuncisión.* Madrid, 1998.

———. *Seis coplas sefardíes de 'castiguerio' de Hayim Yom-Tob Magula.* Madrid, 2003.

Romeu Ferré, Pilar. *Las llaves del Meam loez.* Barcelona, 2000.

———. *Moisés Almosnino: Crónica de los reyes otomanos.* Barcelona, 1998.

Rosanes, Salomon. *Qorot ha-yehudim be-Turqiyah ve-artsot ha-qedem.* Vol. 5. Sofia, 1937–38.

Rosman, Moshe. "Innovative Tradition: Jewish Culture in the Polish-Lithuanian Commonwealth." In *Cultures of the Jews,* ed. David Biale, 519–570. New York, 2002.

Roth, Klaus. "Populare Lesestoffe in Südosteuropa." In *Südosteuropäische Popularliteratur im 19. und 20. Jahrhundert,* ed. Klaus Roth, 11–32. Munich, 1993.

Rozen, Minna. "Contest and Rivalry in Mediterranean Maritime Commerce in the First Half of the Eighteenth Century: The Jews of Salonika and the European Presence." *Revue des Études juives* 147 (1988), 309–352.

———. *A History of the Jewish Community in Istanbul: The Formative Years, 1453–1566.* Leiden, 2002.

———. "Individual and Community in the Jewish Society of the Ottoman Empire: Salonica in the Sixteenth Century." In *The Jews of the Ottoman Empire,* ed. Avigdor Levy, 215–273. Princeton, 1994.

———. "Public Space and Private Space among the Jews of Istanbul in the Sixteenth and Seventeenth Centuries." *Turcica* 30 (1998), 331–346.

———. "Strangers in a Strange Land: The Extraterritorial Status of Jews in Italy and the Ottoman Empire in the Sixteenth to the Eighteenth Centuries." In *Ottoman and Turkish Jewry: Community and Leadership,* ed. Aron Rodrigue, 123–166. Bloomington, 1992.

Ruderman, David B. *Jewish Thought and Scientific Discovery in Early Modern Europe.* New Haven, 1995.

Saloniqi: ʿIr va-em be-Yisraʾel. Ed. Centre for Research into Salonikan Jewry. Jerusalem and Tel Aviv, 1967.

Saperstein, Marc. *Jewish Preaching, 1200–1800: An Anthology.* New Haven, 1989.

Schäfer, Peter. "Research into Rabbinic Literature: An Attempt to Define the Status Quaestionis." *Journal of Jewish Studies* 37 (1986), 139–152.

Scholem, Gershom. "Eliyahu ha-Kohen ha-Itamari ve-ha-shabtaʾut." In Gershom Scholem, *Mehqare Shabtaʾut,* 453–477. Tel Aviv, 1991.

———. *Major Trends in Jewish Mysticism.* New York, 1941, 1961 printing.

———. *Sabbatai Sevi.* Princeton, 1973. Enlarged translation from the Hebrew original, Jerusalem, 1957.

Schroeter, Daniel. "Orientalism and the Jews of the Mediterranean." *Journal of Mediterranean Studies* 4 (1994), 183–196.

———. *The Sultan's Jew: Morocco and the Sephardi World.* Stanford, 2002.

Schroeter, Daniel J., and Joseph Chetrit. "The Transformation of the Jewish Community of Essaouria (Mogador) in the Nineteenth and Twentieth Centuries." In *Sephardi and Middle Eastern Jewries: History and Culture in the Modern Era,* ed. Harvey E. Goldberg, 99–116. Bloomington, 1996.

Schulze, Reinhard. "Das islamische achtzehnte Jahrhundert: Versuch einer historiographischen Kritik." *Die Welt des Islams* 30 (1990), 140–159.

Schwarzfuchs, Simon. *L'"Alliance" dans les communautés du bassin méditerranéen à la fin du 19ème siècle et son influence sur la situation sociale et culturelle.* Jerusalem, 1987 (Fr. and Hebr.).

Séphiha, Haïm Vidal. "Ladino et Djudezmo." In *Salonique, 1850–1918: La "ville des Juifs" et le réveil des Balkans,* ed. Gilles Veinstein, 79–95. Editions Autrement, série Mémoires 12. Paris, 1993.

Shaw, Stanford. *The Jews of the Ottoman Empire and the Turkish Republic.* New York, 1991.

Shmuelevitz, Aryeh. *The Jews of the Ottoman Empire in the Late Fifteenth and Sixteenth Centuries.* Leiden, 1984.

Shohat, Azriel. "Hevrot limud ba-meʾot ha-16–18 be-erets Yisraʾel, be-Folin-Lita uve-Germanyah." In *Mehqarim be-toldot ʿam Yisraʾel ve-erets Yisraʾel,* part 1, 214–240. Haifa, 1978.

———. "The King's Cloth in Salonika." *Sefunot* 12 (1971–78), 168–188 (Hebr.).

Silber, Michael. "The Emergence of Ultra-Orthodoxy: The Invention of a Tradition." In *The Uses of Tradition: Jewish Continuity in the Modern Era,* ed. Jack Wertheimer, 23–84. New York, 1992.

Silberstein, Laurence. "Others Within and Others Without: Rethinking Jewish Identity and Culture." In *The Other in Jewish Thought and History: Constructions of Jewish*

Culture and Identity, ed. Laurence Silberstein and Robert L. Cohn, 1–34. New York, 1994.

Simon, Reeva Spector, Michael Menachem Laskier, and Sara Reguer, eds. *The Jews of the Middle East and North Africa in Modern Times.* New York, 2003.

Sorkin, David. "The Port Jew: Notes toward a Social Type." *Journal of Jewish Studies* 50 (1999), 87–97.

———. *The Transformation of German Jewry, 1870–1840.* 2nd ed. Detroit, 1999.

Stampfer, Shaul. "Gender Differentiation and Education of the Jewish Woman in Nineteenth-Century Eastern Europe." *Polin* 7 (1992), 63–87.

Stein, Sarah Abrevaya. *Making Jews Modern: The Yiddish and Ladino Press in the Russian and Ottoman Empires.* Bloomington, 2004.

———. "Sephardi and Middle Eastern Jewries since 1492." In *The Oxford Handbook of Jewish Studies,* ed. Martin Goodman, 327–362. Oxford, 2002.

Stern, David. "Introduction: The Anthological Imagination in Jewish Literature." *Prooftexts* 17 (1997), 1–7.

———. *Midrash and Theory: Ancient Jewish Exegesis and Contemporary Literary Studies.* Evanston, 1996.

Stillman, Norman A. *The Jews of Arab Lands.* Philadelphia, 1979.

———. *The Jews of Arab Lands in Modern Times.* Philadelphia, 1991.

———. "Middle Eastern and North African Jewries Confront Modernity: Orientation, Disorientation, Reorientation." In *Sephardi and Middle Eastern Jewries: History and Culture in the Modern Era,* ed. Harvey E. Goldberg, 59–72. Bloomington, 1996.

———. *Sephardi Religious Responses to Modernity.* Luxembourg, 1995.

Stillman, Yedida K., and Norman A. Stillman, eds. *From Iberia to Diaspora: Studies in Sephardic History and Culture.* Leiden, 1998.

Tishby, Isaiah, and Joseph Dan. *Mivhar sifrut ha-musar.* Jerusalem, 1970.

Twersky, Isadore, ed. *A Maimonides Reader.* New York, 1972.

———. "Religion and Law." In *Religion in a Religious Age,* ed. S. D. Goitein, 69–82. Cambridge, 1974.

Ursinus, Michael. "Zur Diskussion um 'millet' im Osmanischen Reich." *Südostforschungen* 48 (1989), 195–207.

Veinstein, Gilles. "Un paradoxe séculaire." In *Salonique, 1850–1918: La "ville des Juifs" et le réveil des Balkans,* ed. Gilles Veinstein, 42–63. Editions Autrement, série Mémoires 12. Paris, 1993.

———. "Les provinces balkaniques (1606–1774)." In *Histoire de l'Empire ottoman,* ed. Robert Mantran, 287–340. Paris, 1989.

Wallach, Joan Scott. "Gender: A Useful Category of Historical Analysis." *American Historical Review* 91 (1986), 1053–1075.

Wegner, Judith Romney. *Chattel or Person? The Status of Women in the Mishnah.* New York, 1988.

Wehler, Hans-Ulrich. "Modernisierungstheorie und Geschichte." In Hans-Ulrich Wehler, *Die Gegenwart als Geschichte,* 13–59, endnotes 266–284. Munich, 1995.

Weiker, Walter. *Ottomans, Turks, and the Jewish Polity: A History of the Jews of Turkey.* Lanham, Md., 1992.

Werblowsky, Zvi. *Joseph Karo: Lawyer and Mystic.* Oxford, 1962.

Wolfson, Elliot. *Circle in the Square: Studies in the Use of Gender in Kabbalistic Symbolism.* Albany, 1995.

Yaʿari, Abraham. *Hebrew Printing in Constantinople.* Jerusalem, 1967 (Hebr.).

———. "Hebrew Printing at Izmir." *Aresheth* 1 (1958), 97–222 (Hebr.).

———. *Reshimat sifre ladino ha-nimtsaʾim be-vet ha-sefarim ha-leʾumi ve-ha-universitaʾi bi-Yerushalayim.* Jerusalem, 1934.

———. *Sheluhe Erets Yisraʾel: Toldot ha-shelihut meha-arets la-golah.* Jerusalem, 1997.

Yerushalmi, Yosef Haim. "Kastilianit, portugezit, ladino: ha-sifruyot ha-loʿaziyot shel ha-yahadut ha-sefaradit." In *Meʾaz ve-ʿad ʿatah,* ed. Tsvi Ankori, 35–53. Tel Aviv, 1984.

———. *Zakhor: Jewish History and Jewish Memory.* Seattle, 1982.

Zilfi, Madeline C., ed. *Women in the Ottoman Empire: Middle Eastern Women in the Early Modern Era.* Leiden, 1997.

Zinberg, Israel. *A History of Jewish Literature.* Vol. 7: *Old Yiddish Literature from Its Origins to the Haskalah Period.* Cincinnati and New York, 1975.

Zohar, Zvi. *Tradition and Change: Halakhic Responses of Middle Eastern Rabbis to Legal and Technological Change (Egypt and Syria, 1880–1920).* Jerusalem, 1993 (Hebr.).

INDEX

Matthias B. Lehmann is Assistant Professor of Jewish Studies and History at Indiana University, Bloomington.